At the front, we'd kill snakes this big around, hack 'em into pieces, and stew 'em in a sweet and sour sauce of soy sauce and sugar!

Aaaaah!

Elephant meat is tough! It's like chewing on rubber!

In researching this volume, I interviewed veterans who had been at the front during World War II. I read countless books, examined film footage, and listened to many detailed and intense stories firsthand, but the one comment that affected me the most came from a former soldier who lowered his gaze to the tabletop and said, "I never watch war movies."

—Hiromu Arakawa, 2006

Born in Hokkaido (northern Japan), Hiromu Arakawa first attracted national attention in 1999 with her award-winning manga *Stray Dog*. Her series *Fullmetal Alchemist* debuted in 2001 in Square Enix's monthly manga anthology *Shonen Gangan*.

FULLMETAL ALCHEMIST
VOL. 15

Story and Art by Hiromu Arakawa

Translation/Akira Watanabe
English Adaptation/Jake Forbes
Touch-up Art & Lettering/Wayne Truman
Design/Amy Martin
Editor/Annette Roman

VP, Production/Alvin Lu
VP, Sales & Product Marketing/Gonzalo Ferreyra
VP, Creative/Linda Espinosa
Publisher/Hyoe Narita

Printed in the U.S.A.

Published by VIZ Media, LLC
P.O. Box 77010
San Francisco, CA 94107

10 9 8 7 6 5 4 3 2
First printing, December 2007
Second printing, October 2009

www.viz.com

鋼の錬金術師

FULLMETAL ALCHEMIST

15

荒川弘

HIROMU ARAKAWA

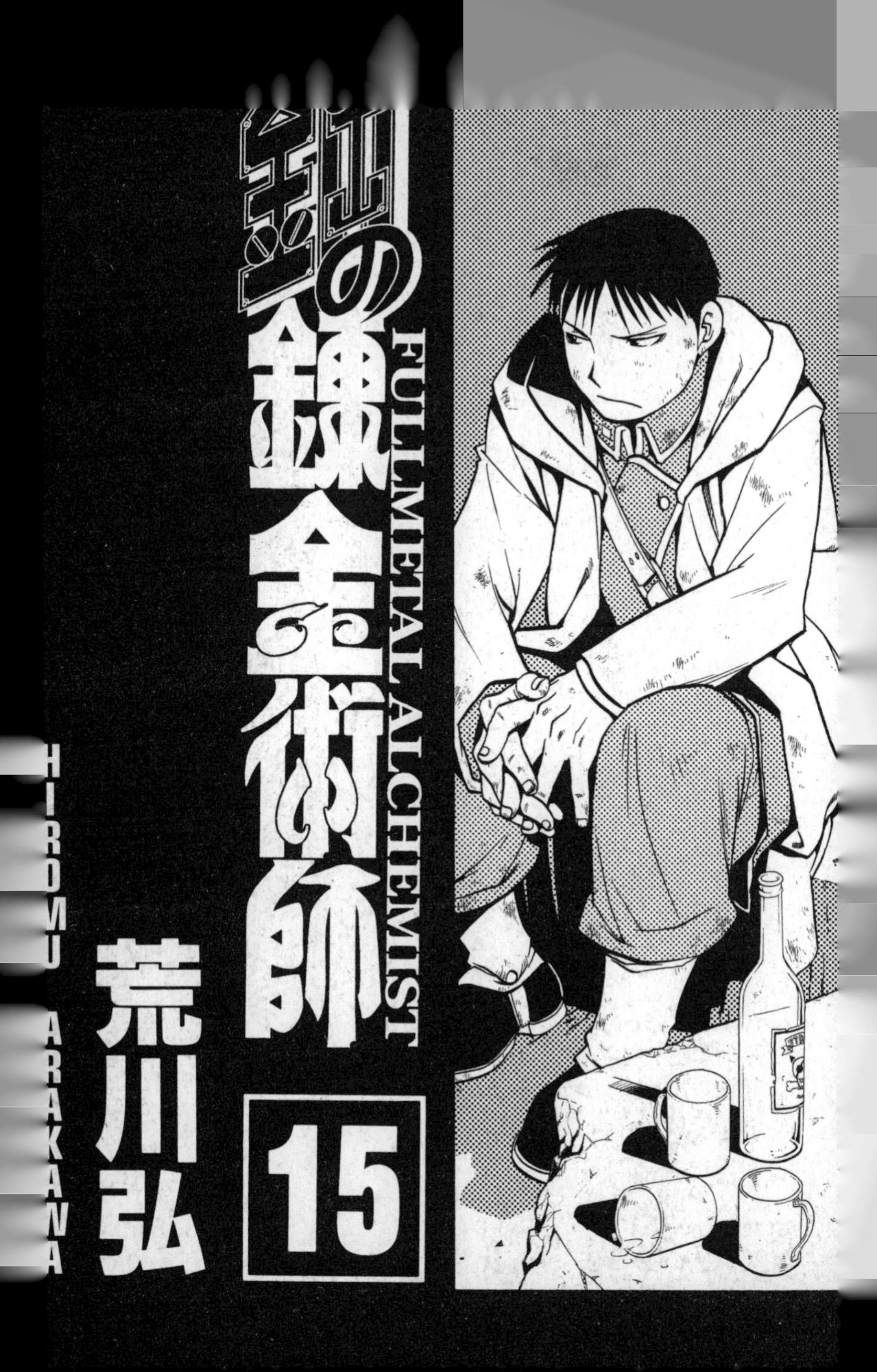

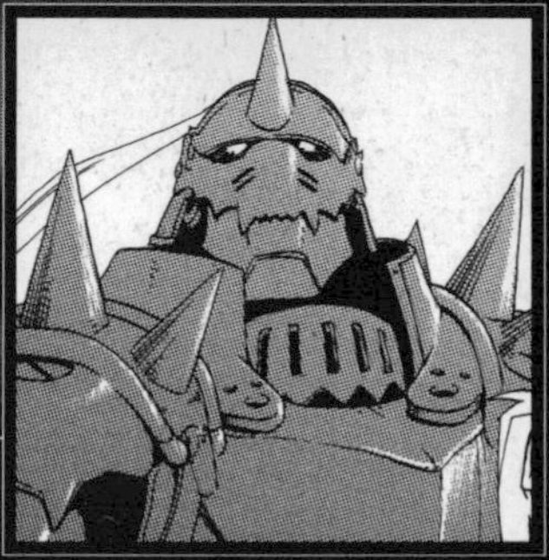

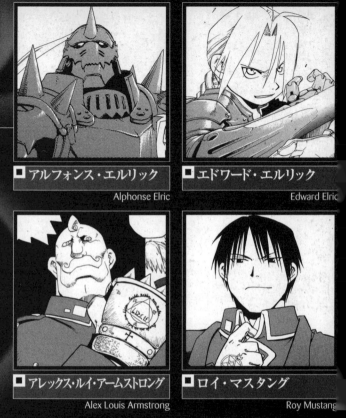

アルフォンス・エルリック

Alphonse Elric

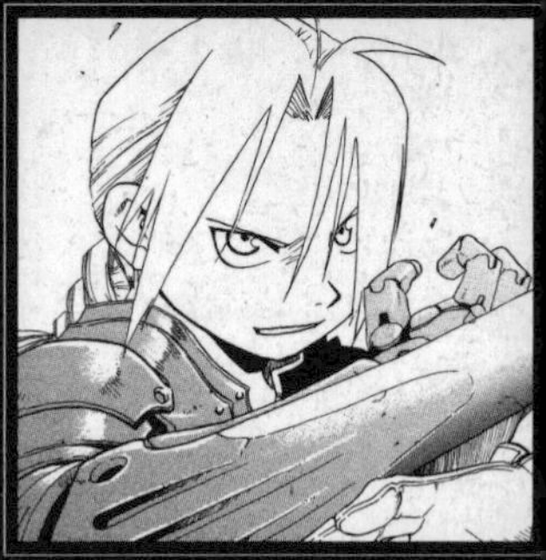

エドワード・エルリック

Edward Elric

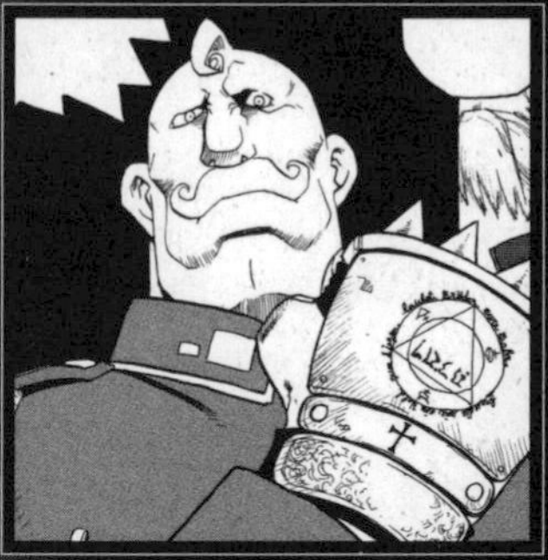

アレックス・ルイ・アームストロング

Alex Louis Armstrong

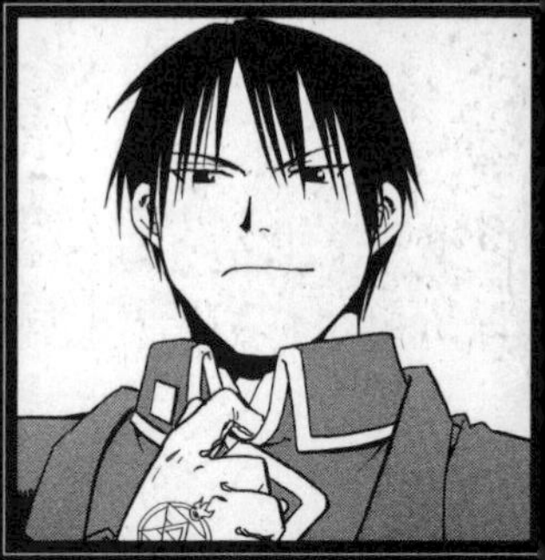

ロイ・マスタング

Roy Mustang

OUTLINE

FULLMETAL ALCHEMIST

The Elrics' plan to capture and interrogate Gluttony, one of the evil and nigh-invulnerable homunculi, goes awry when his "sibling" Envy crashes the party. Gluttony reveals his true bestial form and, in a rage, swallows Ed, Lin, and Envy, sending the three of them into a dark void eerily containing a larg amount of rubble and…blood. Al, fearing his brother lost forever, demands that Gluttony take him to the mysterious "father" of the homunculi…

The Elric Brothers have made a shocking discovery–the Amestris President King Bradley, is a Homunculus–an artificial human born of the Philosopher' Stone. Even more shocking, Bradley's rise to power was orchestrated by th military, and his master, the mysterious "Father," wants the Elrics alive for s nefarious purpose. Meanwhile, Lin, in his quest to discover the secret to immortality, has done the unthinkable–surrendered his body to "Greed," giving new life to the fallen Homunculus.

鋼の錬金術師
FULLMETAL ALCHEMIST

| CHARACTERS
FULLMETAL ALCHEMIST

■ ウィンリィ・ロックベル

Winry Rockbell

■ スカー

Scar

■ リザ・ホークアイ

Riza Hawkeye

■ キング・ブラッドレイ

King Bradley

■ ゾルフ・J・キンブリー

Solf J. Kimblee

■ マース・ヒューズ

Maes Hughes

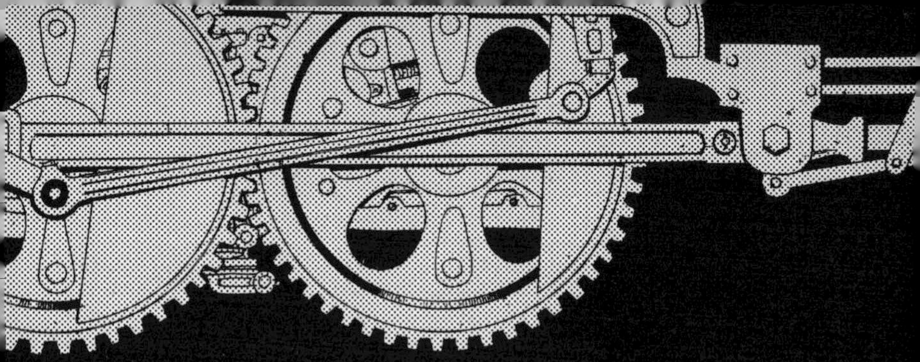

CONTENTS

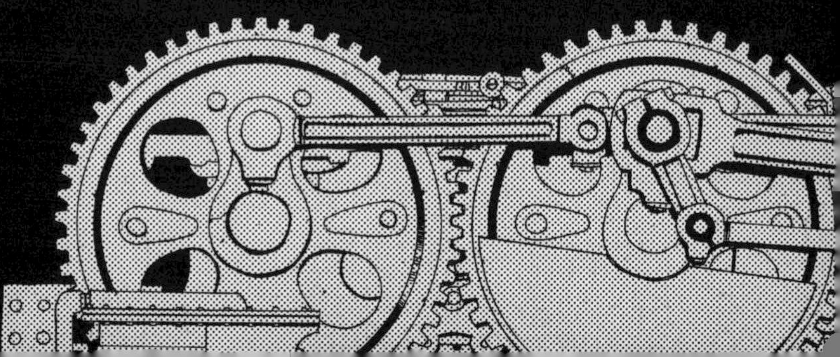

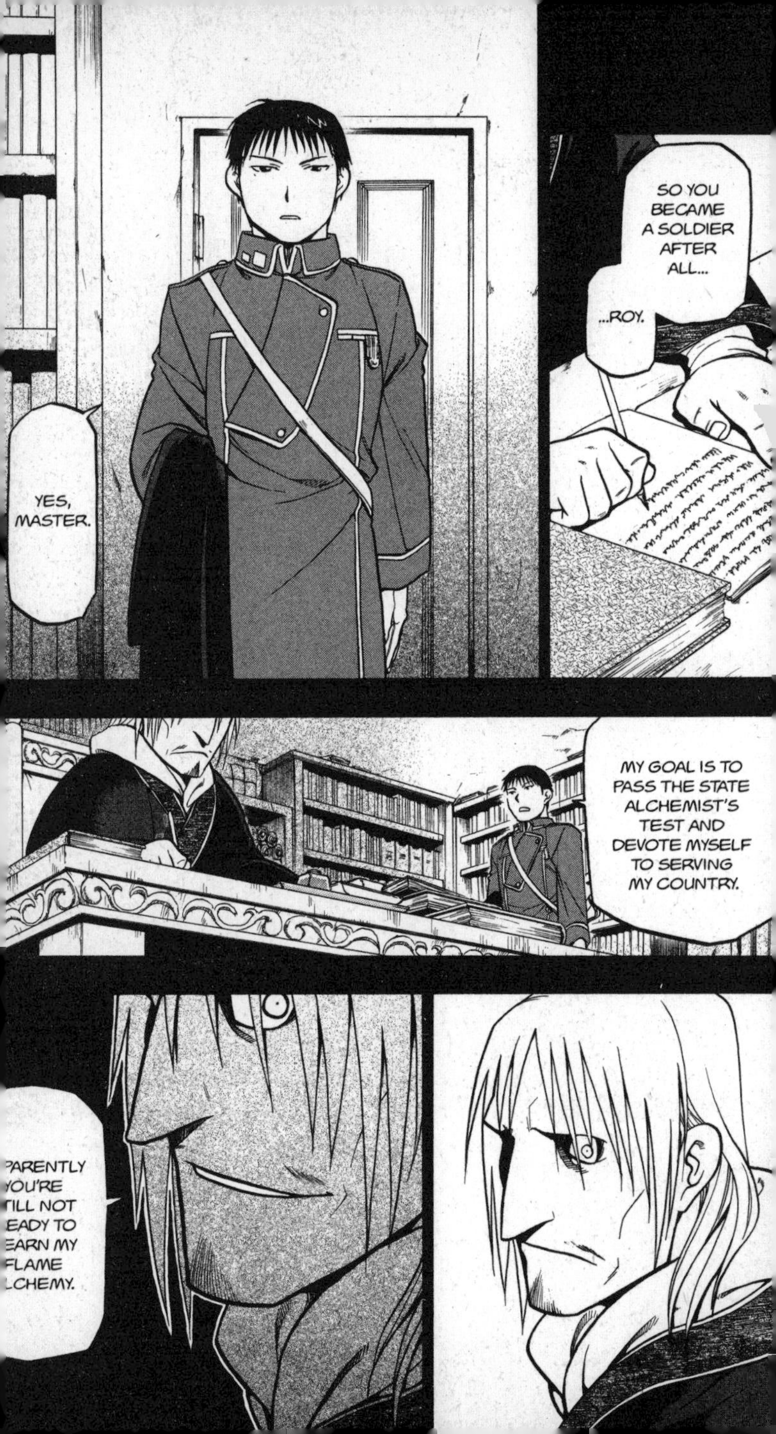
SO YOU BECAME A SOLDIER AFTER ALL...
...ROY.
YES, MASTER.
MY GOAL IS TO PASS THE STATE ALCHEMIST'S TEST AND DEVOTE MYSELF TO SERVING MY COUNTRY.
PARENTLY YOU'RE TILL NOT EADY TO EARN MY FLAME LCHEMY.

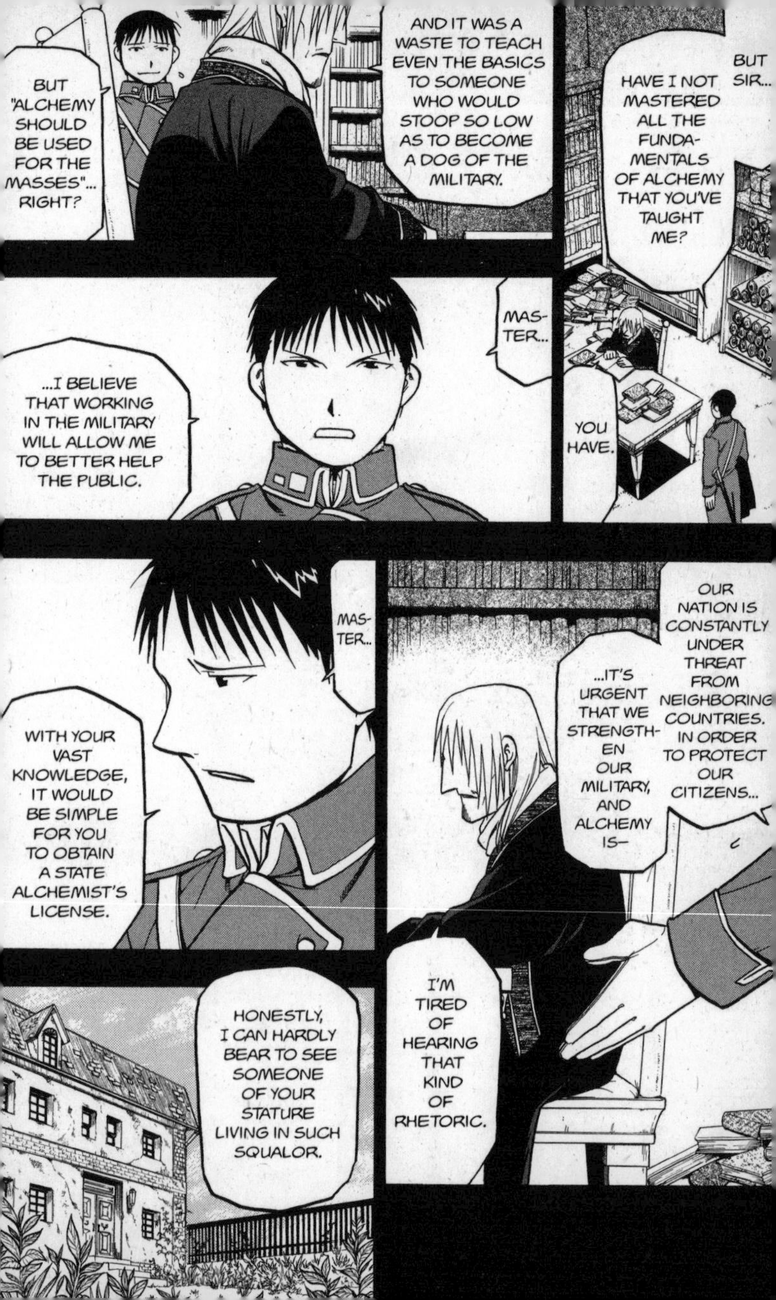
BUT SIR...
HAVE I NOT MASTERED ALL THE FUNDA-MENTALS OF ALCHEMY THAT YOU'VE TAUGHT ME?
YOU HAVE.
AND IT WAS A WASTE TO TEACH EVEN THE BASICS TO SOMEONE WHO WOULD STOOP SO LOW AS TO BECOME A DOG OF THE MILITARY.
BUT "ALCHEMY SHOULD BE USED FOR THE MASSES"... RIGHT?
MAS-TER...
...I BELIEVE THAT WORKING IN THE MILITARY WILL ALLOW ME TO BETTER HELP THE PUBLIC.
OUR NATION IS CONSTANTLY UNDER THREAT FROM NEIGHBORING COUNTRIES. IN ORDER TO PROTECT OUR CITIZENS...
...IT'S URGENT THAT WE STRENGTH-EN OUR MILITARY, AND ALCHEMY IS—
I'M TIRED OF HEARING THAT KIND OF RHETORIC.
MAS-TER...
WITH YOUR VAST KNOWLEDGE, IT WOULD BE SIMPLE FOR YOU TO OBTAIN A STATE ALCHEMIST'S LICENSE.
HONESTLY, I CAN HARDLY BEAR TO SEE SOMEONE OF YOUR STATURE LIVING IN SUCH SQUALOR.

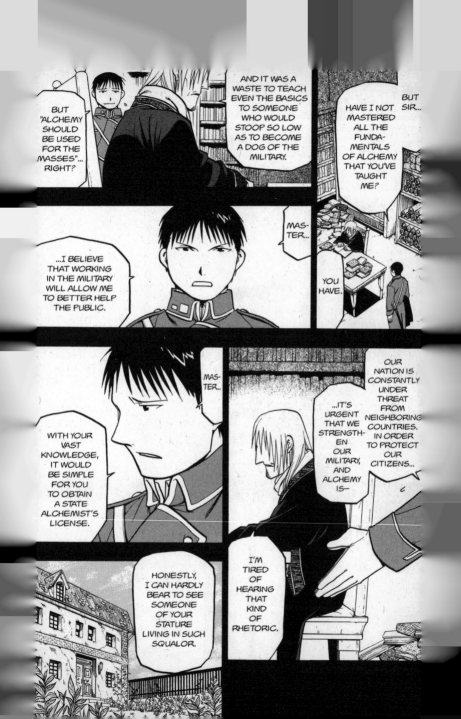

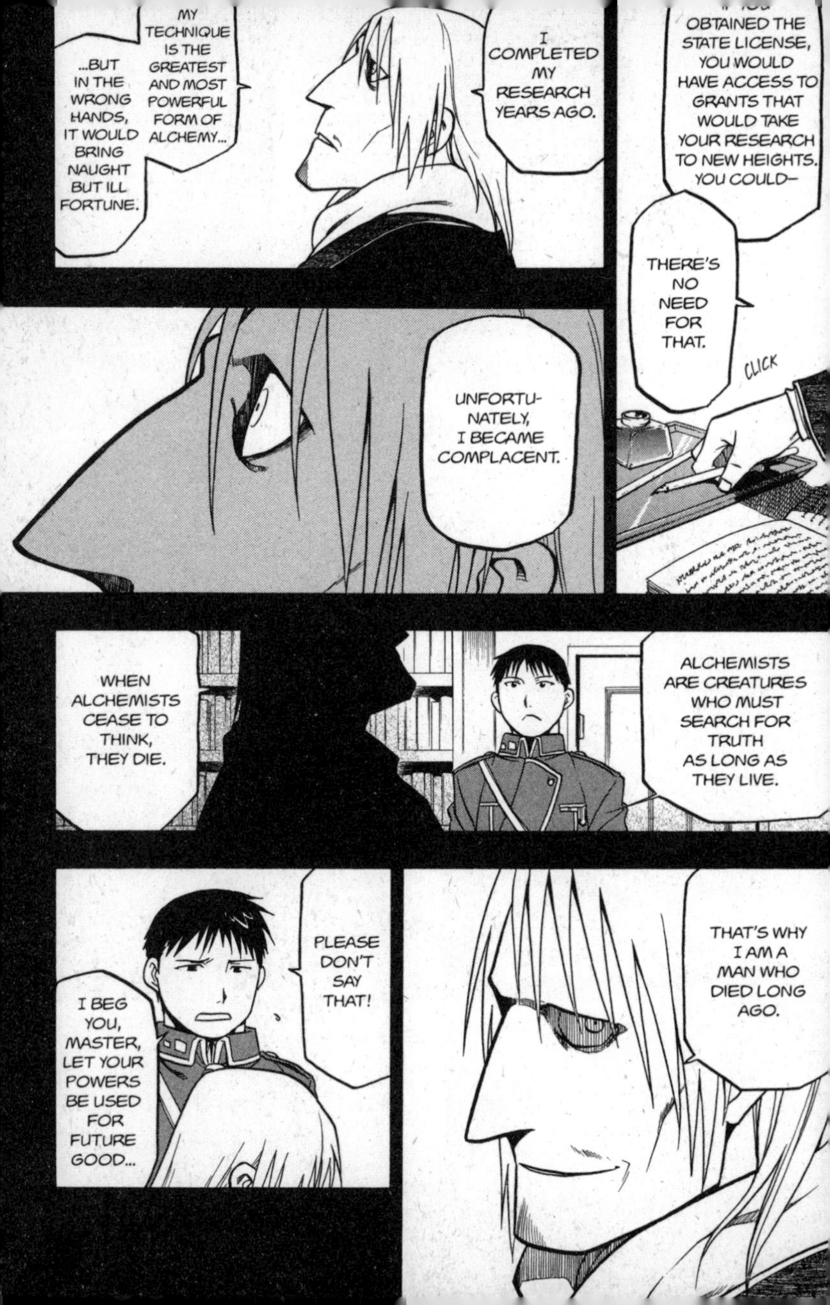
OBTAINED THE STATE LICENSE, YOU WOULD HAVE ACCESS TO GRANTS THAT WOULD TAKE YOUR RESEARCH TO NEW HEIGHTS. YOU COULD–
THERE'S NO NEED FOR THAT.
CLICK
I COMPLETED MY RESEARCH YEARS AGO.
MY TECHNIQUE IS THE GREATEST AND MOST POWERFUL FORM OF ALCHEMY...
...BUT IN THE WRONG HANDS, IT WOULD BRING NAUGHT BUT ILL FORTUNE.
UNFORTU-NATELY, I BECAME COMPLACENT.
ALCHEMISTS ARE CREATURES WHO MUST SEARCH FOR TRUTH AS LONG AS THEY LIVE.
WHEN ALCHEMISTS CEASE TO THINK, THEY DIE.
THAT'S WHY I AM A MAN WHO DIED LONG AGO.
PLEASE DON'T SAY THAT!
I BEG YOU, MASTER, LET YOUR POWERS BE USED FOR FUTURE GOOD...

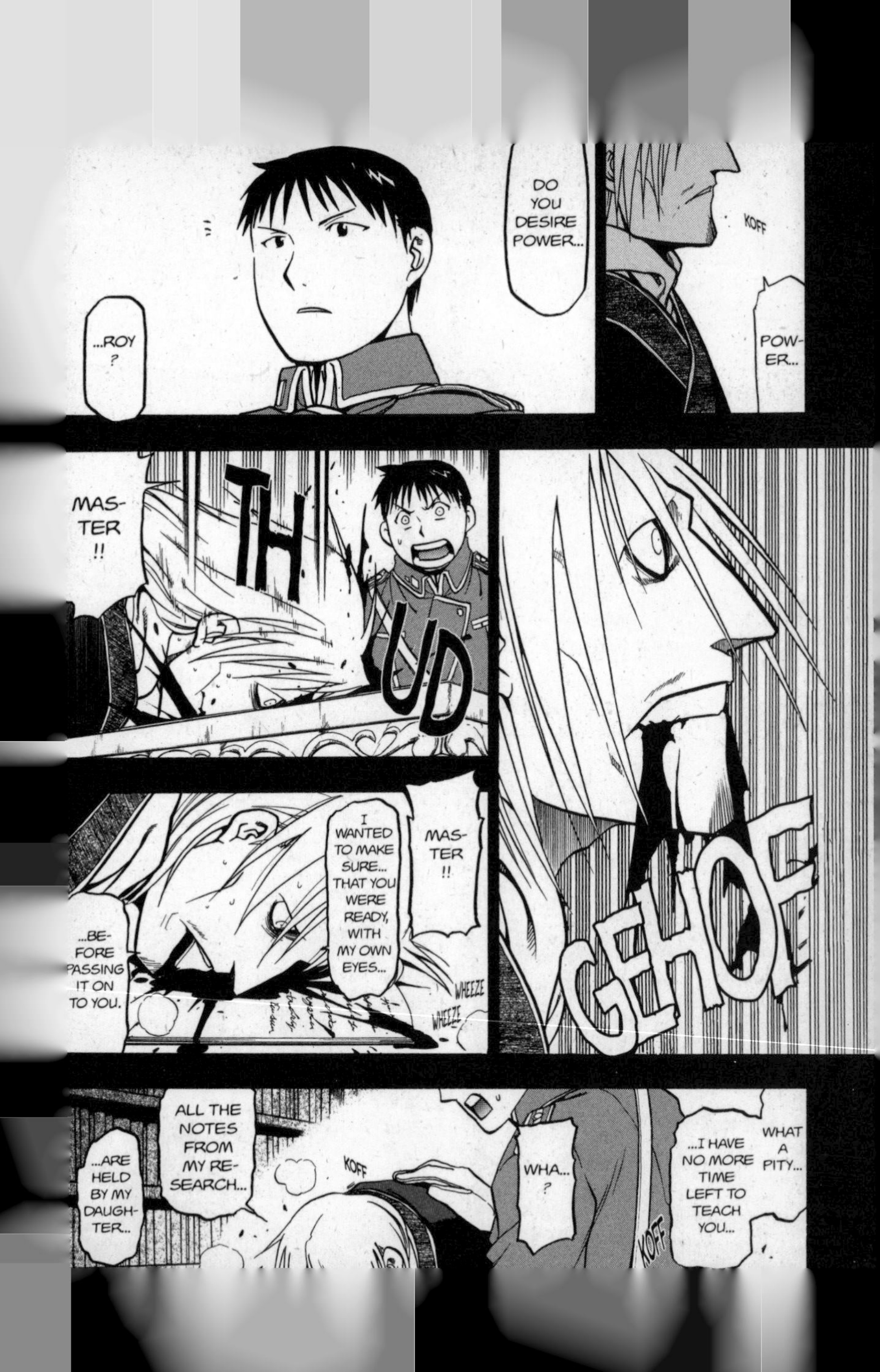
DO YOU DESIRE POWER...
KOFF
POW-ER...
...ROY ?
GEHOF
TH
UD
MAS-TER !!
MAS-TER !!
I WANTED TO MAKE SURE... THAT YOU WERE READY, WITH MY OWN EYES...
...BE-FORE PASSING IT ON TO YOU.
WHEEZE
WHEEZE
WHAT A PITY...
...I HAVE NO MORE TIME LEFT TO TEACH YOU...
KOFF
WHA... ?
ALL THE NOTES FROM MY RE-SEARCH...
KOFF
...ARE HELD BY MY DAUGH-TER...

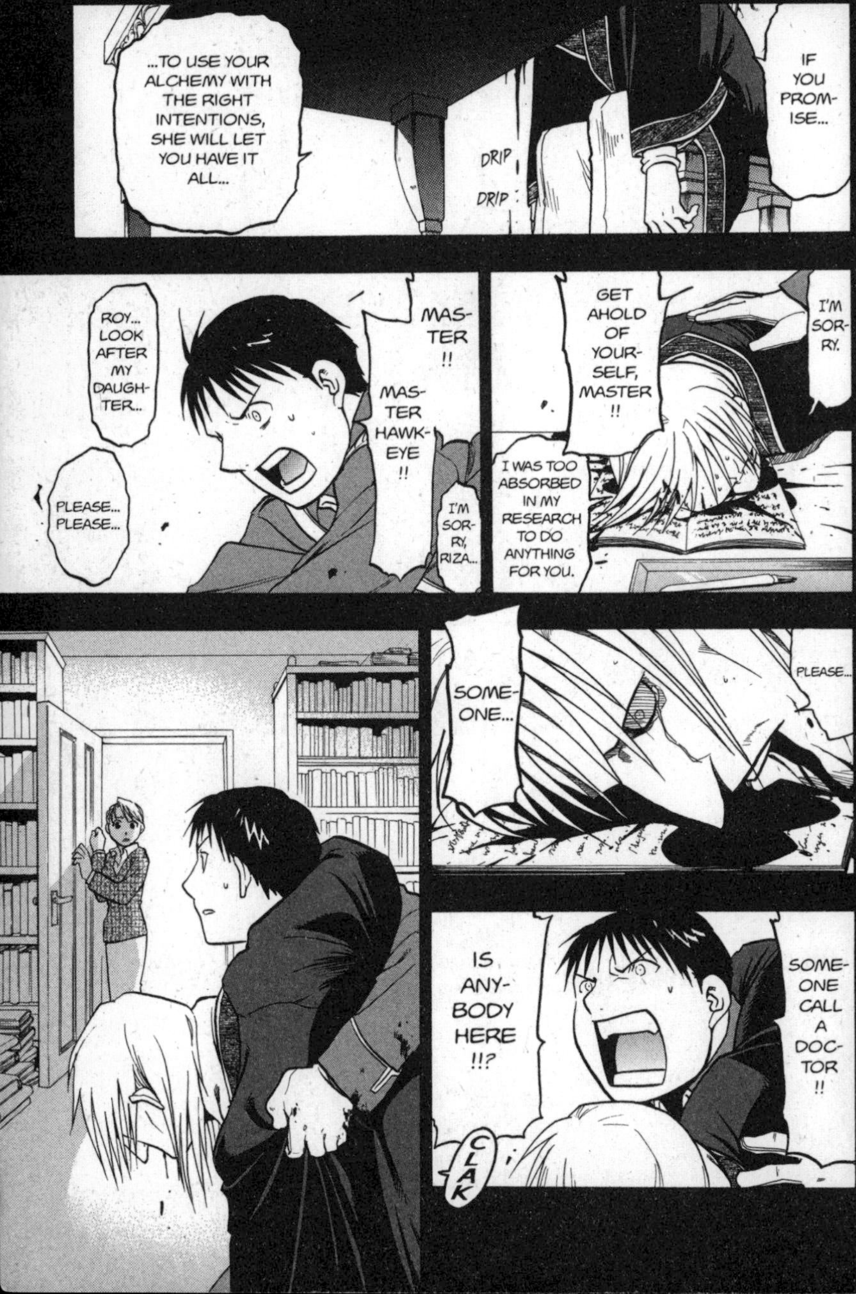
IF YOU PROMISE...
DRIP
DRIP
...TO USE YOUR ALCHEMY WITH THE RIGHT INTENTIONS, SHE WILL LET YOU HAVE IT ALL...
I'M SORRY.
GET AHOLD OF YOURSELF, MASTER!!
I WAS TOO ABSORBED IN MY RESEARCH TO DO ANYTHING FOR YOU.
MASTER!!
MASTER HAWKEYE!!
I'M SORRY, RIZA...
ROY... LOOK AFTER MY DAUGHTER...
PLEASE... PLEASE...
PLEASE...
SOMEONE...
SOMEONE CALL A DOCTOR!!
IS ANYBODY HERE!!?
CLAK

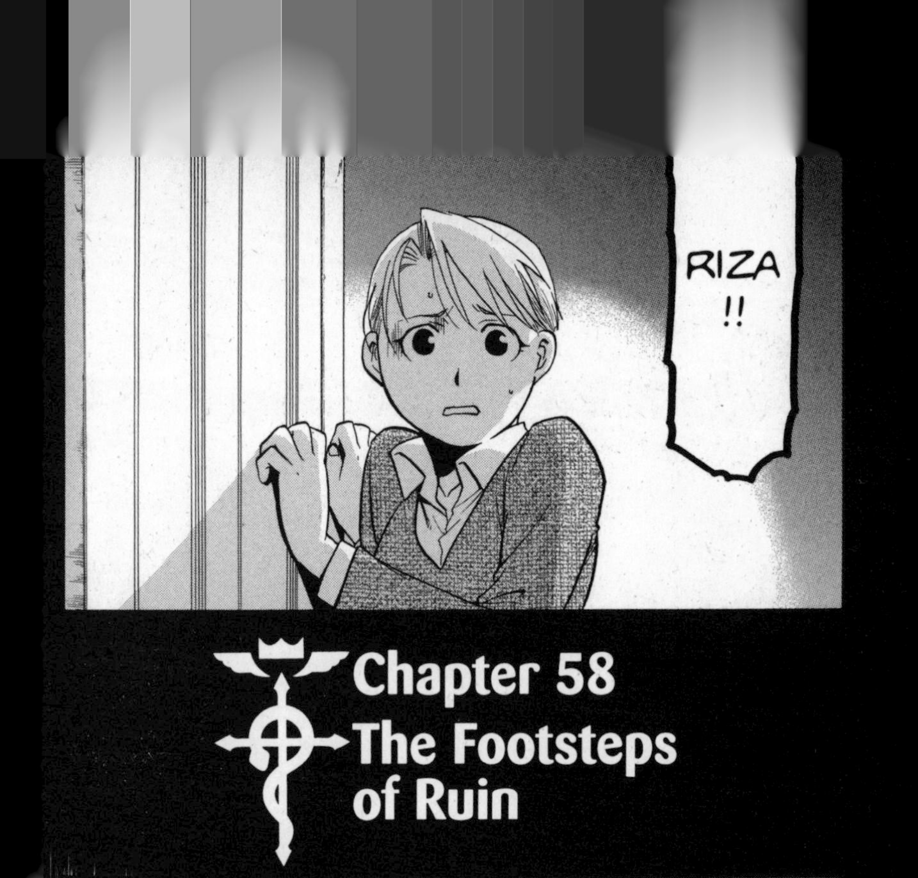
RIZA !!

Chapter 58 The Footsteps of Ruin

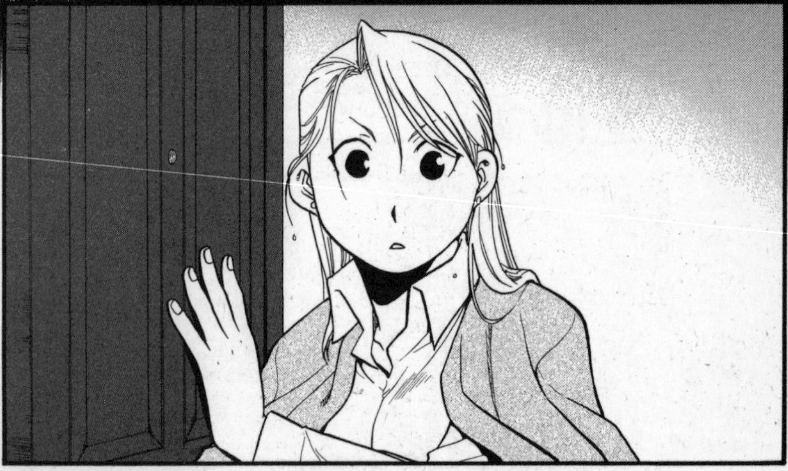

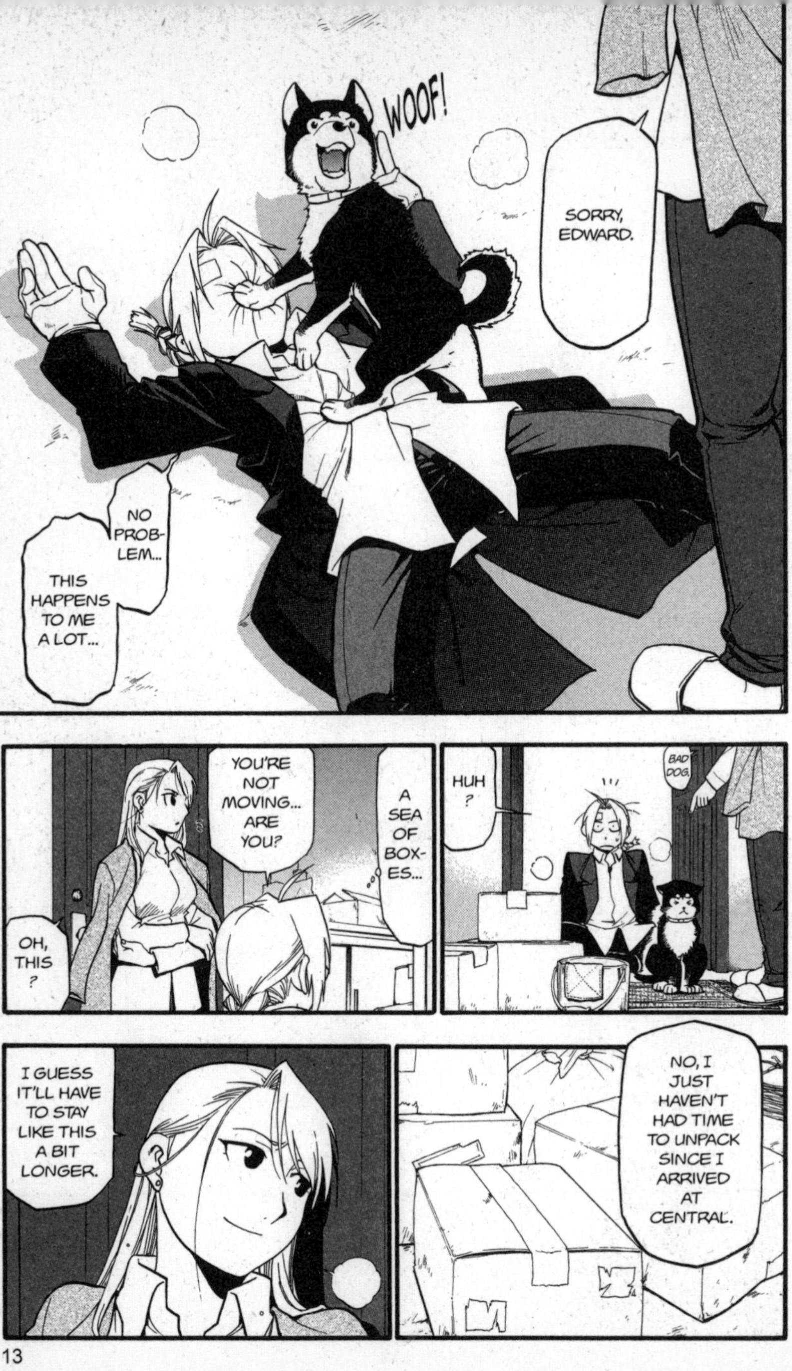
SORRY, EDWARD.
WOOF!
NO PROBLEM...
THIS HAPPENS TO ME A LOT...
BAD DOG.
HUH?
A SEA OF BOXES...
YOU'RE NOT MOVING... ARE YOU?
OH, THIS?
NO, I JUST HAVEN'T HAD TIME TO UNPACK SINCE I ARRIVED AT CENTRAL.
I GUESS IT'LL HAVE TO STAY LIKE THIS A BIT LONGER.

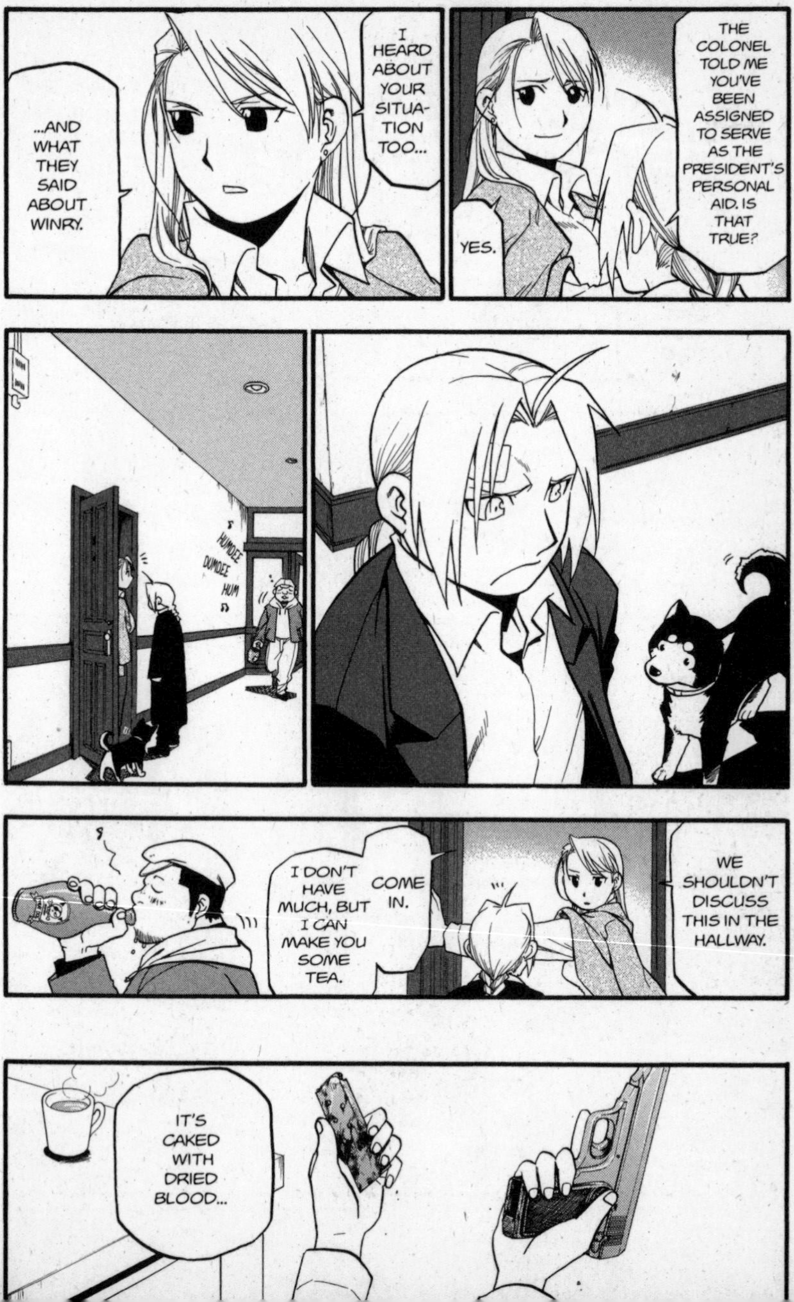
THE COLONEL TOLD ME YOU'VE BEEN ASSIGNED TO SERVE AS THE PRESIDENT'S PERSONAL AID. IS THAT TRUE?
YES.
I HEARD ABOUT YOUR SITUATION TOO...
...AND WHAT THEY SAID ABOUT WINRY.
HUMDEE DUMDEE HUM
WE SHOULDN'T DISCUSS THIS IN THE HALLWAY.
COME IN.
I DON'T HAVE MUCH, BUT I CAN MAKE YOU SOME TEA.
IT'S CAKED WITH DRIED BLOOD...

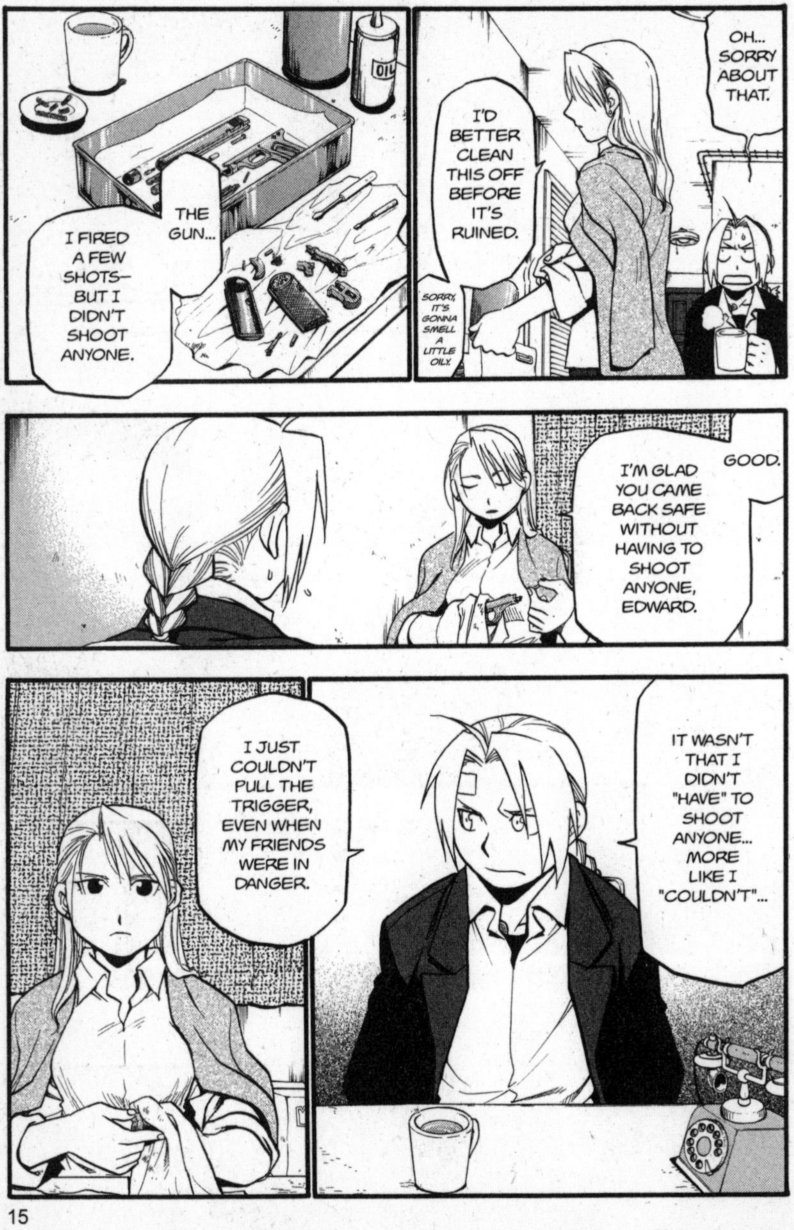
OH... SORRY ABOUT THAT.
I'D BETTER CLEAN THIS OFF BEFORE IT'S RUINED.
SORRY, IT'S GONNA SMELL A LITTLE OILY.
THE GUN...
I FIRED A FEW SHOTS— BUT I DIDN'T SHOOT ANYONE.
GOOD.
I'M GLAD YOU CAME BACK SAFE WITHOUT HAVING TO SHOOT ANYONE, EDWARD.
IT WASN'T THAT I DIDN'T "HAVE" TO SHOOT ANYONE... MORE LIKE I "COULDN'T"...
I JUST COULDN'T PULL THE TRIGGER, EVEN WHEN MY FRIENDS WERE IN DANGER.

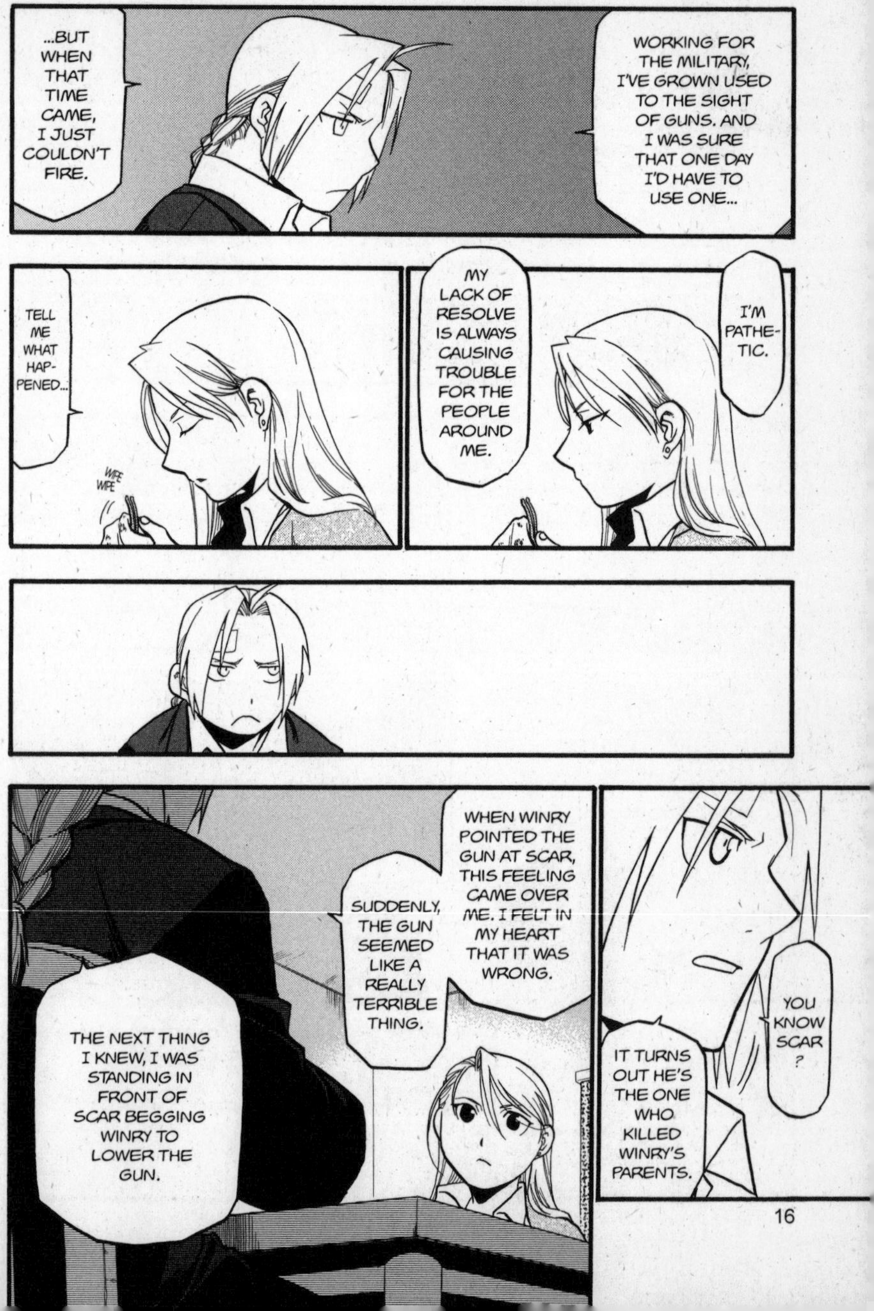
WORKING FOR THE MILITARY, I'VE GROWN USED TO THE SIGHT OF GUNS. AND I WAS SURE THAT ONE DAY I'D HAVE TO USE ONE...
...BUT WHEN THAT TIME CAME, I JUST COULDN'T FIRE.
I'M PATHETIC.
MY LACK OF RESOLVE IS ALWAYS CAUSING TROUBLE FOR THE PEOPLE AROUND ME.
TELL ME WHAT HAPPENED...
WIPE WIPE
YOU KNOW SCAR?
IT TURNS OUT HE'S THE ONE WHO KILLED WINRY'S PARENTS.
WHEN WINRY POINTED THE GUN AT SCAR, THIS FEELING CAME OVER ME. I FELT IN MY HEART THAT IT WAS WRONG.
SUDDENLY, THE GUN SEEMED LIKE A REALLY TERRIBLE THING.
THE NEXT THING I KNEW, I WAS STANDING IN FRONT OF SCAR BEGGING WINRY TO LOWER THE GUN.

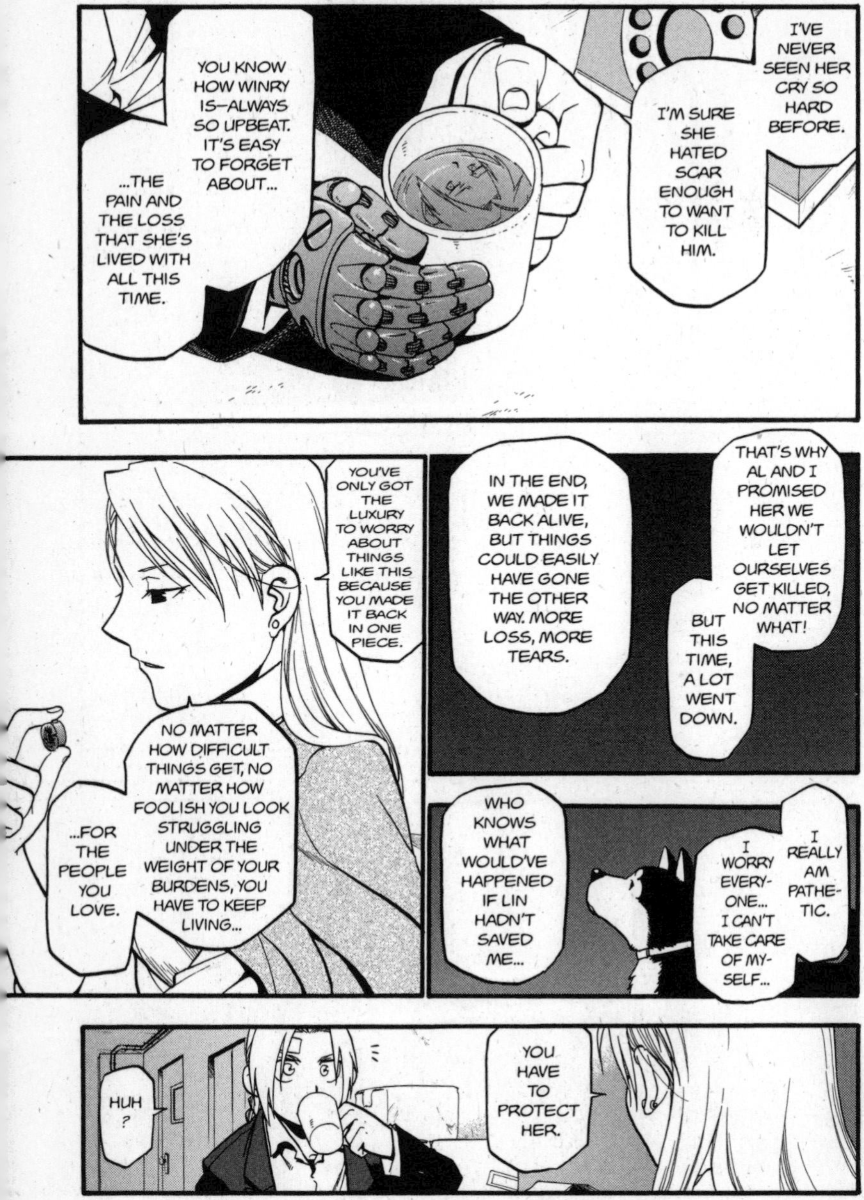
I'VE NEVER SEEN HER CRY SO HARD BEFORE.
I'M SURE SHE HATED SCAR ENOUGH TO WANT TO KILL HIM.
YOU KNOW HOW WINRY IS—ALWAYS SO UPBEAT. IT'S EASY TO FORGET ABOUT...
...THE PAIN AND THE LOSS THAT SHE'S LIVED WITH ALL THIS TIME.
THAT'S WHY AL AND I PROMISED HER WE WOULDN'T LET OURSELVES GET KILLED, NO MATTER WHAT!
BUT THIS TIME, A LOT WENT DOWN.
IN THE END, WE MADE IT BACK ALIVE, BUT THINGS COULD EASILY HAVE GONE THE OTHER WAY. MORE LOSS, MORE TEARS.
I REALLY AM PATHETIC.
I WORRY EVERYONE... I CAN'T TAKE CARE OF MYSELF...
WHO KNOWS WHAT WOULD'VE HAPPENED IF LIN HADN'T SAVED ME...
YOU'VE ONLY GOT THE LUXURY TO WORRY ABOUT THINGS LIKE THIS BECAUSE YOU MADE IT BACK IN ONE PIECE.
NO MATTER HOW DIFFICULT THINGS GET, NO MATTER HOW FOOLISH YOU LOOK STRUGGLING UNDER THE WEIGHT OF YOUR BURDENS, YOU HAVE TO KEEP LIVING...
...FOR THE PEOPLE YOU LOVE.
YOU HAVE TO PROTECT HER.
HUH?

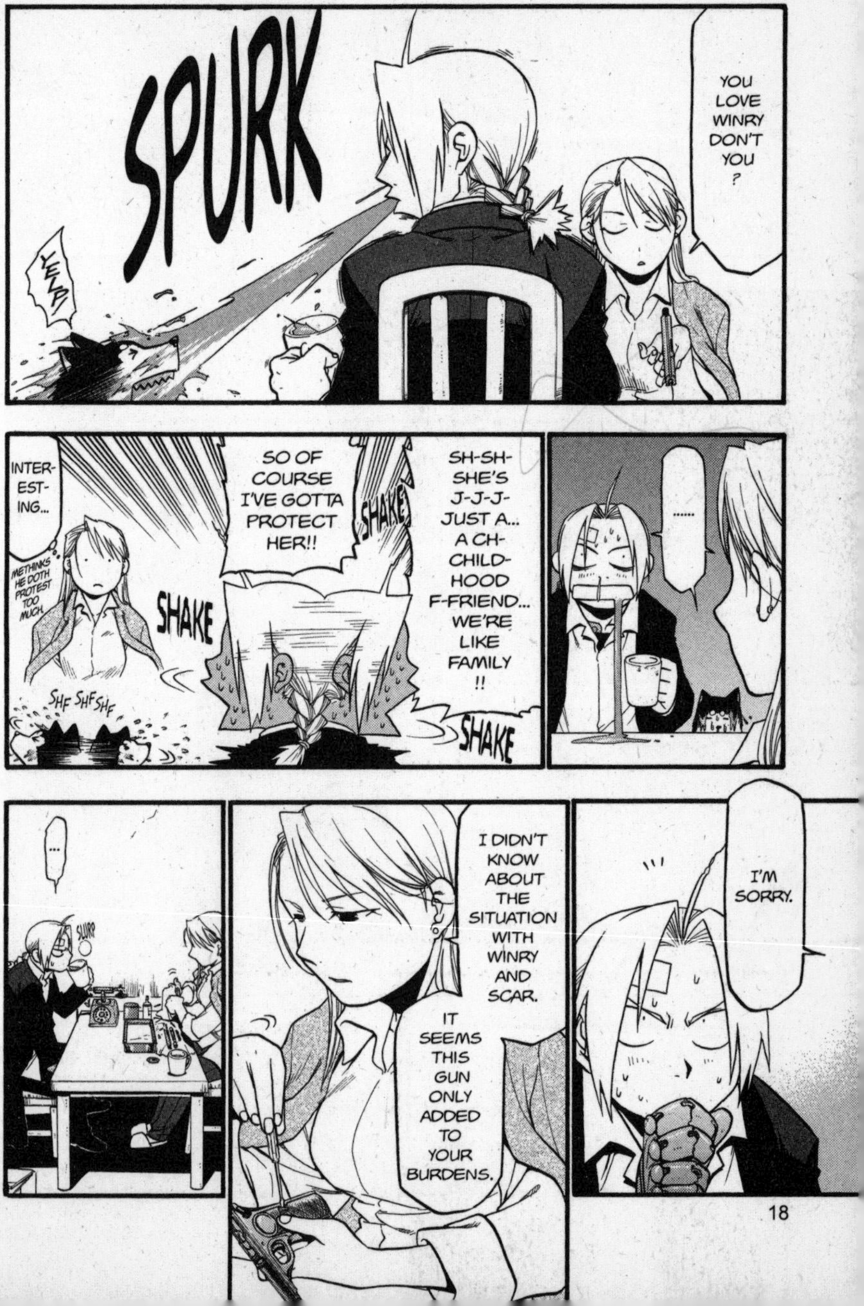
YOU LOVE WINRY DON'T YOU ?
SPURK
YELP!
......
SH-SH-SHE'S J-J-J-JUST A... A CH-CHILDHOOD F-FRIEND... WE'RE LIKE FAMILY !!
SHAKE
SO OF COURSE I'VE GOTTA PROTECT HER!!
SHAKE
SHAKE
INTER-EST-ING...
METHINKS HE DOTH PROTEST TOO MUCH.
SHF SHF SHF
I'M SORRY.
I DIDN'T KNOW ABOUT THE SITUATION WITH WINRY AND SCAR.
IT SEEMS THIS GUN ONLY ADDED TO YOUR BURDENS.
...
SLURP

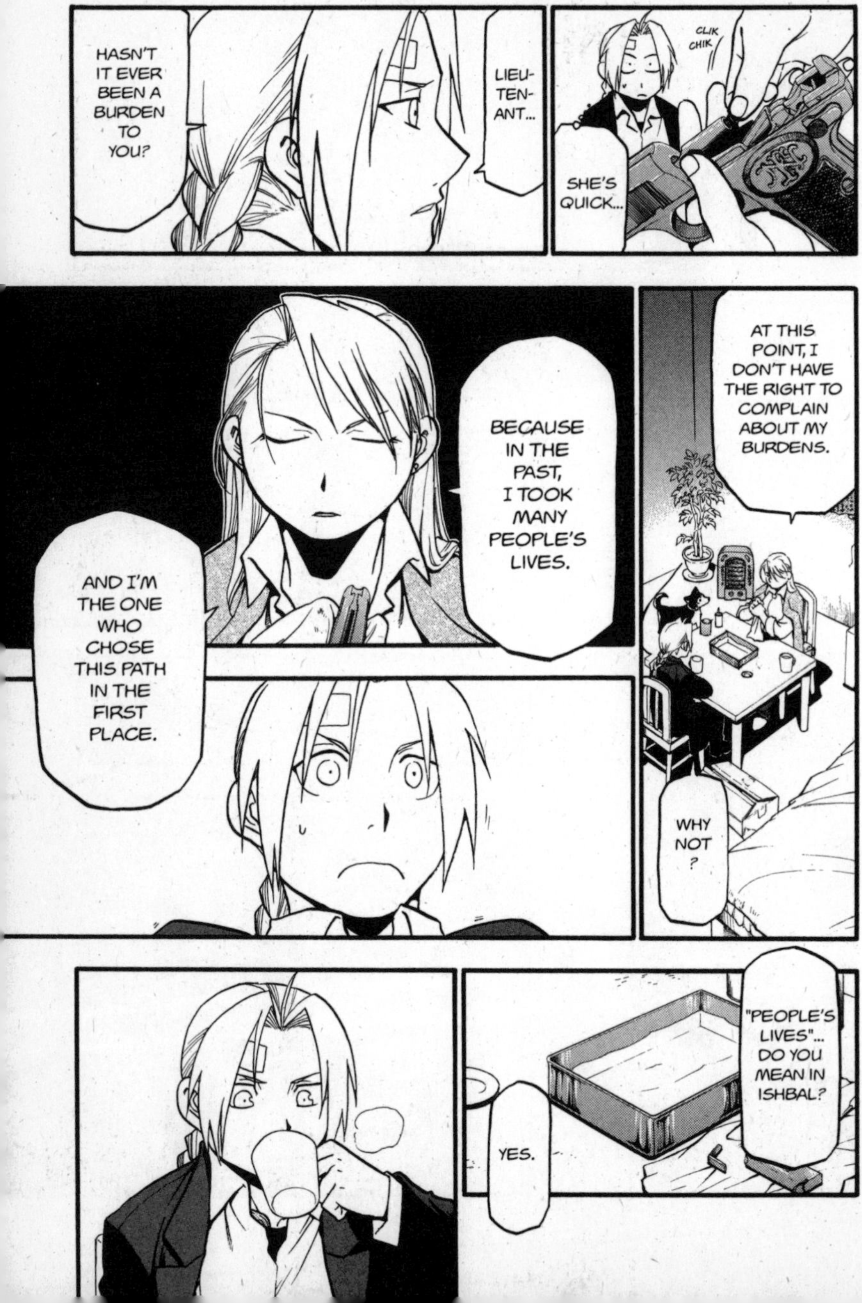
CLIK CHIK
SHE'S QUICK...
LIEU-TEN-ANT...
HASN'T IT EVER BEEN A BURDEN TO YOU?
AT THIS POINT, I DON'T HAVE THE RIGHT TO COMPLAIN ABOUT MY BURDENS.
WHY NOT ?
BECAUSE IN THE PAST, I TOOK MANY PEOPLE'S LIVES.
AND I'M THE ONE WHO CHOSE THIS PATH IN THE FIRST PLACE.
"PEOPLE'S LIVES"... DO YOU MEAN IN ISHBAL?
YES.

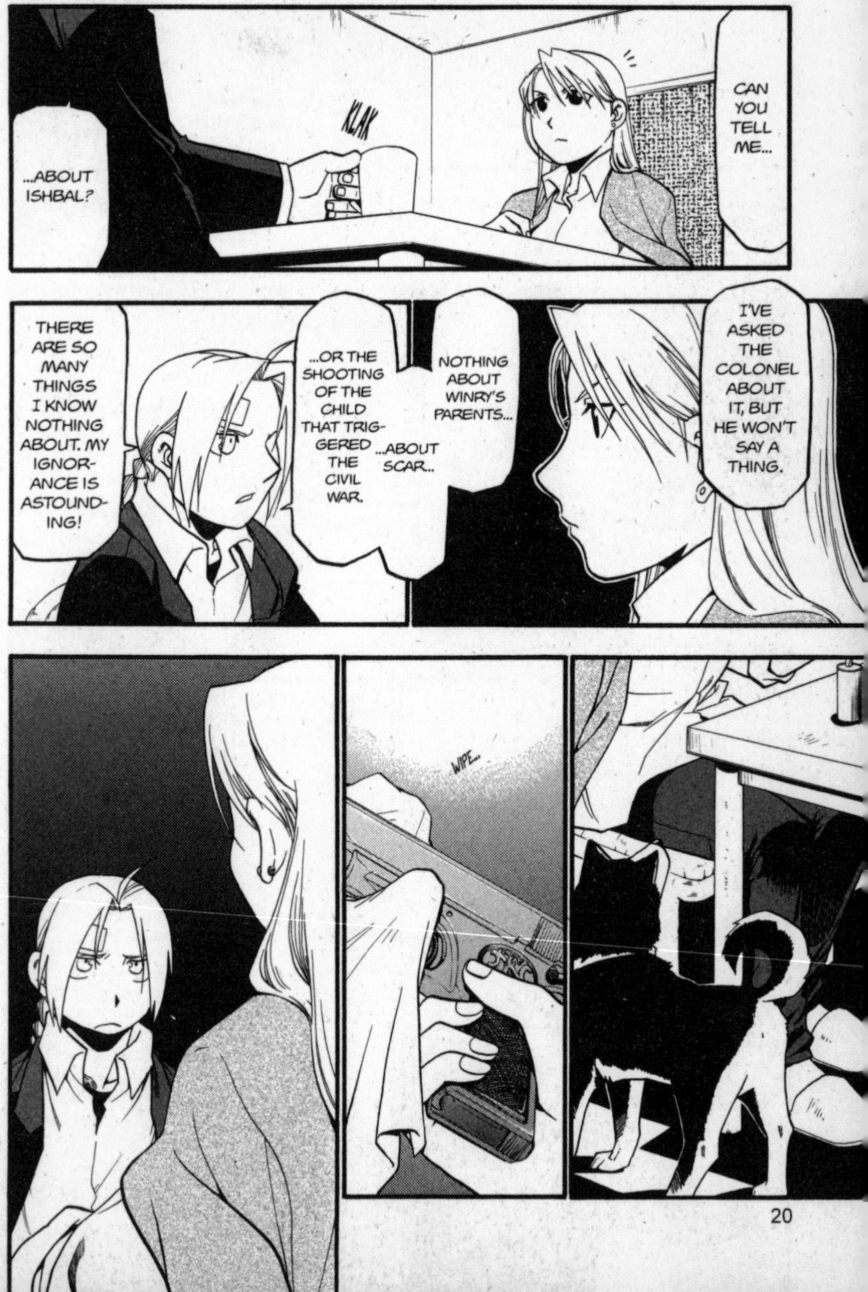
CAN YOU TELL ME...
KLAK
...ABOUT ISHBAL?
I'VE ASKED THE COLONEL ABOUT IT, BUT HE WON'T SAY A THING.
NOTHING ABOUT WINRY'S PARENTS...
...ABOUT SCAR...
...OR THE SHOOTING OF THE CHILD THAT TRIG-GERED THE CIVIL WAR.
THERE ARE SO MANY THINGS I KNOW NOTHING ABOUT. MY IGNOR-ANCE IS ASTOUND-ING!
WIPE...

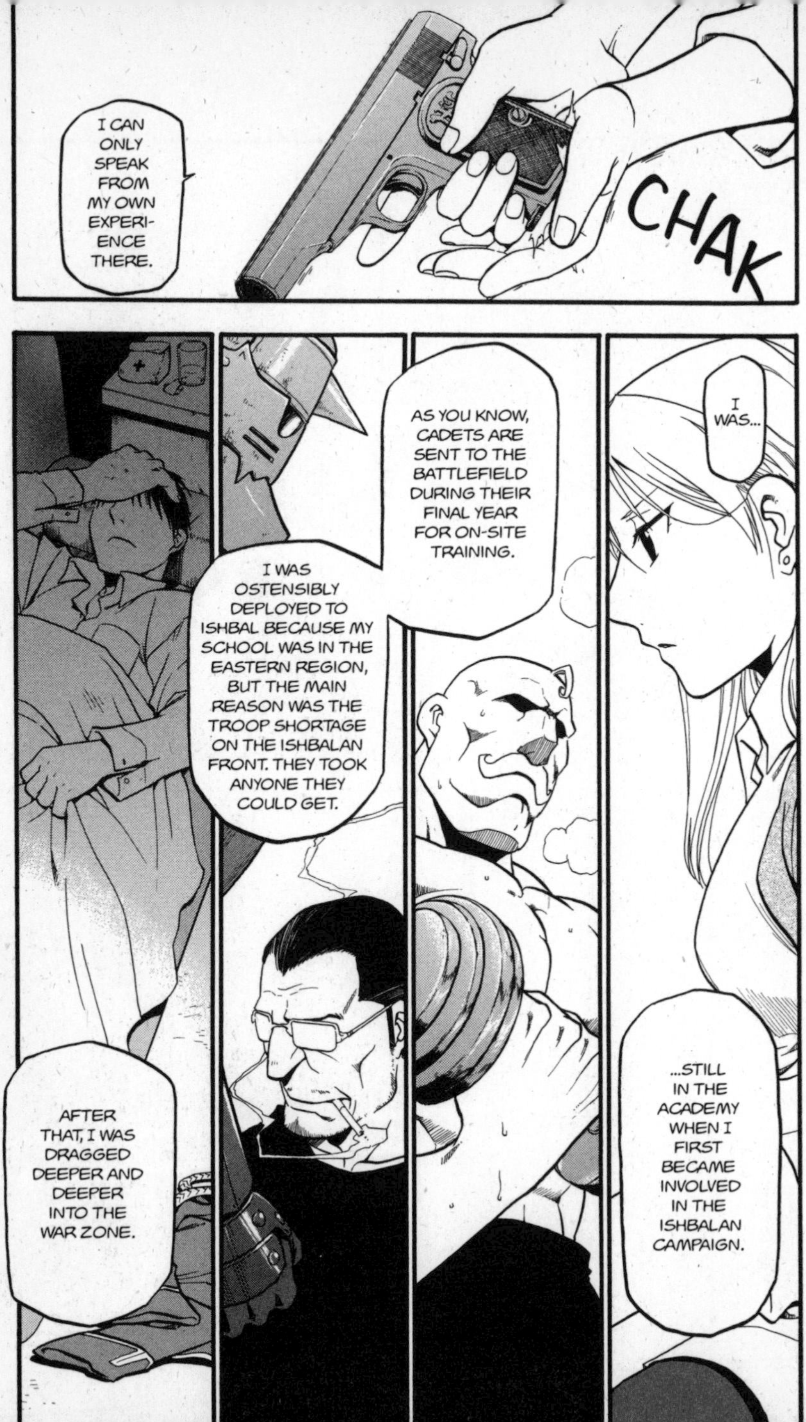
CHAK
I CAN ONLY SPEAK FROM MY OWN EXPERIENCE THERE.
I WAS...
...STILL IN THE ACADEMY WHEN I FIRST BECAME INVOLVED IN THE ISHBALAN CAMPAIGN.
AS YOU KNOW, CADETS ARE SENT TO THE BATTLEFIELD DURING THEIR FINAL YEAR FOR ON-SITE TRAINING.
I WAS OSTENSIBLY DEPLOYED TO ISHBAL BECAUSE MY SCHOOL WAS IN THE EASTERN REGION, BUT THE MAIN REASON WAS THE TROOP SHORTAGE ON THE ISHBALAN FRONT. THEY TOOK ANYONE THEY COULD GET.
AFTER THAT, I WAS DRAGGED DEEPER AND DEEPER INTO THE WAR ZONE.

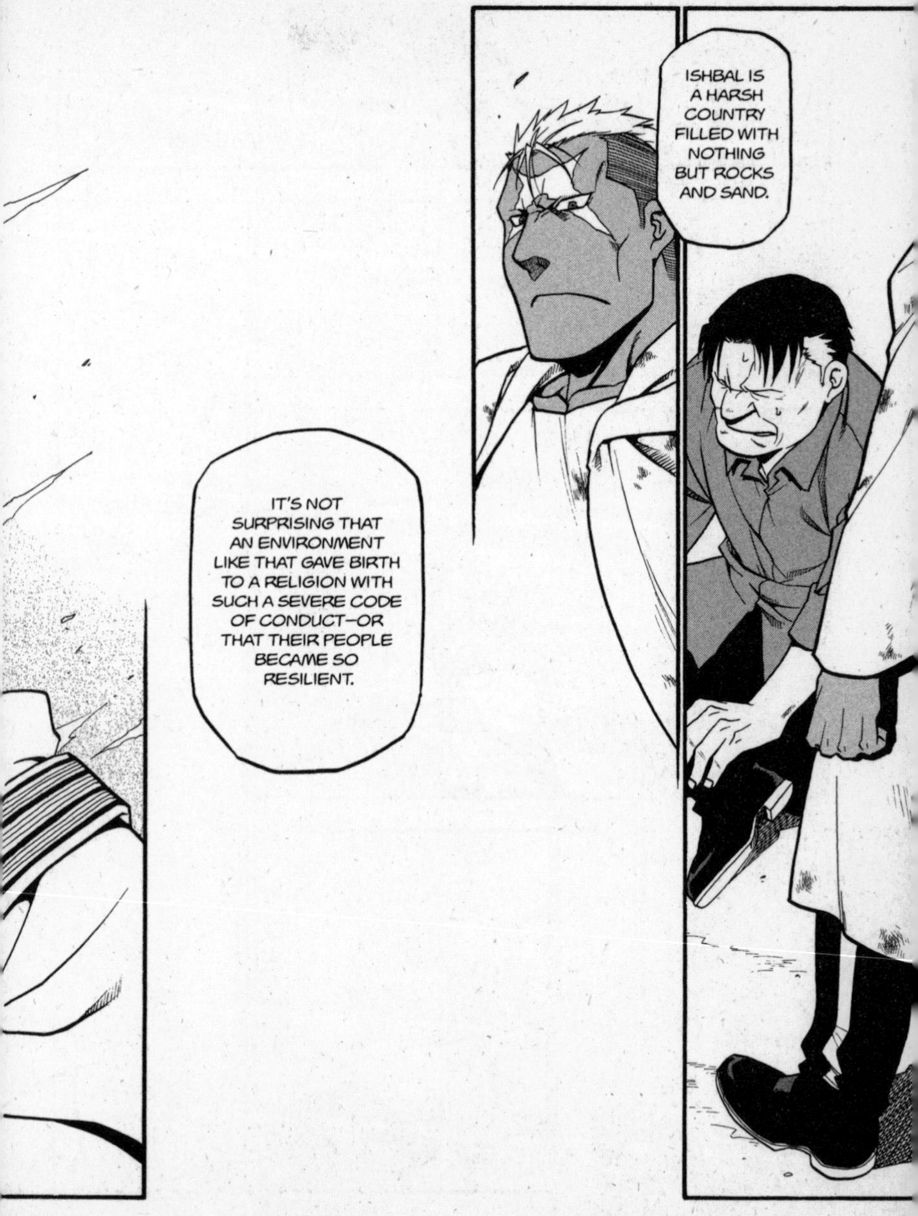
ISHBAL IS A HARSH COUNTRY FILLED WITH NOTHING BUT ROCKS AND SAND.
IT'S NOT SURPRISING THAT AN ENVIRONMENT LIKE THAT GAVE BIRTH TO A RELIGION WITH SUCH A SEVERE CODE OF CONDUCT—OR THAT THEIR PEOPLE BECAME SO RESILIENT.

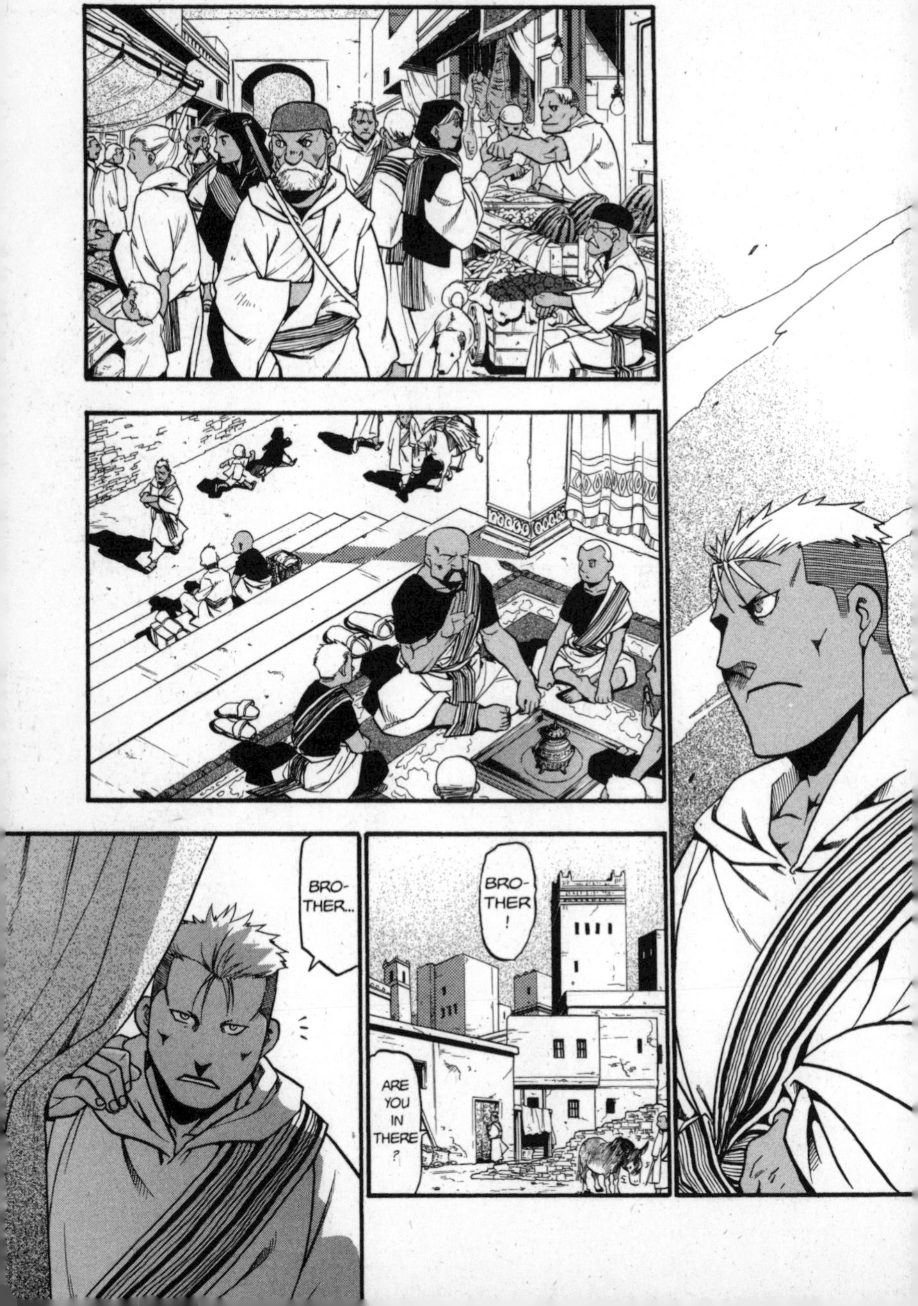
BRO-THER!
ARE YOU IN THERE?
BRO-THER...

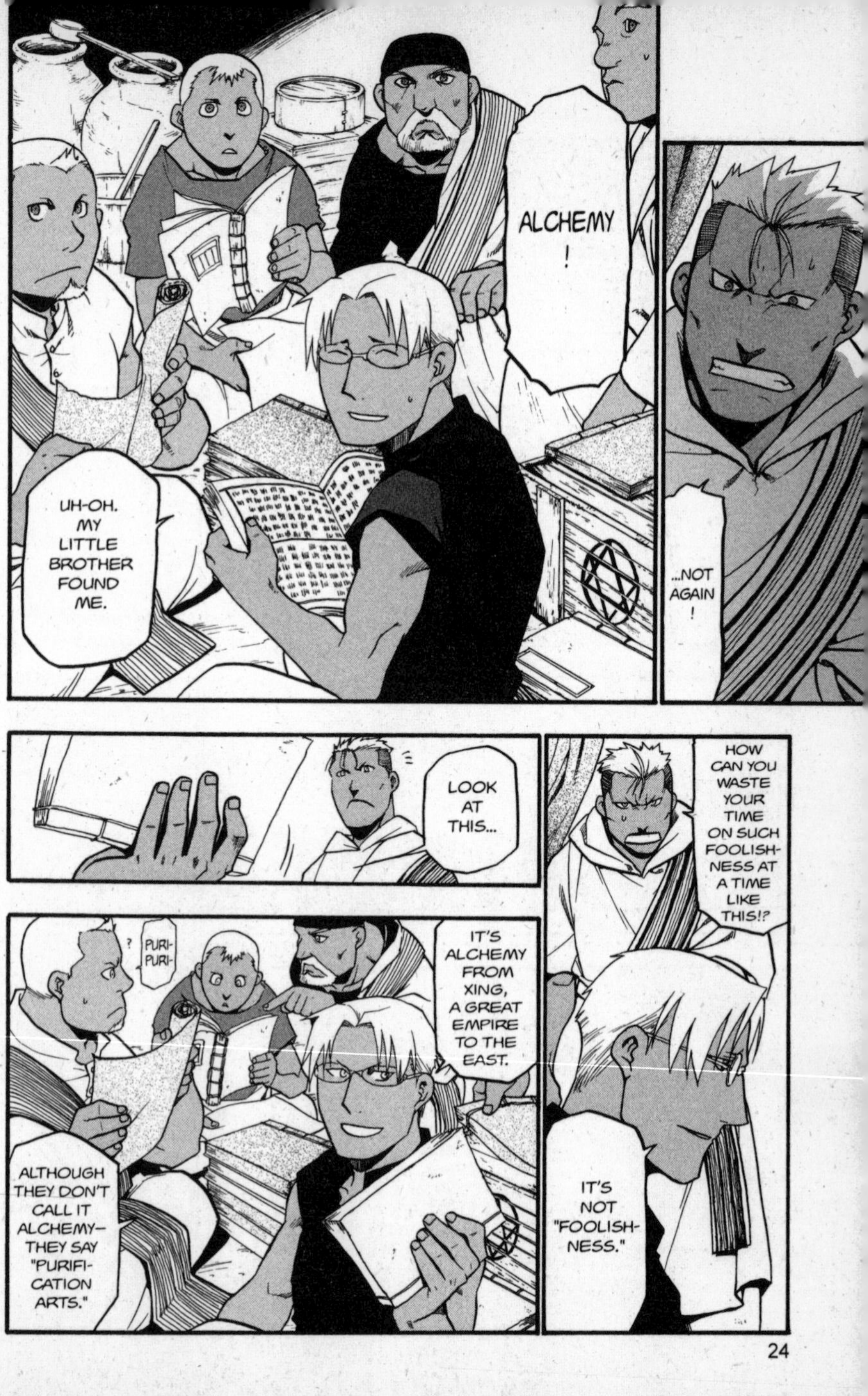
...NOT AGAIN!
ALCHEMY!
UH-OH. MY LITTLE BROTHER FOUND ME.
HOW CAN YOU WASTE YOUR TIME ON SUCH FOOLISHNESS AT A TIME LIKE THIS!?
IT'S NOT "FOOLISHNESS."
LOOK AT THIS...
IT'S ALCHEMY FROM XING, A GREAT EMPIRE TO THE EAST.
PURI-PURI-
?
ALTHOUGH THEY DON'T CALL IT ALCHEMY— THEY SAY "PURIFICATION ARTS."

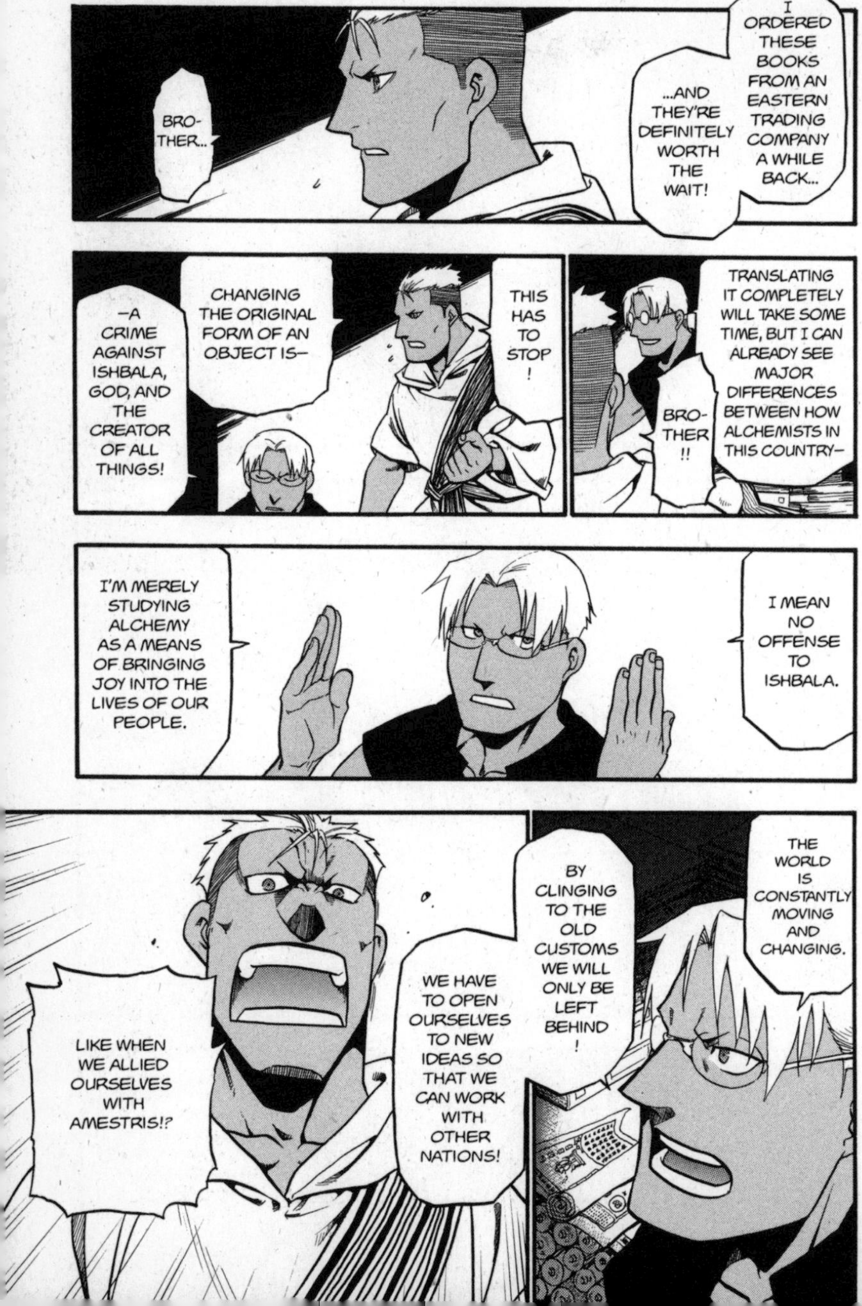
I ORDERED THESE BOOKS FROM AN EASTERN TRADING COMPANY A WHILE BACK...
...AND THEY'RE DEFINITELY WORTH THE WAIT!
BRO-THER...
TRANSLATING IT COMPLETELY WILL TAKE SOME TIME, BUT I CAN ALREADY SEE MAJOR DIFFERENCES BETWEEN HOW ALCHEMISTS IN THIS COUNTRY—
BRO-THER!!
THIS HAS TO STOP!
CHANGING THE ORIGINAL FORM OF AN OBJECT IS—
—A CRIME AGAINST ISHBALA, GOD, AND THE CREATOR OF ALL THINGS!
I MEAN NO OFFENSE TO ISHBALA.
I'M MERELY STUDYING ALCHEMY AS A MEANS OF BRINGING JOY INTO THE LIVES OF OUR PEOPLE.
THE WORLD IS CONSTANTLY MOVING AND CHANGING.
BY CLINGING TO THE OLD CUSTOMS WE WILL ONLY BE LEFT BEHIND!
WE HAVE TO OPEN OURSELVES TO NEW IDEAS SO THAT WE CAN WORK WITH OTHER NATIONS!
LIKE WHEN WE ALLIED OURSELVES WITH AMESTRIS!?

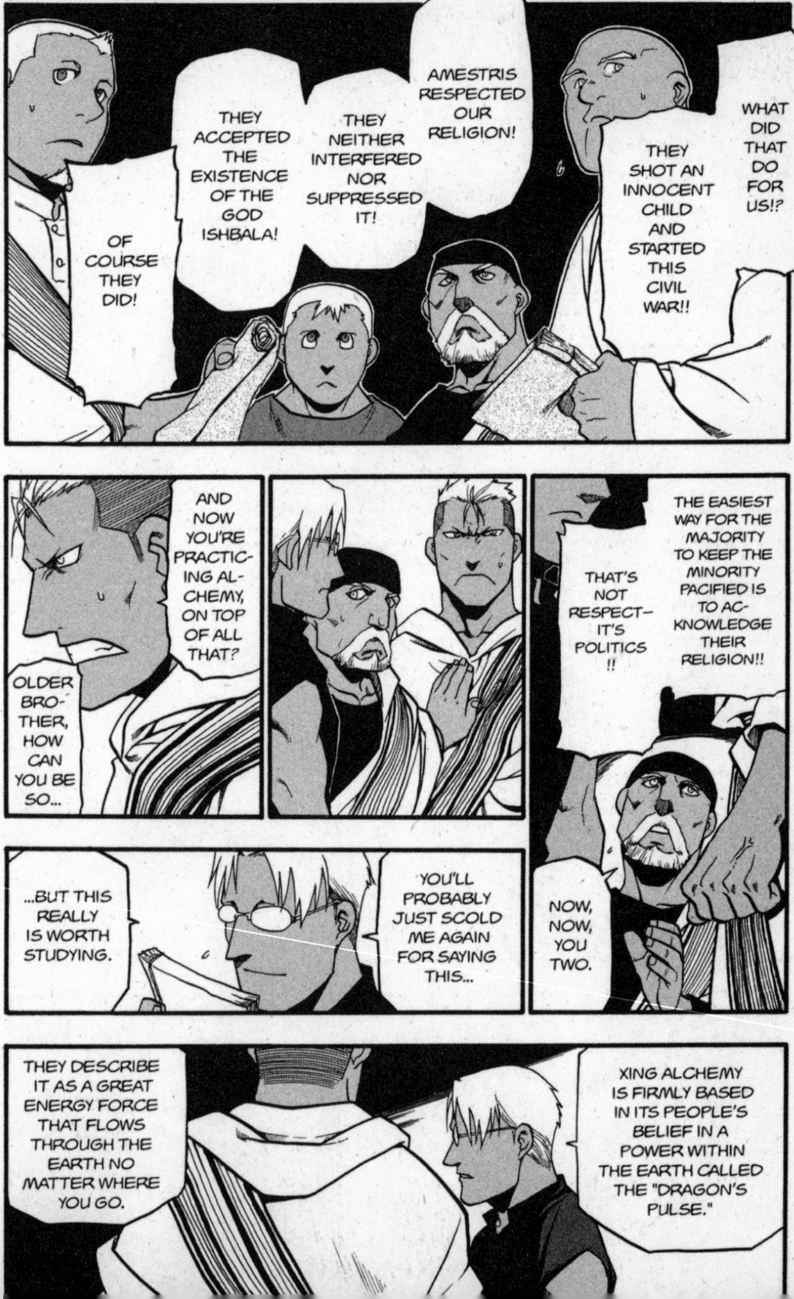
WHAT DID THAT DO FOR US!?
THEY SHOT AN INNOCENT CHILD AND STARTED THIS CIVIL WAR!!
AMESTRIS RESPECTED OUR RELIGION!
THEY NEITHER INTERFERED NOR SUPPRESSED IT!
THEY ACCEPTED THE EXISTENCE OF THE GOD ISHBALA!
OF COURSE THEY DID!
THE EASIEST WAY FOR THE MAJORITY TO KEEP THE MINORITY PACIFIED IS TO ACKNOWLEDGE THEIR RELIGION!!
THAT'S NOT RESPECT—IT'S POLITICS!!
NOW, NOW, YOU TWO.
AND NOW YOU'RE PRACTICING ALCHEMY, ON TOP OF ALL THAT?
OLDER BROTHER, HOW CAN YOU BE SO...
YOU'LL PROBABLY JUST SCOLD ME AGAIN FOR SAYING THIS...
...BUT THIS REALLY IS WORTH STUDYING.
XING ALCHEMY IS FIRMLY BASED IN ITS PEOPLE'S BELIEF IN A POWER WITHIN THE EARTH CALLED THE "DRAGON'S PULSE."
THEY DESCRIBE IT AS A GREAT ENERGY FORCE THAT FLOWS THROUGH THE EARTH NO MATTER WHERE YOU GO.

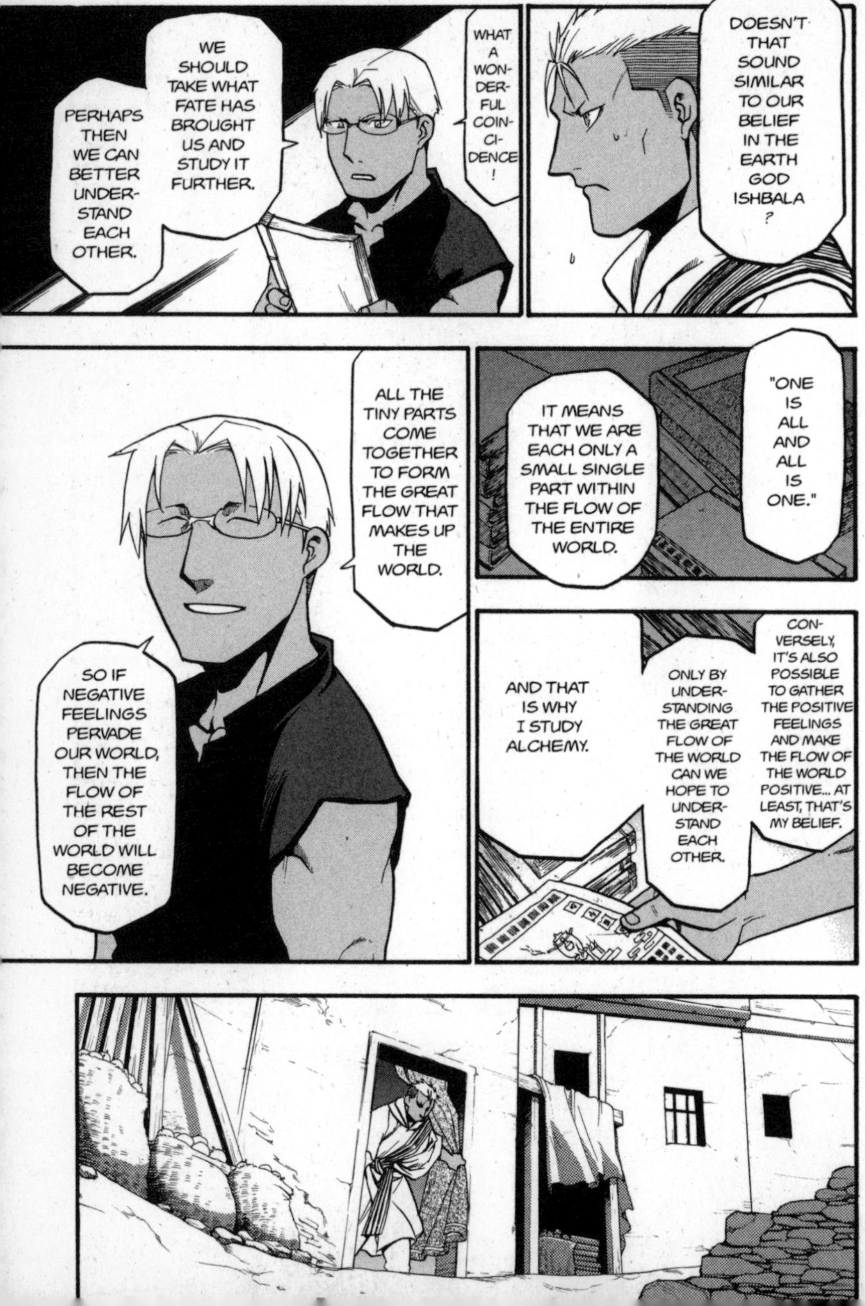
DOESN'T THAT SOUND SIMILAR TO OUR BELIEF IN THE EARTH GOD ISHBALA?
WHAT A WONDERFUL COINCIDENCE!
WE SHOULD TAKE WHAT FATE HAS BROUGHT US AND STUDY IT FURTHER.
PERHAPS THEN WE CAN BETTER UNDERSTAND EACH OTHER.
"ONE IS ALL AND ALL IS ONE."
IT MEANS THAT WE ARE EACH ONLY A SMALL SINGLE PART WITHIN THE FLOW OF THE ENTIRE WORLD.
CONVERSELY, IT'S ALSO POSSIBLE TO GATHER THE POSITIVE FEELINGS AND MAKE THE FLOW OF THE WORLD POSITIVE... AT LEAST, THAT'S MY BELIEF.
ONLY BY UNDERSTANDING THE GREAT FLOW OF THE WORLD CAN WE HOPE TO UNDERSTAND EACH OTHER.
AND THAT IS WHY I STUDY ALCHEMY.
ALL THE TINY PARTS COME TOGETHER TO FORM THE GREAT FLOW THAT MAKES UP THE WORLD.
SO IF NEGATIVE FEELINGS PERVADE OUR WORLD, THEN THE FLOW OF THE REST OF THE WORLD WILL BECOME NEGATIVE.

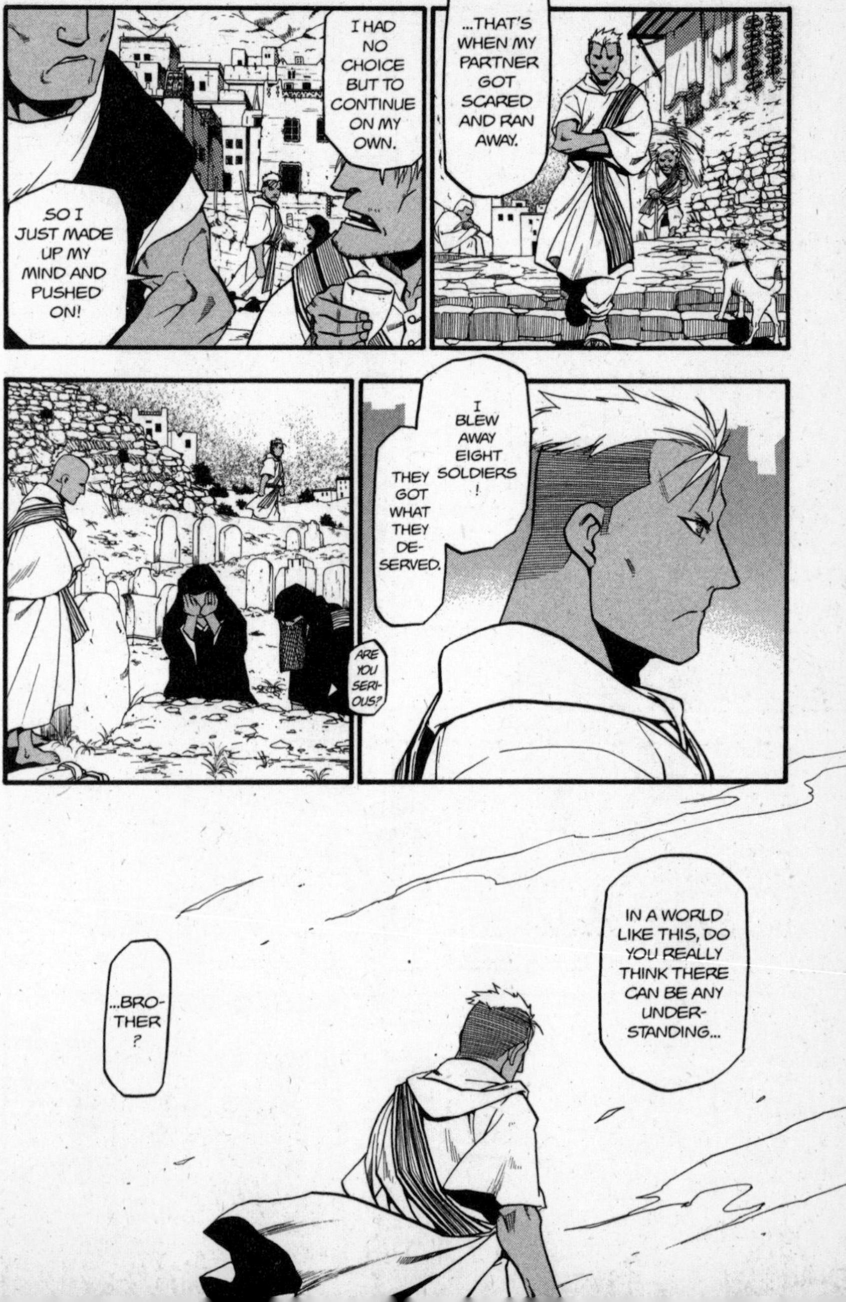
...THAT'S WHEN MY PARTNER GOT SCARED AND RAN AWAY.
I HAD NO CHOICE BUT TO CONTINUE ON MY OWN.
SO I JUST MADE UP MY MIND AND PUSHED ON!
I BLEW AWAY EIGHT SOLDIERS!
THEY GOT WHAT THEY DE-SERVED.
ARE YOU SERI-OUS?
IN A WORLD LIKE THIS, DO YOU REALLY THINK THERE CAN BE ANY UNDER-STANDING...
...BRO-THER?

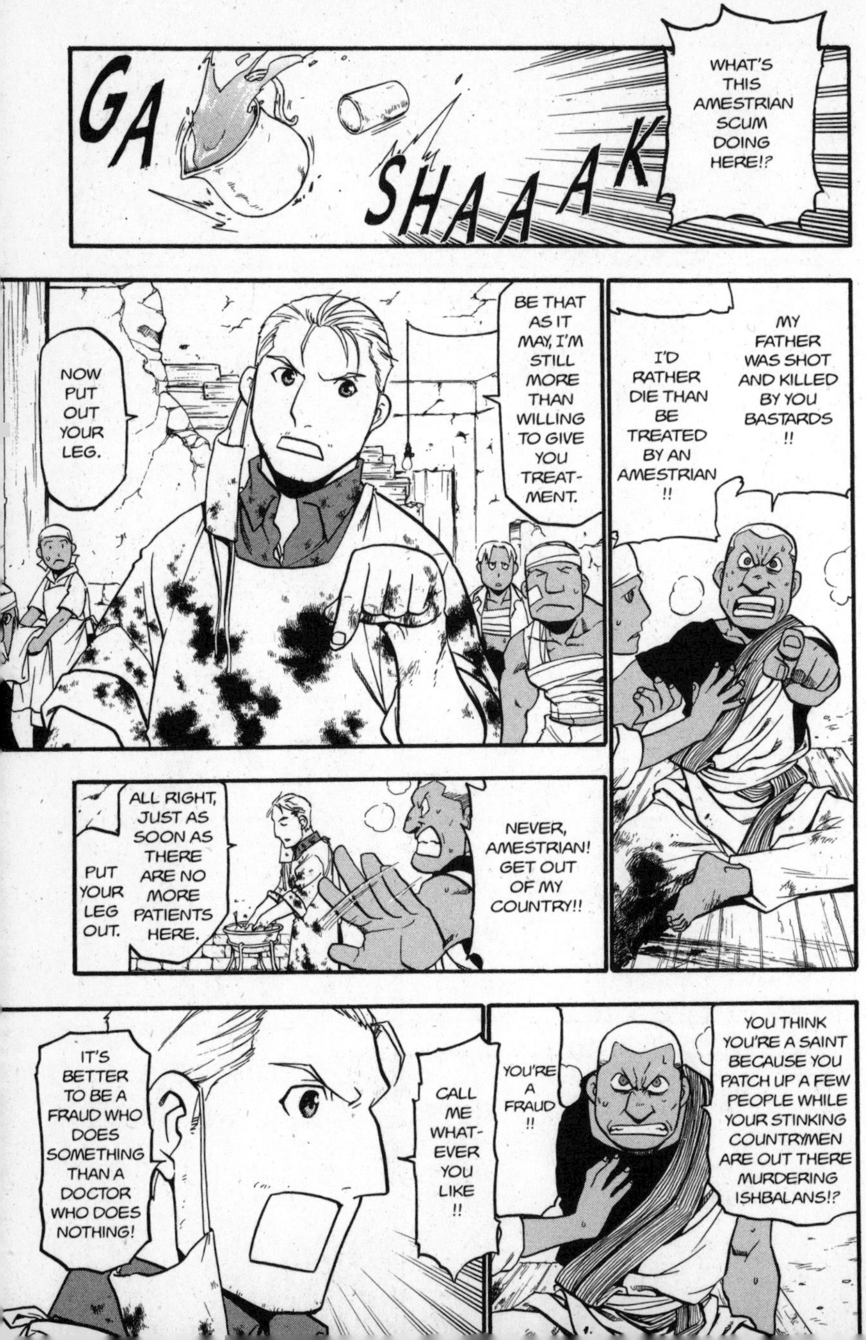
WHAT'S THIS AMESTRIAN SCUM DOING HERE!?
GA
SHAAAK
MY FATHER WAS SHOT AND KILLED BY YOU BASTARDS!!
I'D RATHER DIE THAN BE TREATED BY AN AMESTRIAN!!
BE THAT AS IT MAY, I'M STILL MORE THAN WILLING TO GIVE YOU TREAT-MENT.
NOW PUT OUT YOUR LEG.
NEVER, AMESTRIAN! GET OUT OF MY COUNTRY!!
ALL RIGHT, JUST AS SOON AS THERE ARE NO MORE PATIENTS HERE.
PUT YOUR LEG OUT.
YOU THINK YOU'RE A SAINT BECAUSE YOU PATCH UP A FEW PEOPLE WHILE YOUR STINKING COUNTRYMEN ARE OUT THERE MURDERING ISHBALANS!?
YOU'RE A FRAUD!!
CALL ME WHATEVER YOU LIKE!!
IT'S BETTER TO BE A FRAUD WHO DOES SOMETHING THAN A DOCTOR WHO DOES NOTHING!

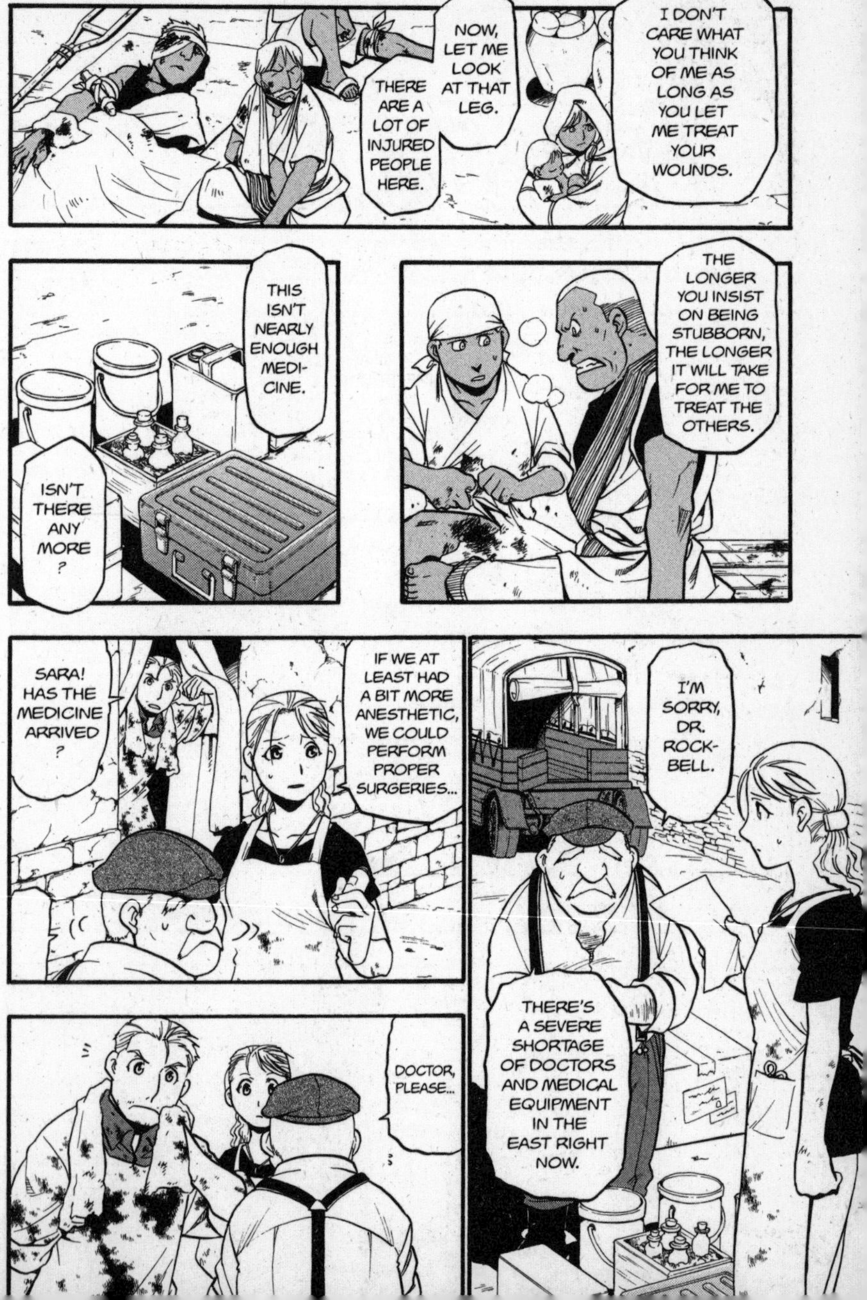
I DON'T CARE WHAT YOU THINK OF ME AS LONG AS YOU LET ME TREAT YOUR WOUNDS.
NOW, LET ME LOOK AT THAT LEG.
THERE ARE A LOT OF INJURED PEOPLE HERE.
THE LONGER YOU INSIST ON BEING STUBBORN, THE LONGER IT WILL TAKE FOR ME TO TREAT THE OTHERS.
THIS ISN'T NEARLY ENOUGH MEDI-CINE.
ISN'T THERE ANY MORE?
I'M SORRY, DR. ROCK-BELL.
THERE'S A SEVERE SHORTAGE OF DOCTORS AND MEDICAL EQUIPMENT IN THE EAST RIGHT NOW.
IF WE AT LEAST HAD A BIT MORE ANESTHETIC, WE COULD PERFORM PROPER SURGERIES...
SARA! HAS THE MEDICINE ARRIVED?
DOCTOR, PLEASE...

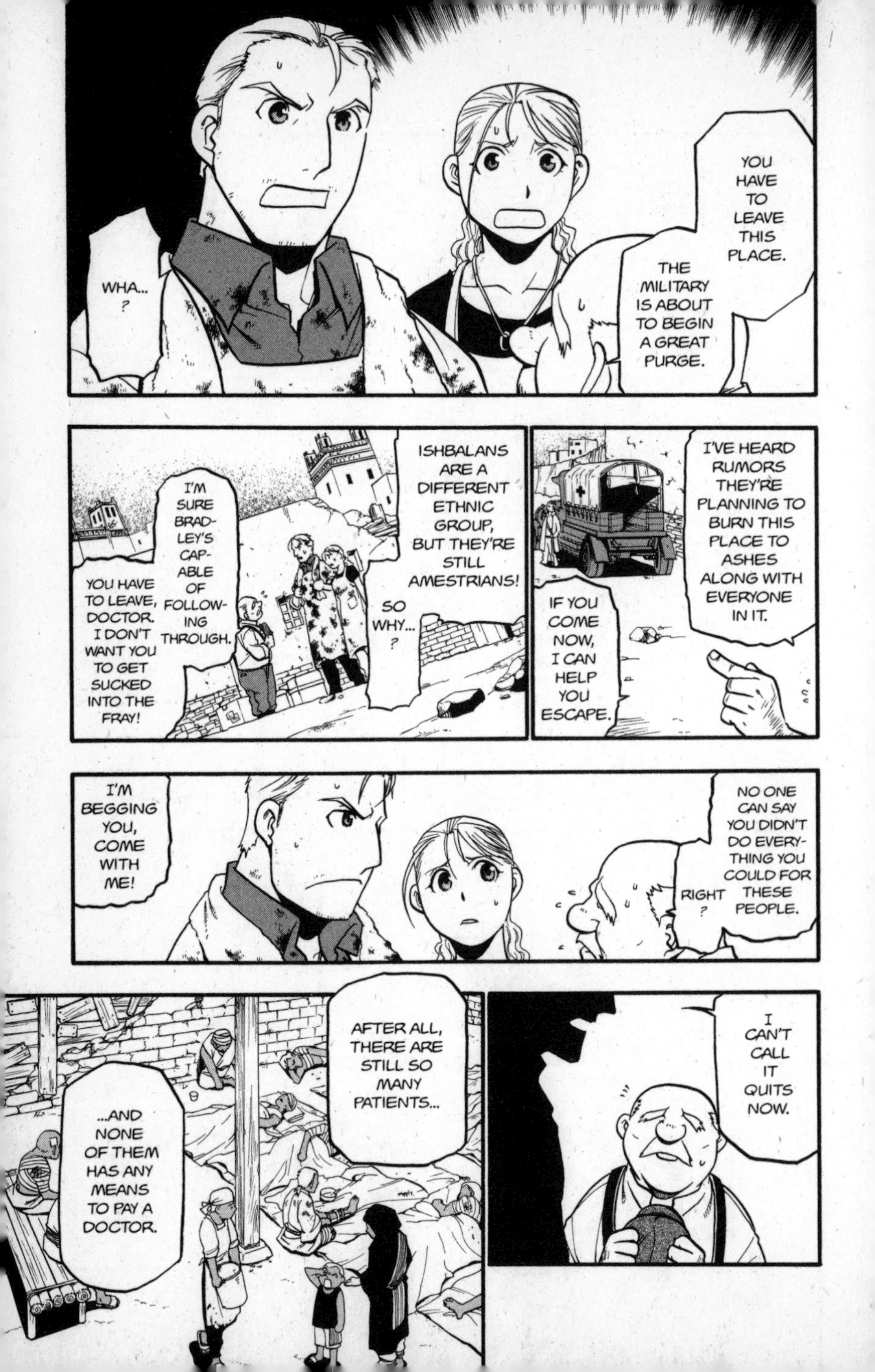
YOU HAVE TO LEAVE THIS PLACE.
THE MILITARY IS ABOUT TO BEGIN A GREAT PURGE.
WHA...?
I'VE HEARD RUMORS THEY'RE PLANNING TO BURN THIS PLACE TO ASHES ALONG WITH EVERYONE IN IT.
IF YOU COME NOW, I CAN HELP YOU ESCAPE.
ISHBALANS ARE A DIFFERENT ETHNIC GROUP, BUT THEY'RE STILL AMESTRIANS!
SO WHY...?
I'M SURE BRADLEY'S CAPABLE OF FOLLOWING THROUGH.
YOU HAVE TO LEAVE, DOCTOR. I DON'T WANT YOU TO GET SUCKED INTO THE FRAY!
NO ONE CAN SAY YOU DIDN'T DO EVERYTHING YOU COULD FOR THESE PEOPLE.
RIGHT?
I'M BEGGING YOU, COME WITH ME!
I CAN'T CALL IT QUITS NOW.
AFTER ALL, THERE ARE STILL SO MANY PATIENTS...
...AND NONE OF THEM HAS ANY MEANS TO PAY A DOCTOR.

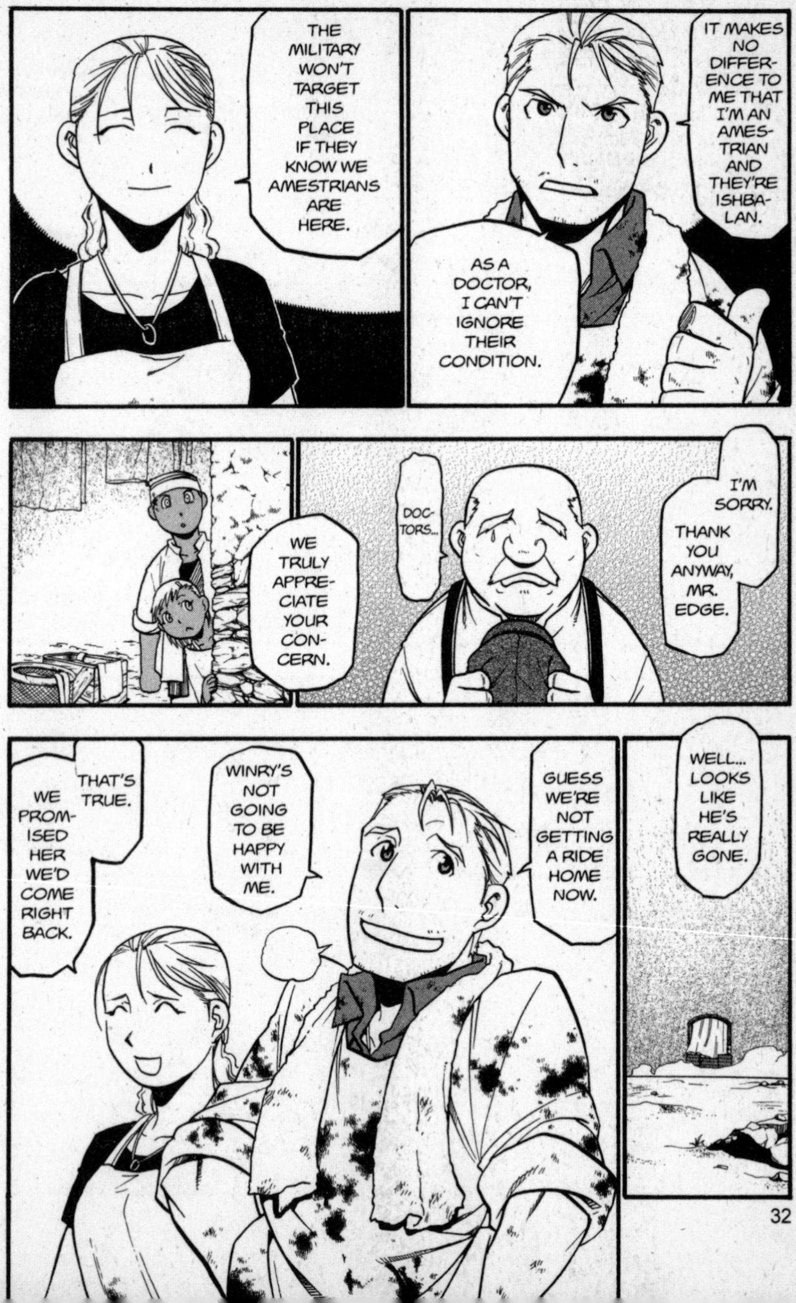
IT MAKES NO DIFFERENCE TO ME THAT I'M AN AMESTRIAN AND THEY'RE ISHBALAN.
AS A DOCTOR, I CAN'T IGNORE THEIR CONDITION.
THE MILITARY WON'T TARGET THIS PLACE IF THEY KNOW WE AMESTRIANS ARE HERE.
I'M SORRY.
THANK YOU ANYWAY, MR. EDGE.
DOCTORS...
WE TRULY APPRECIATE YOUR CONCERN.
WELL... LOOKS LIKE HE'S REALLY GONE.
GUESS WE'RE NOT GETTING A RIDE HOME NOW.
WINRY'S NOT GOING TO BE HAPPY WITH ME.
THAT'S TRUE.
WE PROMISED HER WE'D COME RIGHT BACK.

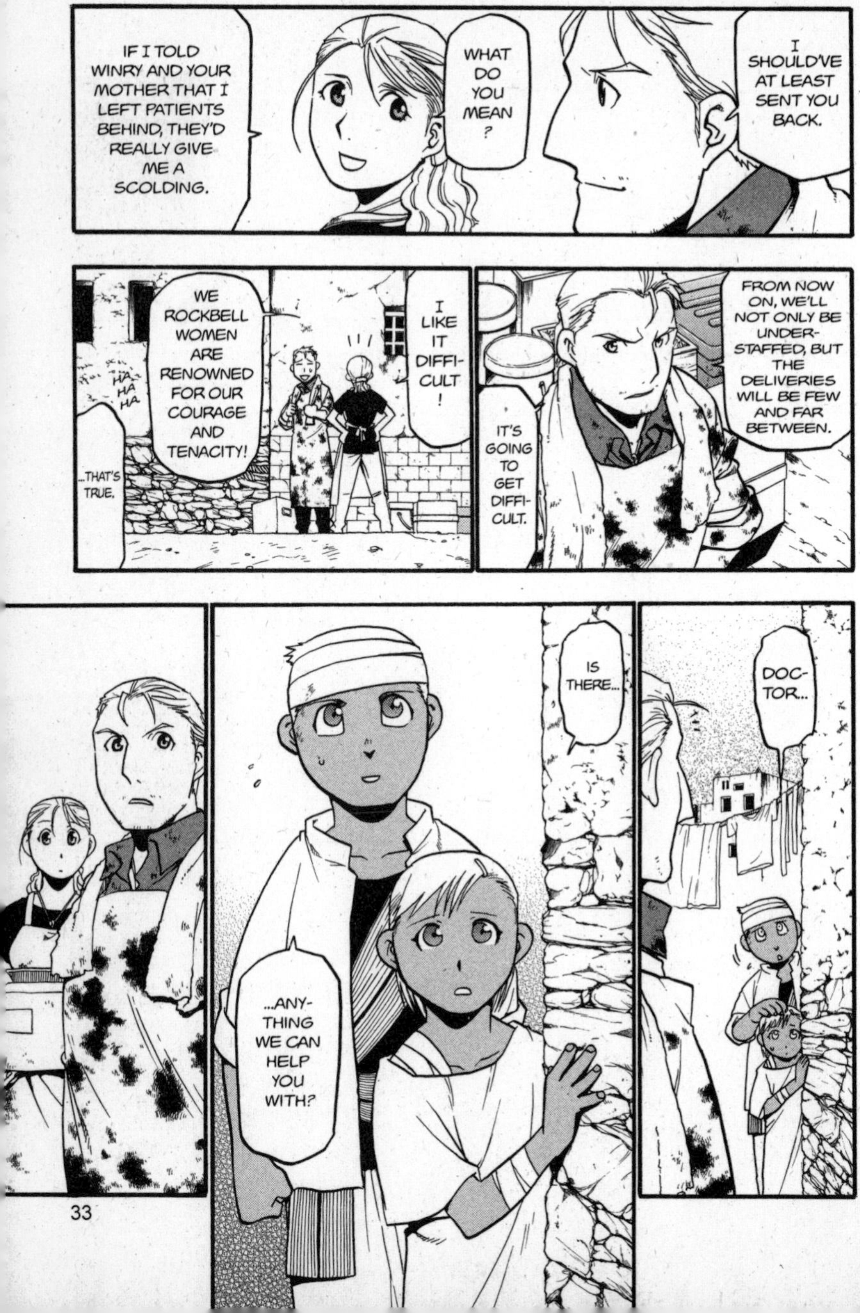
I SHOULD'VE AT LEAST SENT YOU BACK.
WHAT DO YOU MEAN?
IF I TOLD WINRY AND YOUR MOTHER THAT I LEFT PATIENTS BEHIND, THEY'D REALLY GIVE ME A SCOLDING.
FROM NOW ON, WE'LL NOT ONLY BE UNDER-STAFFED, BUT THE DELIVERIES WILL BE FEW AND FAR BETWEEN.
IT'S GOING TO GET DIFFI-CULT.
I LIKE IT DIFFI-CULT!
WE ROCKBELL WOMEN ARE RENOWNED FOR OUR COURAGE AND TENACITY!
HA HA HA
...THAT'S TRUE.
DOC-TOR...
IS THERE...
...ANY-THING WE CAN HELP YOU WITH?

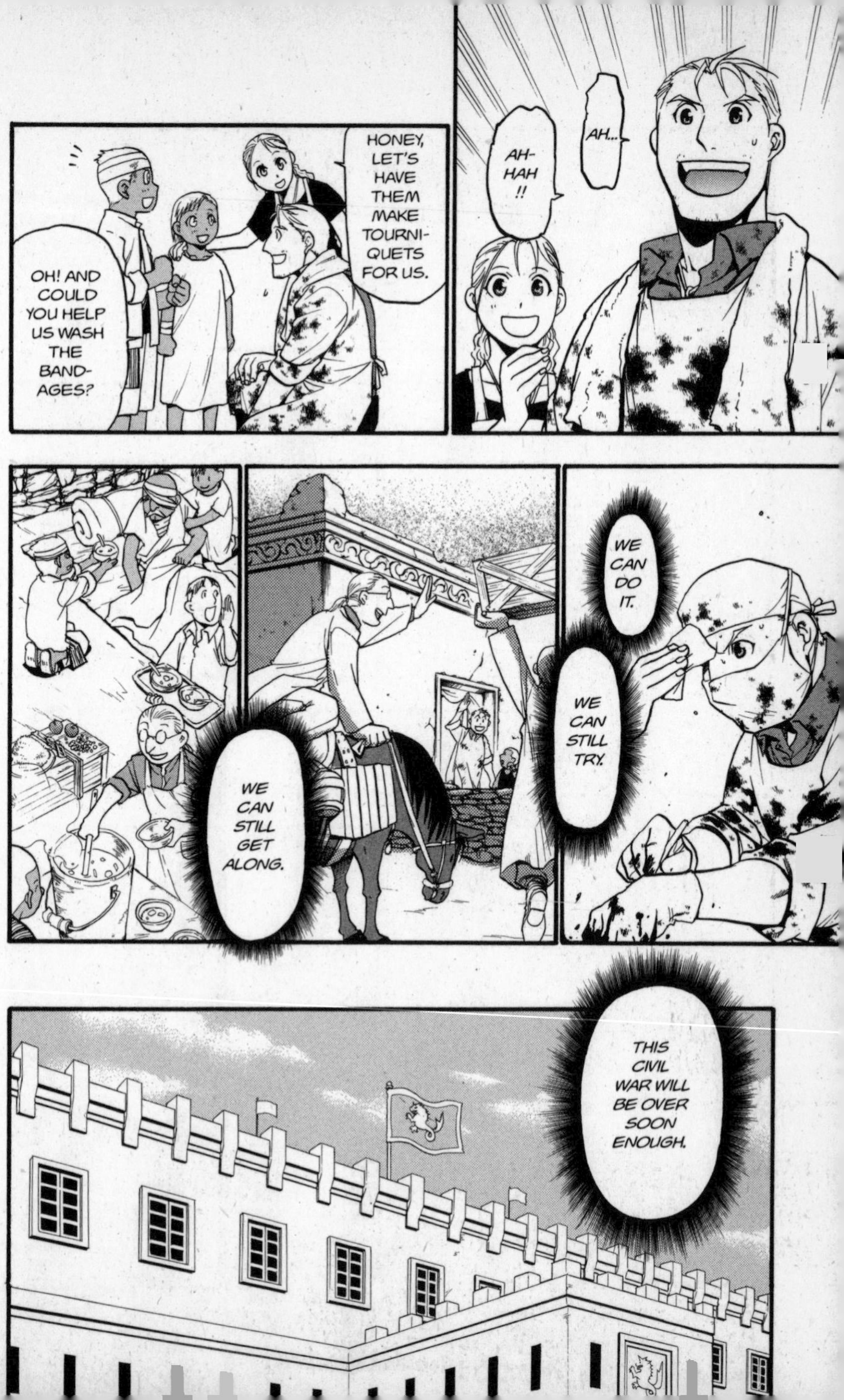
AH...
AH-HAH!!
HONEY, LET'S HAVE THEM MAKE TOURNIQUETS FOR US.
OH! AND COULD YOU HELP US WASH THE BANDAGES?
WE CAN DO IT.
WE CAN STILL TRY.
WE CAN STILL GET ALONG.
THIS CIVIL WAR WILL BE OVER SOON ENOUGH.

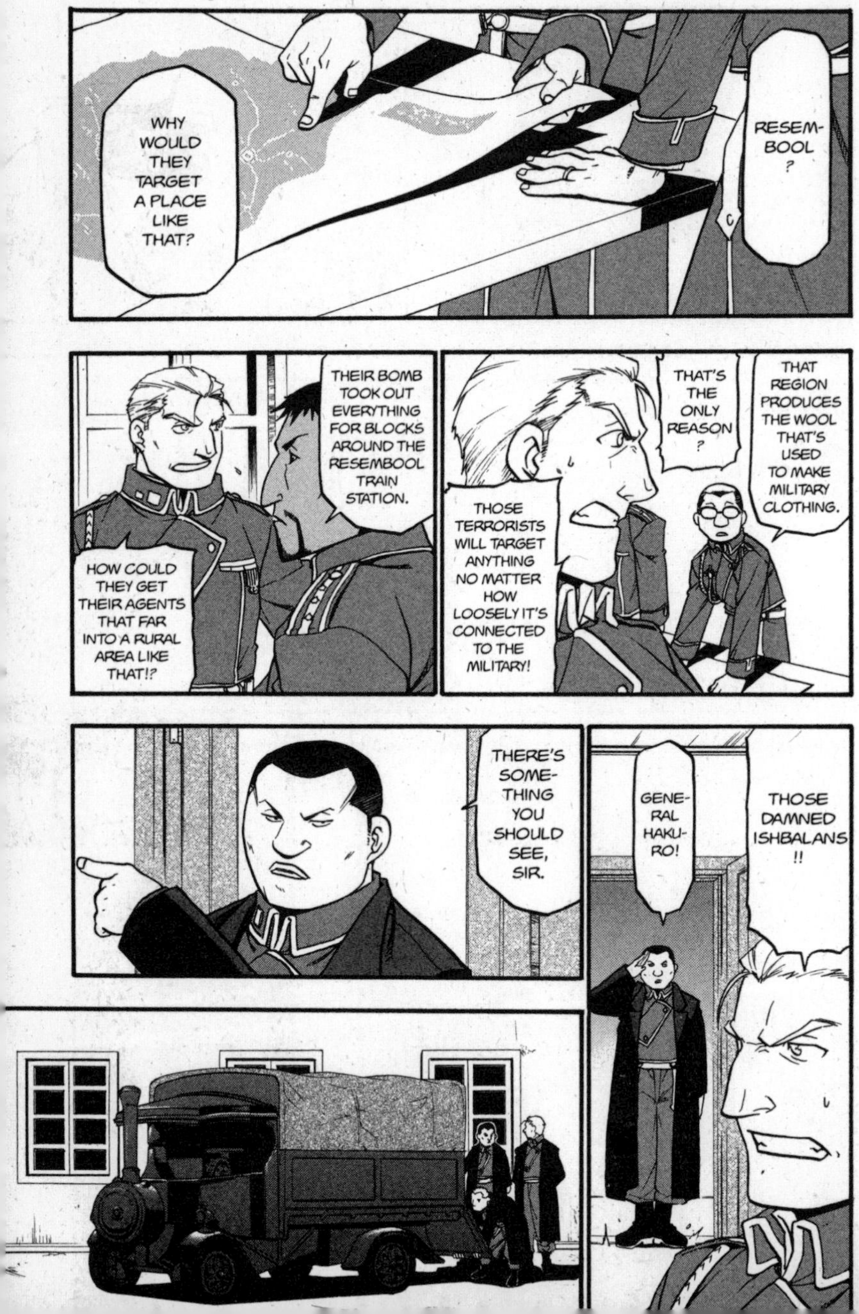
RESEM-BOOL?
WHY WOULD THEY TARGET A PLACE LIKE THAT?
THAT REGION PRODUCES THE WOOL THAT'S USED TO MAKE MILITARY CLOTHING.
THAT'S THE ONLY REASON?
THOSE TERRORISTS WILL TARGET ANYTHING NO MATTER HOW LOOSELY IT'S CONNECTED TO THE MILITARY!
THEIR BOMB TOOK OUT EVERYTHING FOR BLOCKS AROUND THE RESEMBOOL TRAIN STATION.
HOW COULD THEY GET THEIR AGENTS THAT FAR INTO A RURAL AREA LIKE THAT!?
THOSE DAMNED ISHBALANS!!
GENE-RAL HAKU-RO!
THERE'S SOME-THING YOU SHOULD SEE, SIR.

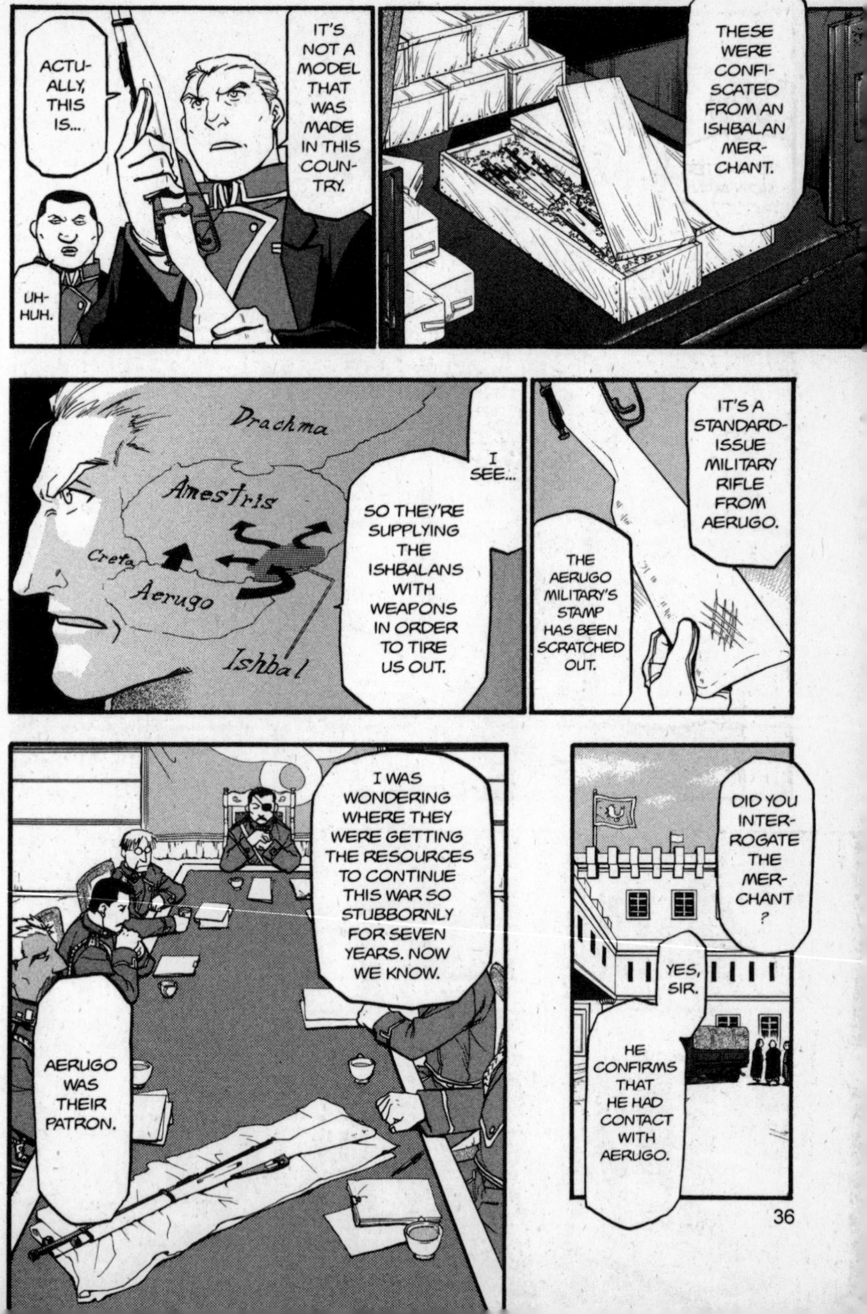
THESE WERE CONFISCATED FROM AN ISHBALAN MERCHANT.
IT'S NOT A MODEL THAT WAS MADE IN THIS COUNTRY.
ACTUALLY, THIS IS...
UH-HUH.
IT'S A STANDARD-ISSUE MILITARY RIFLE FROM AERUGO.
THE AERUGO MILITARY'S STAMP HAS BEEN SCRATCHED OUT.
I SEE...
SO THEY'RE SUPPLYING THE ISHBALANS WITH WEAPONS IN ORDER TO TIRE US OUT.
Drachma
Amestris
Creta
Aerugo
Ishbal
DID YOU INTERROGATE THE MERCHANT?
YES, SIR.
HE CONFIRMS THAT HE HAD CONTACT WITH AERUGO.
I WAS WONDERING WHERE THEY WERE GETTING THE RESOURCES TO CONTINUE THIS WAR SO STUBBORNLY FOR SEVEN YEARS. NOW WE KNOW.
AERUGO WAS THEIR PATRON.

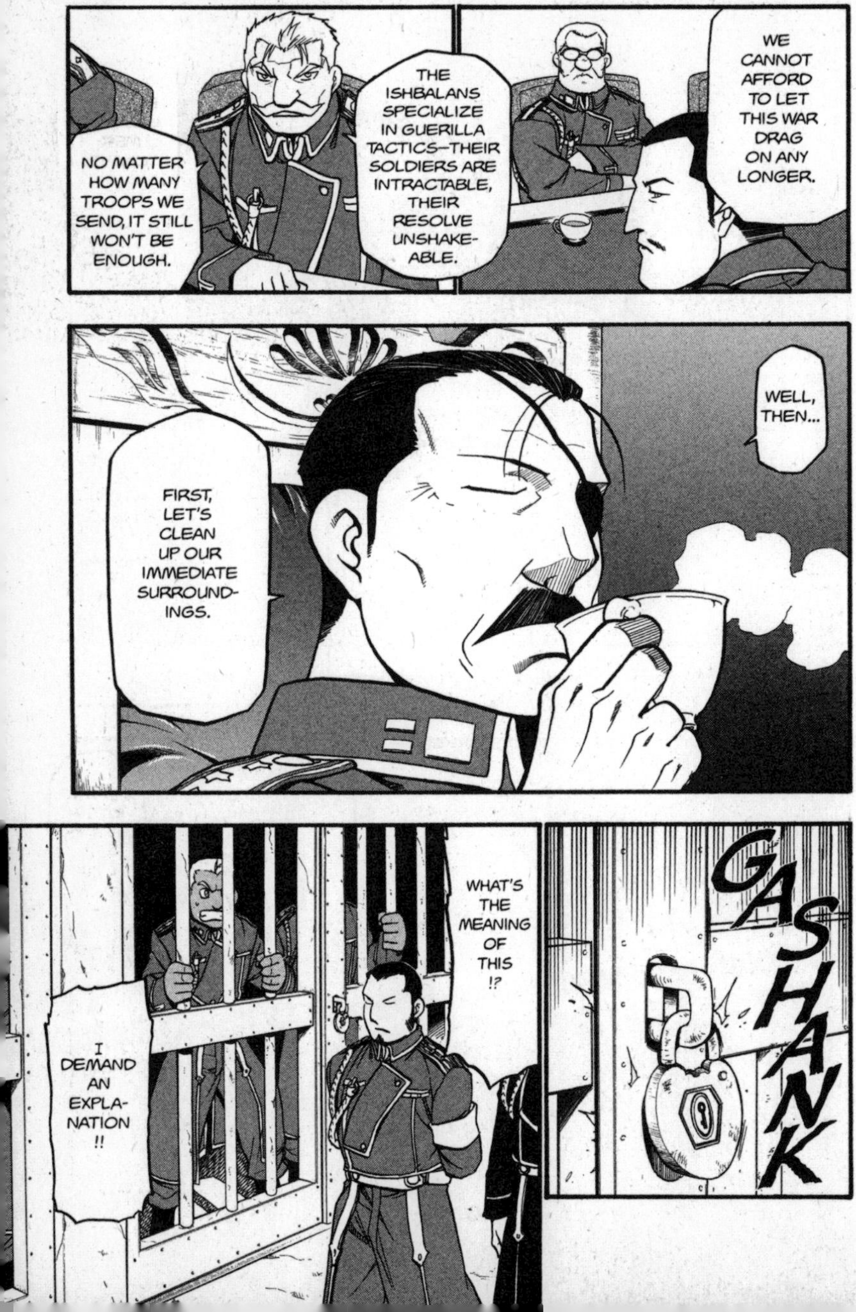
WE CANNOT AFFORD TO LET THIS WAR DRAG ON ANY LONGER.
THE ISHBALANS SPECIALIZE IN GUERILLA TACTICS—THEIR SOLDIERS ARE INTRACTABLE, THEIR RESOLVE UNSHAKE-ABLE.
NO MATTER HOW MANY TROOPS WE SEND, IT STILL WON'T BE ENOUGH.
WELL, THEN...
FIRST, LET'S CLEAN UP OUR IMMEDIATE SURROUND-INGS.
GASHANK
WHAT'S THE MEANING OF THIS !?
I DEMAND AN EXPLA-NATION !!

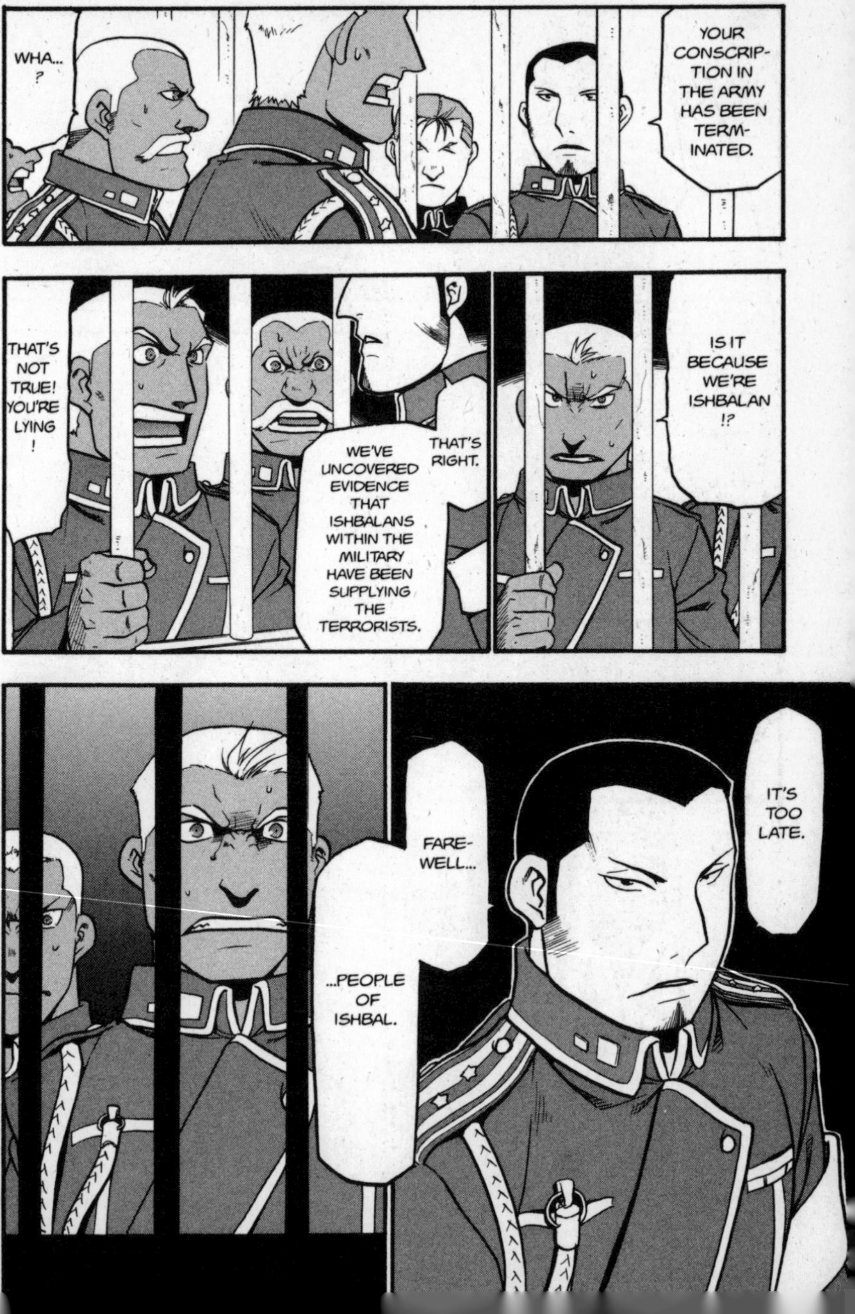
YOUR CONSCRIPTION IN THE ARMY HAS BEEN TERMINATED.
WHA...?
IS IT BECAUSE WE'RE ISHBALAN!?
THAT'S RIGHT.
WE'VE UNCOVERED EVIDENCE THAT ISHBALANS WITHIN THE MILITARY HAVE BEEN SUPPLYING THE TERRORISTS.
THAT'S NOT TRUE! YOU'RE LYING!
IT'S TOO LATE.
FAREWELL...
...PEOPLE OF ISHBAL.

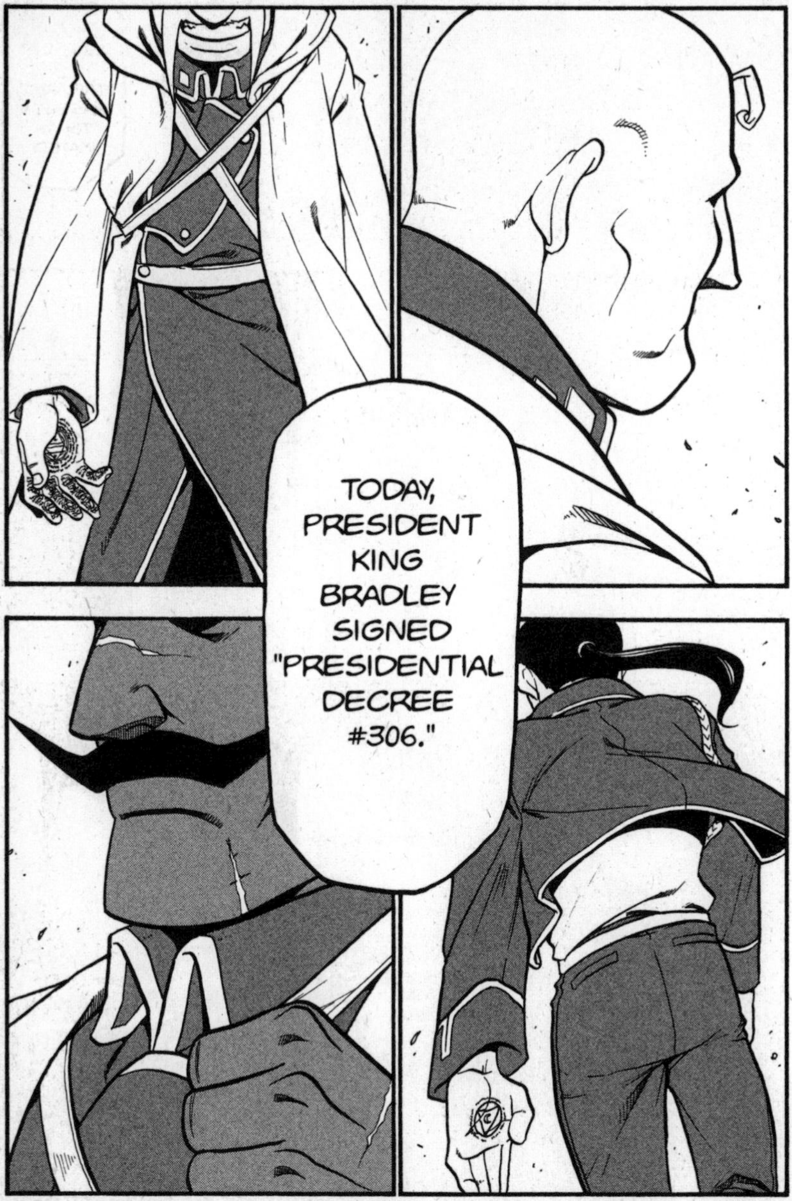
TODAY, PRESIDENT KING BRADLEY SIGNED "PRESIDENTIAL DECREE #306."

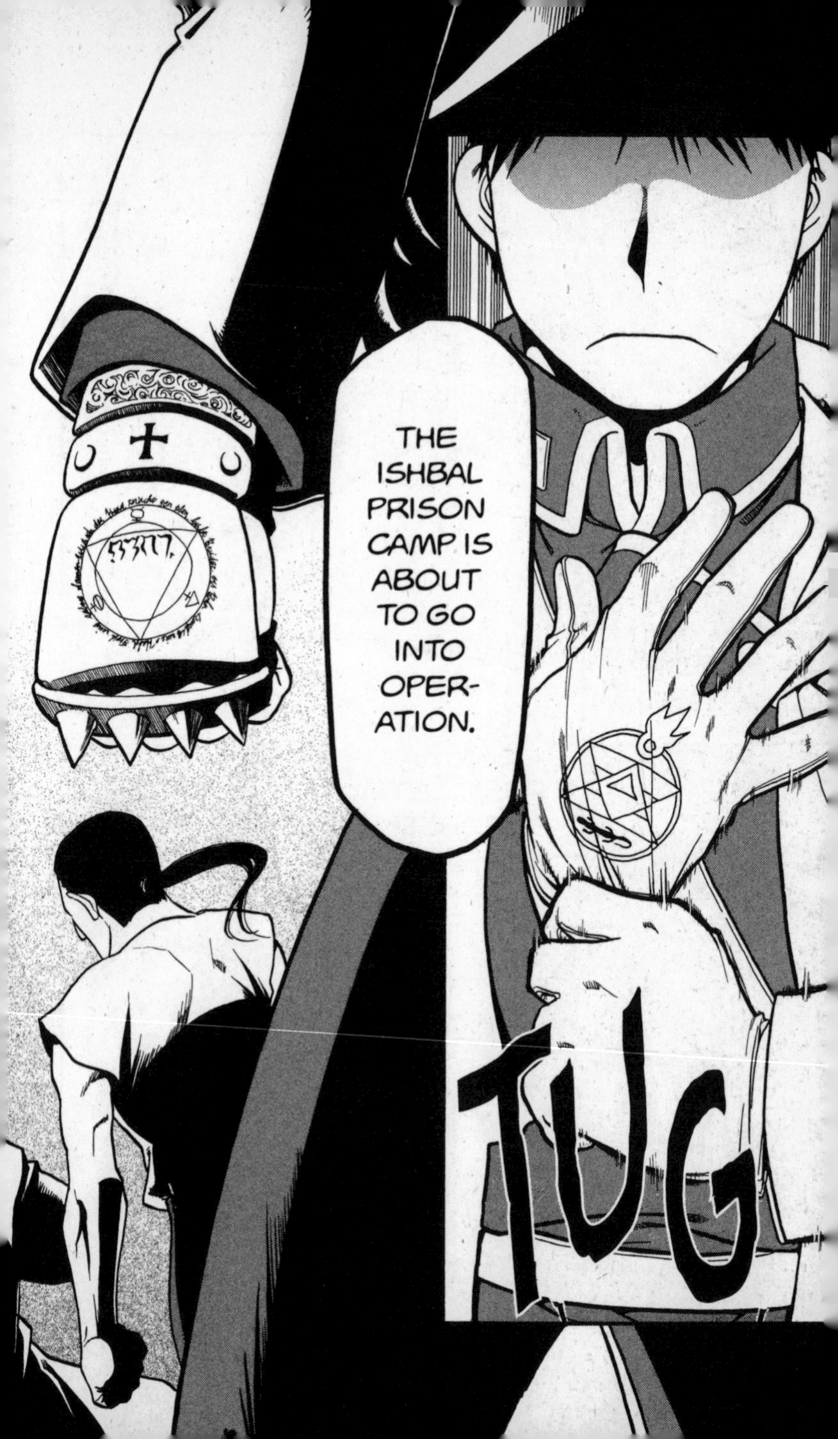
THE ISHBAL PRISON CAMP IS ABOUT TO GO INTO OPERATION.
TUG

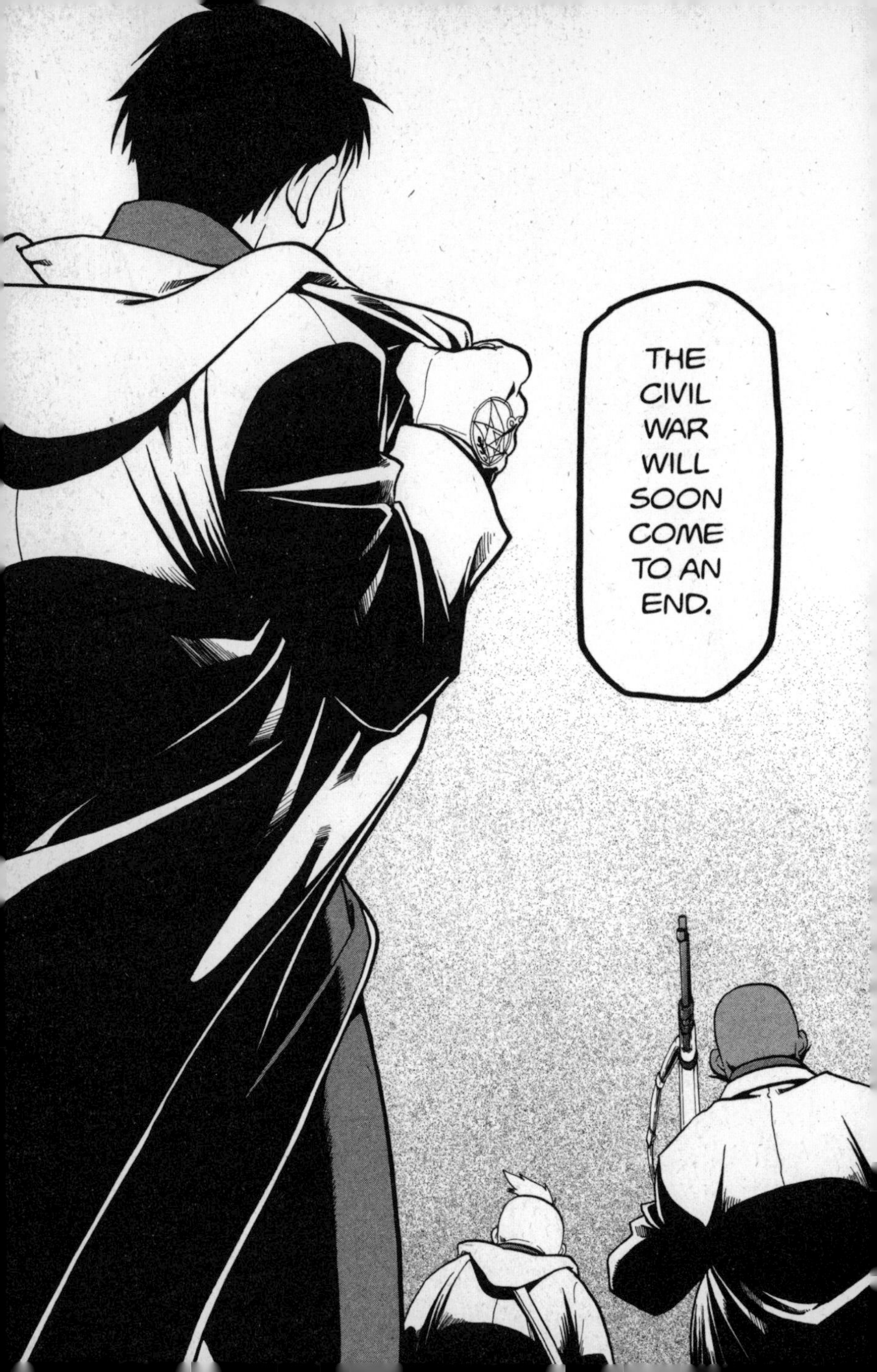
THE CIVIL WAR WILL SOON COME TO AN END.

FULLMETAL
ALCHEMIST

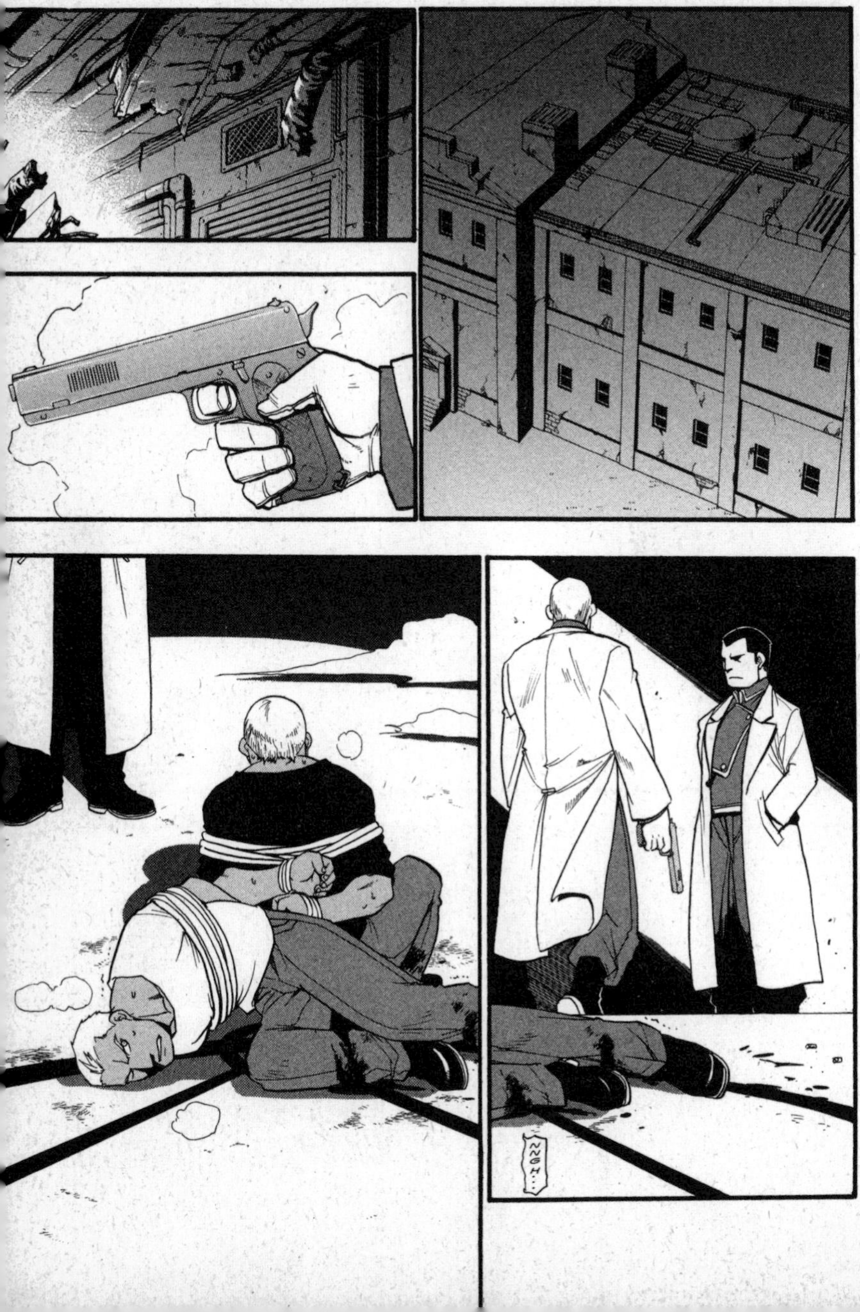
NNGH...

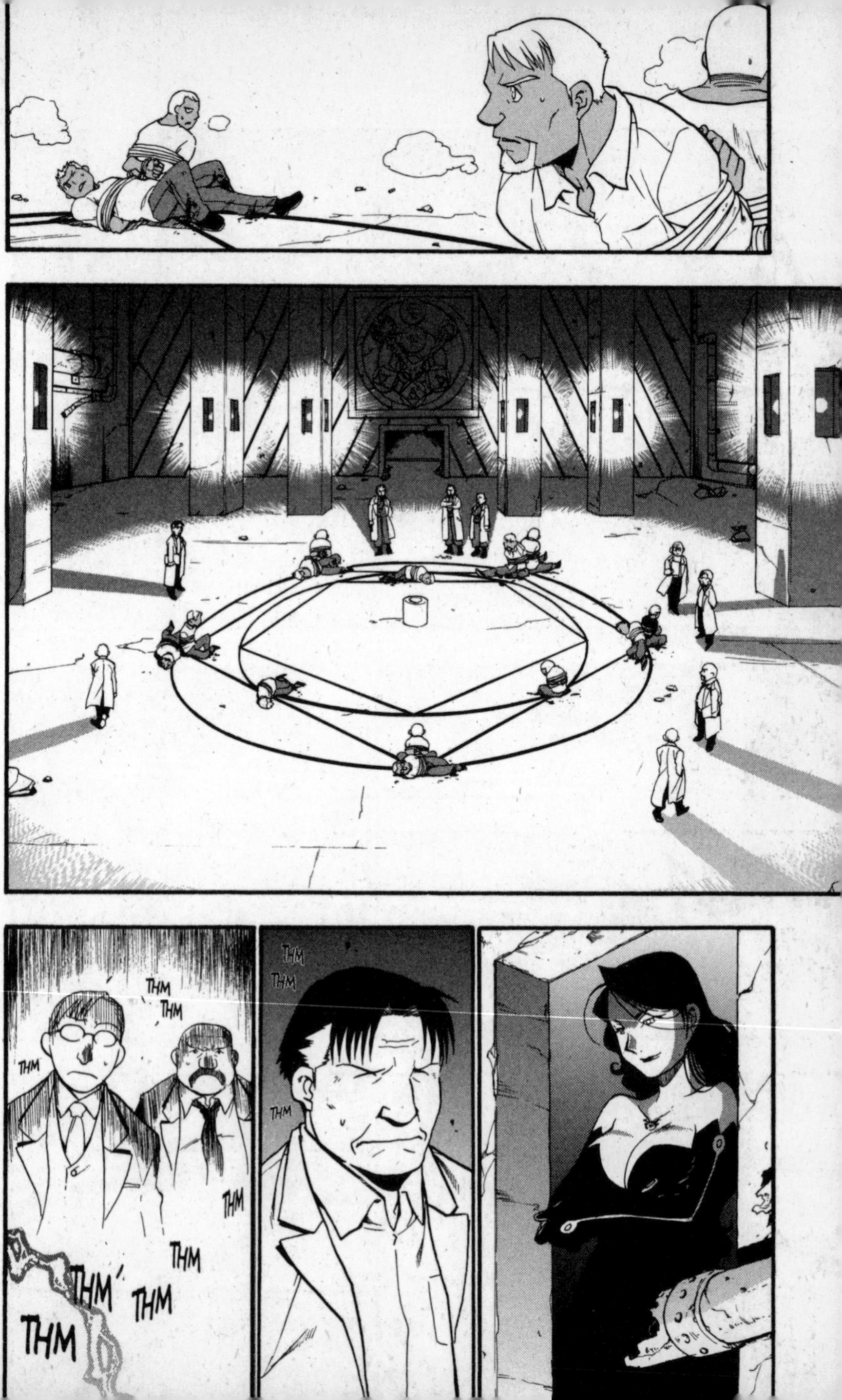
THM
THM
THM
THM
THM
THM
THM
THM
THM
THM
THM

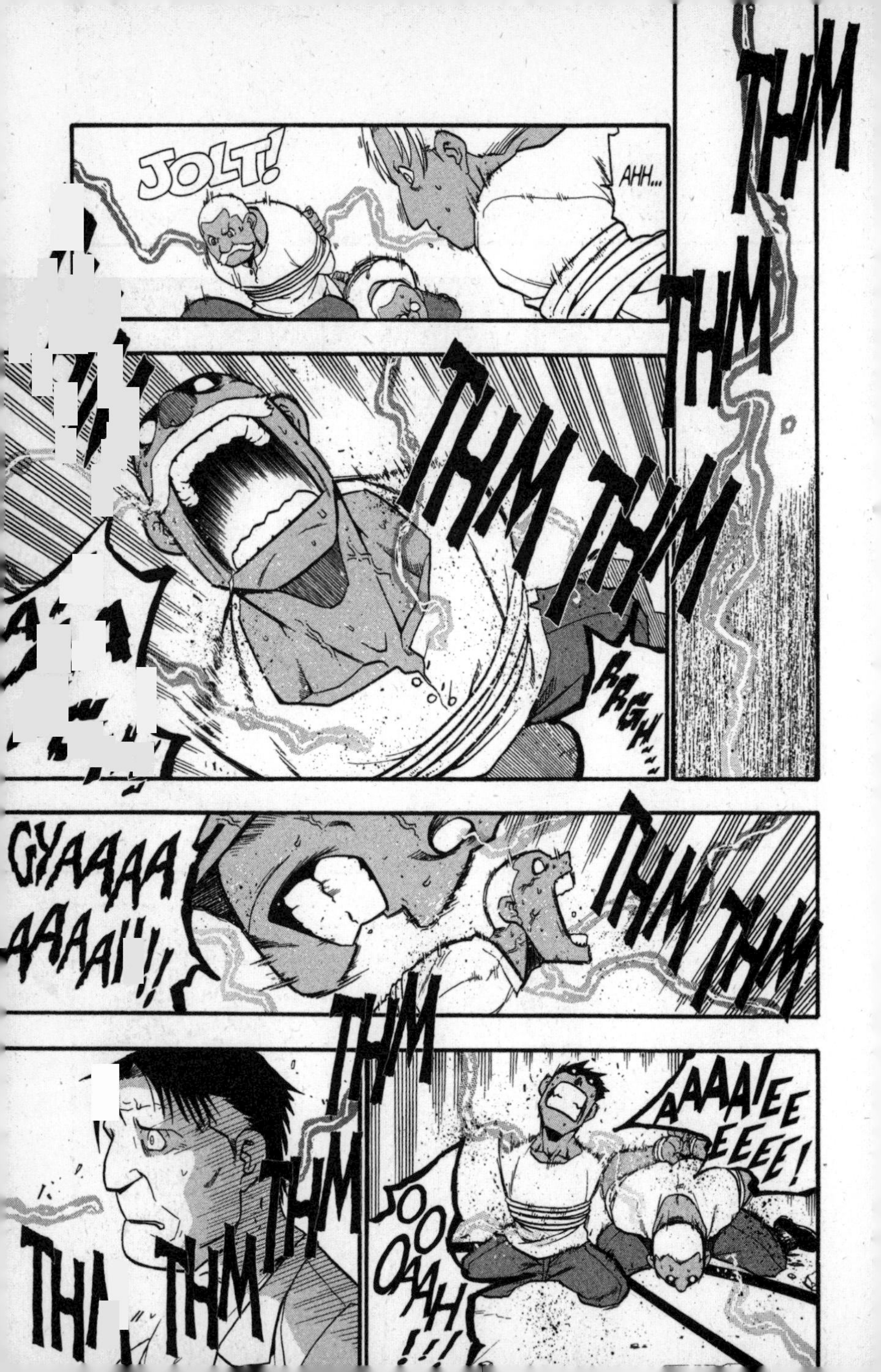

THM
THM
AHH...
JOLT!
THM THM THM
ARRGH...
THM THM THM
GYAAAAAAAAAI!!
AAAAIEEEEEEE!
SOOOOAAAH!!!
THM
THM THM

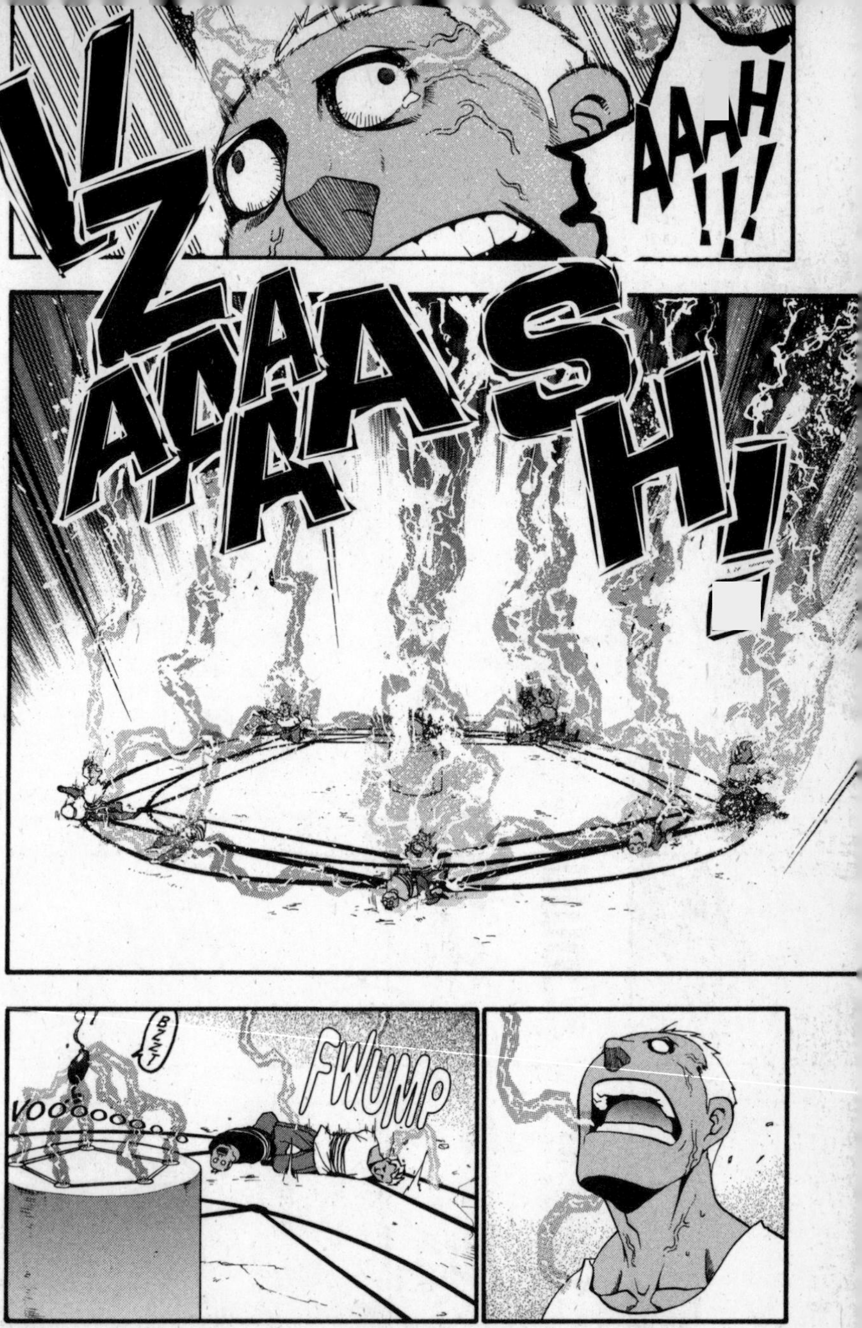
AAAH!!!
LZAAAAASH!
FWUMP
BZZT
VOOOOOOOO

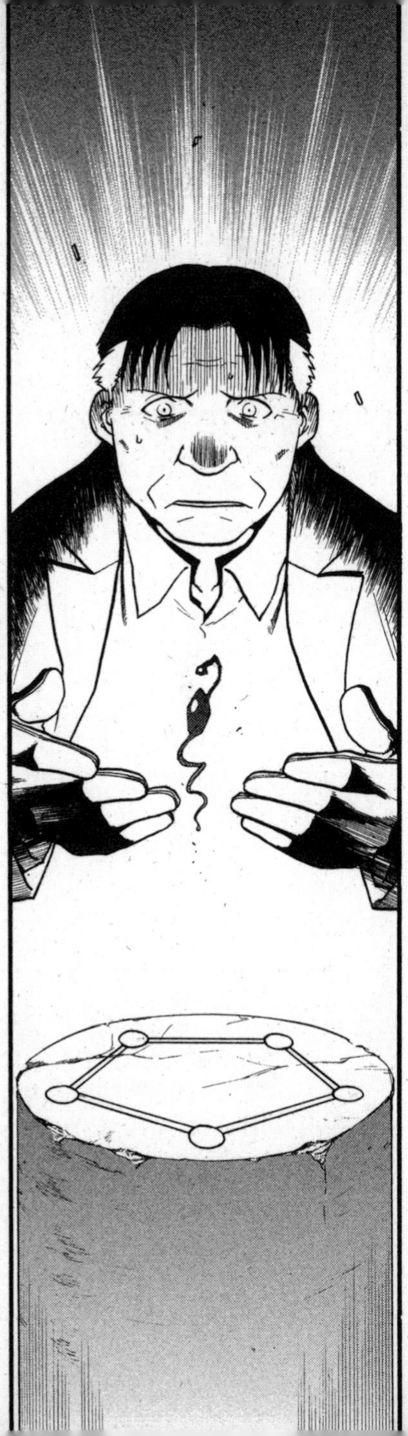

Chapter 59 The Immoral Alchemist

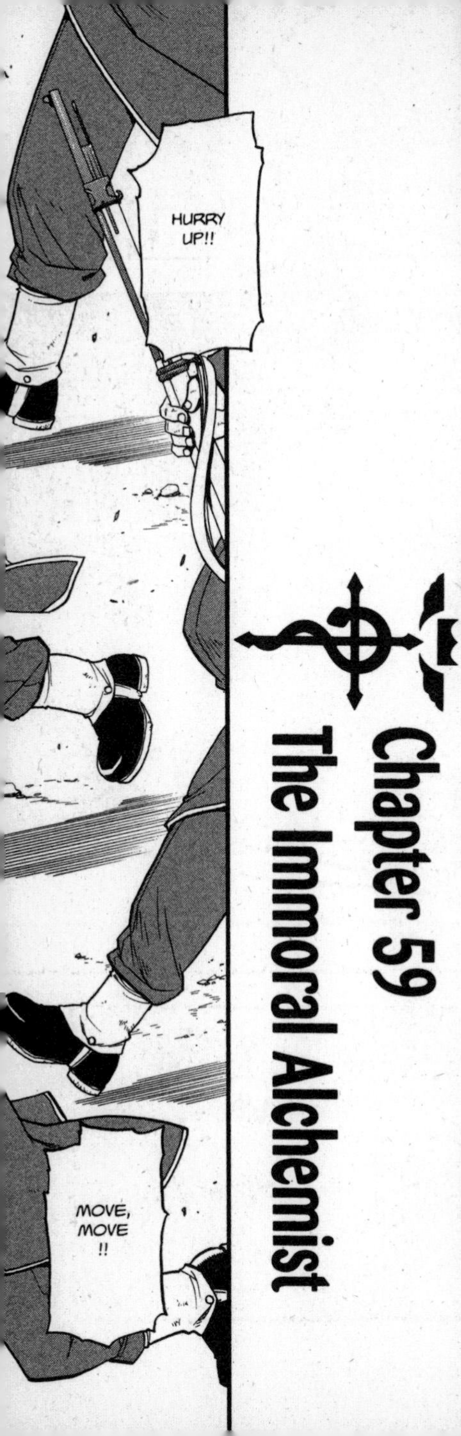
HURRY UP!!
MOVE, MOVE !!

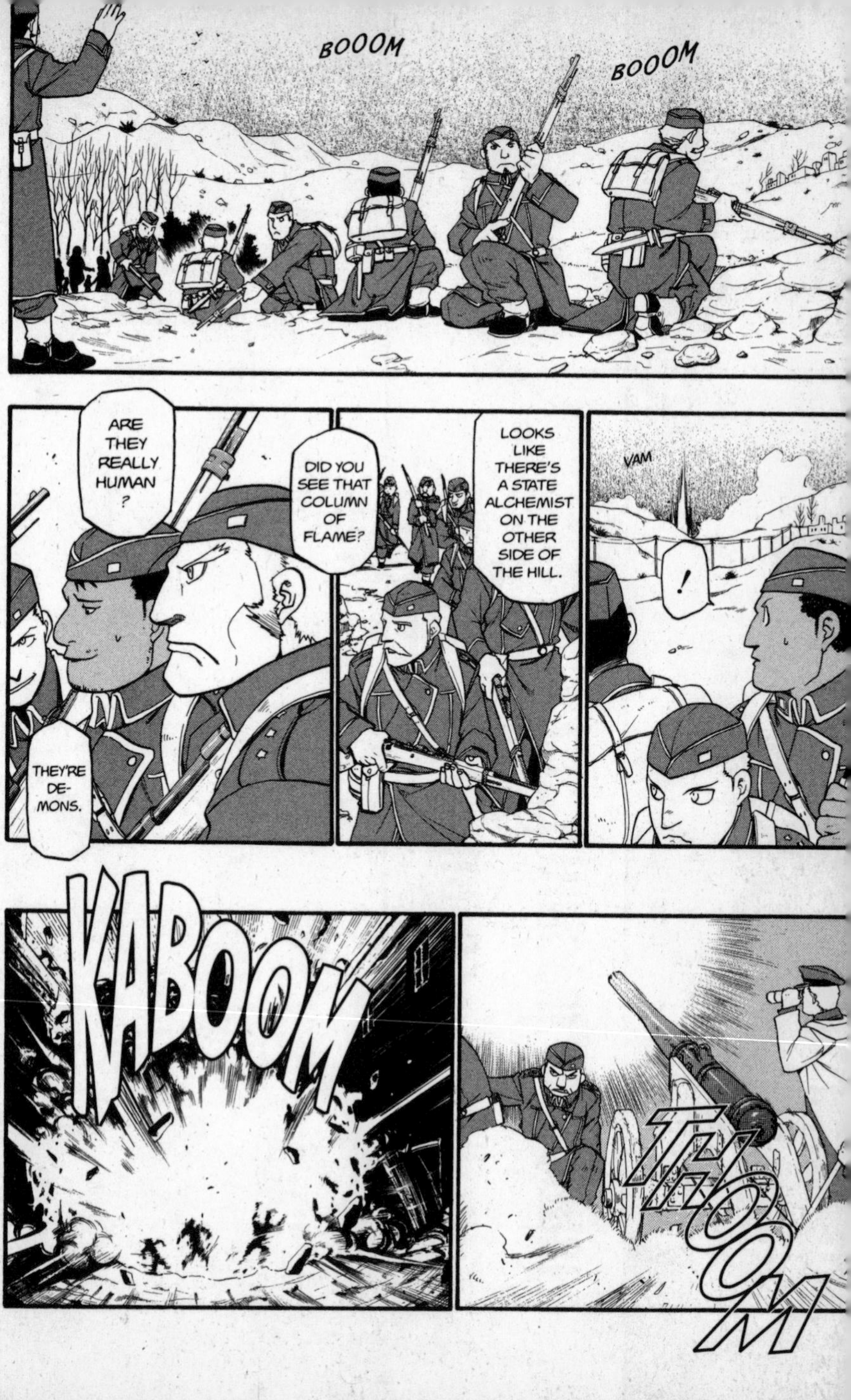
BOOOM
BOOOM
VAM
!
LOOKS LIKE THERE'S A STATE ALCHEMIST ON THE OTHER SIDE OF THE HILL.
DID YOU SEE THAT COLUMN OF FLAME?
ARE THEY REALLY HUMAN?
THEY'RE DE-MONS.
THOOM
KABOOM

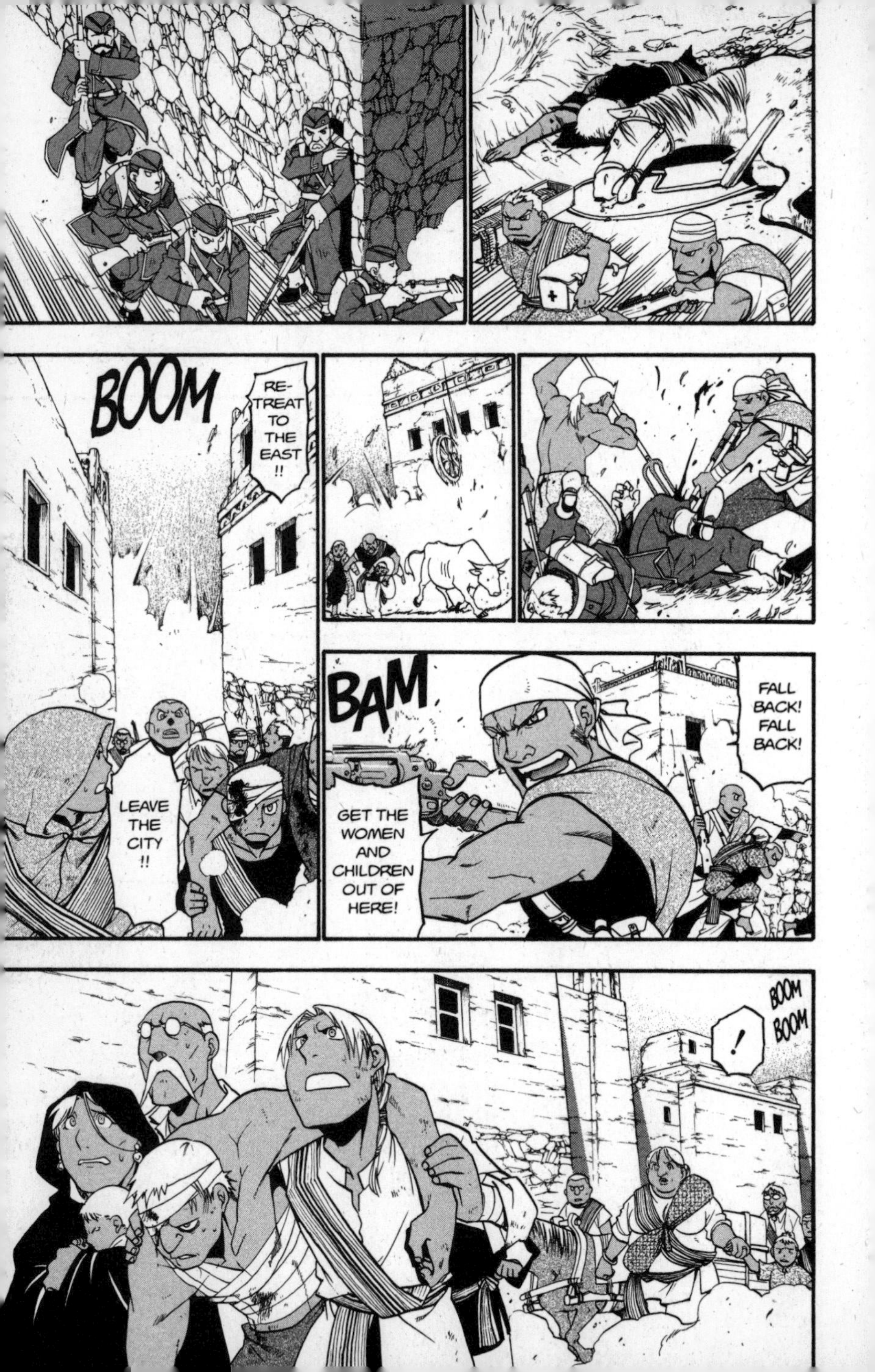
FALL BACK! FALL BACK!
BAM
GET THE WOMEN AND CHILDREN OUT OF HERE!
RE-TREAT TO THE EAST !!
BOOM
LEAVE THE CITY !!
BOOM BOOM
!

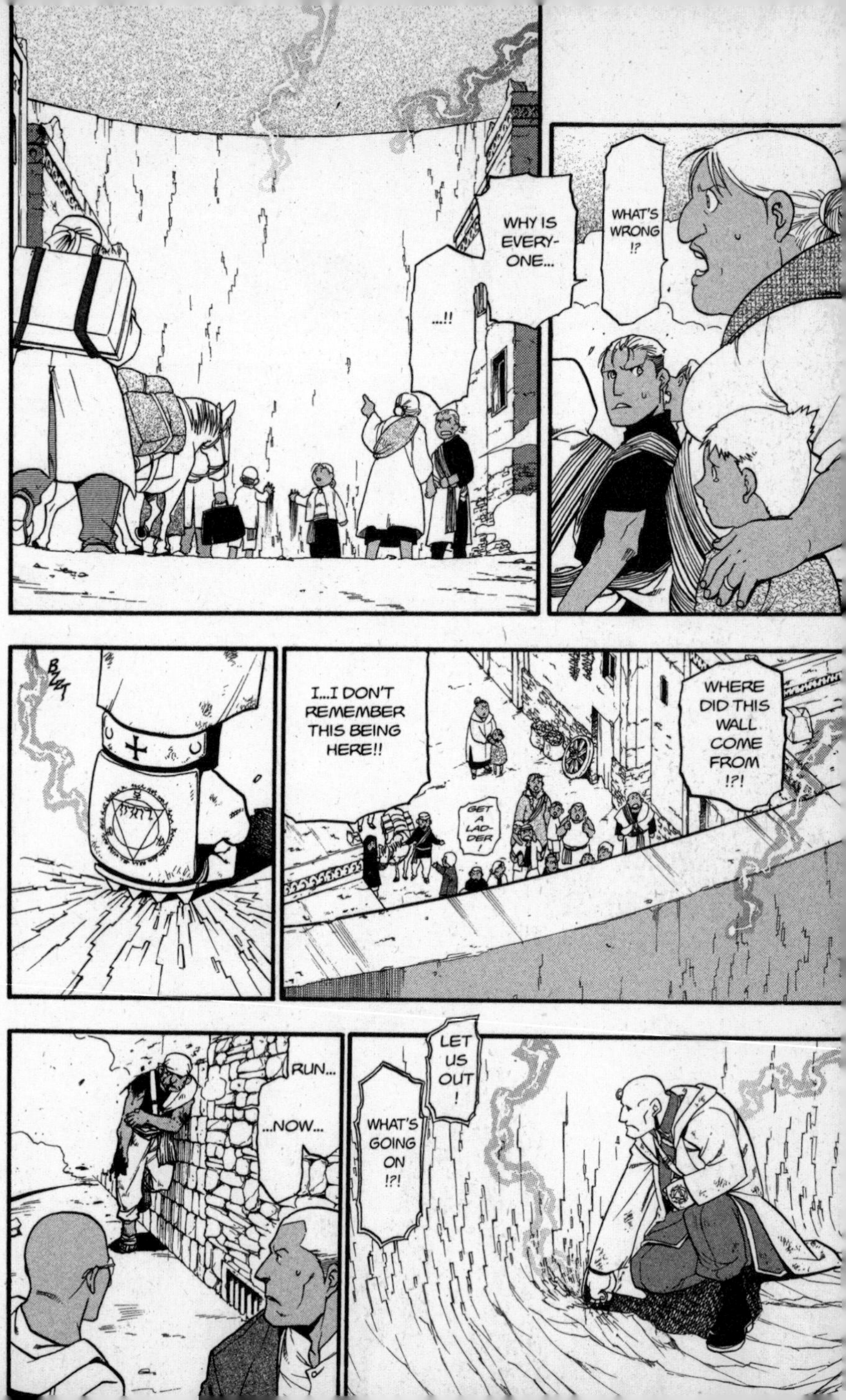
WHAT'S WRONG !?
WHY IS EVERY-ONE...
...!!
WHERE DID THIS WALL COME FROM !?!
I...I DON'T REMEMBER THIS BEING HERE!!
GET A LAD-DER !
BZZT
LET US OUT !
WHAT'S GOING ON !?!
RUN...
...NOW...

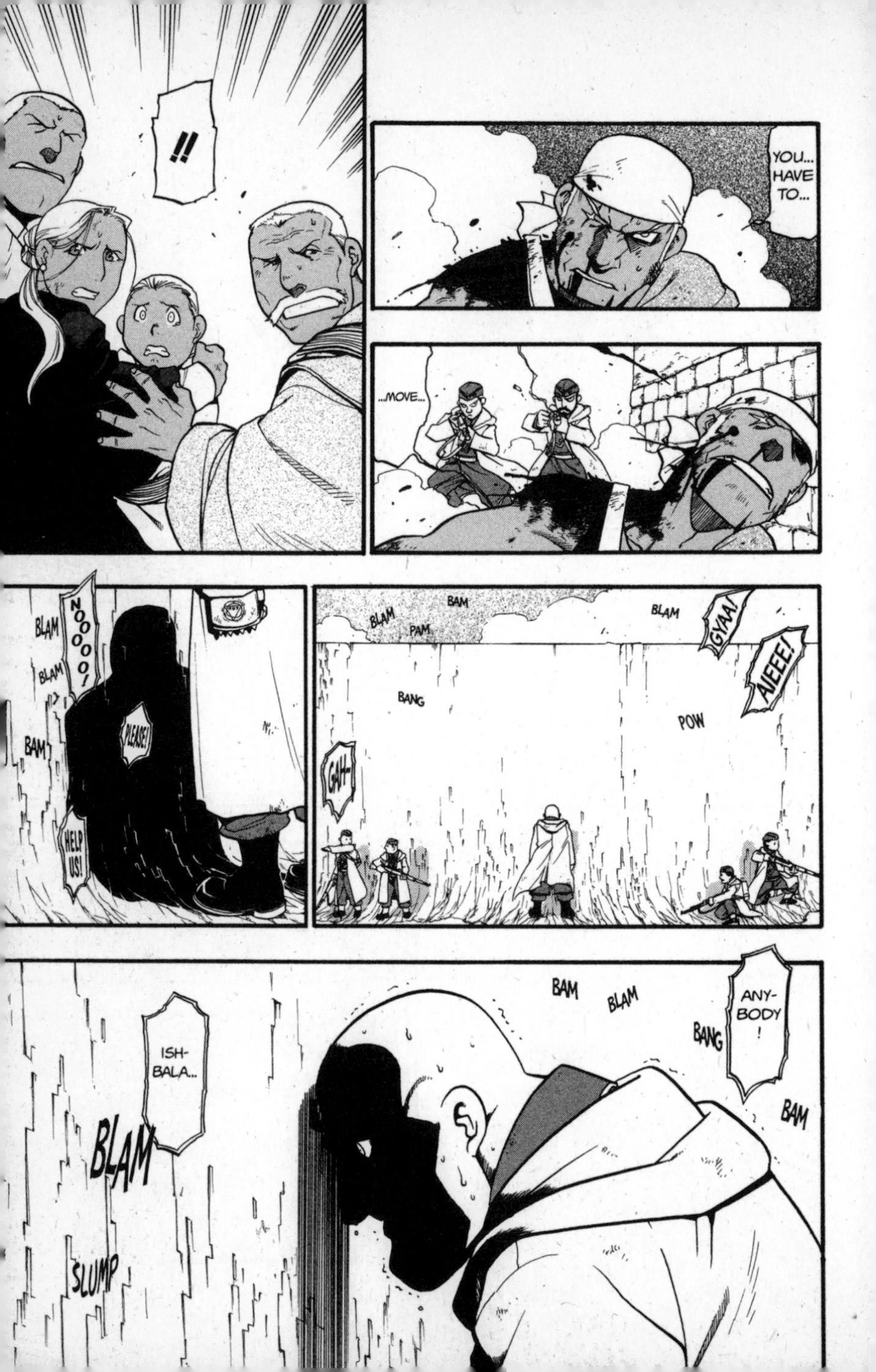
YOU... HAVE TO...
...MOVE...
!!
GYAA!
BLAM
AIEEE!
BAM
PAM
BLAM
BANG
POW
GAH--
NOOOOO!
BLAM
BLAM
PLEASE!
BAM
HELP US!
ANY-BODY!
BAM
BLAM
BANG
BAM
ISH-BALA...
BLAM
SLUMP

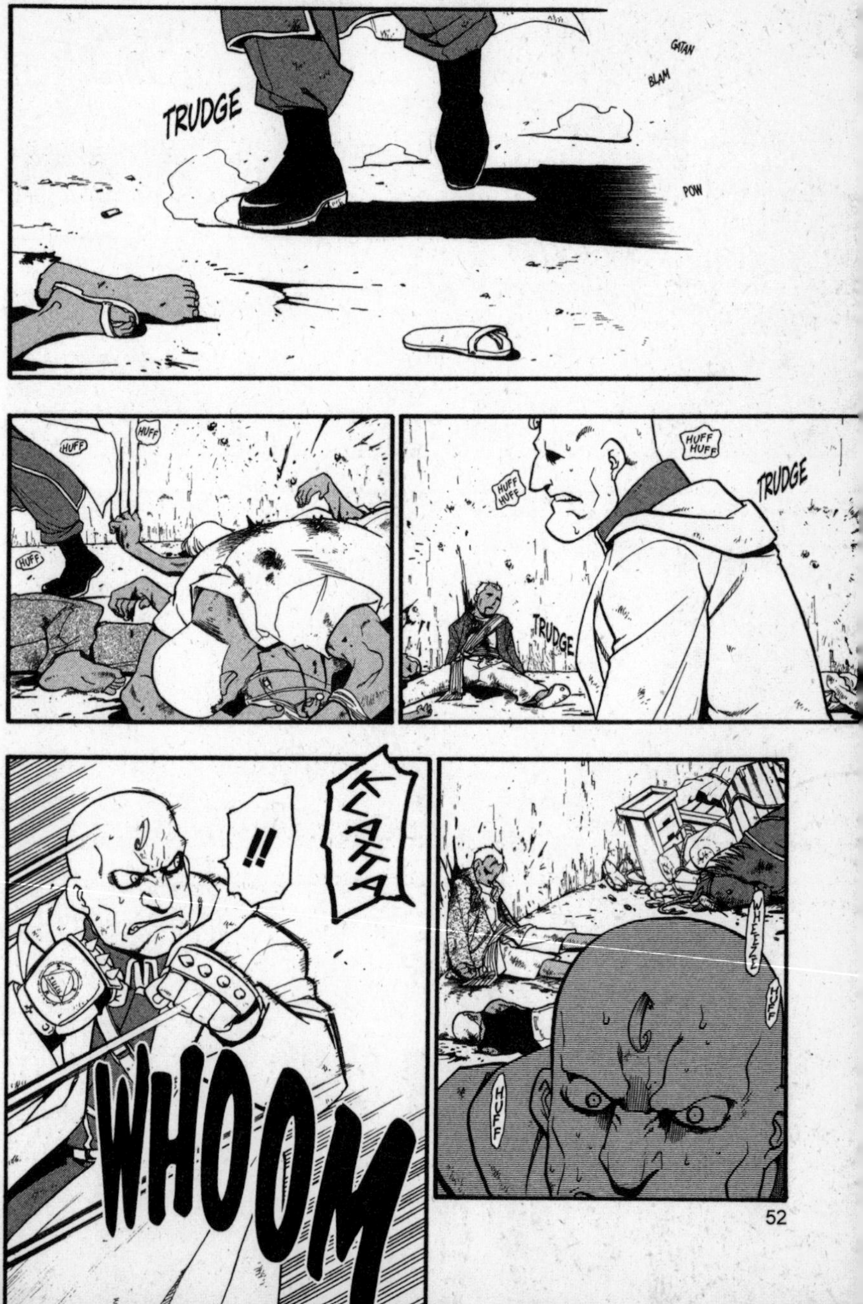
GATAN
BLAM
POW
TRUDGE
HUFF HUFF
TRUDGE
HUFF HUFF
TRUDGE
HUFF
HUFF
HUFF
WHEEZE
HUFF
HUFF
KLAKA
!!
WHOOM

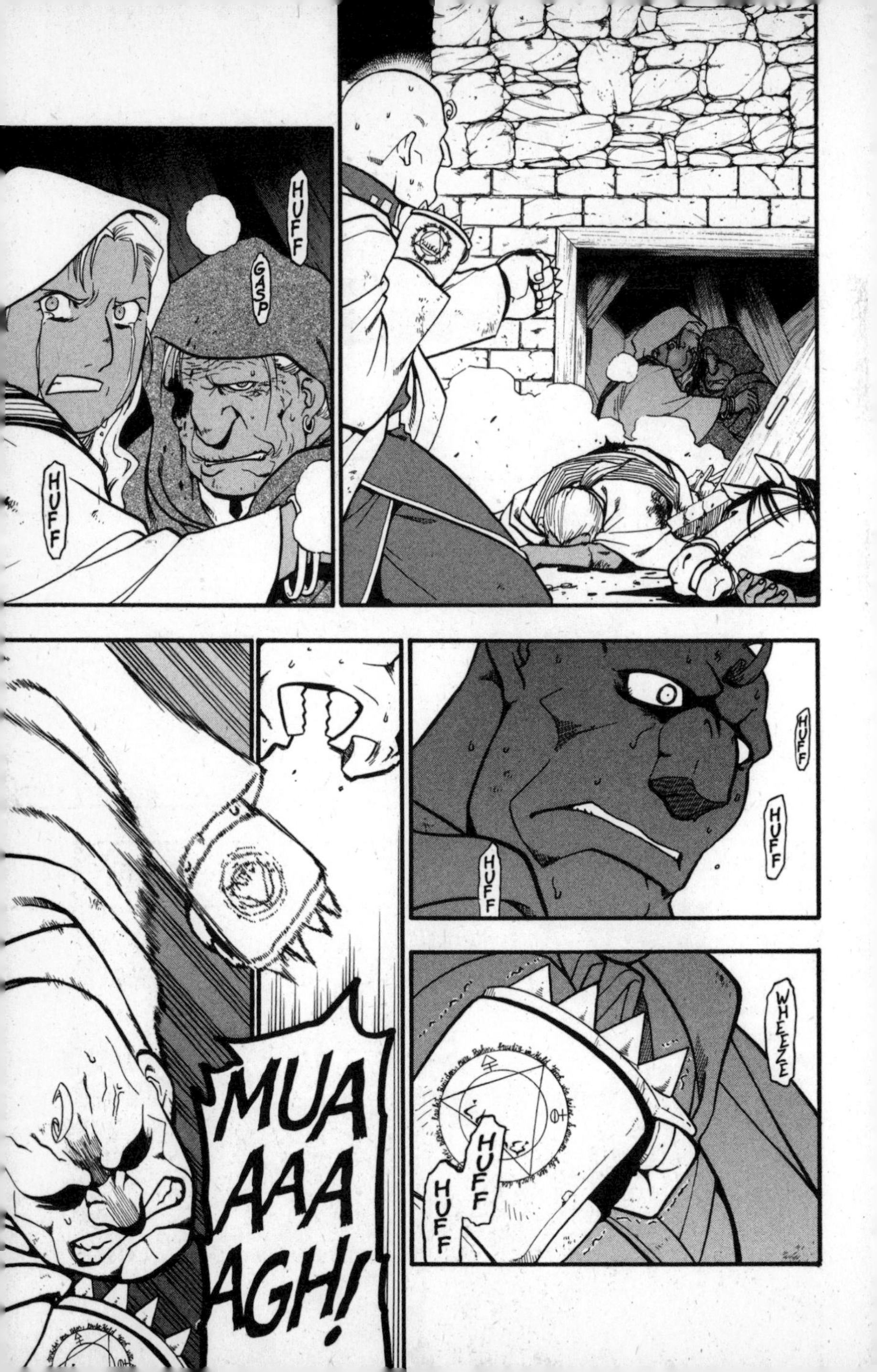
HUFF
GASP
HUFF
HUFF
HUFF
HUFF
WHEEZE
HUFF
HUFF
MUA AAA AGH!

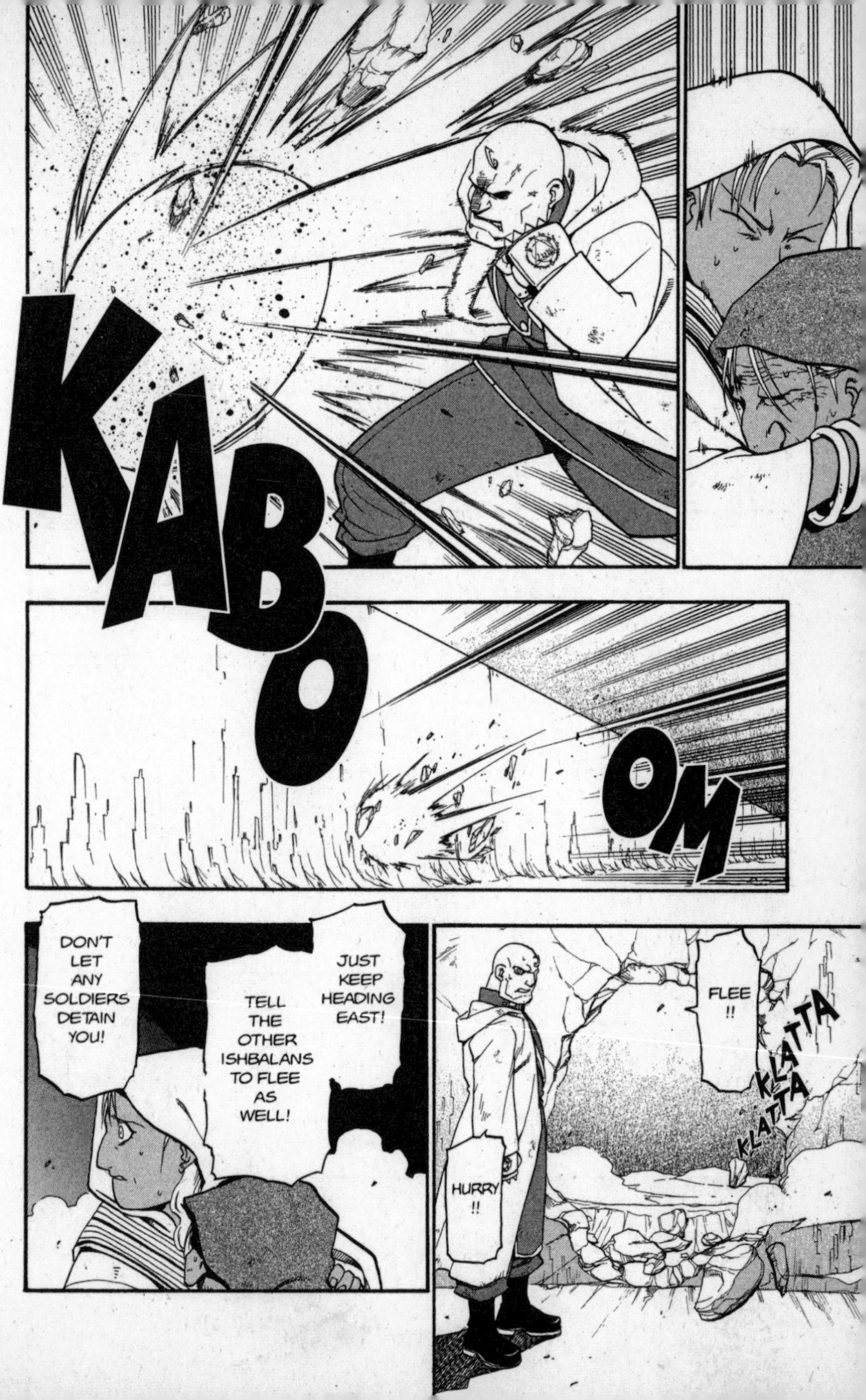
KABOOM
FLEE !!
KLATTA KLATTA
HURRY !!
JUST KEEP HEADING EAST!
TELL THE OTHER ISHBALANS TO FLEE AS WELL!
DON'T LET ANY SOLDIERS DETAIN YOU!

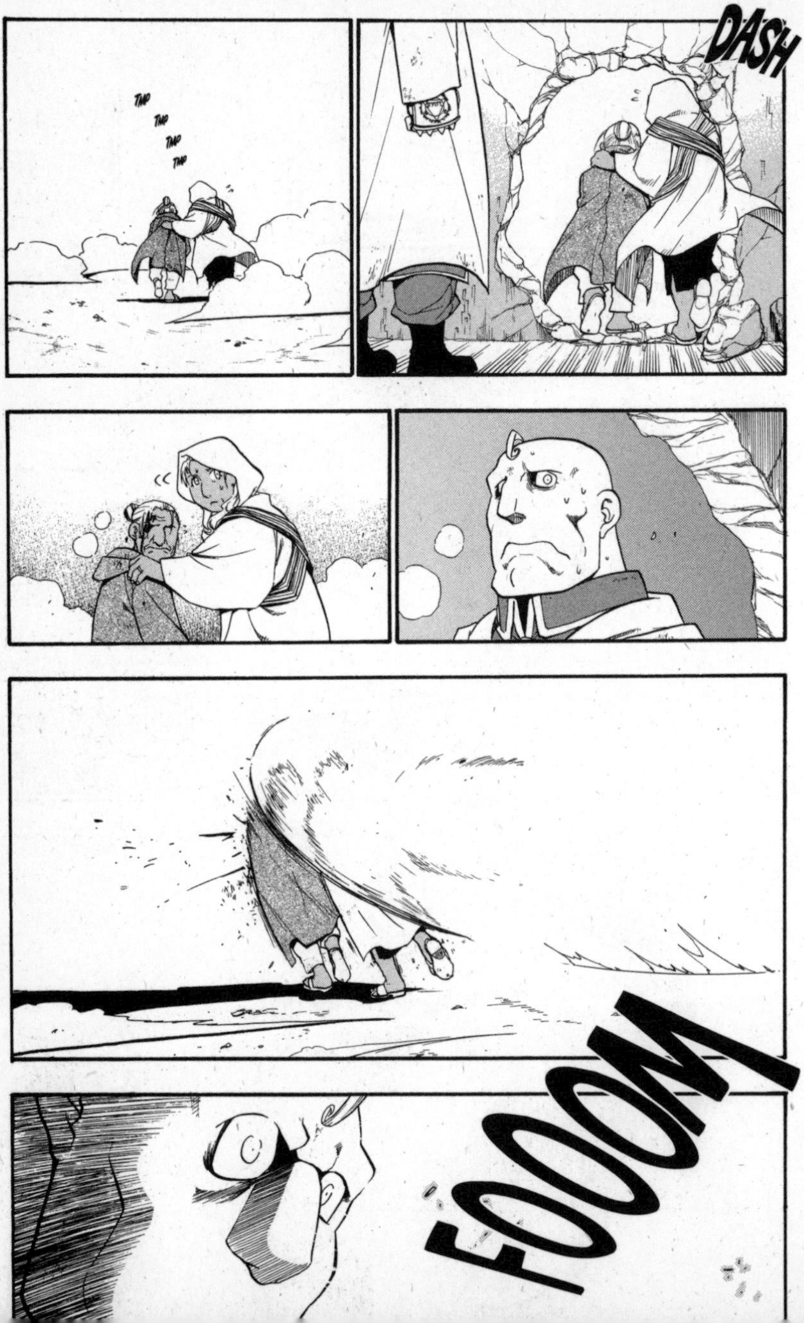
DASH
TMP
TMP
TMP
TMP
FOOOM

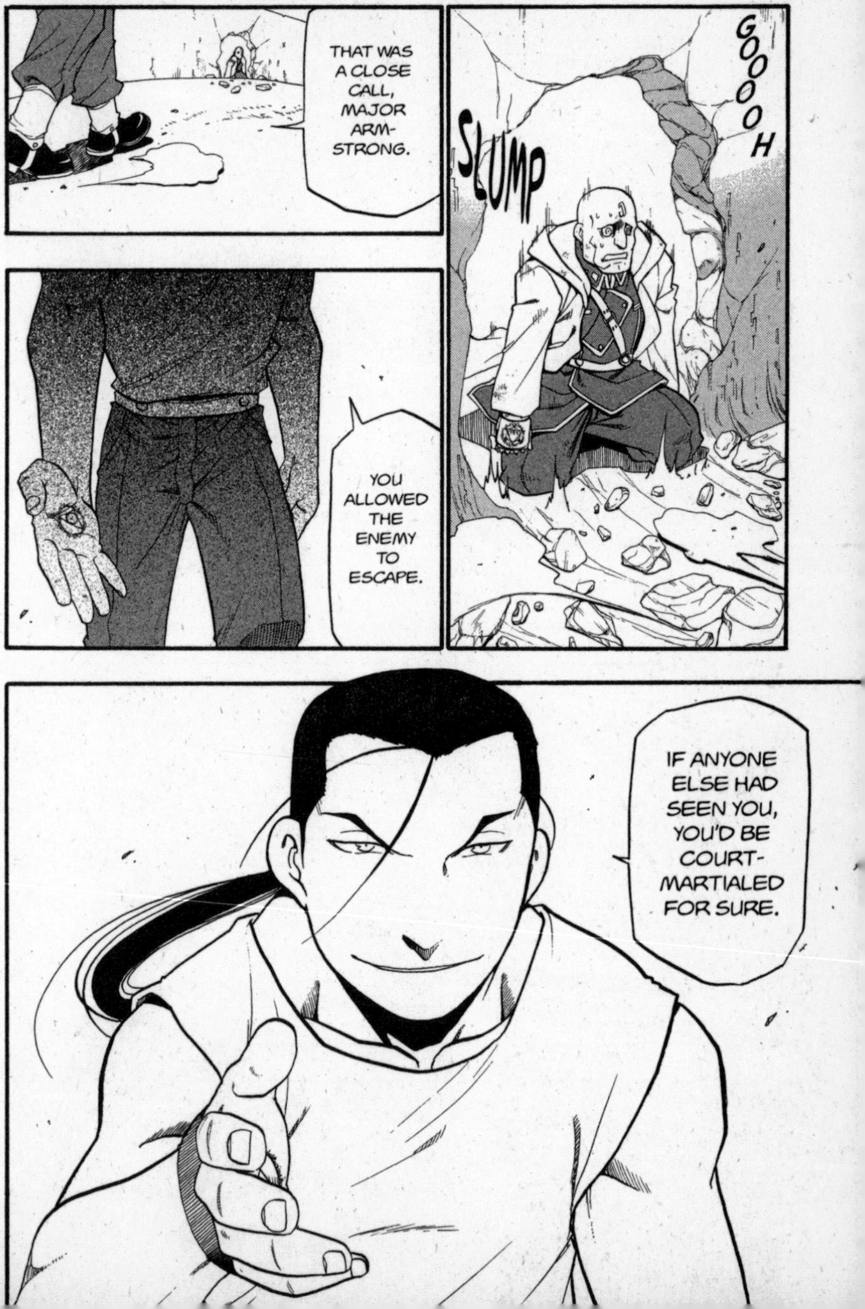
GOOOOOH
SLUMP
THAT WAS A CLOSE CALL, MAJOR ARM-STRONG.
YOU ALLOWED THE ENEMY TO ESCAPE.
IF ANYONE ELSE HAD SEEN YOU, YOU'D BE COURT-MARTIALED FOR SURE.

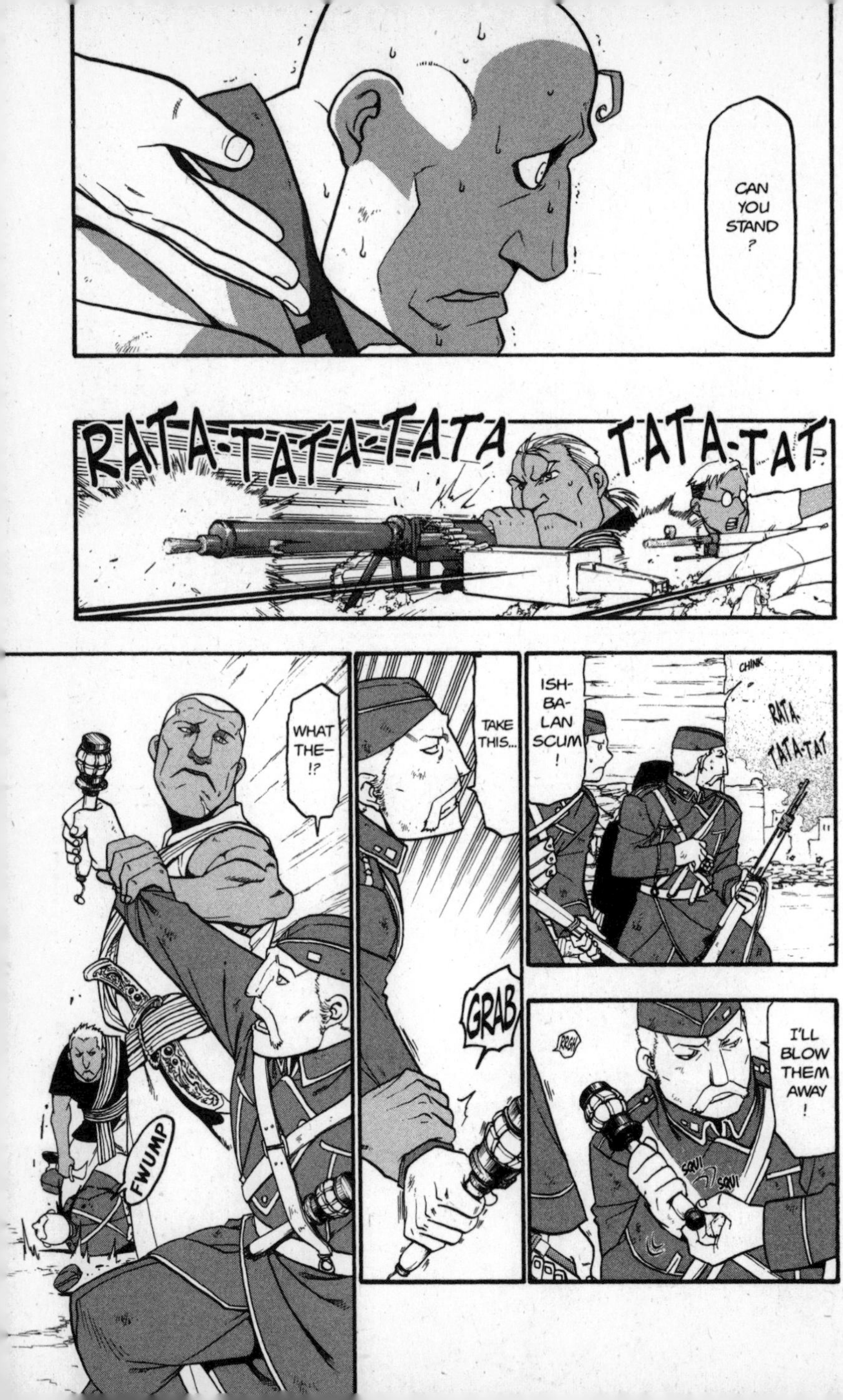

CAN YOU STAND ?
TATA-TAT
RATA-TATA-TATA
CHINK
RATA-TATA-TAT
ISH-BA-LAN SCUM !
I'LL BLOW THEM AWAY !
RRGH
SQUI SQUI
TAKE THIS...
GRAB
WHAT THE-!?
FWUMP

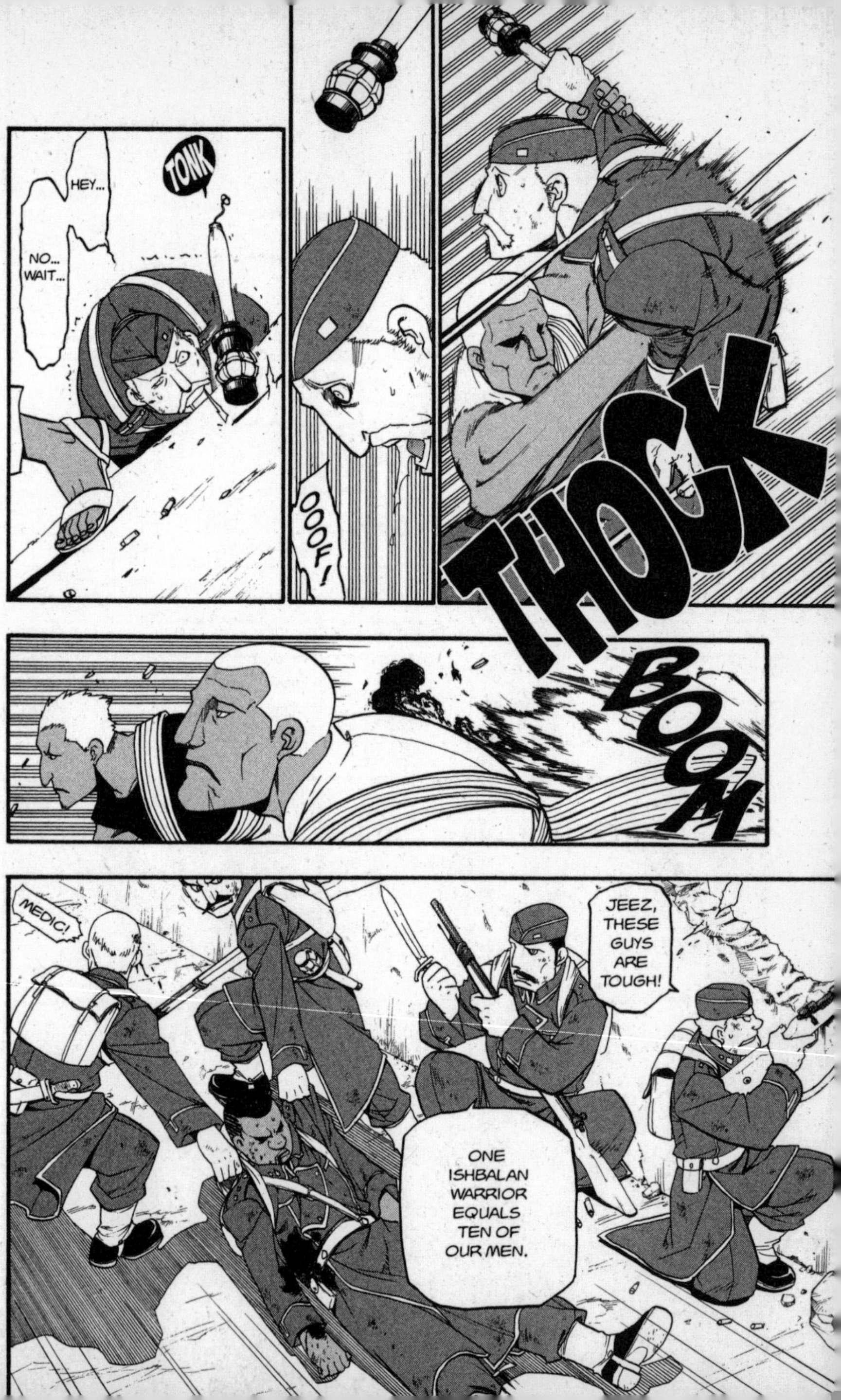
THOCK
OOOF!
TONK
HEY...
NO... WAIT...
BOOM
JEEZ, THESE GUYS ARE TOUGH!
MEDIC!
ONE ISHBALAN WARRIOR EQUALS TEN OF OUR MEN.

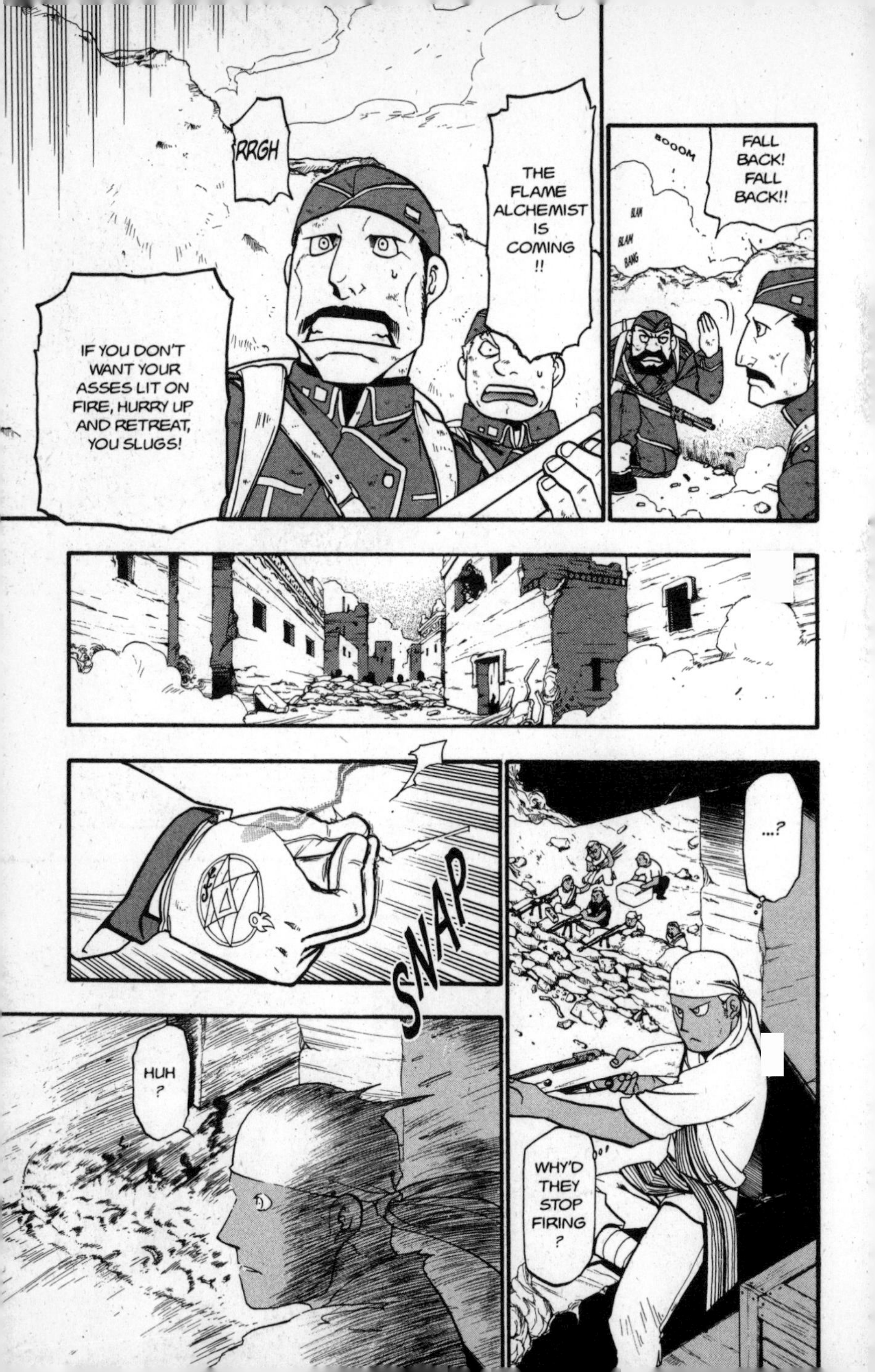
BOOOM
FALL BACK! FALL BACK!!
BLAM
BLAM
BANG
THE FLAME ALCHEMIST IS COMING!!
RRGH
IF YOU DON'T WANT YOUR ASSES LIT ON FIRE, HURRY UP AND RETREAT, YOU SLUGS!
...?
WHY'D THEY STOP FIRING?
SNAP
HUH?

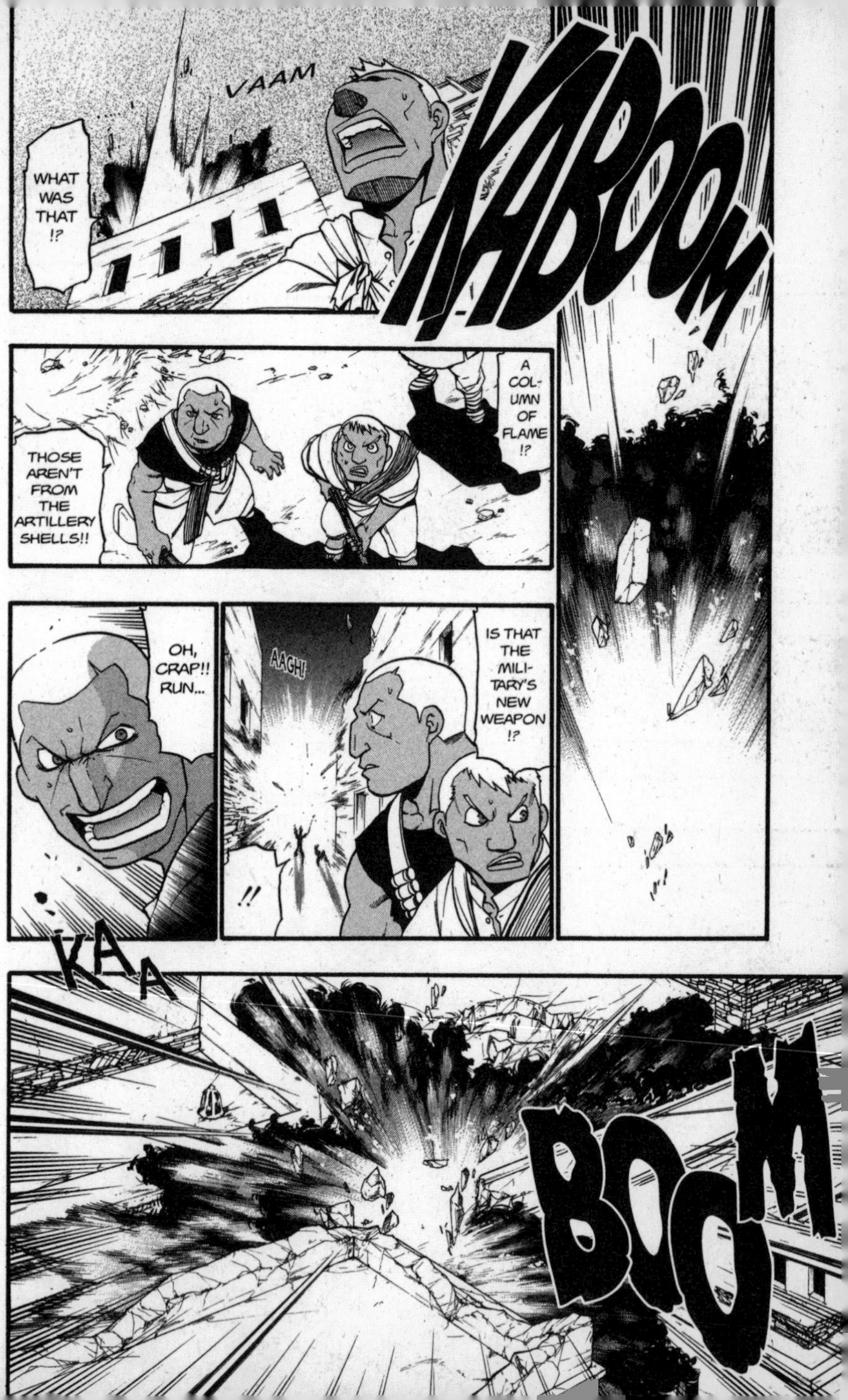
KABOOM
VAAM
WHAT WAS THAT!?
A COL-UMN OF FLAME!?
THOSE AREN'T FROM THE ARTILLERY SHELLS!!
IS THAT THE MILI-TARY'S NEW WEAPON!?
AAGH!
!!
OH, CRAP!! RUN...
BOOM
KAA

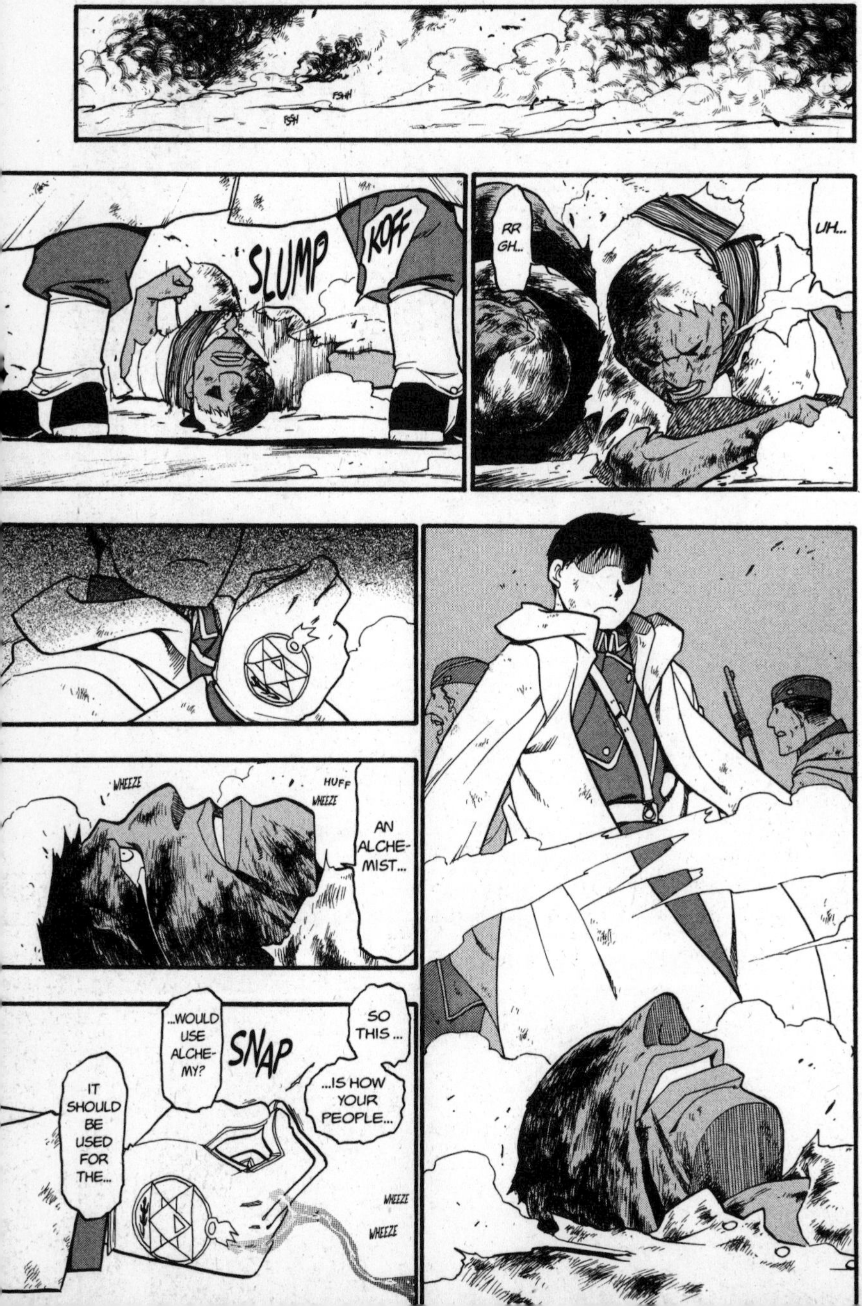
FSHH
FSH
UH...
RR GH...
KOFF
SLUMP
HUFF
WHEEZE
AN ALCHEMIST...
WHEEZE
SO THIS...
...IS HOW YOUR PEOPLE...
...WOULD USE ALCHEMY?
SNAP
IT SHOULD BE USED FOR THE...
WHEEZE
WHEEZE

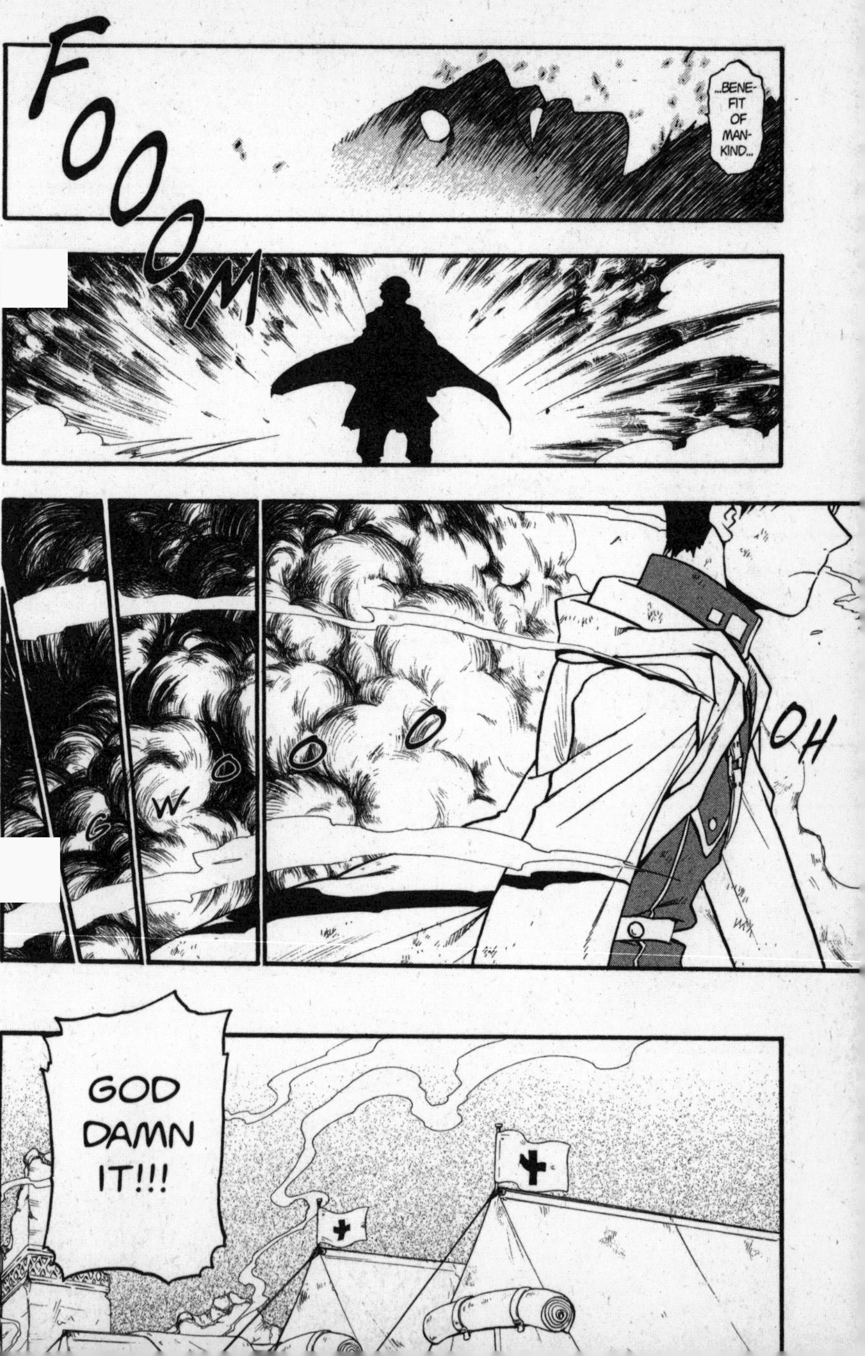
...BENE-FIT OF MAN-KIND...
FOOOM
GWOOOOH
GOD DAMN IT!!!

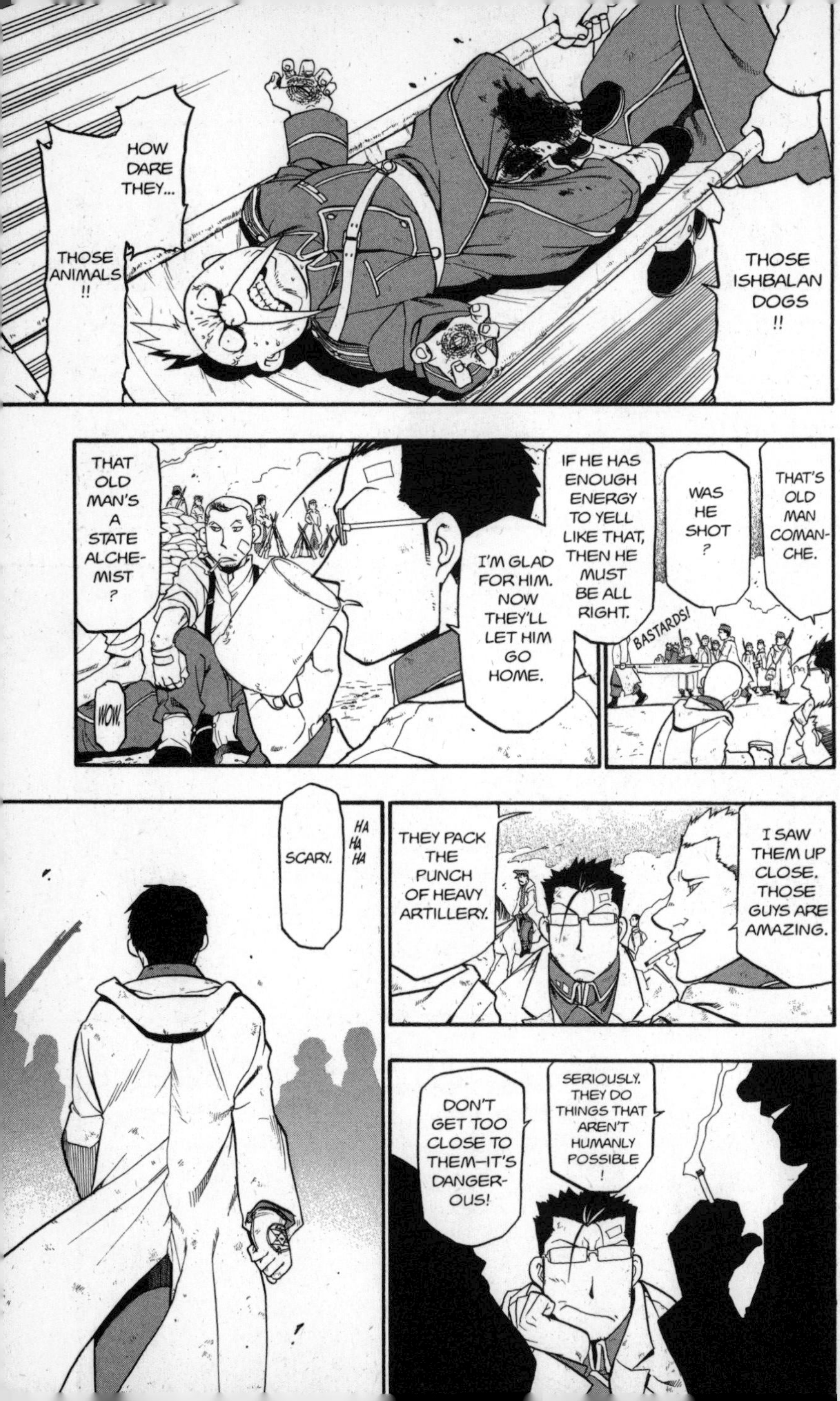
THOSE ISHBALAN DOGS !!
HOW DARE THEY...
THOSE ANIMALS !!
THAT'S OLD MAN COMANCHE.
WAS HE SHOT ?
BASTARDS!
IF HE HAS ENOUGH ENERGY TO YELL LIKE THAT, THEN HE MUST BE ALL RIGHT.
I'M GLAD FOR HIM. NOW THEY'LL LET HIM GO HOME.
THAT OLD MAN'S A STATE ALCHEMIST ?
WOW.
I SAW THEM UP CLOSE. THOSE GUYS ARE AMAZING.
THEY PACK THE PUNCH OF HEAVY ARTILLERY.
SERIOUSLY. THEY DO THINGS THAT AREN'T HUMANLY POSSIBLE !
DON'T GET TOO CLOSE TO THEM—IT'S DANGER-OUS!
SCARY.
HA HA HA

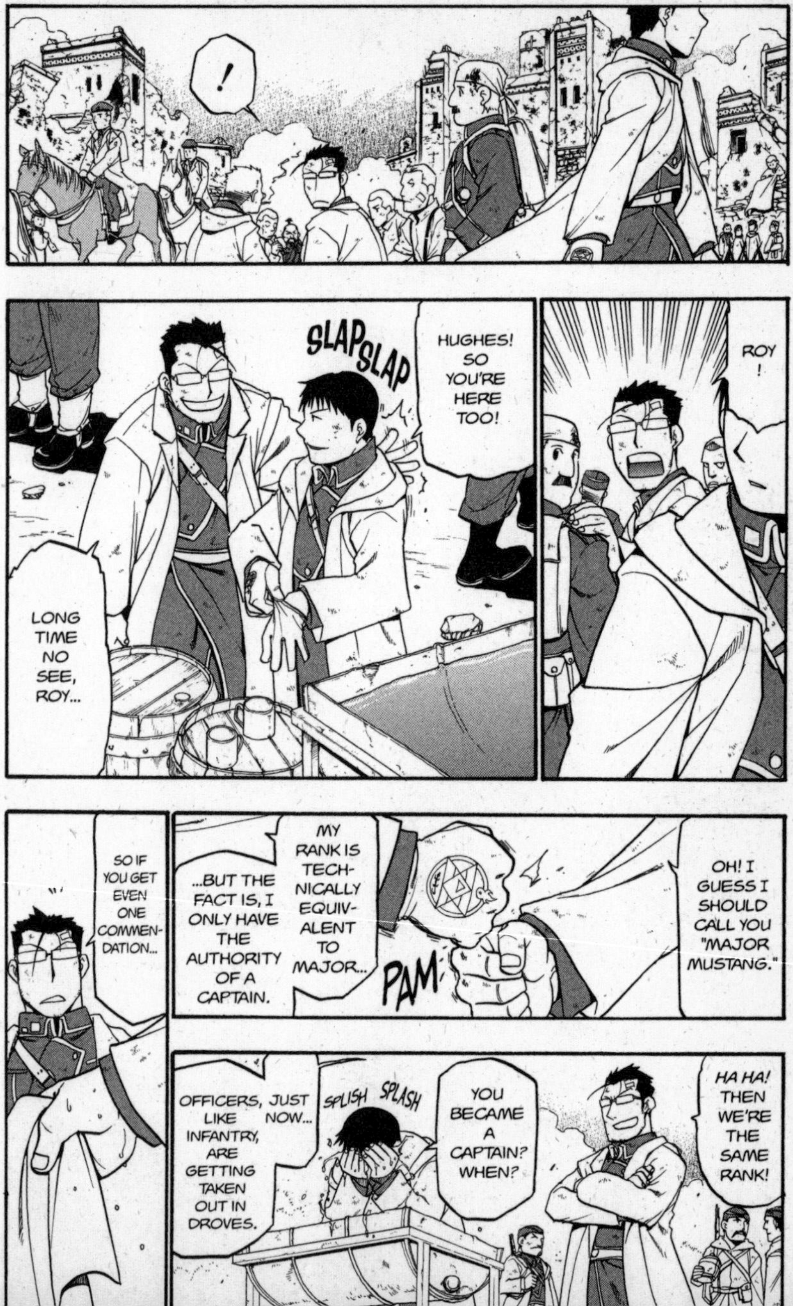
!
ROY!
HUGHES! SO YOU'RE HERE TOO!
SLAP SLAP
LONG TIME NO SEE, ROY...
OH! I GUESS I SHOULD CALL YOU "MAJOR MUSTANG."
PAM
MY RANK IS TECHNICALLY EQUIVALENT TO MAJOR...
...BUT THE FACT IS, I ONLY HAVE THE AUTHORITY OF A CAPTAIN.
HA HA! THEN WE'RE THE SAME RANK!
YOU BECAME A CAPTAIN? WHEN?
SPLASH
SPLISH
JUST NOW...
OFFICERS, LIKE INFANTRY, ARE GETTING TAKEN OUT IN DROVES.
SO IF YOU GET EVEN ONE COMMENDATION...

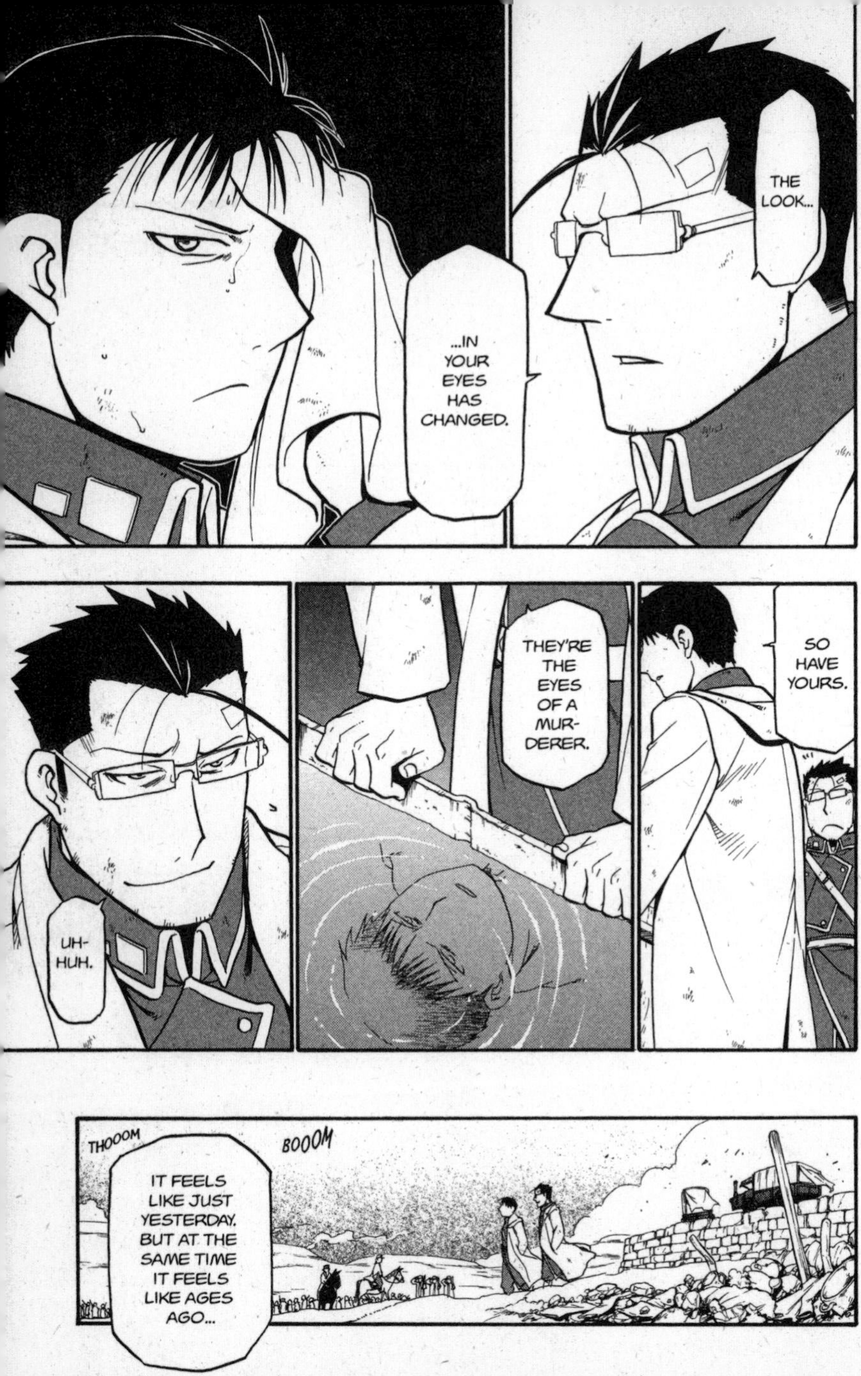
THE LOOK...
...IN YOUR EYES HAS CHANGED.
SO HAVE YOURS.
THEY'RE THE EYES OF A MUR-DERER.
UH-HUH.
BOOOM
THOOOM
IT FEELS LIKE JUST YESTERDAY. BUT AT THE SAME TIME IT FEELS LIKE AGES AGO...

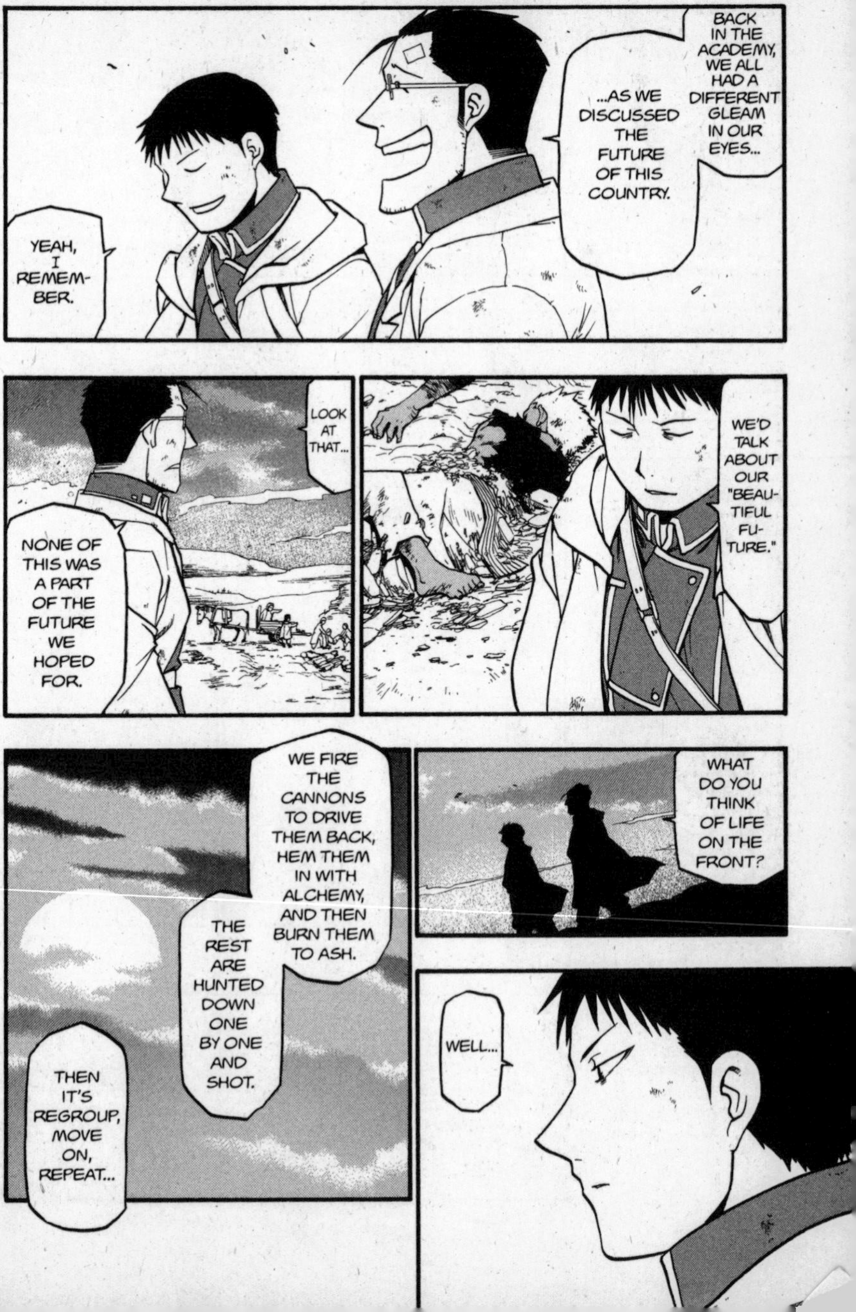
BACK IN THE ACADEMY, WE ALL HAD A DIFFERENT GLEAM IN OUR EYES...
...AS WE DISCUSSED THE FUTURE OF THIS COUNTRY.
YEAH, I REMEMBER.
WE'D TALK ABOUT OUR "BEAUTIFUL FUTURE."
LOOK AT THAT...
NONE OF THIS WAS A PART OF THE FUTURE WE HOPED FOR.
WHAT DO YOU THINK OF LIFE ON THE FRONT?
WELL...
WE FIRE THE CANNONS TO DRIVE THEM BACK, HEM THEM IN WITH ALCHEMY, AND THEN BURN THEM TO ASH.
THE REST ARE HUNTED DOWN ONE BY ONE AND SHOT.
THEN IT'S REGROUP, MOVE ON, REPEAT...

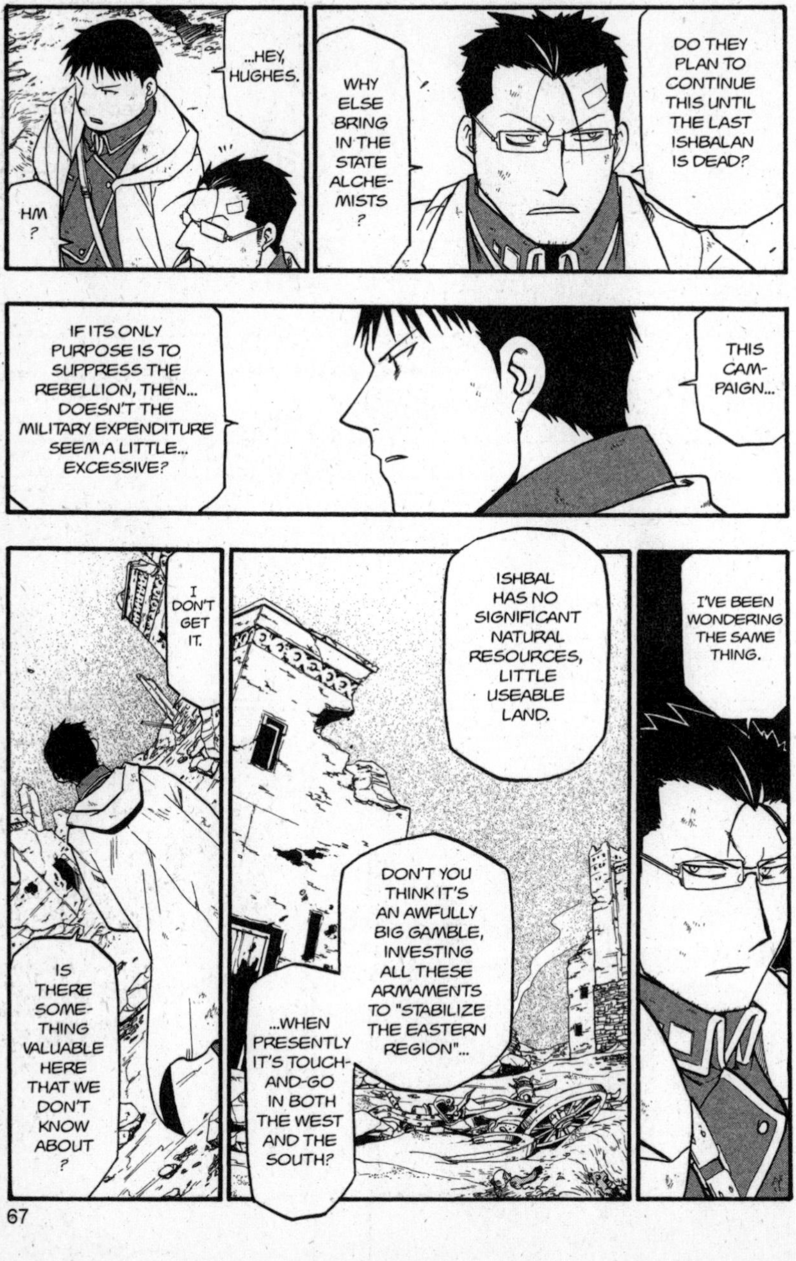
DO THEY PLAN TO CONTINUE THIS UNTIL THE LAST ISHBALAN IS DEAD?
WHY ELSE BRING IN THE STATE ALCHEMISTS?
...HEY, HUGHES.
HM?
THIS CAMPAIGN...
IF ITS ONLY PURPOSE IS TO SUPPRESS THE REBELLION, THEN... DOESN'T THE MILITARY EXPENDITURE SEEM A LITTLE... EXCESSIVE?
I'VE BEEN WONDERING THE SAME THING.
ISHBAL HAS NO SIGNIFICANT NATURAL RESOURCES, LITTLE USEABLE LAND.
DON'T YOU THINK IT'S AN AWFULLY BIG GAMBLE, INVESTING ALL THESE ARMAMENTS TO "STABILIZE THE EASTERN REGION"...
...WHEN PRESENTLY IT'S TOUCH-AND-GO IN BOTH THE WEST AND THE SOUTH?
I DON'T GET IT.
IS THERE SOMETHING VALUABLE HERE THAT WE DON'T KNOW ABOUT?

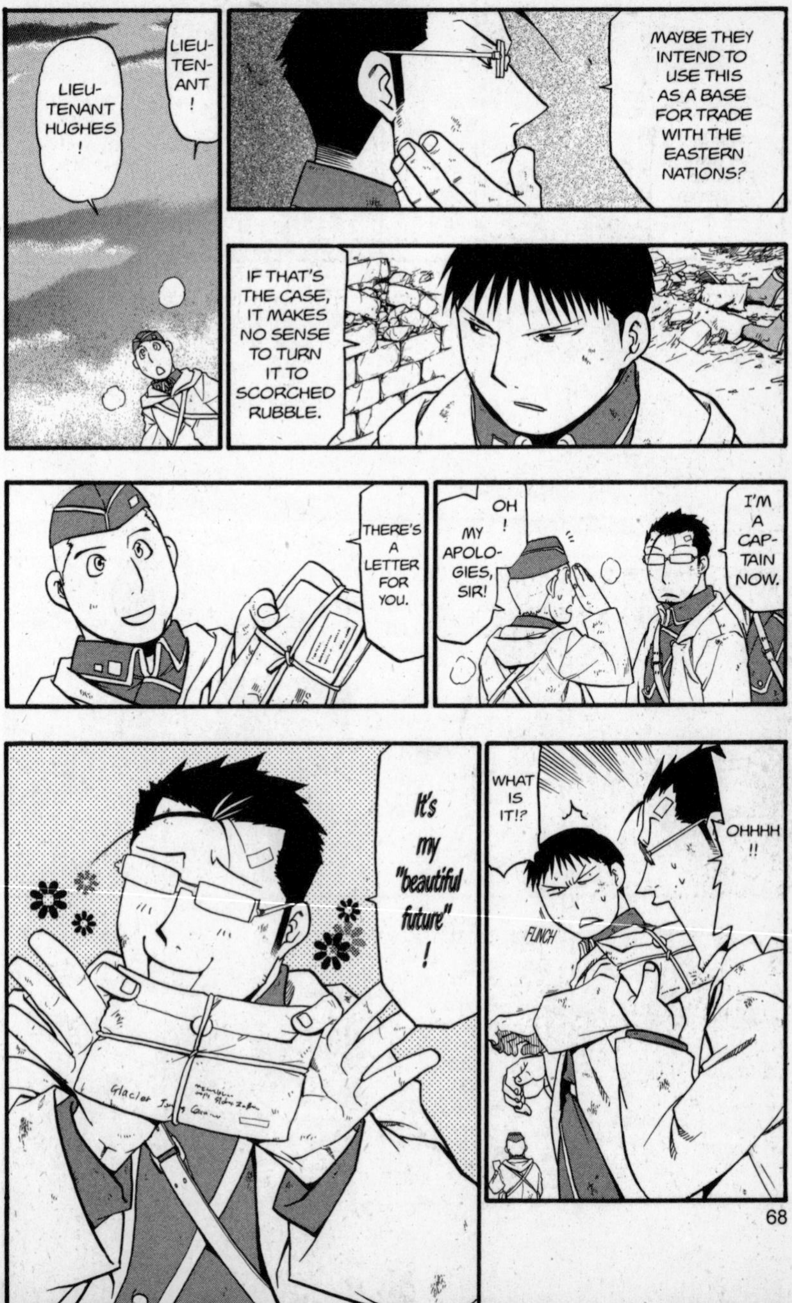
MAYBE THEY INTEND TO USE THIS AS A BASE FOR TRADE WITH THE EASTERN NATIONS?
IF THAT'S THE CASE, IT MAKES NO SENSE TO TURN IT TO SCORCHED RUBBLE.
LIEU-TENANT!
LIEU-TENANT HUGHES!
I'M A CAP-TAIN NOW.
OH! MY APOLO-GIES, SIR!
THERE'S A LETTER FOR YOU.
OHHHH!!
WHAT IS IT!?
FLINCH
It's my "beautiful future"!

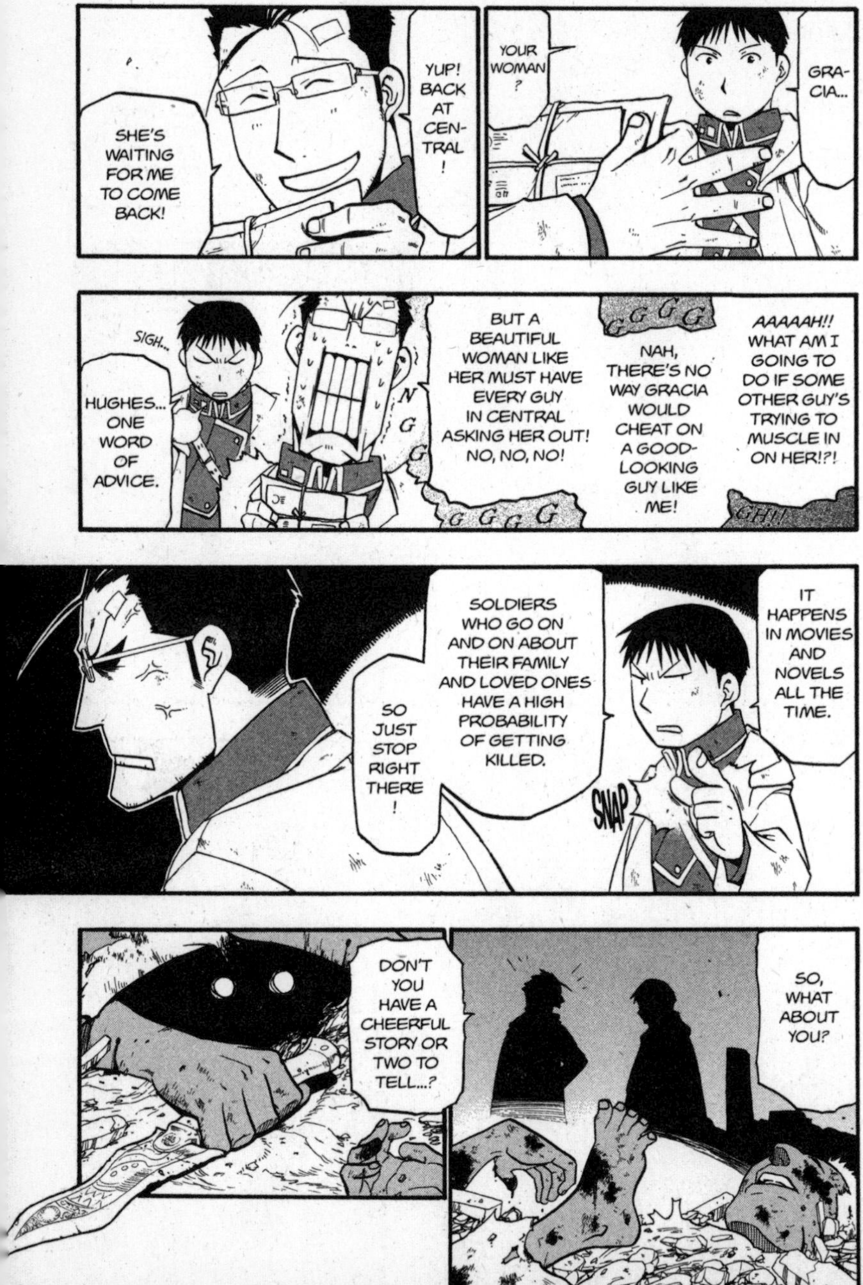
GRA-CIA...
YOUR WOMAN?
YUP! BACK AT CENTRAL!
SHE'S WAITING FOR ME TO COME BACK!
AAAAAH!! WHAT AM I GOING TO DO IF SOME OTHER GUY'S TRYING TO MUSCLE IN ON HER!?!
GH!!
NAH, THERE'S NO WAY GRACIA WOULD CHEAT ON A GOOD-LOOKING GUY LIKE ME!
GGGG
BUT A BEAUTIFUL WOMAN LIKE HER MUST HAVE EVERY GUY IN CENTRAL ASKING HER OUT! NO, NO, NO!
NGG
GGGG
HUGHES... ONE WORD OF ADVICE.
SIGH...
IT HAPPENS IN MOVIES AND NOVELS ALL THE TIME.
SNAP
SOLDIERS WHO GO ON AND ON ABOUT THEIR FAMILY AND LOVED ONES HAVE A HIGH PROBABILITY OF GETTING KILLED.
SO JUST STOP RIGHT THERE!
SO, WHAT ABOUT YOU?
DON'T YOU HAVE A CHEERFUL STORY OR TWO TO TELL...?

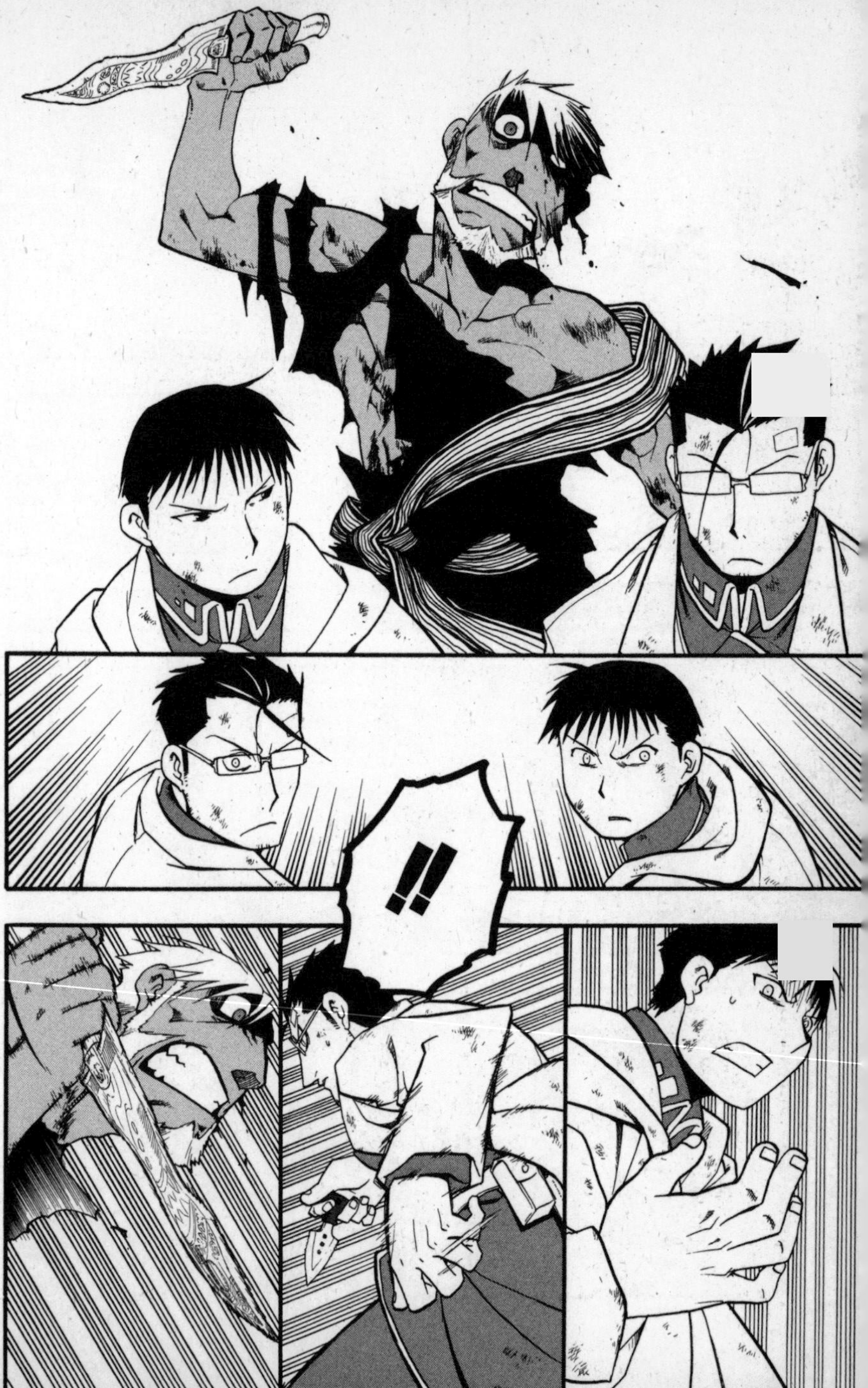
!!

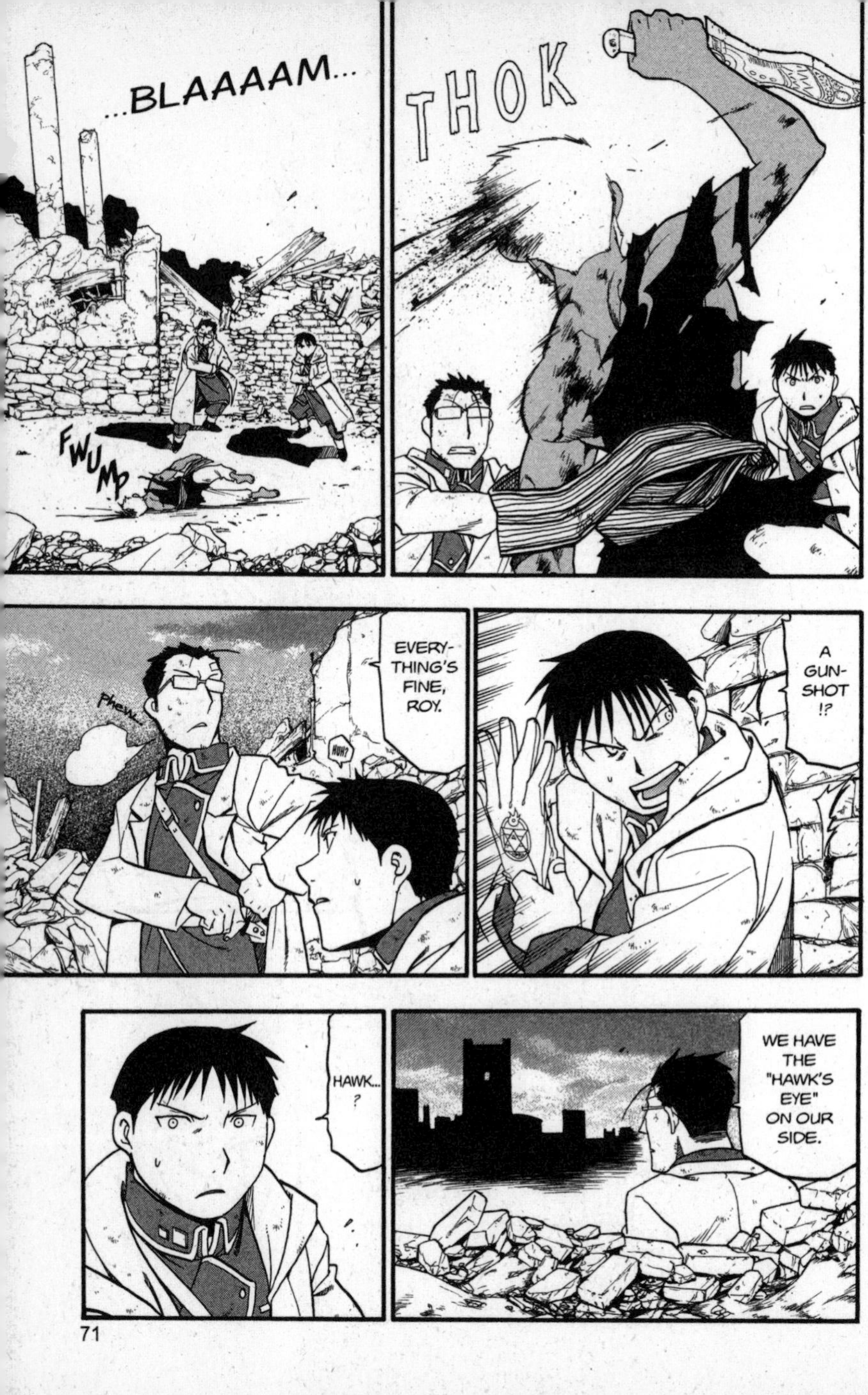
THOK
...BLAAAAM...
FWUMP
A GUN-SHOT !?
EVERY-THING'S FINE, ROY.
phew...
HUH?
WE HAVE THE "HAWK'S EYE" ON OUR SIDE.
HAWK... ?

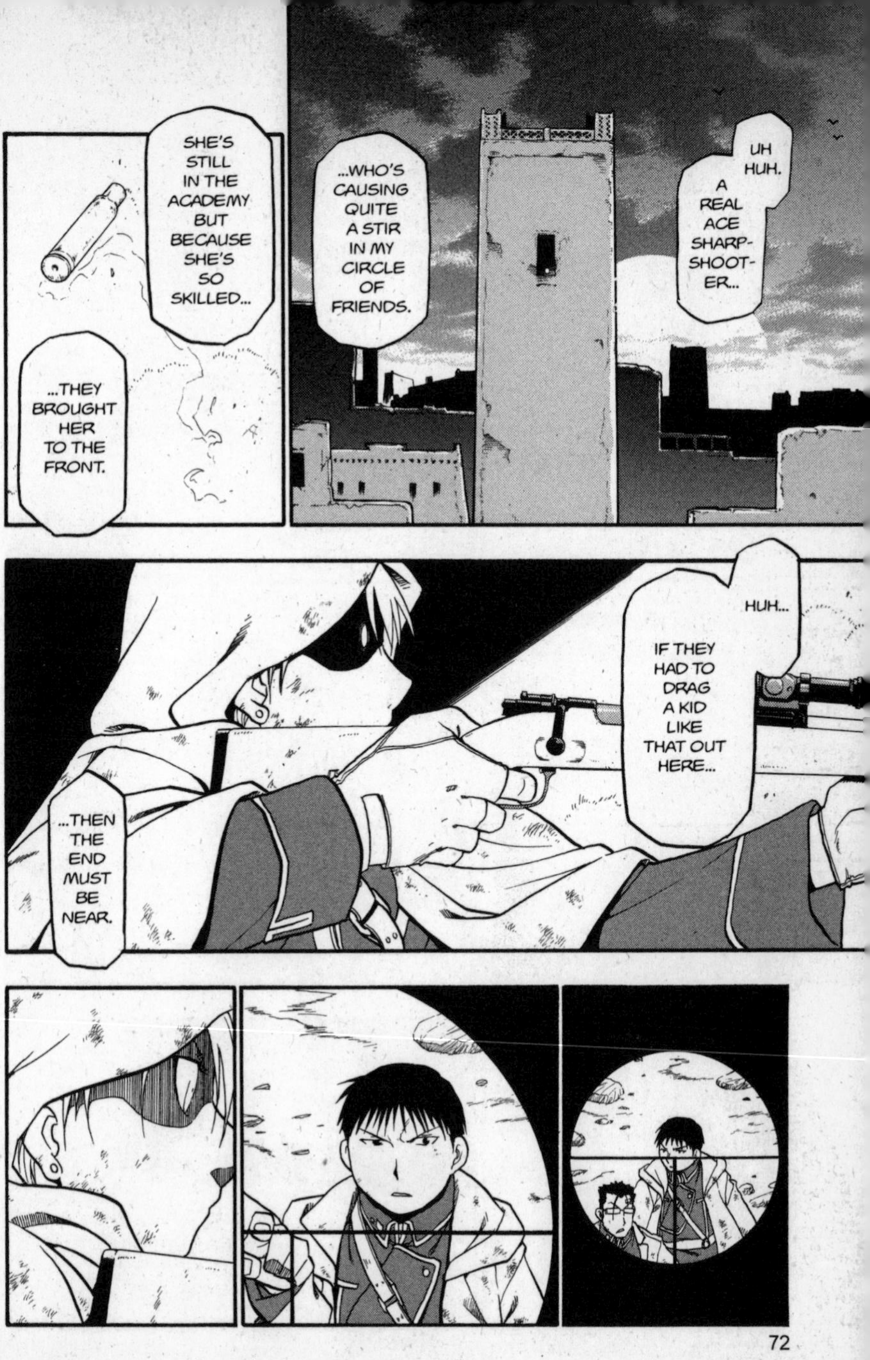

UH HUH. A REAL ACE SHARP-SHOOTER...
...WHO'S CAUSING QUITE A STIR IN MY CIRCLE OF FRIENDS.
SHE'S STILL IN THE ACADEMY BUT BECAUSE SHE'S SO SKILLED...
...THEY BROUGHT HER TO THE FRONT.
HUH...
IF THEY HAD TO DRAG A KID LIKE THAT OUT HERE...
...THEN THE END MUST BE NEAR.

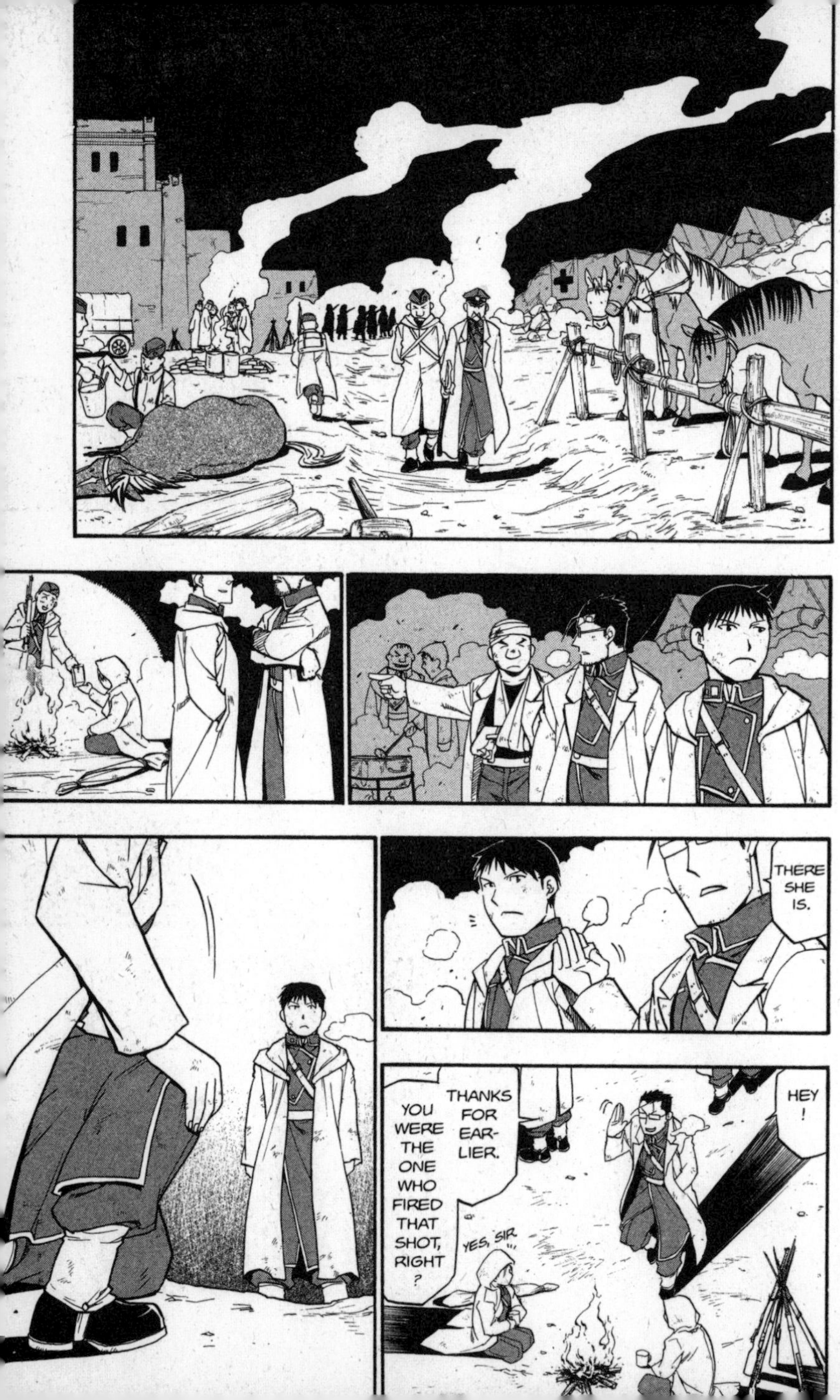
THERE SHE IS.
HEY!
THANKS FOR EARLIER.
YOU WERE THE ONE WHO FIRED THAT SHOT, RIGHT?
YES, SIR...

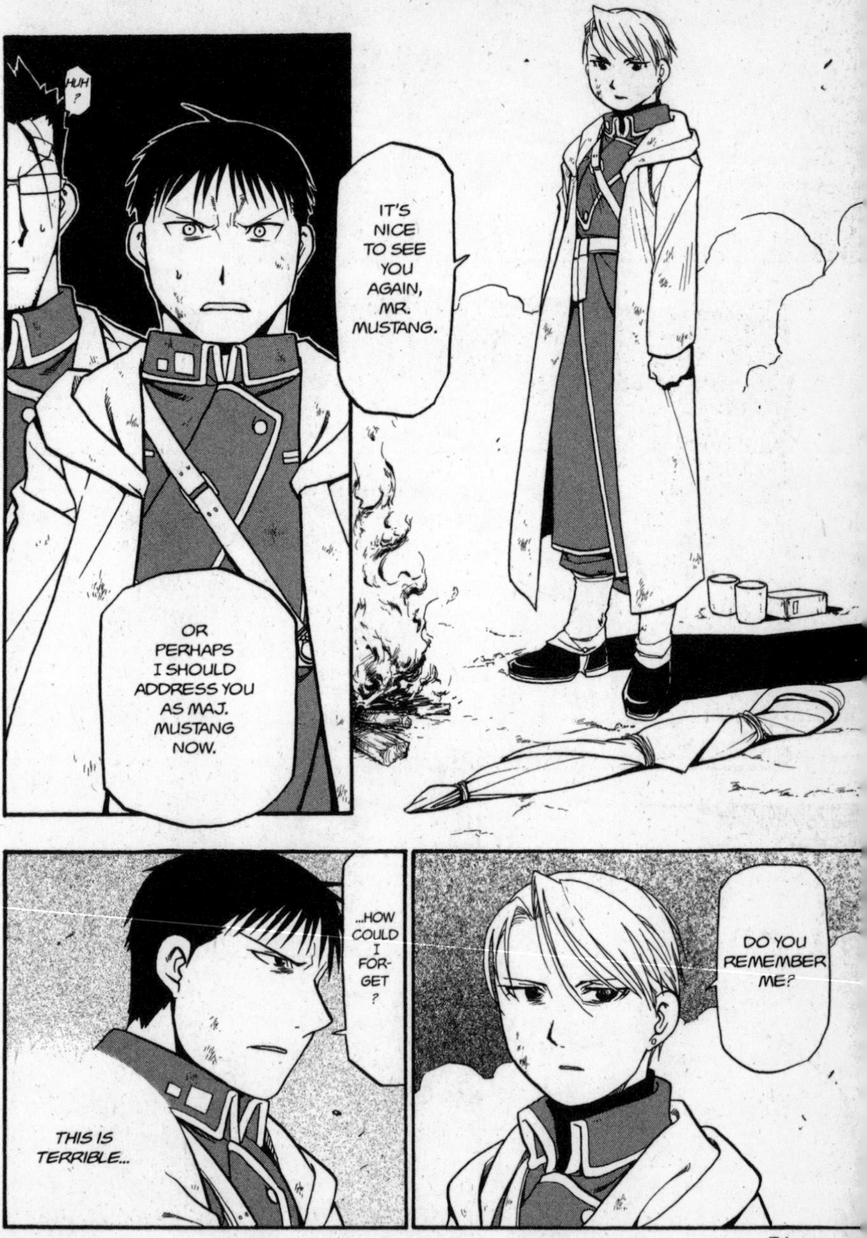
IT'S NICE TO SEE YOU AGAIN, MR. MUSTANG.
HUH?
OR PERHAPS I SHOULD ADDRESS YOU AS MAJ. MUSTANG NOW.
DO YOU REMEMBER ME?
...HOW COULD I FOR-GET?
THIS IS TERRIBLE...

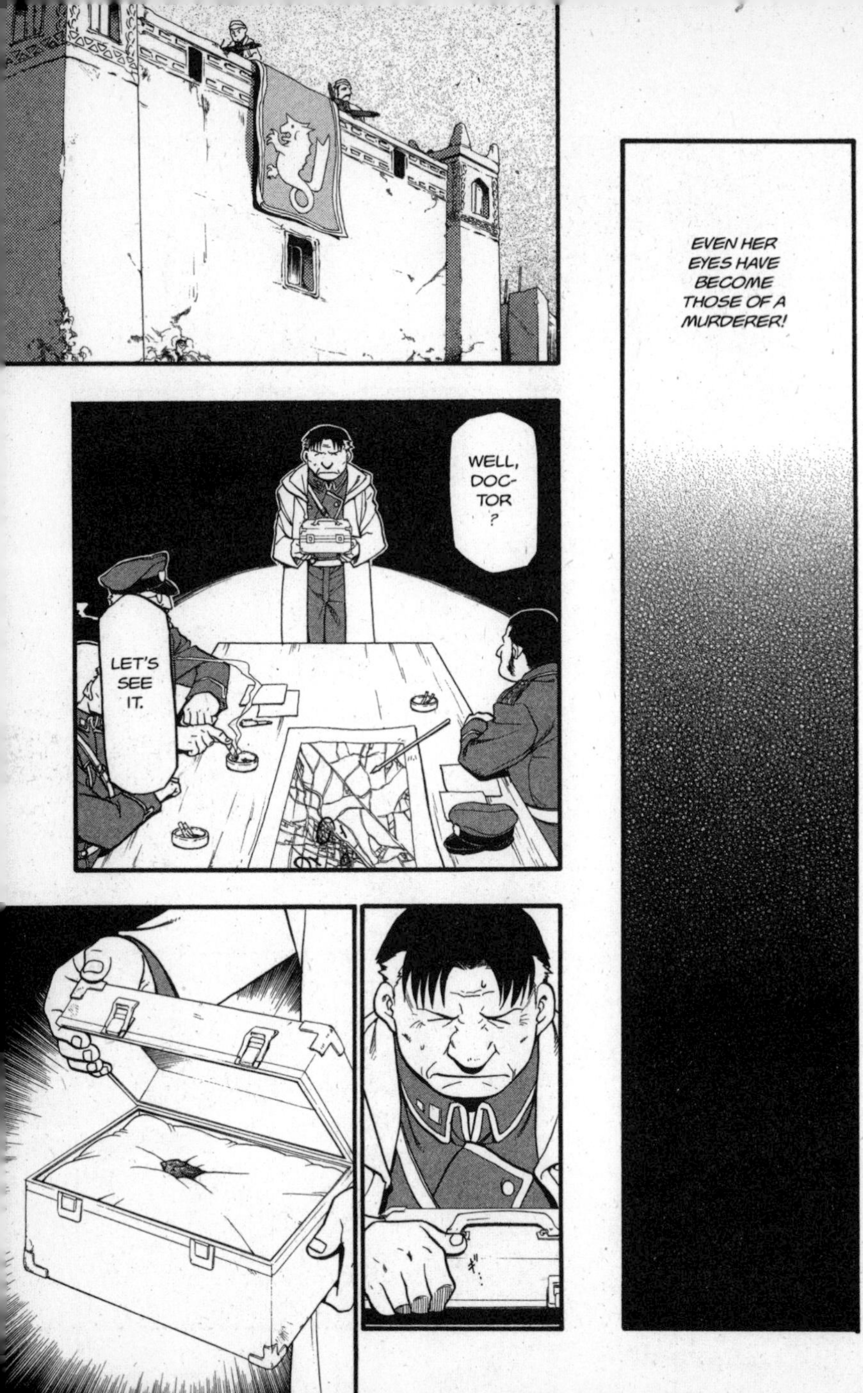
EVEN HER EYES HAVE BECOME THOSE OF A MURDERER!
WELL, DOC-TOR?
LET'S SEE IT.

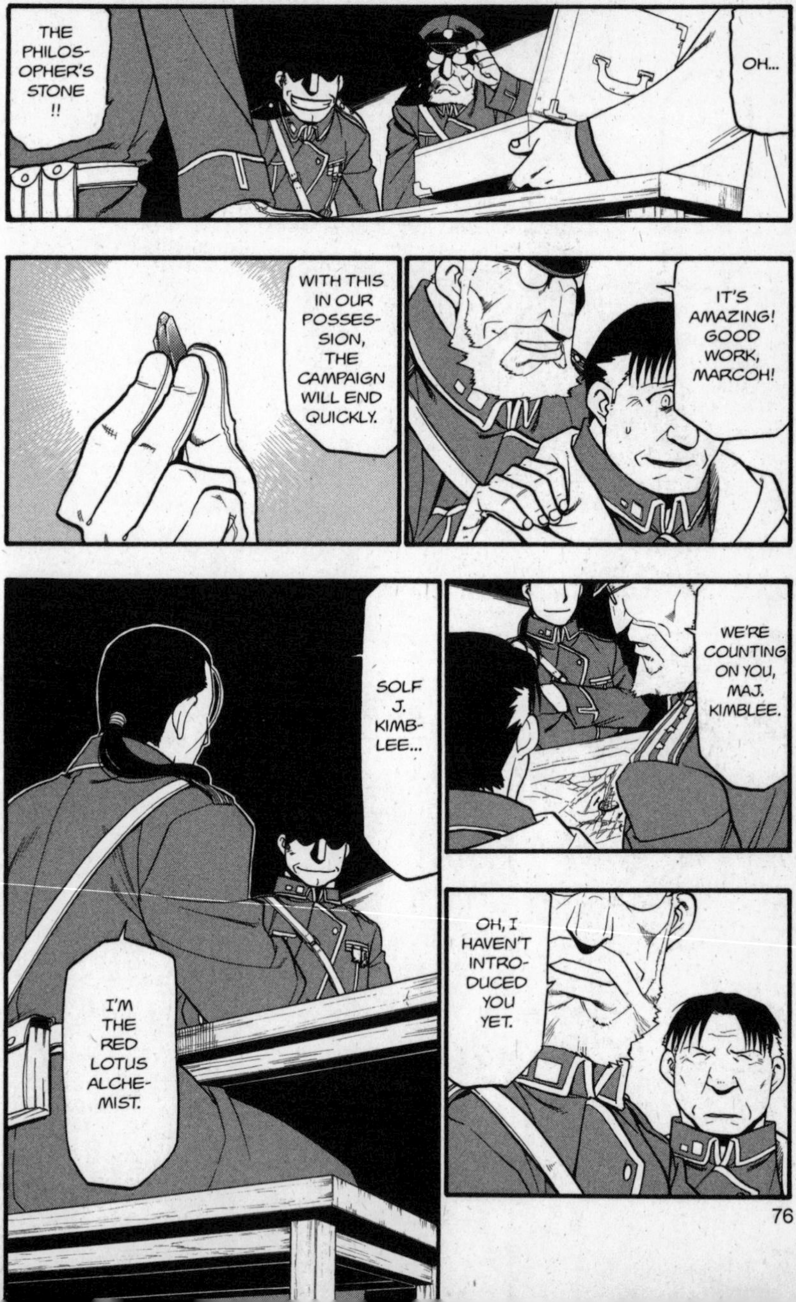
OH...
THE PHILOSOPHER'S STONE !!
IT'S AMAZING! GOOD WORK, MARCOH!
WITH THIS IN OUR POSSESSION, THE CAMPAIGN WILL END QUICKLY.
WE'RE COUNTING ON YOU, MAJ. KIMBLEE.
OH, I HAVEN'T INTRODUCED YOU YET.
SOLF J. KIMBLEE...
I'M THE RED LOTUS ALCHEMIST.

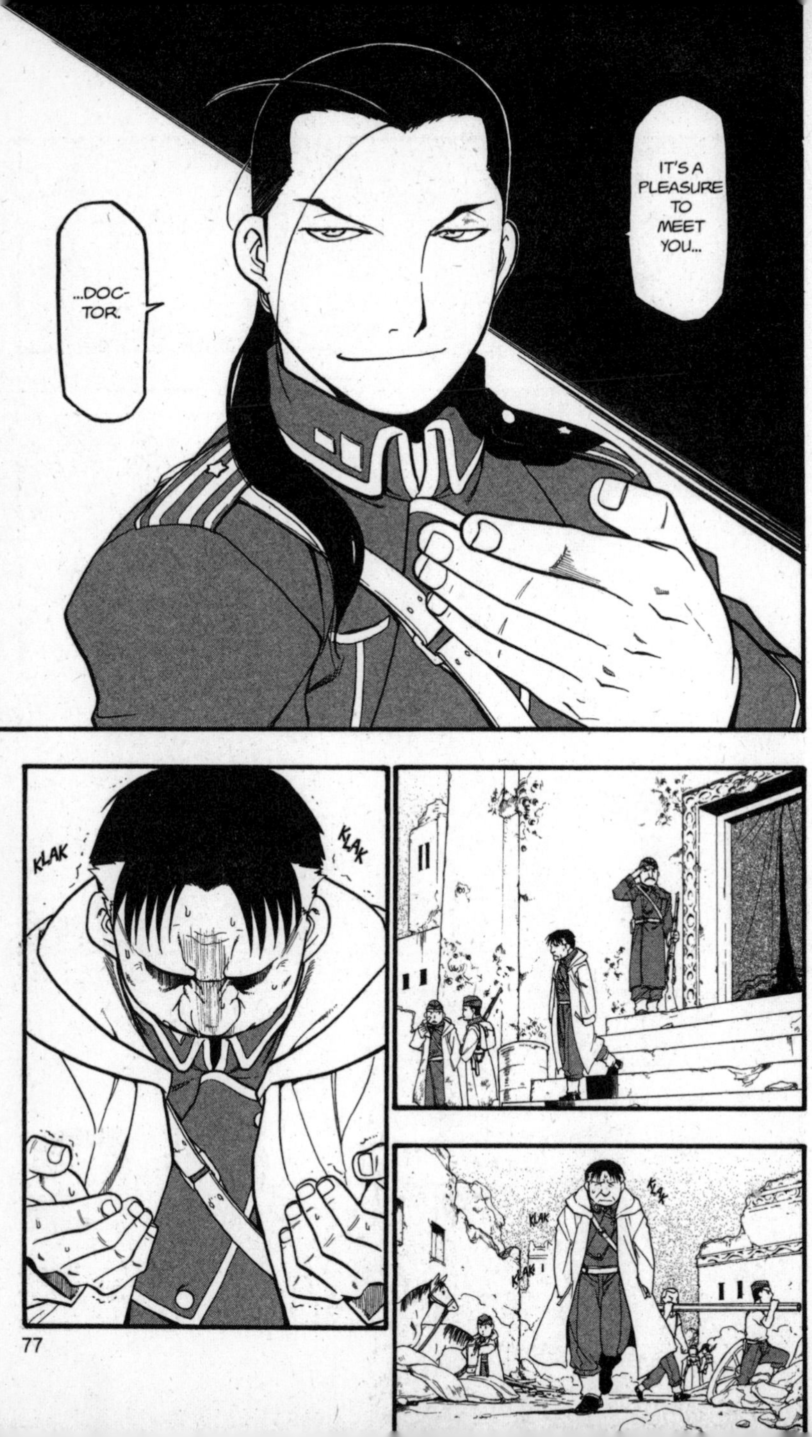
IT'S A PLEASURE TO MEET YOU...
...DOC-TOR.
KLAK
KLAK
KLAK
KLAK
KLAK

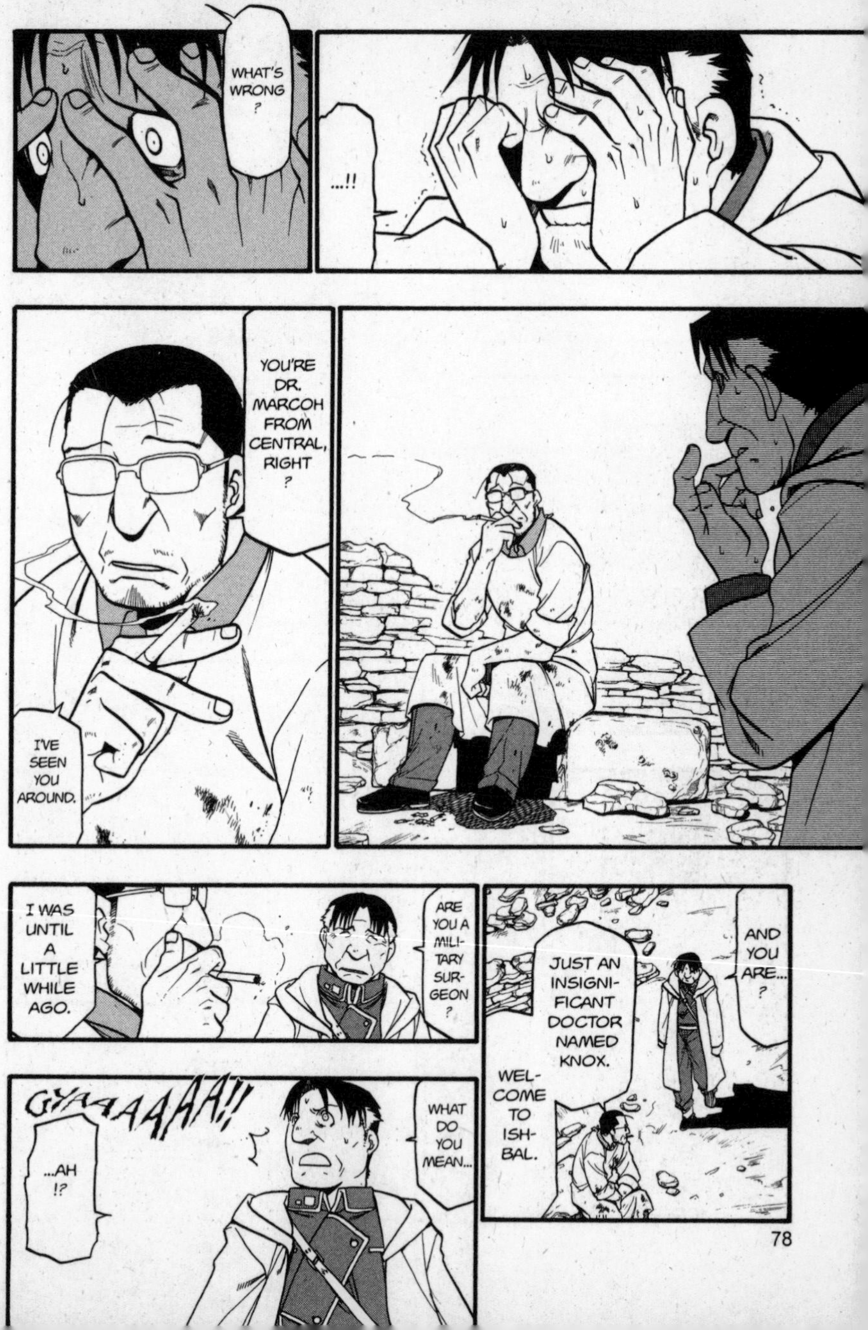
WHAT'S WRONG?
...!!
YOU'RE DR. MARCOH FROM CENTRAL, RIGHT?
I'VE SEEN YOU AROUND.
AND YOU ARE...?
JUST AN INSIGNIFICANT DOCTOR NAMED KNOX.
WELCOME TO ISHBAL.
ARE YOU A MILITARY SURGEON?
I WAS UNTIL A LITTLE WHILE AGO.
WHAT DO YOU MEAN...
GYAAAAAAA!!
...AH!?

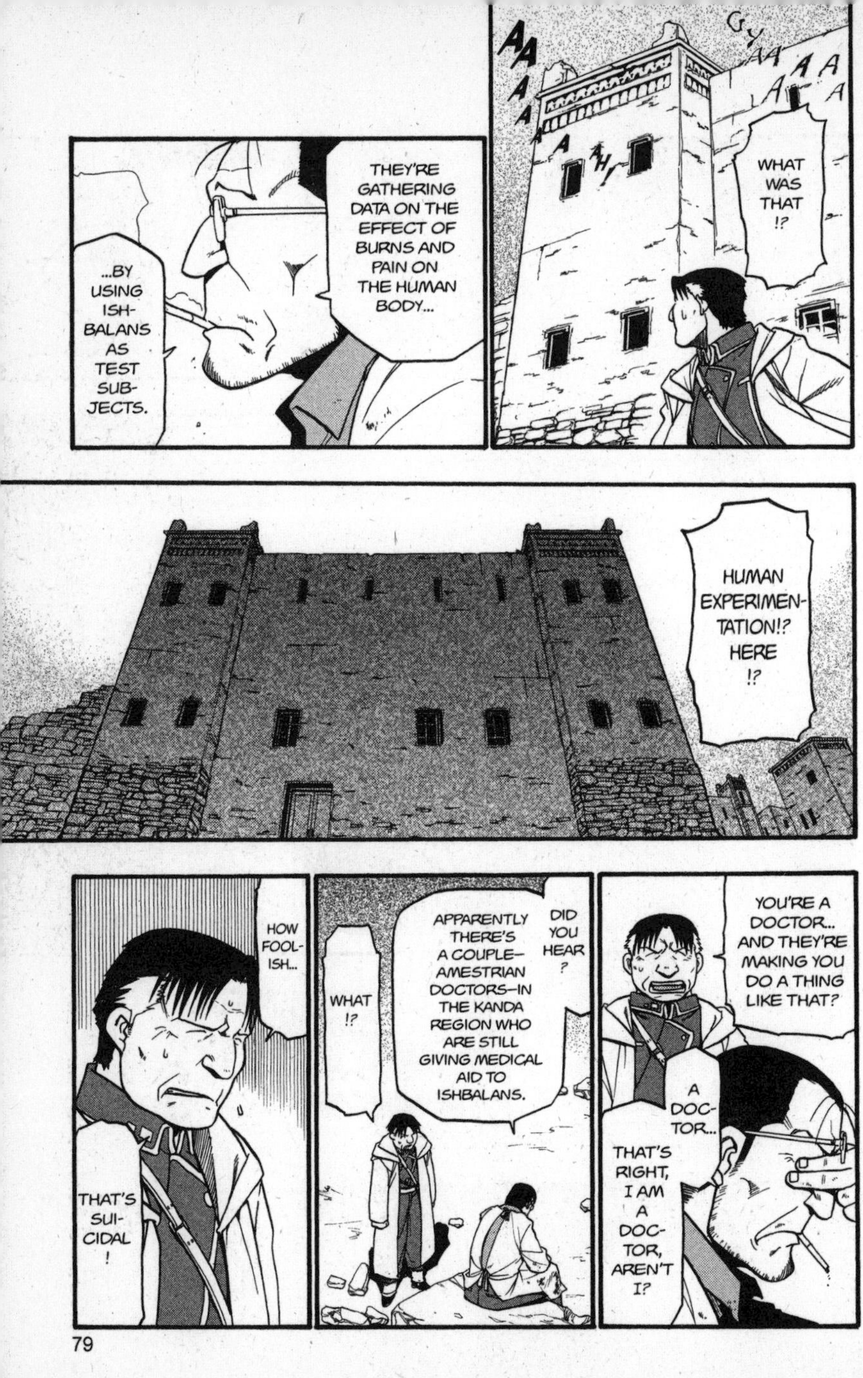
GYAAAAAA
AAAAAAAH!
WHAT WAS THAT!?
THEY'RE GATHERING DATA ON THE EFFECT OF BURNS AND PAIN ON THE HUMAN BODY...
...BY USING ISHBALANS AS TEST SUBJECTS.
HUMAN EXPERIMENTATION!? HERE!?
YOU'RE A DOCTOR... AND THEY'RE MAKING YOU DO A THING LIKE THAT?
A DOCTOR...
THAT'S RIGHT, I AM A DOCTOR, AREN'T I?
DID YOU HEAR?
APPARENTLY THERE'S A COUPLE—AMESTRIAN DOCTORS—IN THE KANDA REGION WHO ARE STILL GIVING MEDICAL AID TO ISHBALANS.
WHAT!?
HOW FOOLISH...
THAT'S SUICIDAL!

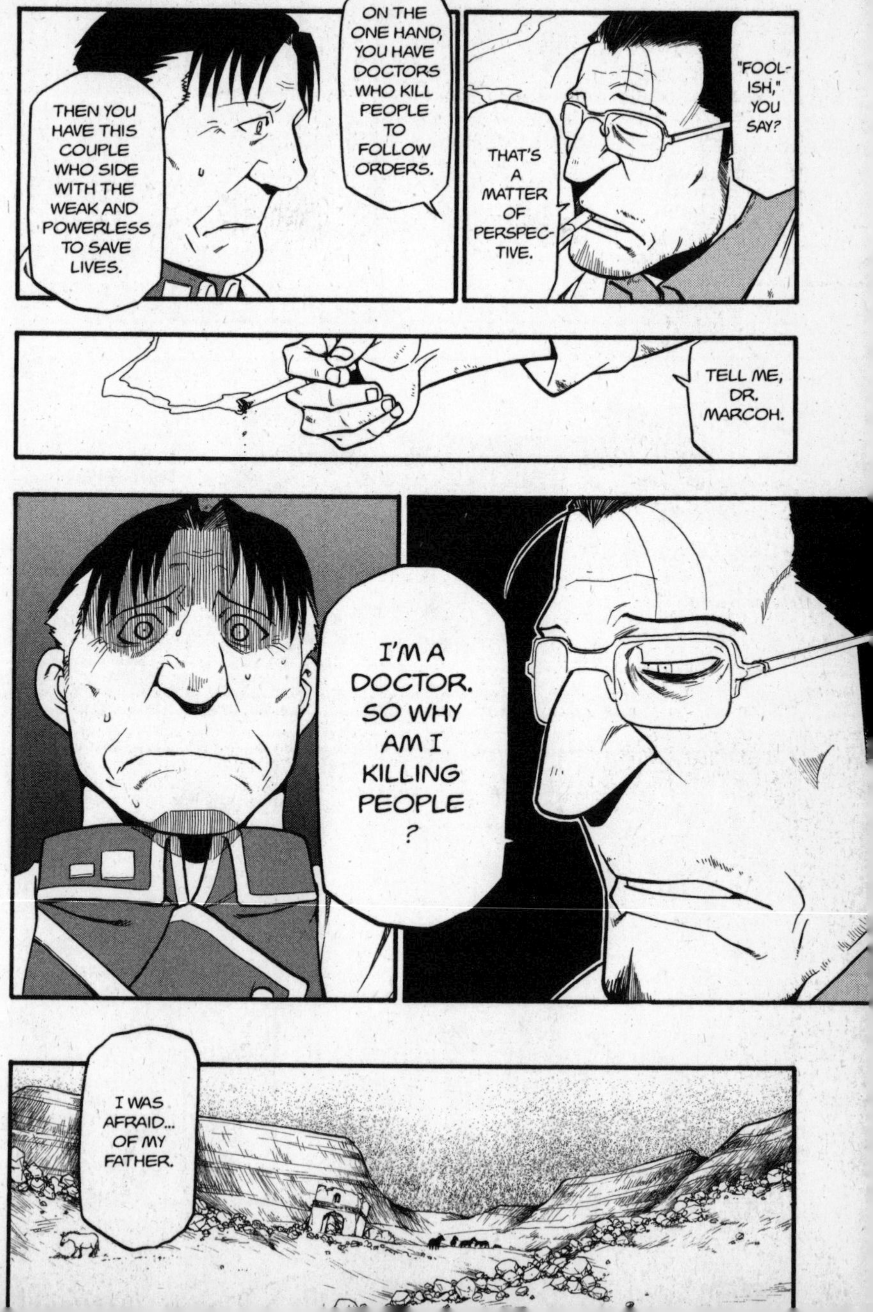
"FOOL-ISH," YOU SAY?
THAT'S A MATTER OF PERSPEC-TIVE.
ON THE ONE HAND, YOU HAVE DOCTORS WHO KILL PEOPLE TO FOLLOW ORDERS.
THEN YOU HAVE THIS COUPLE WHO SIDE WITH THE WEAK AND POWERLESS TO SAVE LIVES.
TELL ME, DR. MARCOH.
I'M A DOCTOR. SO WHY AM I KILLING PEOPLE?
I WAS AFRAID... OF MY FATHER.

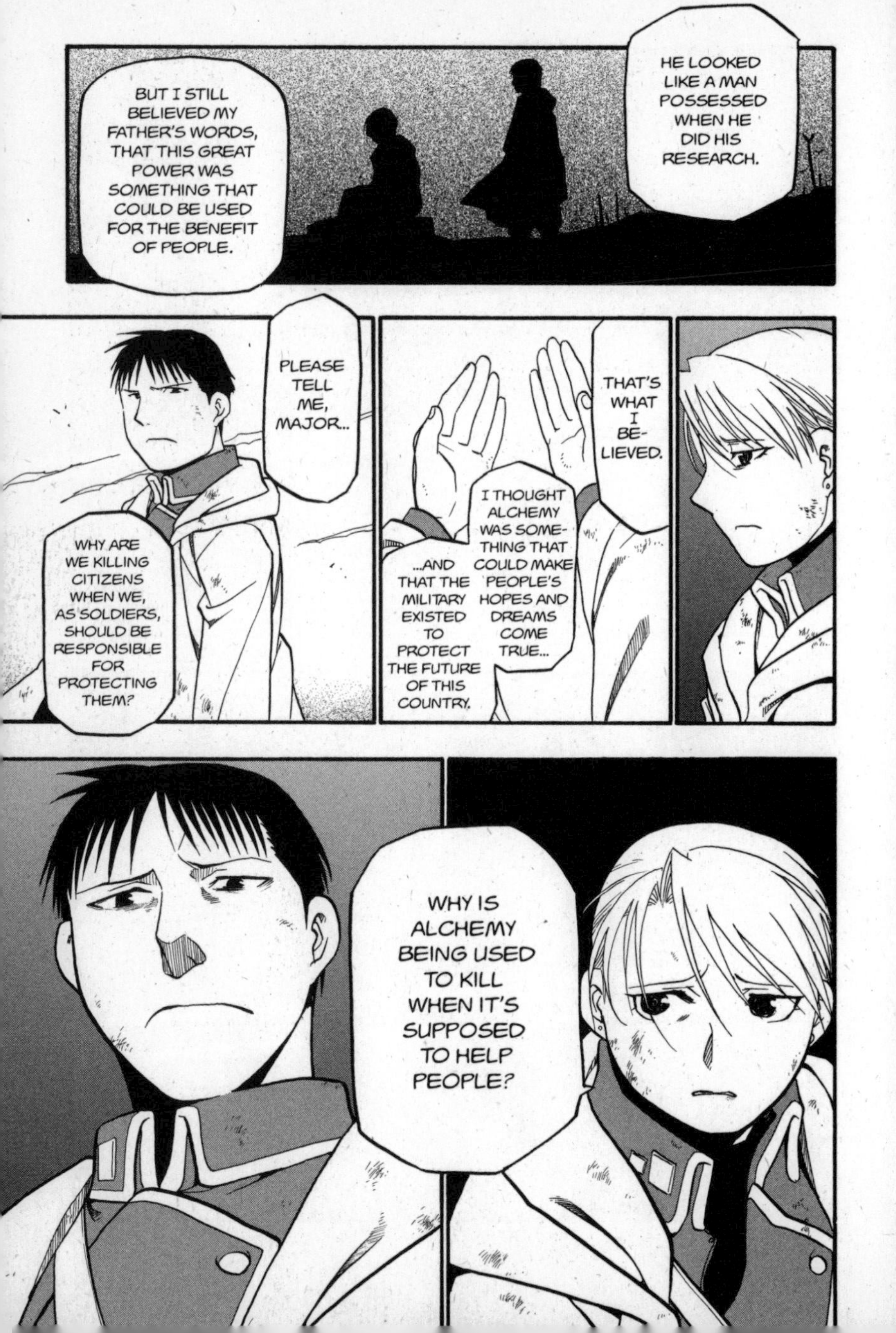
HE LOOKED LIKE A MAN POSSESSED WHEN HE DID HIS RESEARCH.
BUT I STILL BELIEVED MY FATHER'S WORDS, THAT THIS GREAT POWER WAS SOMETHING THAT COULD BE USED FOR THE BENEFIT OF PEOPLE.
THAT'S WHAT I BE-LIEVED.
I THOUGHT ALCHEMY WAS SOME-THING THAT COULD MAKE PEOPLE'S HOPES AND DREAMS COME TRUE...
...AND THAT THE MILITARY EXISTED TO PROTECT THE FUTURE OF THIS COUNTRY.
PLEASE TELL ME, MAJOR...
WHY ARE WE KILLING CITIZENS WHEN WE, AS SOLDIERS, SHOULD BE RESPONSIBLE FOR PROTECTING THEM?
WHY IS ALCHEMY BEING USED TO KILL WHEN IT'S SUPPOSED TO HELP PEOPLE?

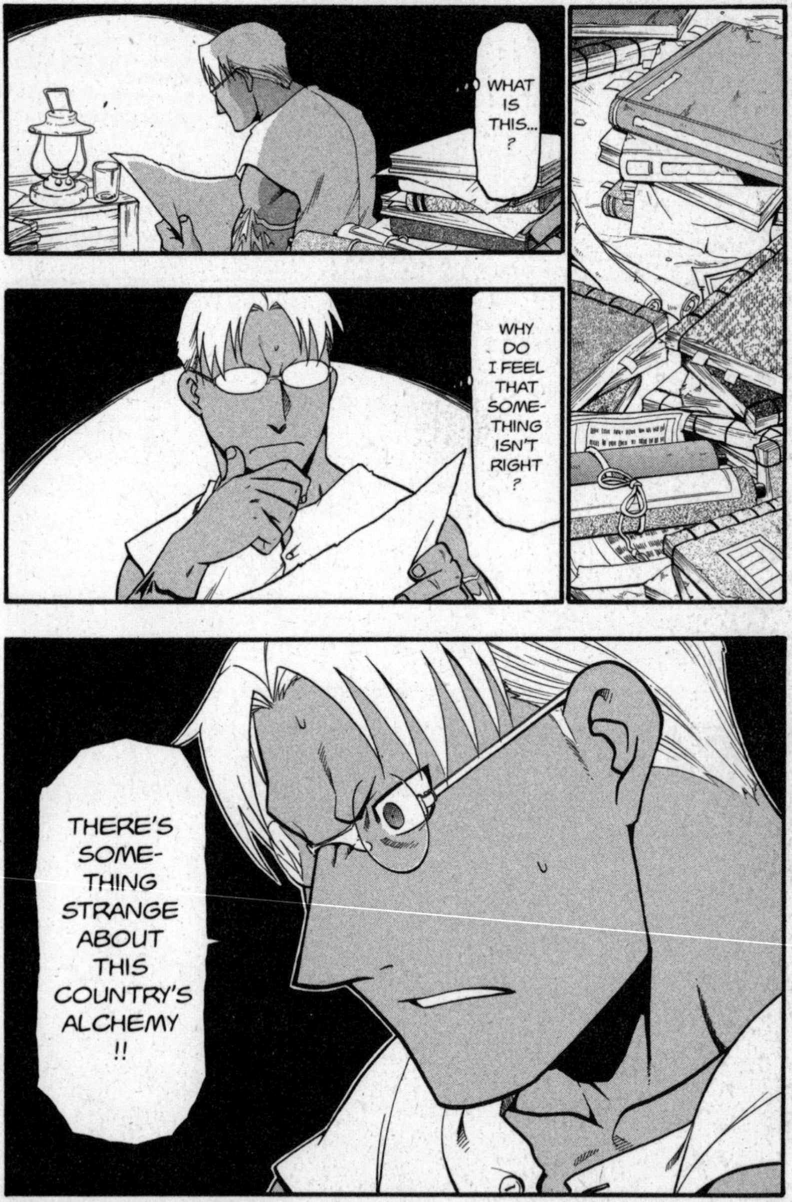
WHAT IS THIS... ?
WHY DO I FEEL THAT SOMETHING ISN'T RIGHT ?
THERE'S SOMETHING STRANGE ABOUT THIS COUNTRY'S ALCHEMY !!

FULLMETAL
ALCHEMIST

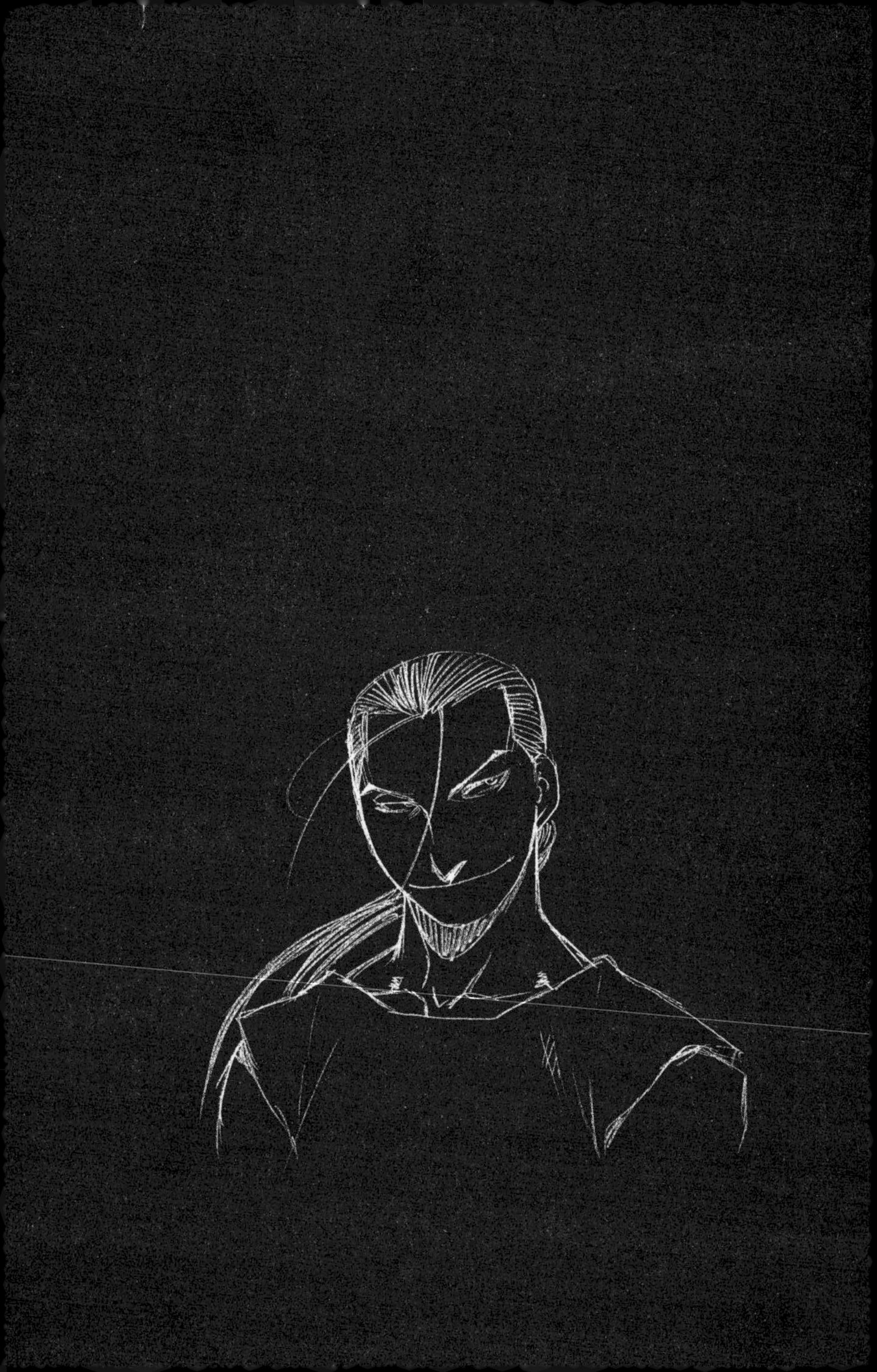

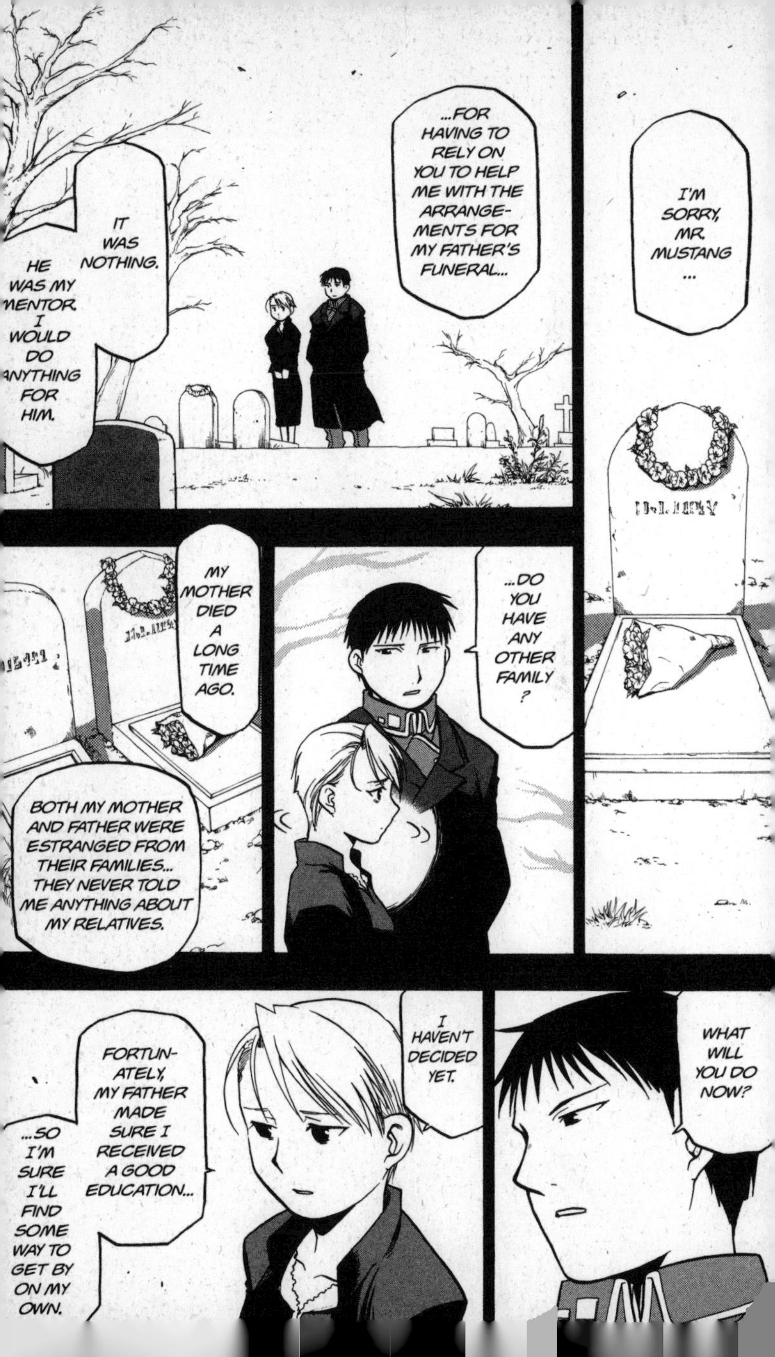
I'M SORRY, MR. MUSTANG ...
...FOR HAVING TO RELY ON YOU TO HELP ME WITH THE ARRANGE-MENTS FOR MY FATHER'S FUNERAL...
IT WAS NOTHING.
HE WAS MY MENTOR. I WOULD DO ANYTHING FOR HIM.
...DO YOU HAVE ANY OTHER FAMILY?
MY MOTHER DIED A LONG TIME AGO.
BOTH MY MOTHER AND FATHER WERE ESTRANGED FROM THEIR FAMILIES... THEY NEVER TOLD ME ANYTHING ABOUT MY RELATIVES.
WHAT WILL YOU DO NOW?
I HAVEN'T DECIDED YET.
FORTUN-ATELY, MY FATHER MADE SURE I RECEIVED A GOOD EDUCATION...
...SO I'M SURE I'LL FIND SOME WAY TO GET BY ON MY OWN.

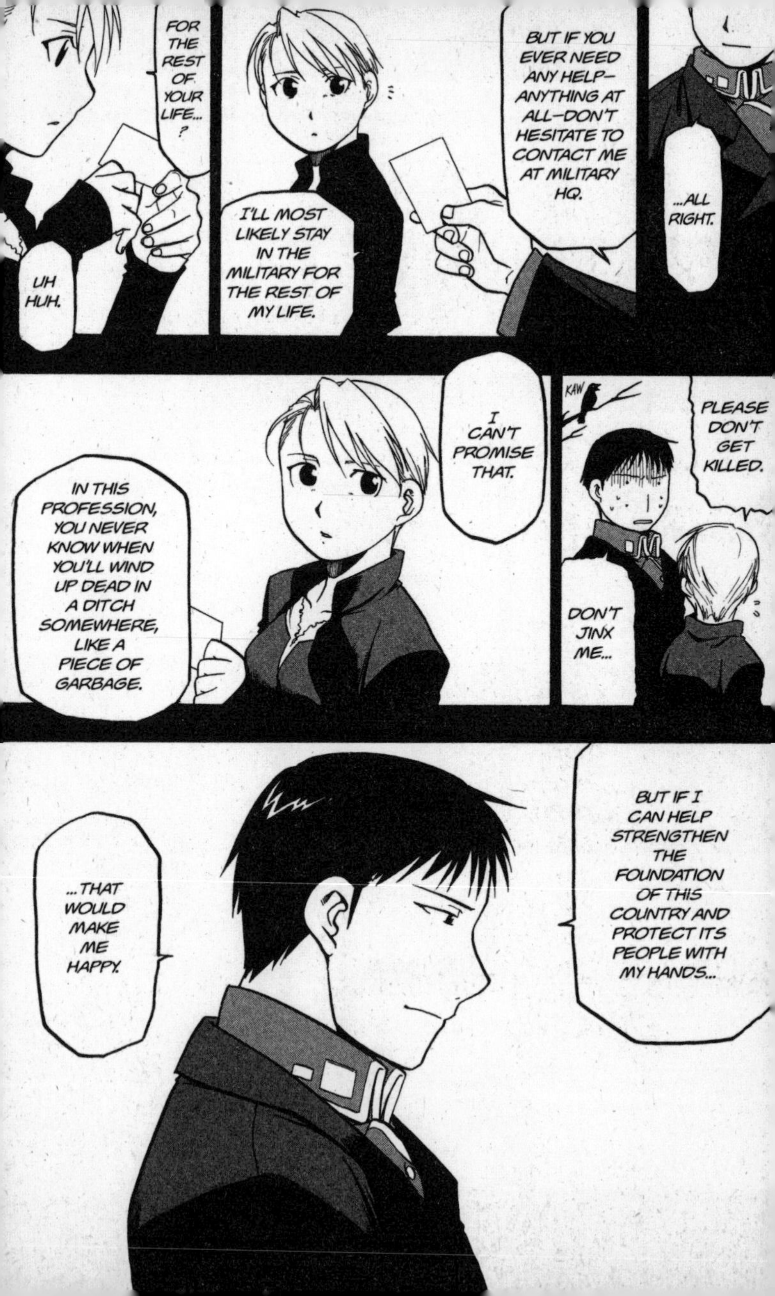
...ALL RIGHT.
BUT IF YOU EVER NEED ANY HELP—ANYTHING AT ALL—DON'T HESITATE TO CONTACT ME AT MILITARY HQ.
I'LL MOST LIKELY STAY IN THE MILITARY FOR THE REST OF MY LIFE.
FOR THE REST OF YOUR LIFE...?
UH HUH.
KAW
PLEASE DON'T GET KILLED.
DON'T JINX ME...
I CAN'T PROMISE THAT.
IN THIS PROFESSION, YOU NEVER KNOW WHEN YOU'LL WIND UP DEAD IN A DITCH SOMEWHERE, LIKE A PIECE OF GARBAGE.
BUT IF I CAN HELP STRENGTHEN THE FOUNDATION OF THIS COUNTRY AND PROTECT ITS PEOPLE WITH MY HANDS...
...THAT WOULD MAKE ME HAPPY.

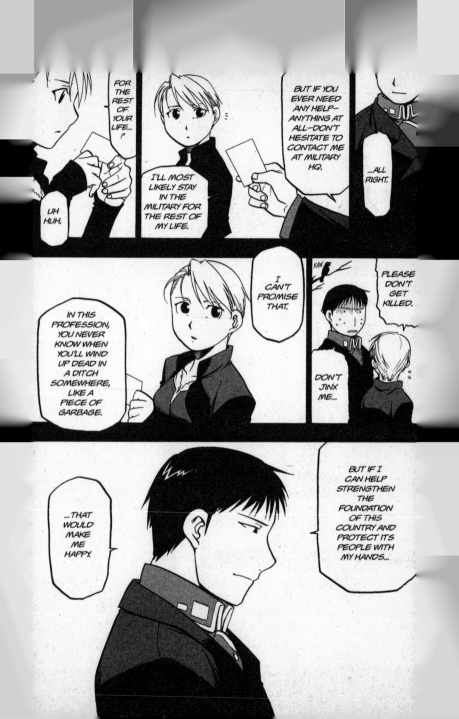

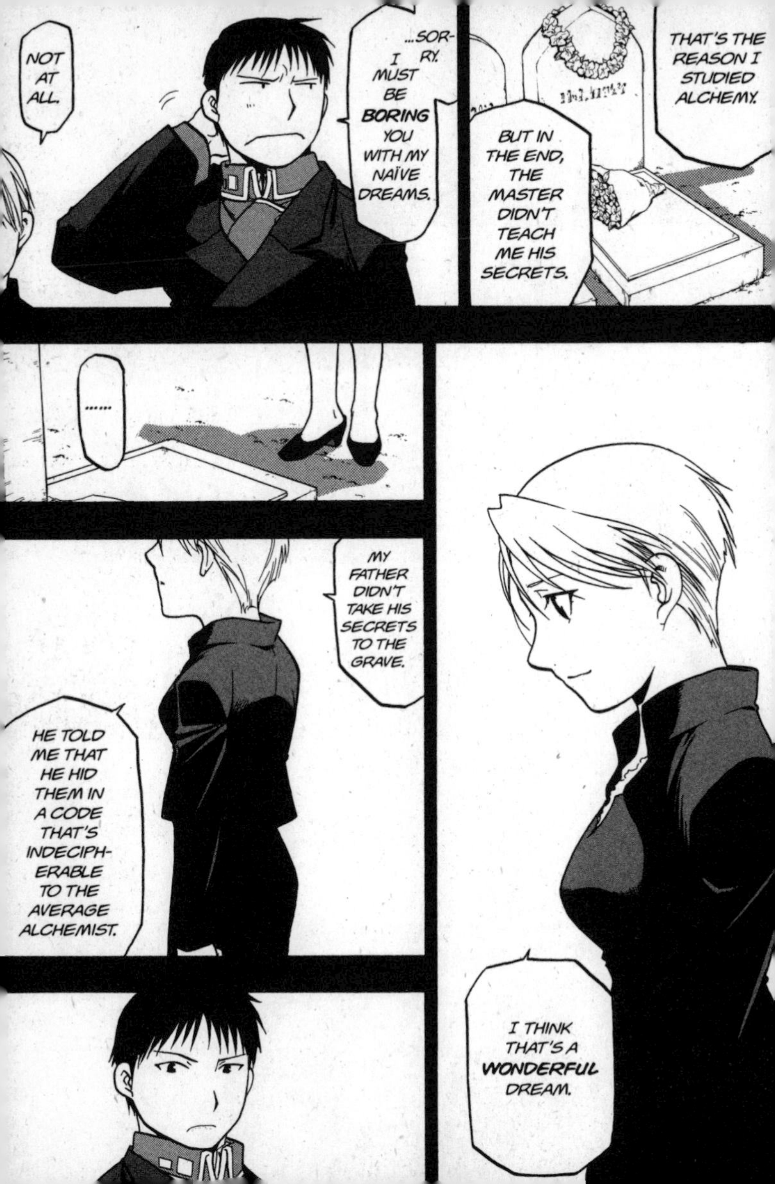
THAT'S THE REASON I STUDIED ALCHEMY.
BUT IN THE END, THE MASTER DIDN'T TEACH ME HIS SECRETS.
...SORRY.
I MUST BE **BORING** YOU WITH MY NAÏVE DREAMS.
NOT AT ALL.
I THINK THAT'S A **WONDERFUL** DREAM.
......
MY FATHER DIDN'T TAKE HIS SECRETS TO THE GRAVE.
HE TOLD ME THAT HE HID THEM IN A CODE THAT'S INDECIPHERABLE TO THE AVERAGE ALCHEMIST.

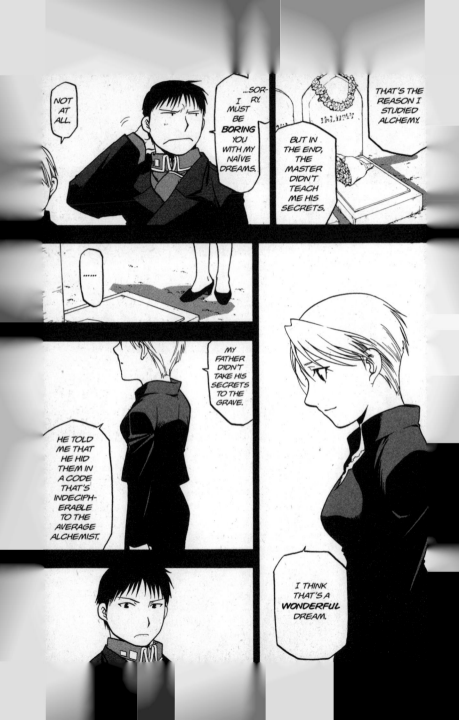

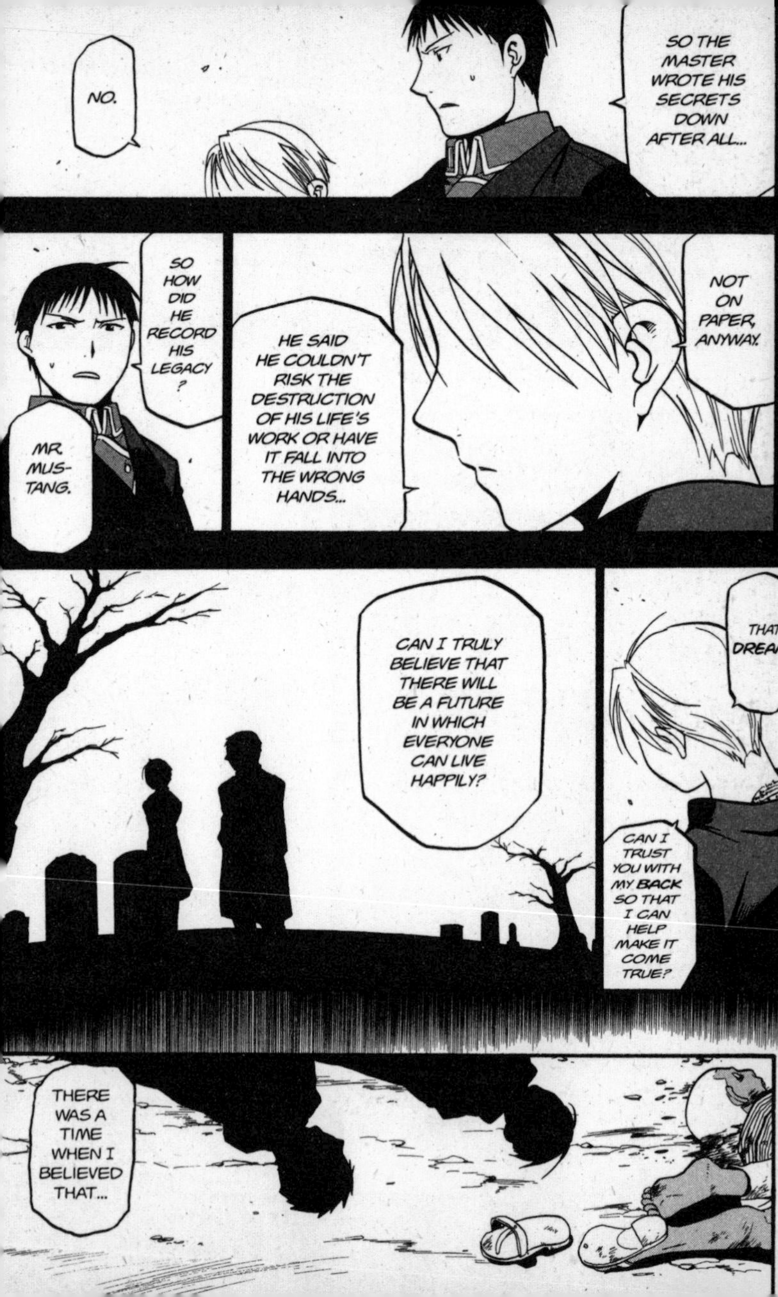
SO THE MASTER WROTE HIS SECRETS DOWN AFTER ALL...
NO.
NOT ON PAPER, ANYWAY.
HE SAID HE COULDN'T RISK THE DESTRUCTION OF HIS LIFE'S WORK OR HAVE IT FALL INTO THE WRONG HANDS...
SO HOW DID HE RECORD HIS LEGACY?
MR. MUS-TANG.
THAT DREAM...
CAN I TRUST YOU WITH MY BACK SO THAT I CAN HELP MAKE IT COME TRUE?
CAN I TRULY BELIEVE THAT THERE WILL BE A FUTURE IN WHICH EVERYONE CAN LIVE HAPPILY?
THERE WAS A TIME WHEN I BELIEVED THAT...

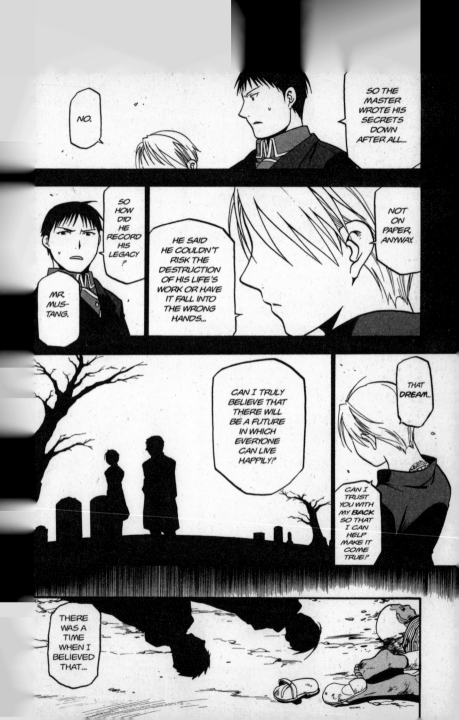

HOW COULD WE HAVE FALLEN THIS LOW?

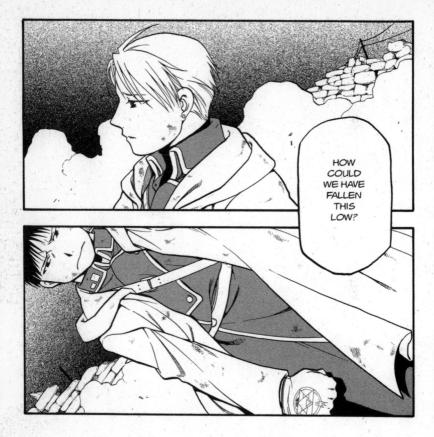

Chapter 60
In the Absence Of God

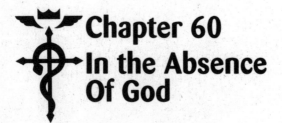

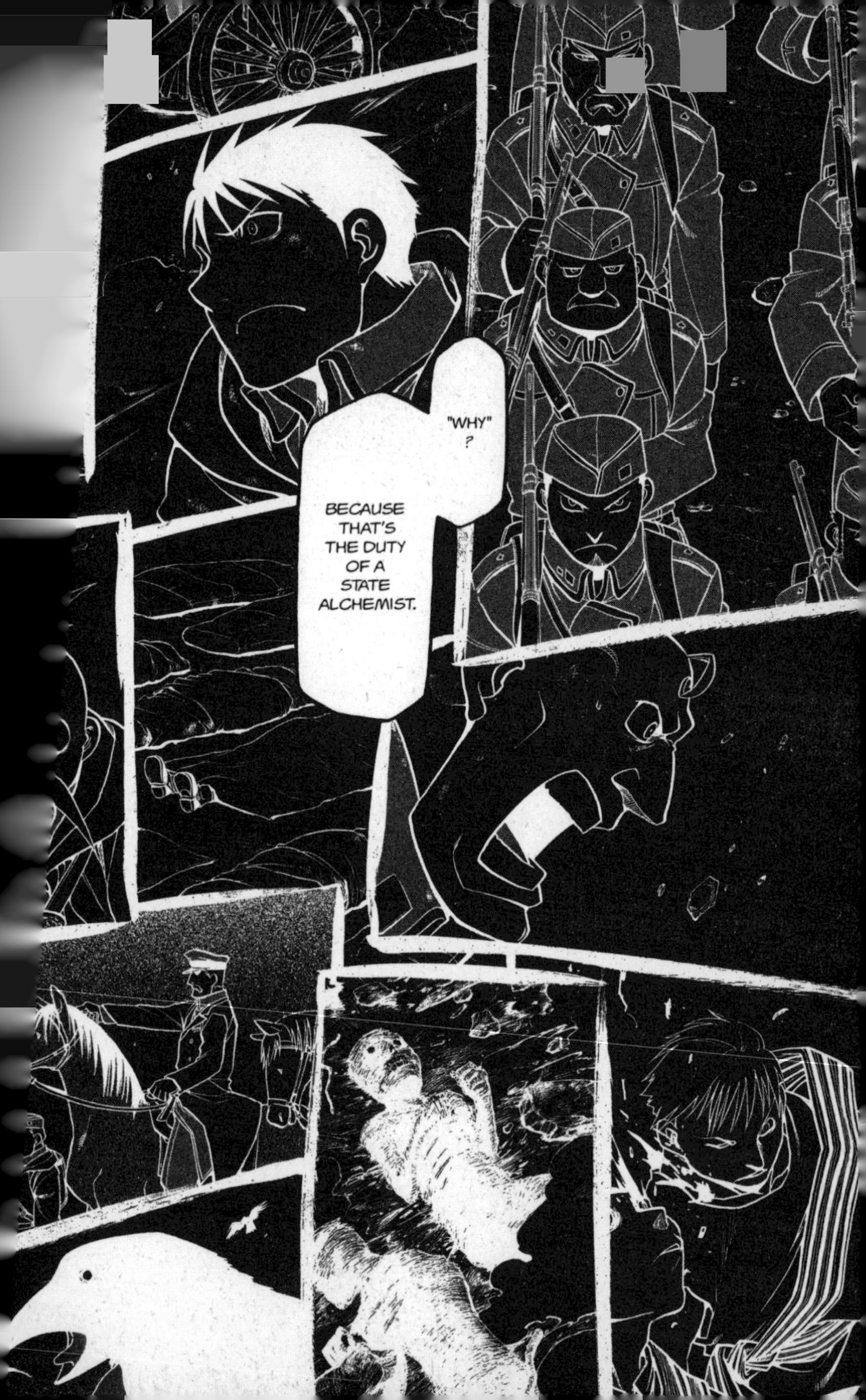
"WHY" ? BECAUSE THAT'S THE DUTY OF A STATE ALCHEMIST.

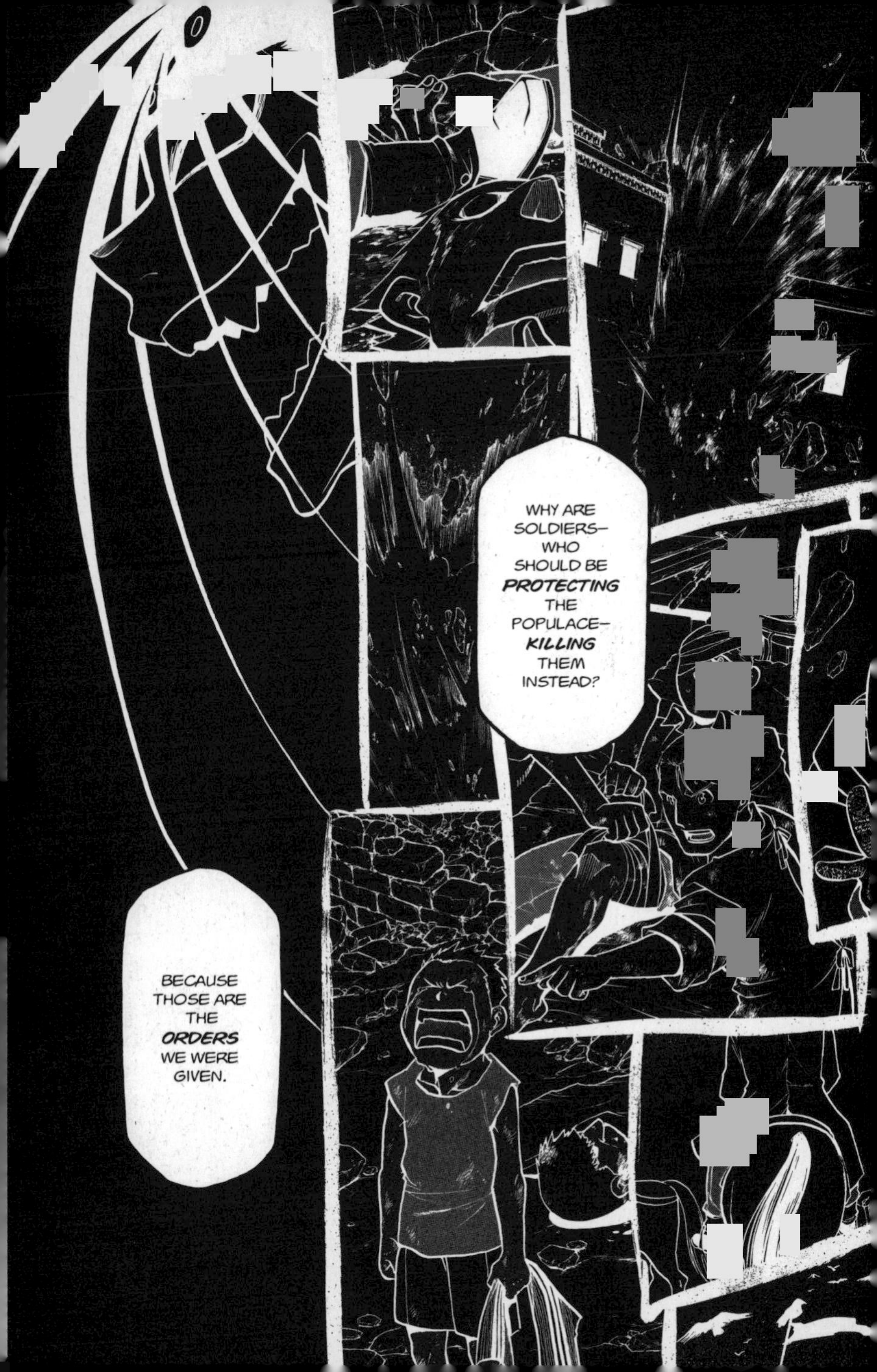
WHY ARE SOLDIERS— WHO SHOULD BE PROTECTING THE POPULACE— KILLING THEM INSTEAD?
BECAUSE THOSE ARE THE ORDERS WE WERE GIVEN.

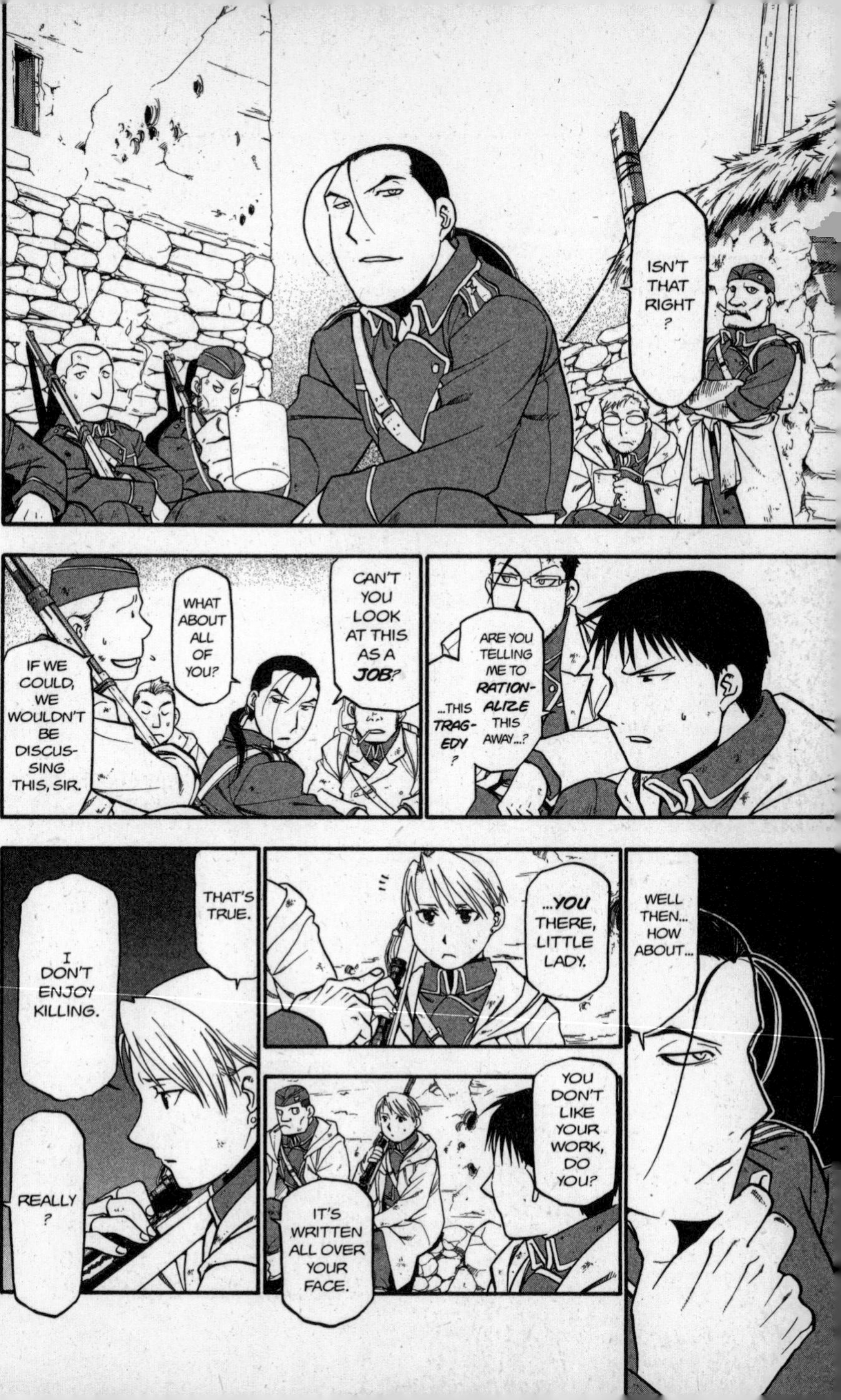
ISN'T THAT RIGHT ?
ARE YOU TELLING ME TO RATION-ALIZE THIS AWAY...?
...THIS TRAG-EDY ?
CAN'T YOU LOOK AT THIS AS A JOB?
WHAT ABOUT ALL OF YOU?
IF WE COULD, WE WOULDN'T BE DISCUS-SING THIS, SIR.
WELL THEN... HOW ABOUT...
...YOU THERE, LITTLE LADY.
YOU DON'T LIKE YOUR WORK, DO YOU?
IT'S WRITTEN ALL OVER YOUR FACE.
THAT'S TRUE.
I DON'T ENJOY KILLING.
REALLY ?

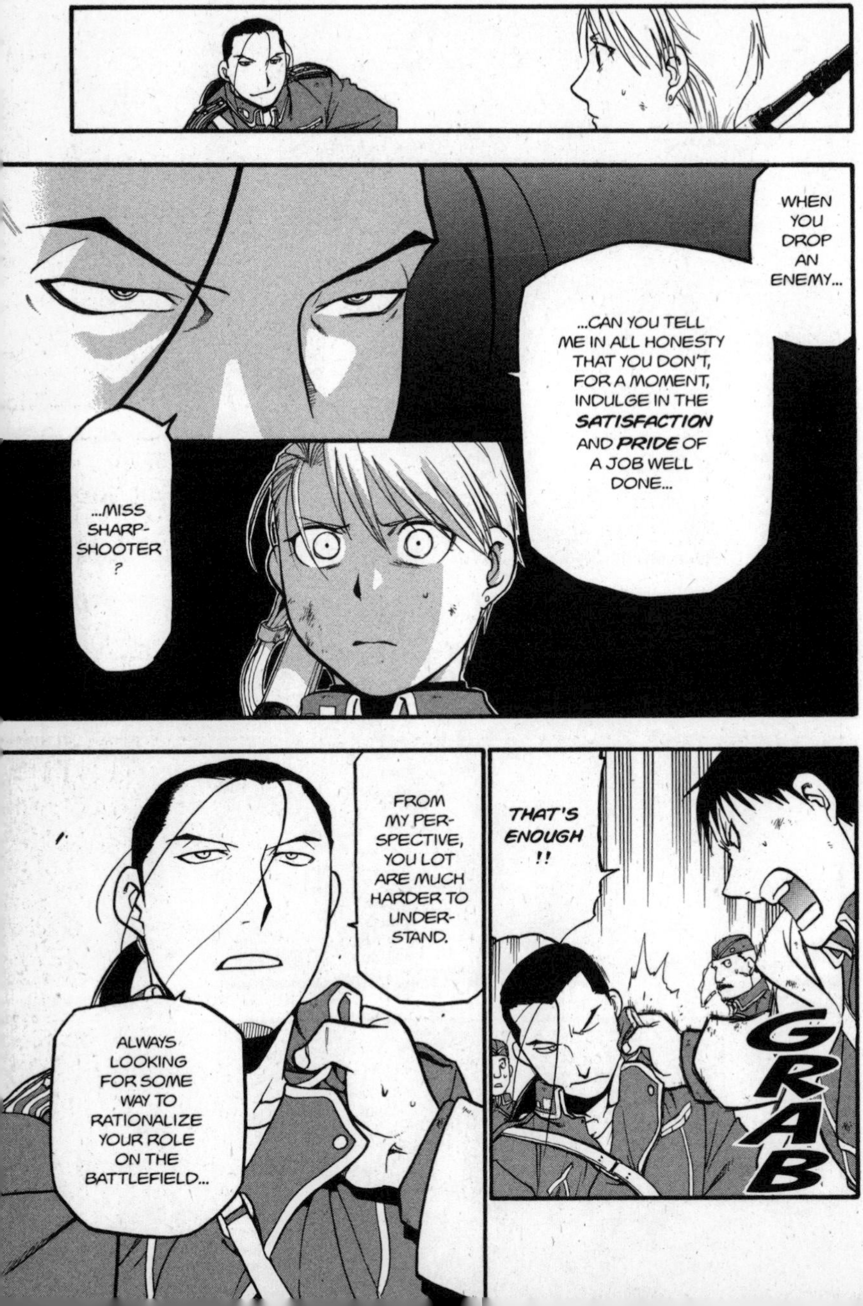
WHEN YOU DROP AN ENEMY...
...CAN YOU TELL ME IN ALL HONESTY THAT YOU DON'T, FOR A MOMENT, INDULGE IN THE SATISFACTION AND PRIDE OF A JOB WELL DONE...
...MISS SHARP-SHOOTER?
THAT'S ENOUGH!!
GRAB
FROM MY PER-SPECTIVE, YOU LOT ARE MUCH HARDER TO UNDER-STAND.
ALWAYS LOOKING FOR SOME WAY TO RATIONALIZE YOUR ROLE ON THE BATTLEFIELD...

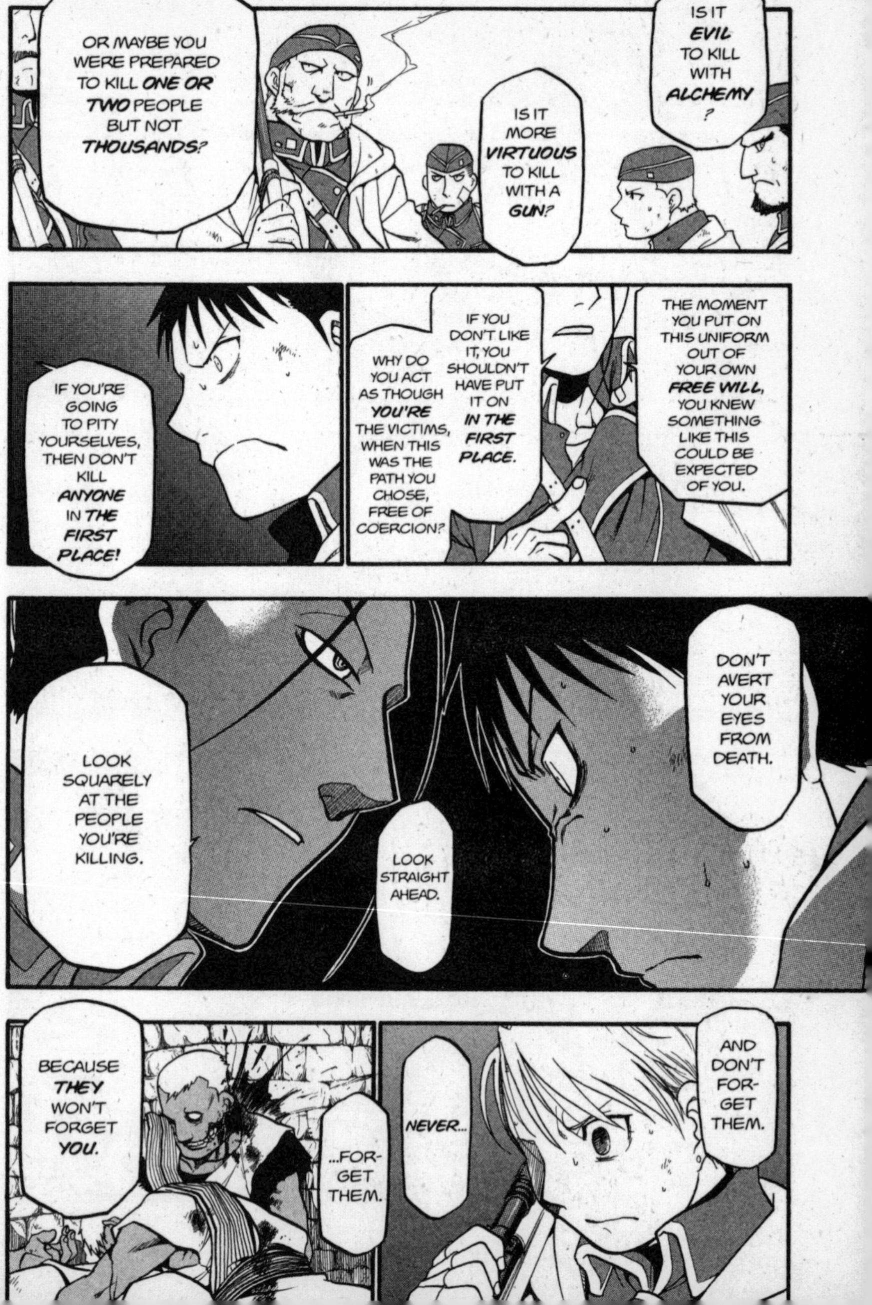
IS IT EVIL TO KILL WITH ALCHEMY?
IS IT MORE VIRTUOUS TO KILL WITH A GUN?
OR MAYBE YOU WERE PREPARED TO KILL ONE OR TWO PEOPLE BUT NOT THOUSANDS?
THE MOMENT YOU PUT ON THIS UNIFORM OUT OF YOUR OWN FREE WILL, YOU KNEW SOMETHING LIKE THIS COULD BE EXPECTED OF YOU.
IF YOU DON'T LIKE IT, YOU SHOULDN'T HAVE PUT IT ON IN THE FIRST PLACE.
WHY DO YOU ACT AS THOUGH YOU'RE THE VICTIMS, WHEN THIS WAS THE PATH YOU CHOSE, FREE OF COERCION?
IF YOU'RE GOING TO PITY YOURSELVES, THEN DON'T KILL ANYONE IN THE FIRST PLACE!
DON'T AVERT YOUR EYES FROM DEATH.
LOOK STRAIGHT AHEAD.
LOOK SQUARELY AT THE PEOPLE YOU'RE KILLING.
AND DON'T FOR-GET THEM.
NEVER...
...FOR-GET THEM.
BECAUSE THEY WON'T FORGET YOU.

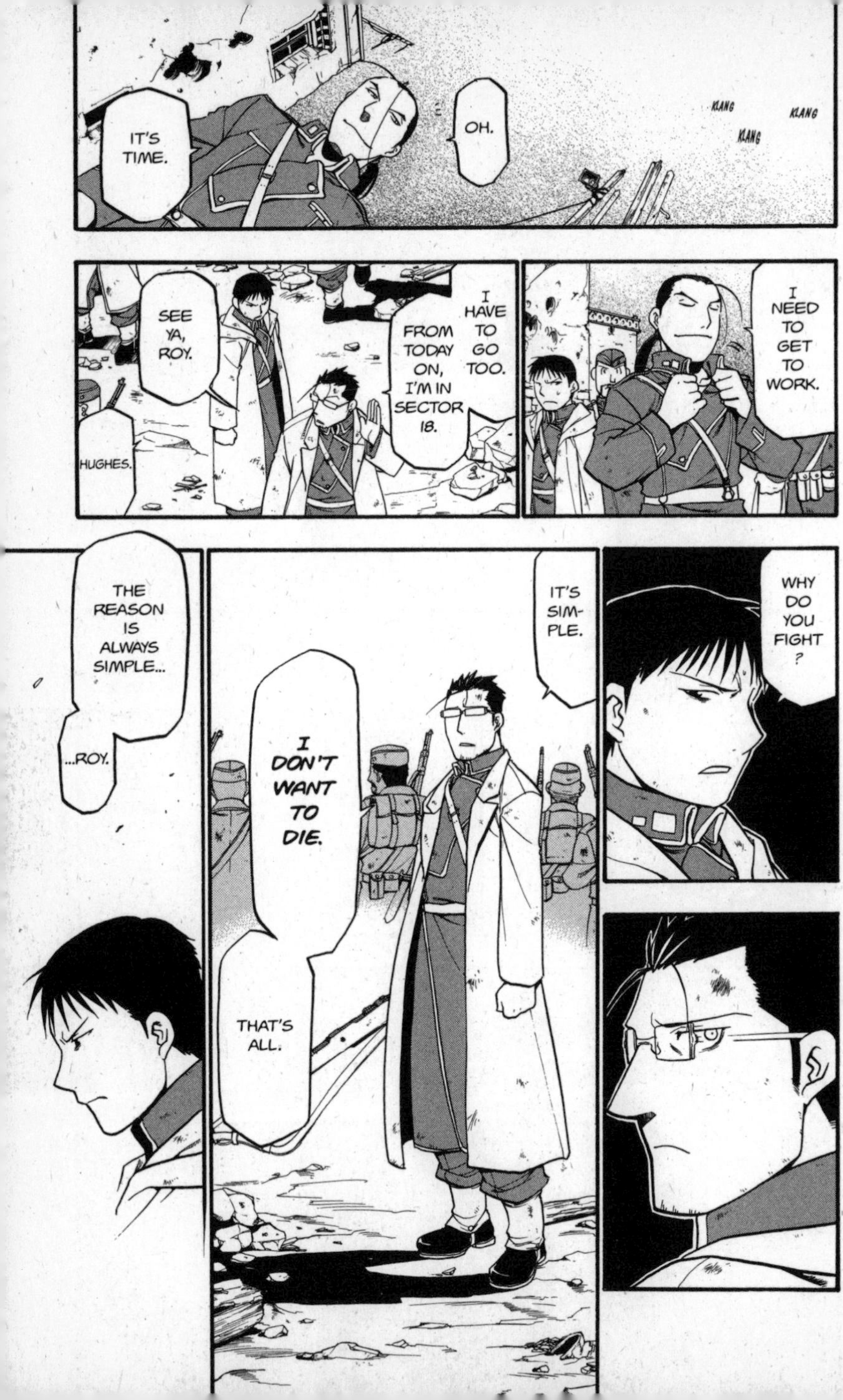
KLANG
KLANG
KLANG
OH.
IT'S TIME.
I NEED TO GET TO WORK.
I HAVE TO GO TOO.
FROM TODAY ON, I'M IN SECTOR 18.
SEE YA, ROY.
HUGHES.
WHY DO YOU FIGHT?
IT'S SIMPLE.
I DON'T WANT TO DIE.
THAT'S ALL.
THE REASON IS ALWAYS SIMPLE...
...ROY.

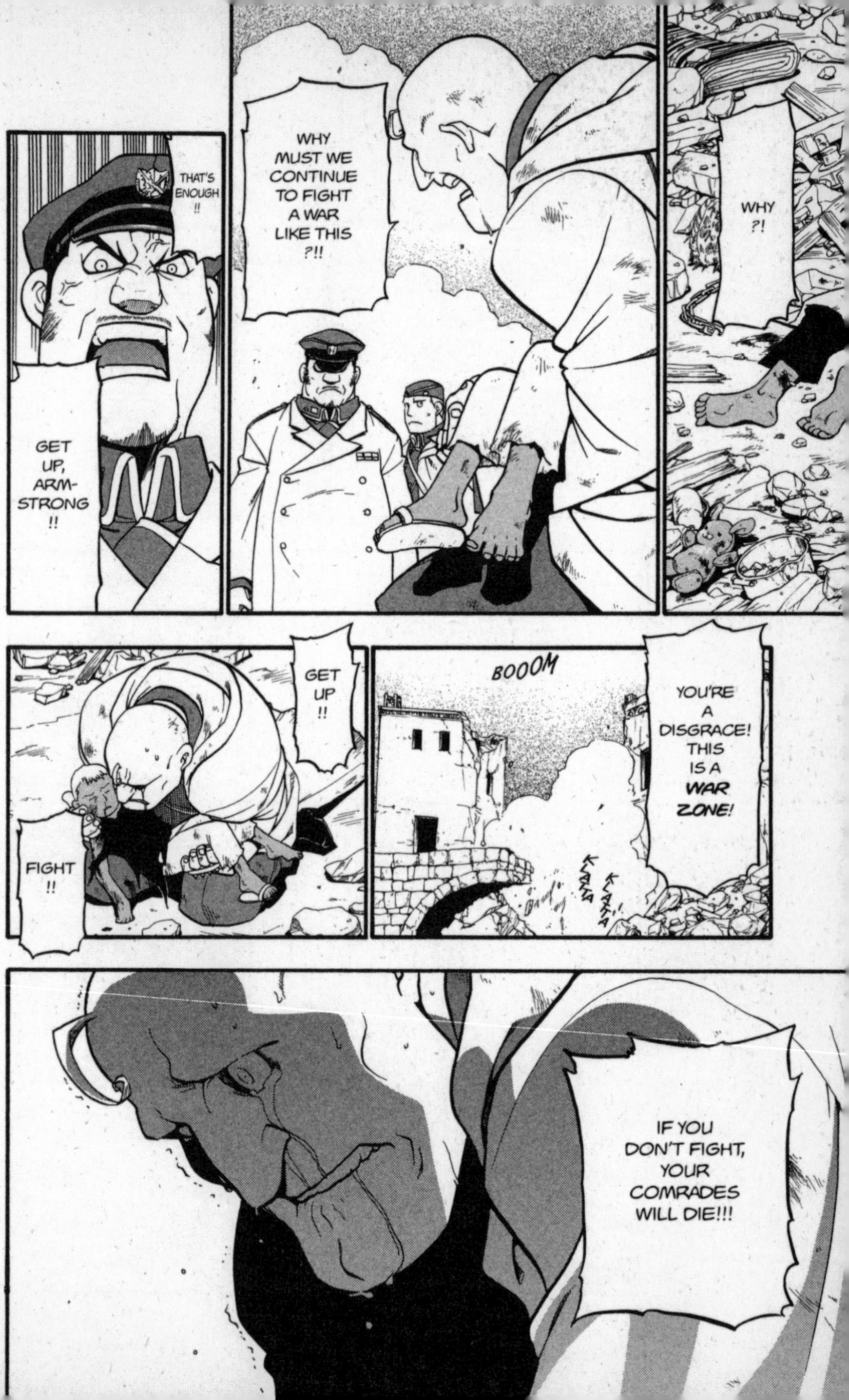
WHY ?!
WHY MUST WE CONTINUE TO FIGHT A WAR LIKE THIS ?!!
THAT'S ENOUGH !!
GET UP, ARMSTRONG !!
BOOOM
YOU'RE A DISGRACE! THIS IS A WAR ZONE!
KLATA KLATA
GET UP !!
FIGHT !!
IF YOU DON'T FIGHT, YOUR COMRADES WILL DIE!!!

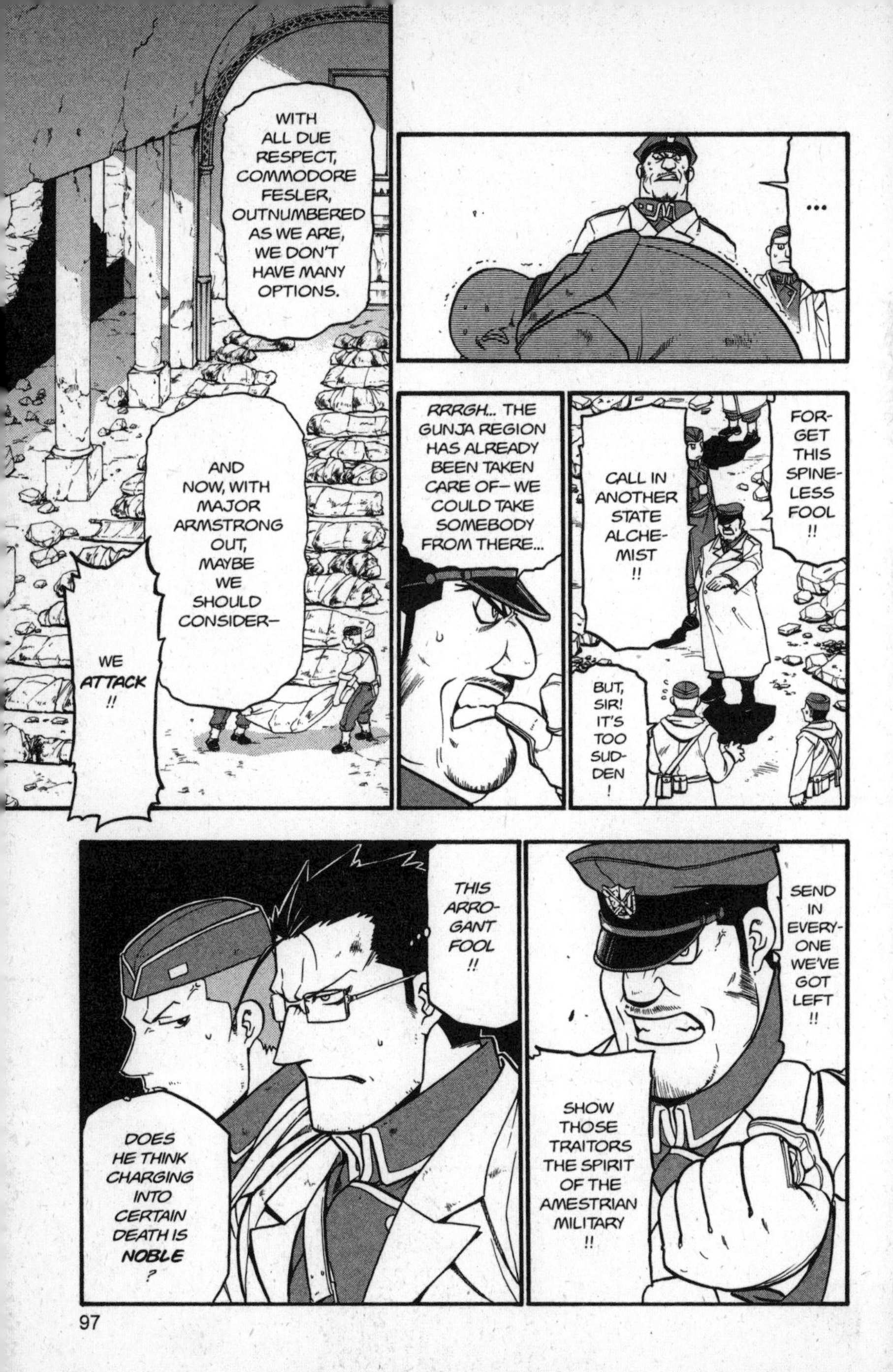
...
FORGET THIS SPINELESS FOOL!!
CALL IN ANOTHER STATE ALCHEMIST!!
BUT, SIR! IT'S TOO SUDDEN!
RRRGH... THE GUNJA REGION HAS ALREADY BEEN TAKEN CARE OF— WE COULD TAKE SOMEBODY FROM THERE...
WITH ALL DUE RESPECT, COMMODORE FESLER, OUTNUMBERED AS WE ARE, WE DON'T HAVE MANY OPTIONS.
AND NOW, WITH MAJOR ARMSTRONG OUT, MAYBE WE SHOULD CONSIDER—
WE ***ATTACK*** !!
SEND IN EVERY-ONE WE'VE GOT LEFT!!
SHOW THOSE TRAITORS THE SPIRIT OF THE AMESTRIAN MILITARY!!
THIS ARROGANT FOOL!!
DOES HE THINK CHARGING INTO CERTAIN DEATH IS ***NOBLE*** *?*

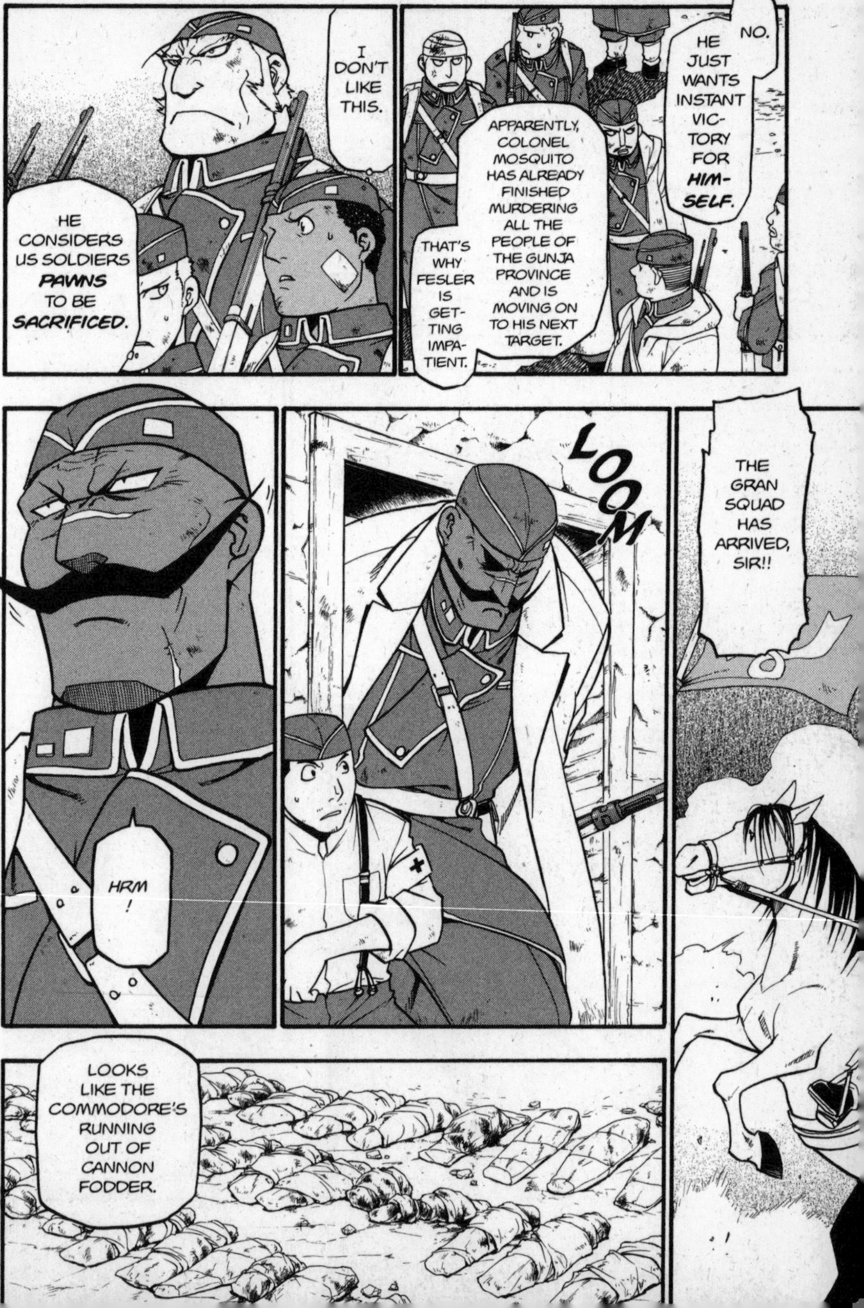
NO.
HE JUST WANTS INSTANT VICTORY FOR HIMSELF.
APPARENTLY, COLONEL MOSQUITO HAS ALREADY FINISHED MURDERING ALL THE PEOPLE OF THE GUNJA PROVINCE AND IS MOVING ON TO HIS NEXT TARGET.
THAT'S WHY FESLER IS GETTING IMPATIENT.
I DON'T LIKE THIS.
HE CONSIDERS US SOLDIERS PAWNS TO BE SACRIFICED.
THE GRAN SQUAD HAS ARRIVED, SIR!!
LOOM
HRM!
LOOKS LIKE THE COMMODORE'S RUNNING OUT OF CANNON FODDER.

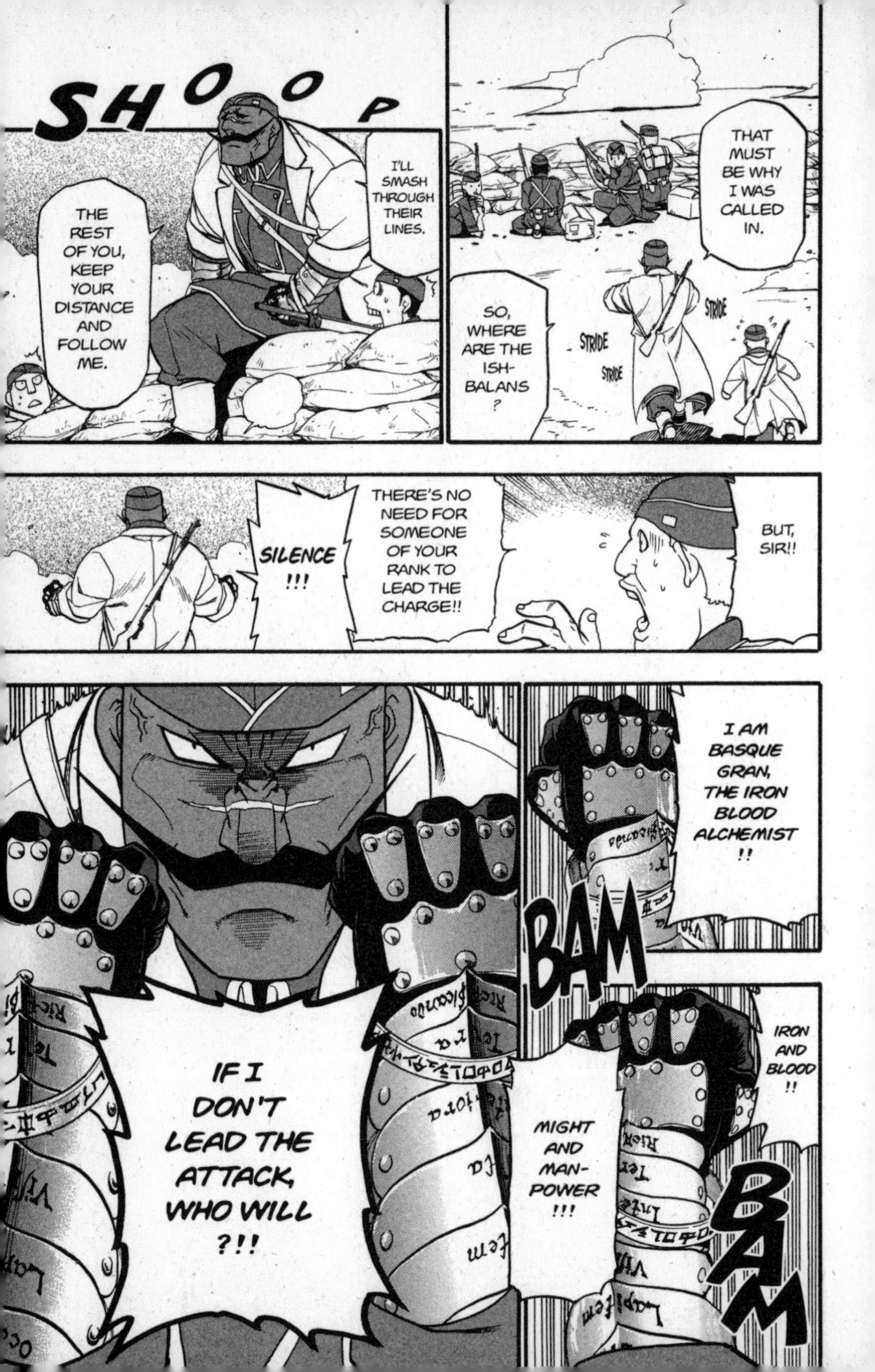
THAT MUST BE WHY I WAS CALLED IN.
SO, WHERE ARE THE ISH-BALANS?
STRIDE
STRIDE
STRIDE
SHOOP
I'LL SMASH THROUGH THEIR LINES.
THE REST OF YOU, KEEP YOUR DISTANCE AND FOLLOW ME.
BUT, SIR!!
THERE'S NO NEED FOR SOMEONE OF YOUR RANK TO LEAD THE CHARGE!!
SILENCE!!!
I AM BASQUE GRAN, THE IRON BLOOD ALCHEMIST!!
BAM
IRON AND BLOOD!!
MIGHT AND MAN-POWER!!!
BAM
IF I DON'T LEAD THE ATTACK, WHO WILL?!!

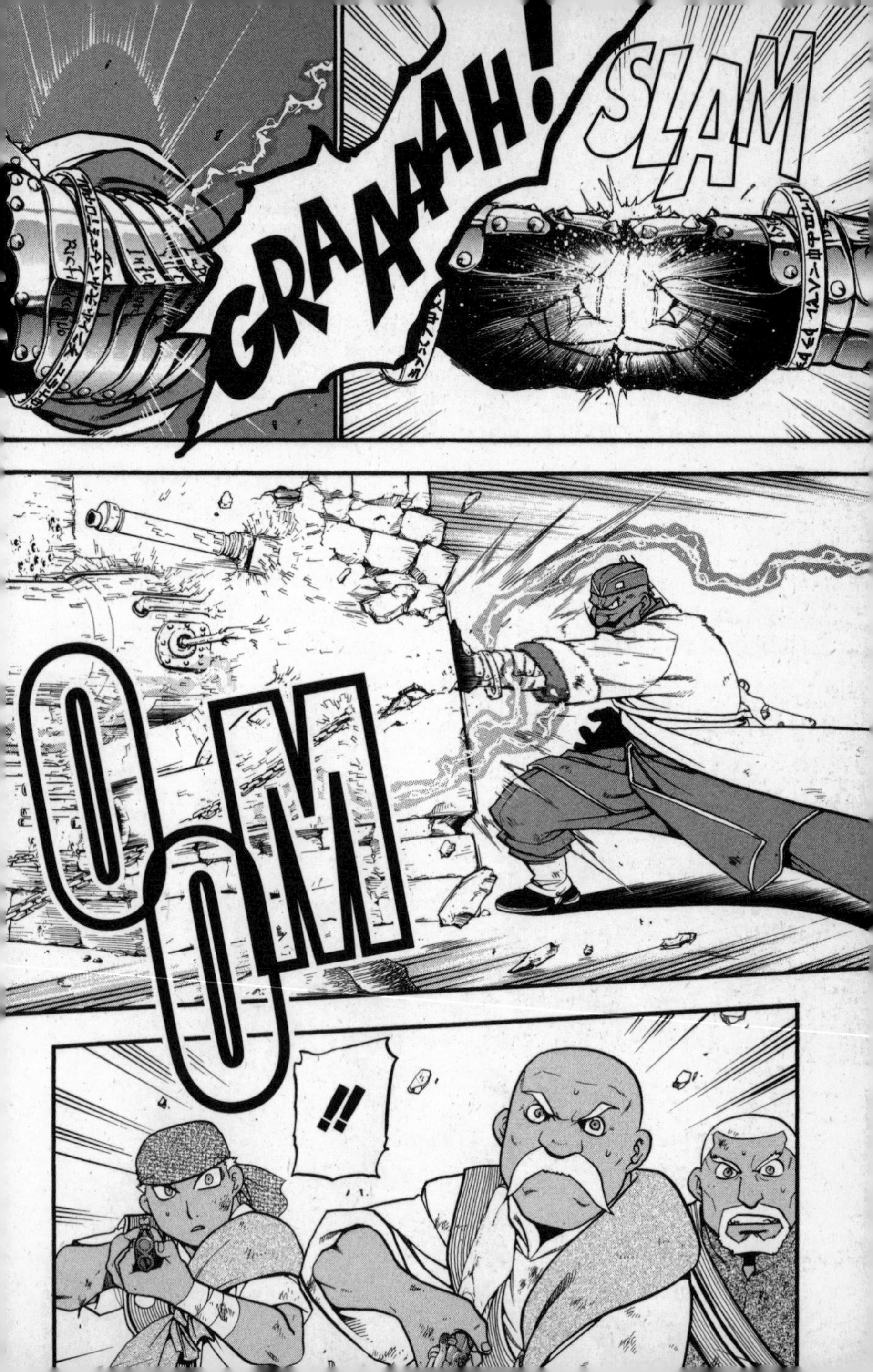
SLAM
GRAAAH!
OOM
!!

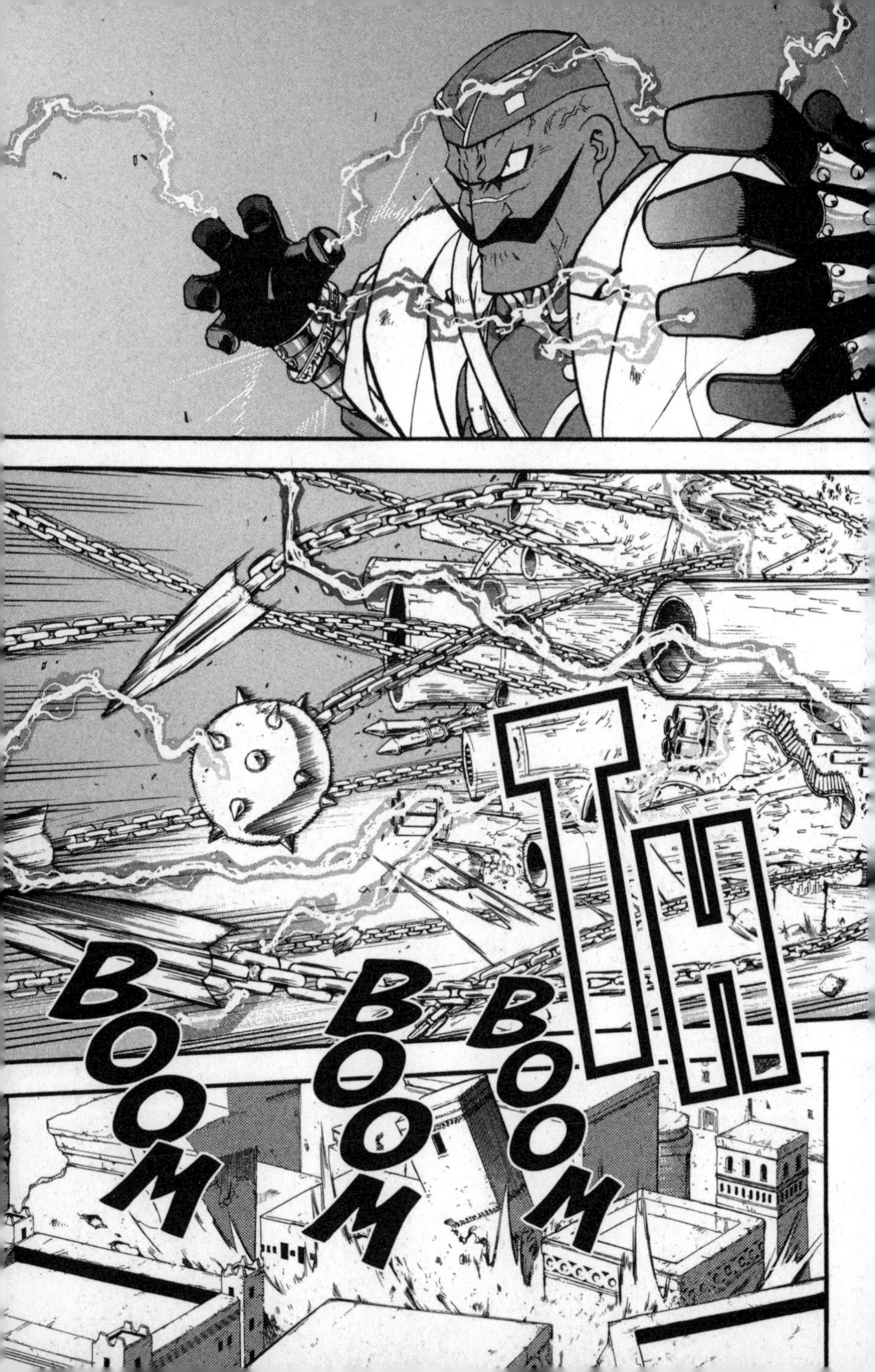
BOOM
BOOM
BOOM

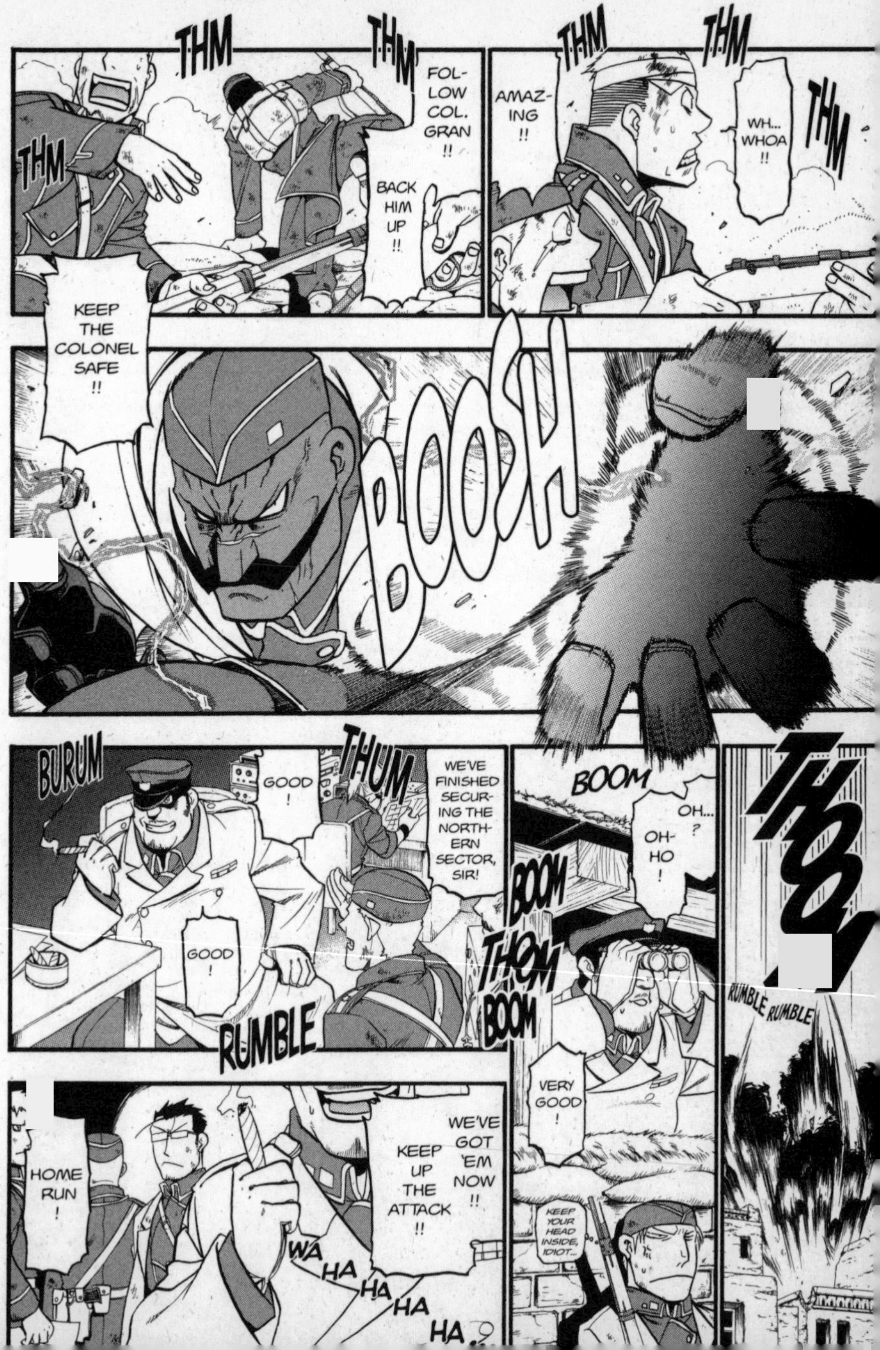
THM
THM
WH... WHOA!!
AMAZING!!
THM
THM
THM
FOLLOW COL. GRAN!!
BACK HIM UP!!
THM
KEEP THE COLONEL SAFE!!
BOOSH
RUMBLE RUMBLE
BOOM
OH...?
OH-HO!
BOOM
THOM
BOOM
THUM
WE'VE FINISHED SECURING THE NORTHERN SECTOR, SIR!
GOOD!
BURUM
GOOD!
RUMBLE
VERY GOOD!
KEEP YOUR HEAD INSIDE, IDIOT...
WE'VE GOT 'EM NOW!!
KEEP UP THE ATTACK!!
HOME RUN!
WA HA HA HA HA...

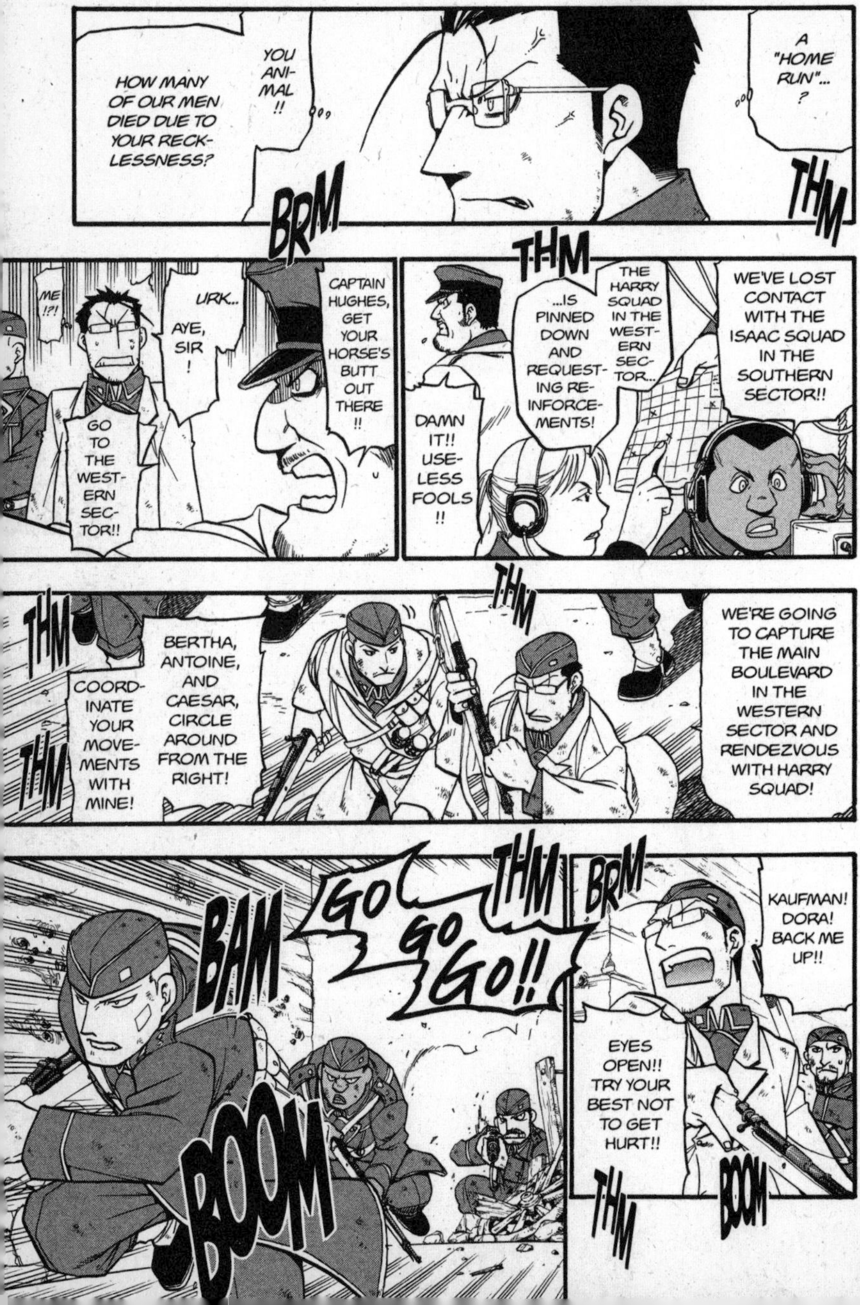
A "HOME RUN"...?
YOU ANIMAL!!
HOW MANY OF OUR MEN DIED DUE TO YOUR RECKLESSNESS?
THM
BRM
WE'VE LOST CONTACT WITH THE ISAAC SQUAD IN THE SOUTHERN SECTOR!!
THE HARRY SQUAD IN THE WESTERN SECTOR...
...IS PINNED DOWN AND REQUESTING REINFORCEMENTS!
THM
DAMN IT!! USELESS FOOLS!!
CAPTAIN HUGHES, GET YOUR HORSE'S BUTT OUT THERE!!
URK... AYE, SIR!
ME!?!
GO TO THE WESTERN SECTOR!!
WE'RE GOING TO CAPTURE THE MAIN BOULEVARD IN THE WESTERN SECTOR AND RENDEZVOUS WITH HARRY SQUAD!
THM
BERTHA, ANTOINE, AND CAESAR, CIRCLE AROUND FROM THE RIGHT!
COORDINATE YOUR MOVEMENTS WITH MINE!
THM
THM
BRM
KAUFMAN! DORA! BACK ME UP!!
EYES OPEN!! TRY YOUR BEST NOT TO GET HURT!!
BOOM
THM
THM
GO GO GO!!
BAM
BOOM

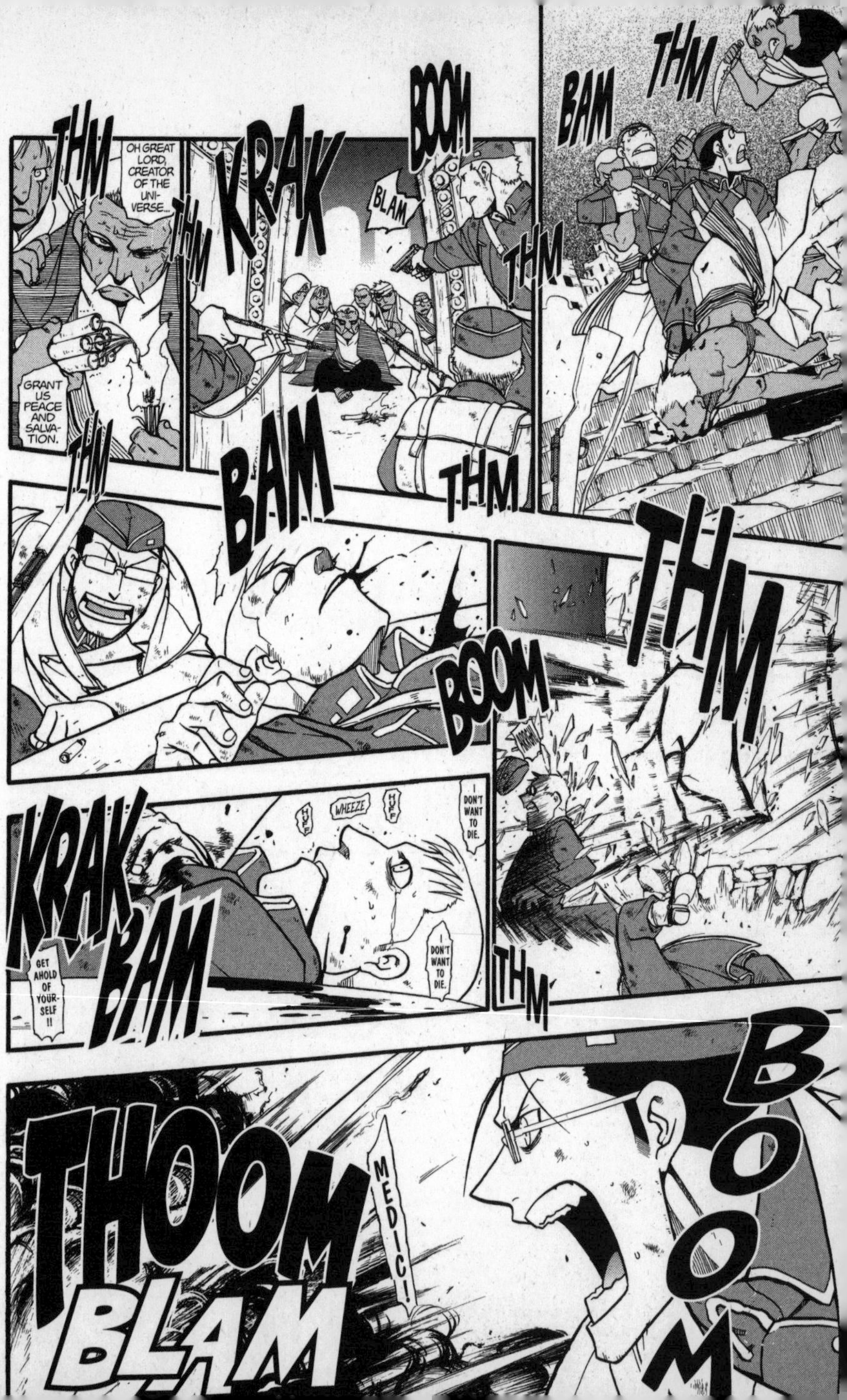
THM
BAM
THM
BOOM
BLAM
KRAK
THM
THM
THM
OH GREAT LORD, CREATOR OF THE UNIVERSE...
GRANT US PEACE AND SALVATION.
THM
BOOM
THM
BAM
THM
THM
I DON'T WANT TO DIE.
HUFF
WHEEZE
HUFF
I DON'T WANT TO DIE.
KRAK
BAM
GET AHOLD OF YOURSELF!!
BOOM
MEDIC!
THOOM
BLAM

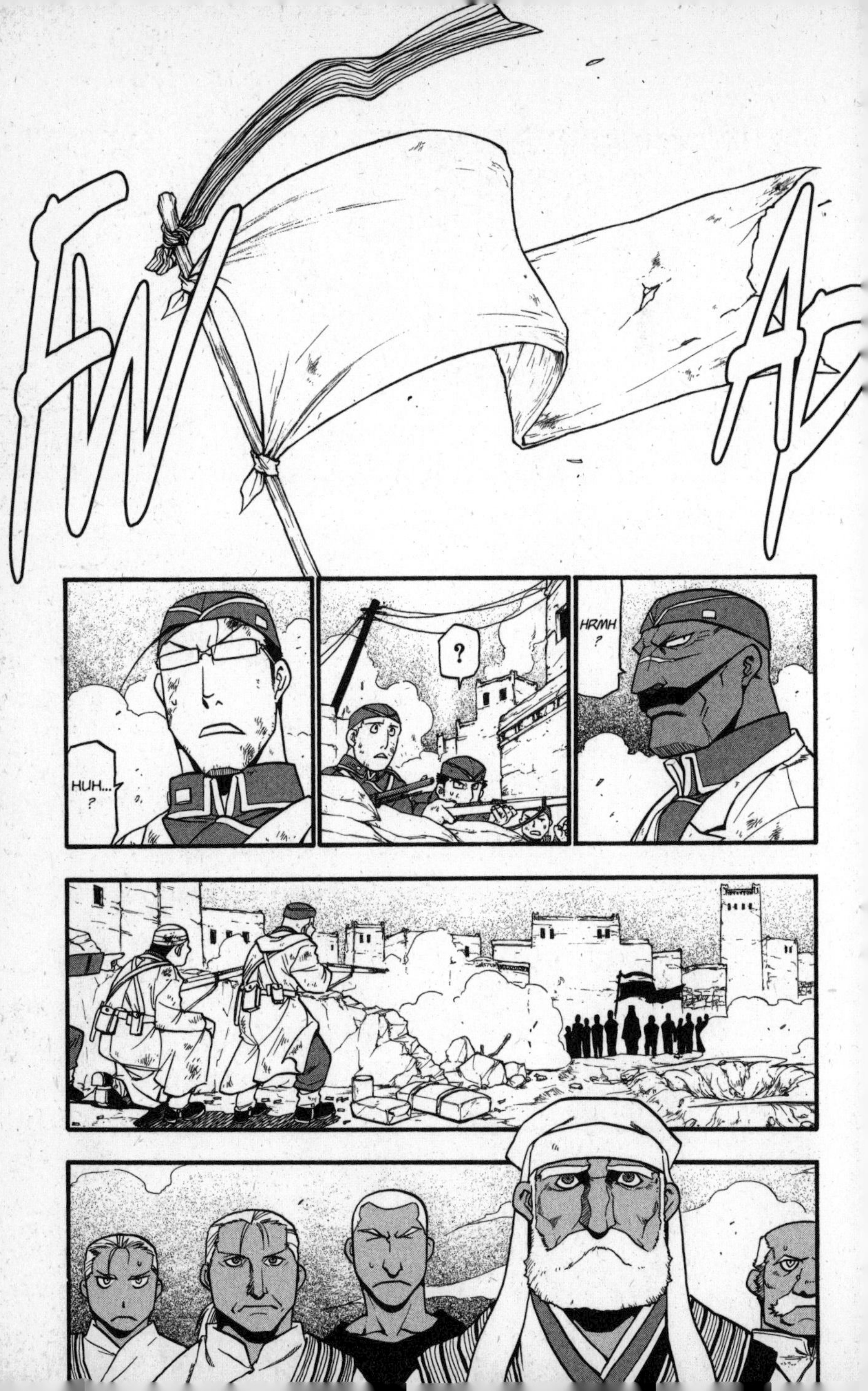
FWAP
HRMH ?
?
HUH... ?

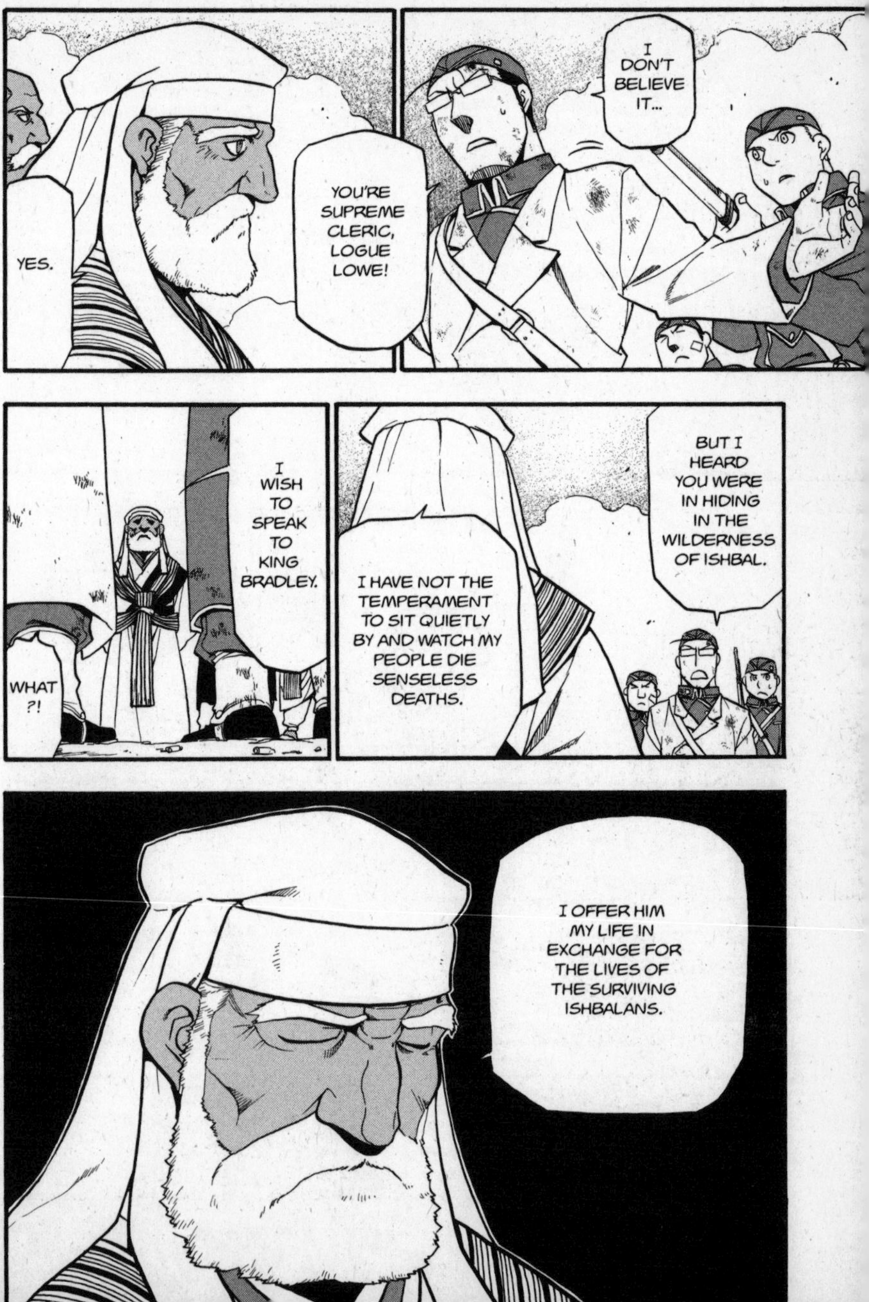
I DON'T BELIEVE IT...
YOU'RE SUPREME CLERIC, LOGUE LOWE!
YES.
BUT I HEARD YOU WERE IN HIDING IN THE WILDERNESS OF ISHBAL.
I HAVE NOT THE TEMPERAMENT TO SIT QUIETLY BY AND WATCH MY PEOPLE DIE SENSELESS DEATHS.
I WISH TO SPEAK TO KING BRADLEY.
WHAT?!
I OFFER HIM MY LIFE IN EXCHANGE FOR THE LIVES OF THE SURVIVING ISHBALANS.

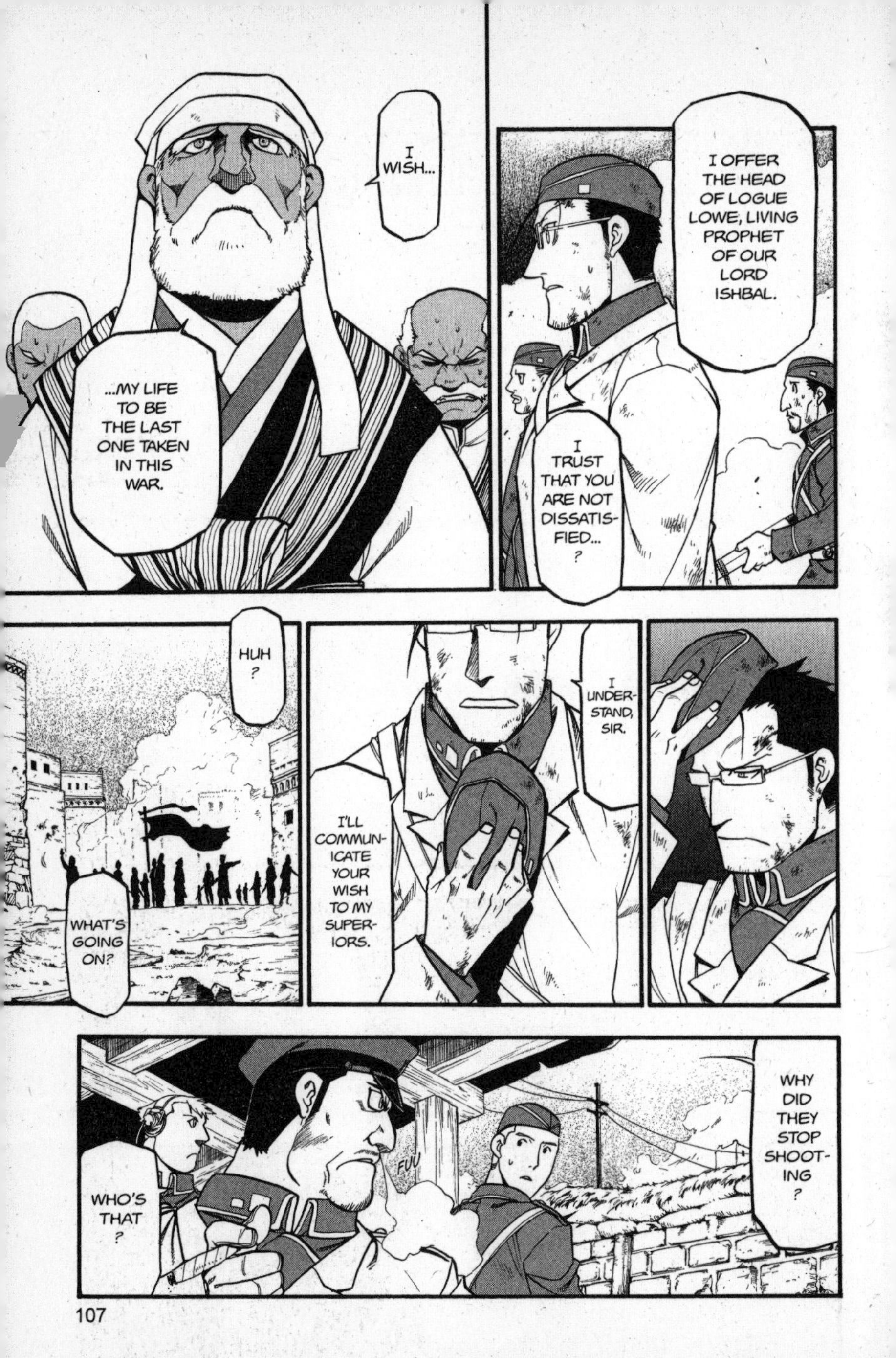
I OFFER THE HEAD OF LOGUE LOWE, LIVING PROPHET OF OUR LORD ISHBAL.
I TRUST THAT YOU ARE NOT DISSATIS-FIED...?
I WISH...
...MY LIFE TO BE THE LAST ONE TAKEN IN THIS WAR.
I UNDER-STAND, SIR.
I'LL COMMUN-ICATE YOUR WISH TO MY SUPER-IORS.
HUH?
WHAT'S GOING ON?
WHY DID THEY STOP SHOOT-ING?
FUU
WHO'S THAT?

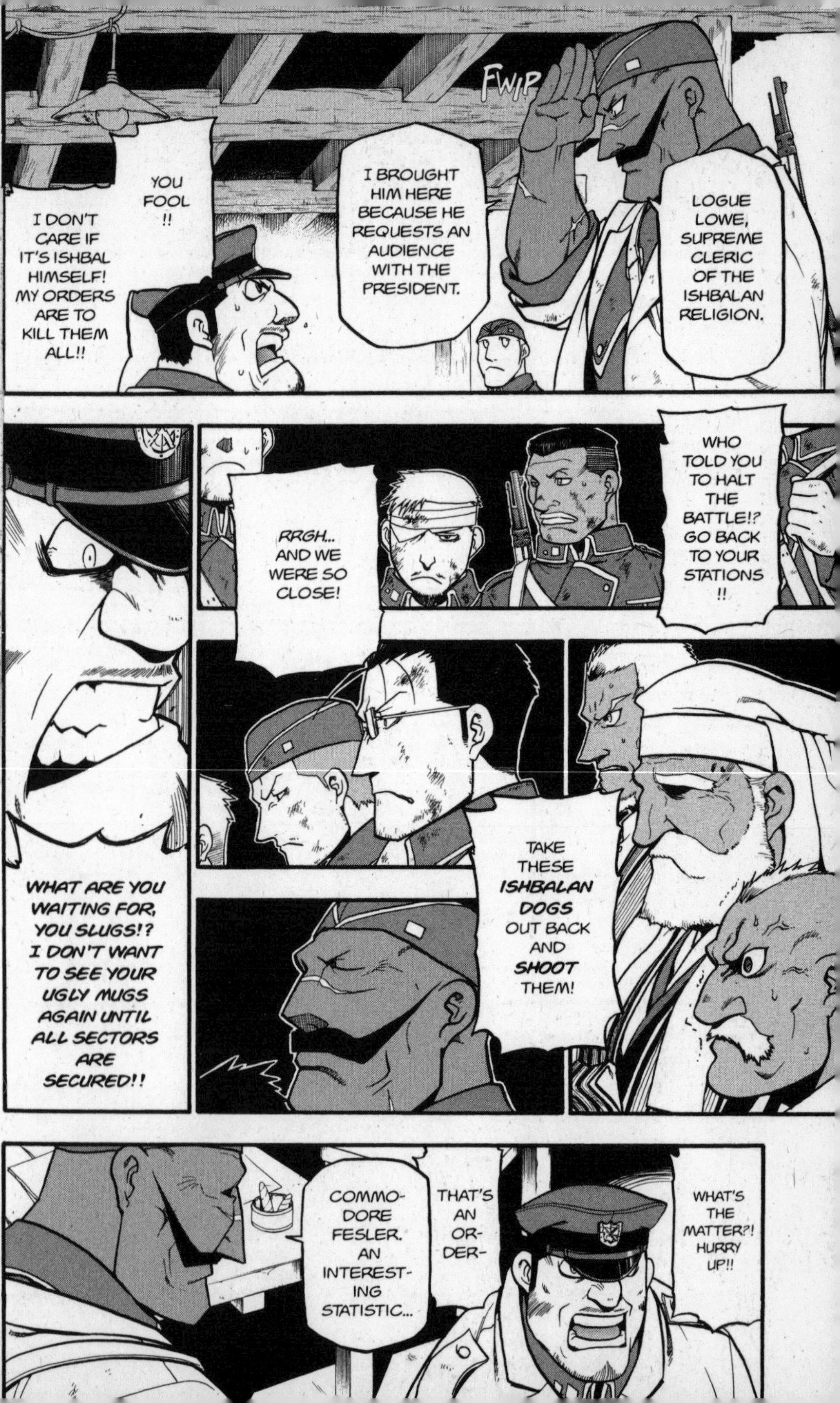
FWIP
LOGUE LOWE, SUPREME CLERIC OF THE ISHBALAN RELIGION.
I BROUGHT HIM HERE BECAUSE HE REQUESTS AN AUDIENCE WITH THE PRESIDENT.
YOU FOOL!!
I DON'T CARE IF IT'S ISHBAL HIMSELF! MY ORDERS ARE TO KILL THEM ALL!!
WHO TOLD YOU TO HALT THE BATTLE!? GO BACK TO YOUR STATIONS!!
RRGH... AND WE WERE SO CLOSE!
TAKE THESE ISHBALAN DOGS OUT BACK AND SHOOT THEM!
WHAT ARE YOU WAITING FOR, YOU SLUGS!? I DON'T WANT TO SEE YOUR UGLY MUGS AGAIN UNTIL ALL SECTORS ARE SECURED!!
WHAT'S THE MATTER?! HURRY UP!!
THAT'S AN ORDER-
COMMODORE FESLER. AN INTERESTING STATISTIC...

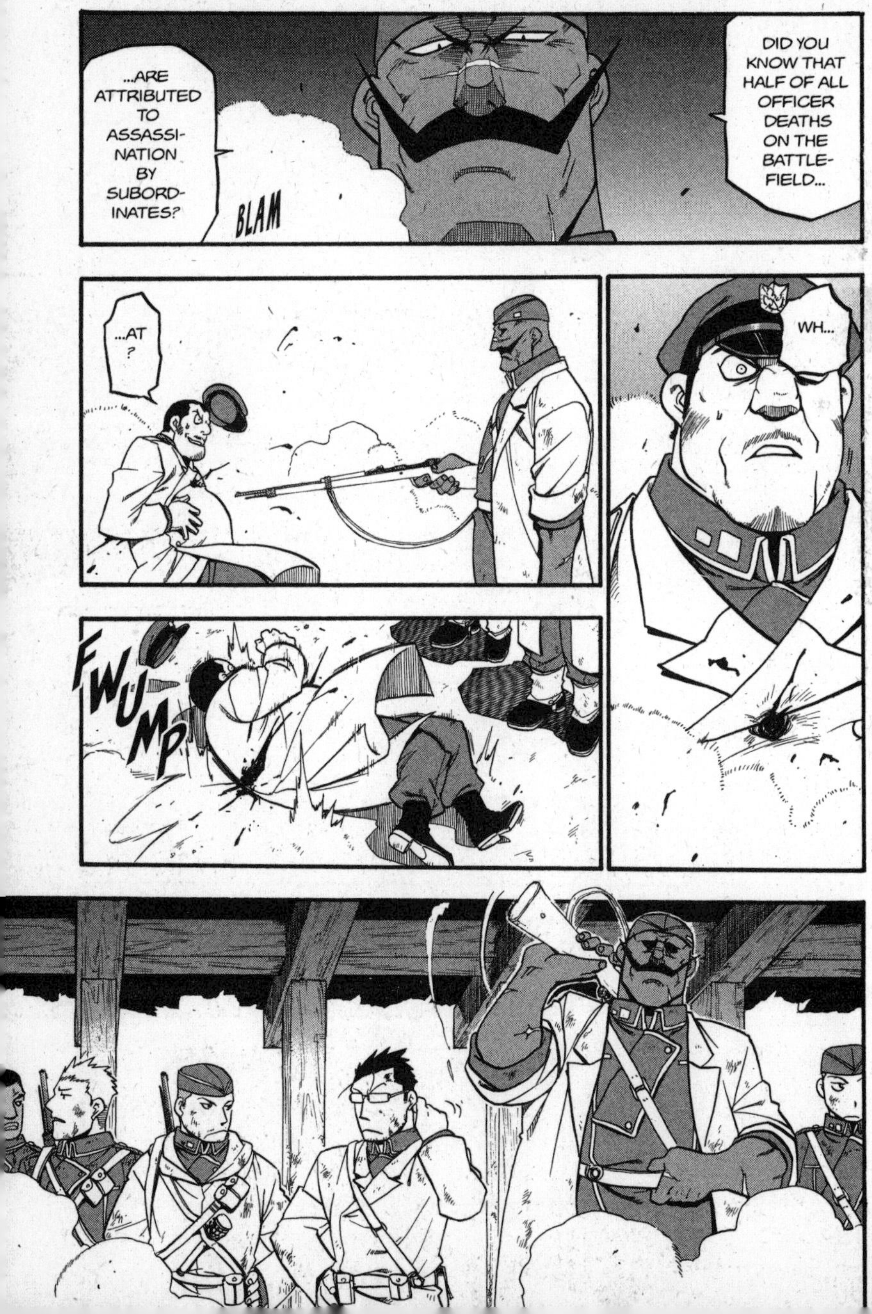
DID YOU KNOW THAT HALF OF ALL OFFICER DEATHS ON THE BATTLE-FIELD...
...ARE ATTRIBUTED TO ASSASSI-NATION BY SUBORD-INATES?
BLAM
WH...
...AT ?
FWUMP

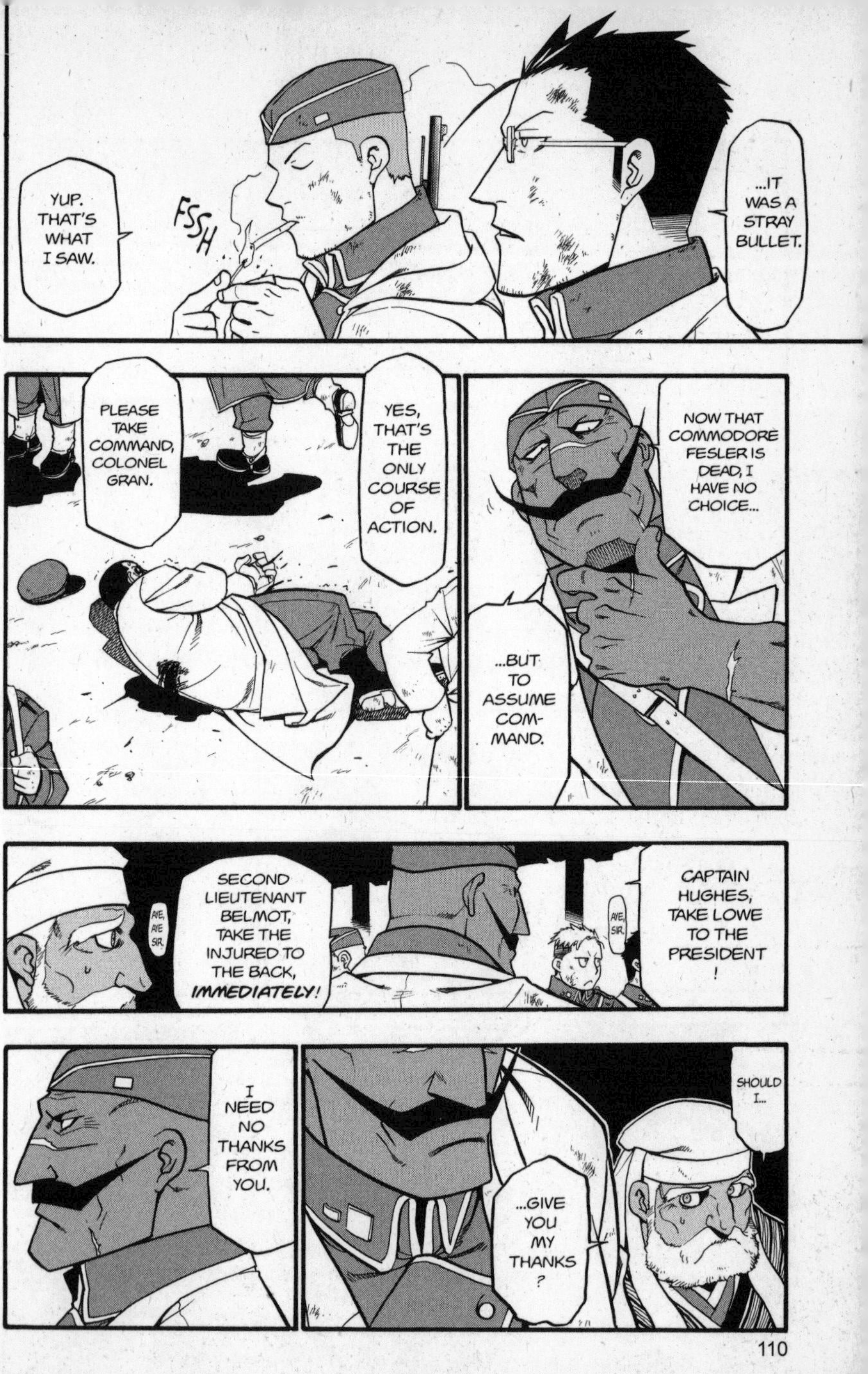
...IT WAS A STRAY BULLET.
FSSH
YUP. THAT'S WHAT I SAW.
NOW THAT COMMODORE FESLER IS DEAD, I HAVE NO CHOICE...
...BUT TO ASSUME COM-MAND.
YES, THAT'S THE ONLY COURSE OF ACTION.
PLEASE TAKE COMMAND, COLONEL GRAN.
CAPTAIN HUGHES, TAKE LOWE TO THE PRESIDENT!
AYE, SIR.
SECOND LIEUTENANT BELMOT, TAKE THE INJURED TO THE BACK, *IMMEDIATELY!*
AYE, AYE SIR.
SHOULD I...
...GIVE YOU MY THANKS?
I NEED NO THANKS FROM YOU.

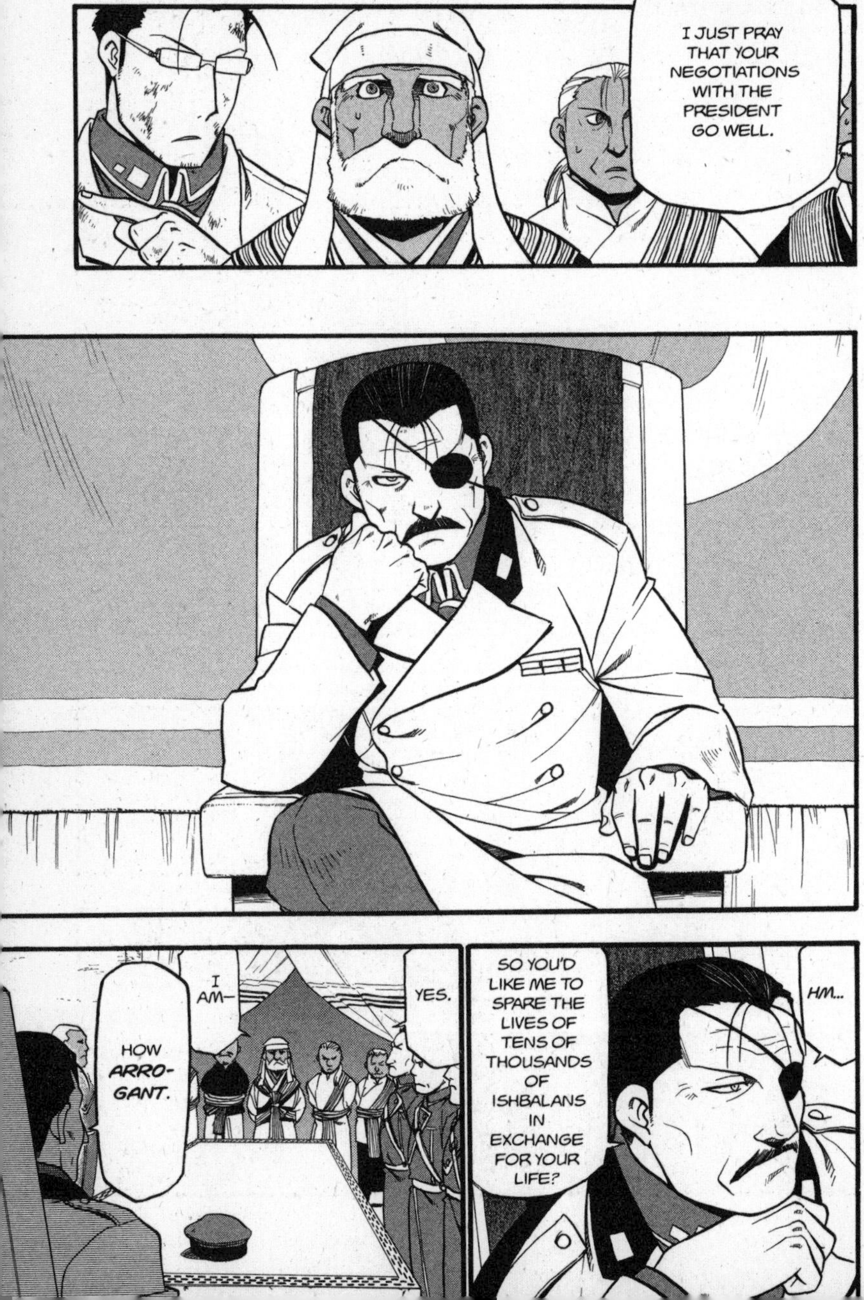
I JUST PRAY THAT YOUR NEGOTIATIONS WITH THE PRESIDENT GO WELL.
HM...
SO YOU'D LIKE ME TO SPARE THE LIVES OF TENS OF THOUSANDS OF ISHBALANS IN EXCHANGE FOR YOUR LIFE?
YES.
I AM—
HOW *ARROGANT*.

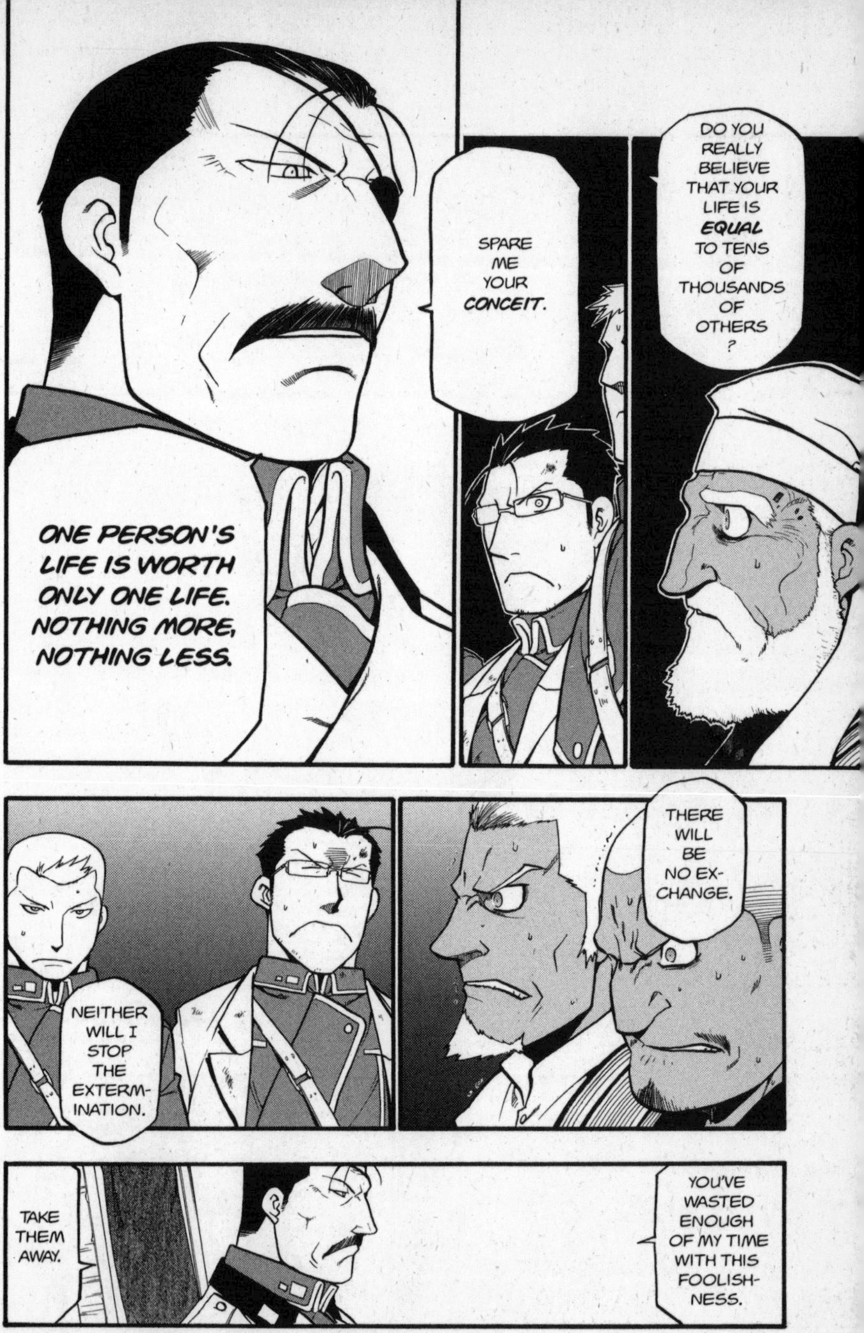
DO YOU REALLY BELIEVE THAT YOUR LIFE IS EQUAL TO TENS OF THOUSANDS OF OTHERS ?
SPARE ME YOUR CONCEIT.
ONE PERSON'S LIFE IS WORTH ONLY ONE LIFE. NOTHING MORE, NOTHING LESS.
THERE WILL BE NO EX-CHANGE.
NEITHER WILL I STOP THE EXTERM-INATION.
YOU'VE WASTED ENOUGH OF MY TIME WITH THIS FOOLISH-NESS.
TAKE THEM AWAY.

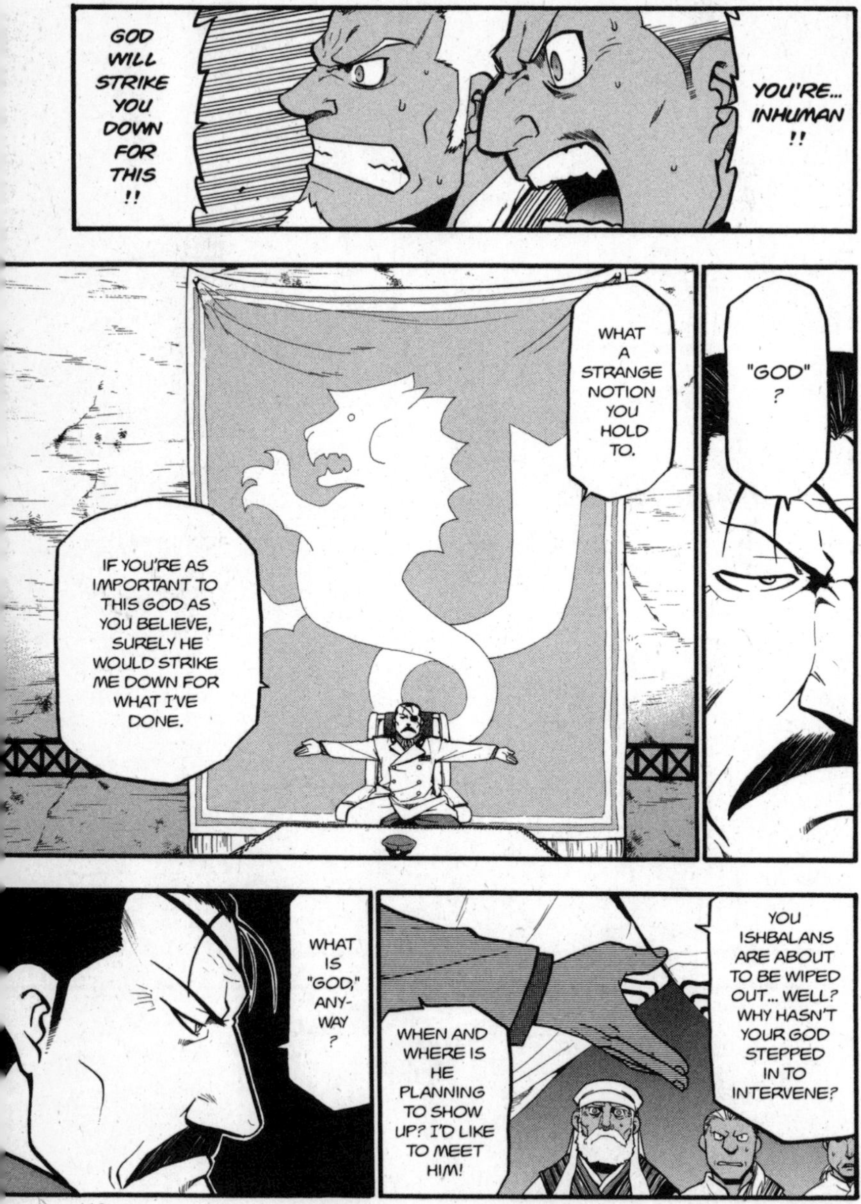
YOU'RE... INHUMAN!!
GOD WILL STRIKE YOU DOWN FOR THIS!!
"GOD"?
WHAT A STRANGE NOTION YOU HOLD TO.
IF YOU'RE AS IMPORTANT TO THIS GOD AS YOU BELIEVE, SURELY HE WOULD STRIKE ME DOWN FOR WHAT I'VE DONE.
YOU ISHBALANS ARE ABOUT TO BE WIPED OUT... WELL? WHY HASN'T YOUR GOD STEPPED IN TO INTERVENE?
WHEN AND WHERE IS HE PLANNING TO SHOW UP? I'D LIKE TO MEET HIM!
WHAT IS "GOD," ANY-WAY?

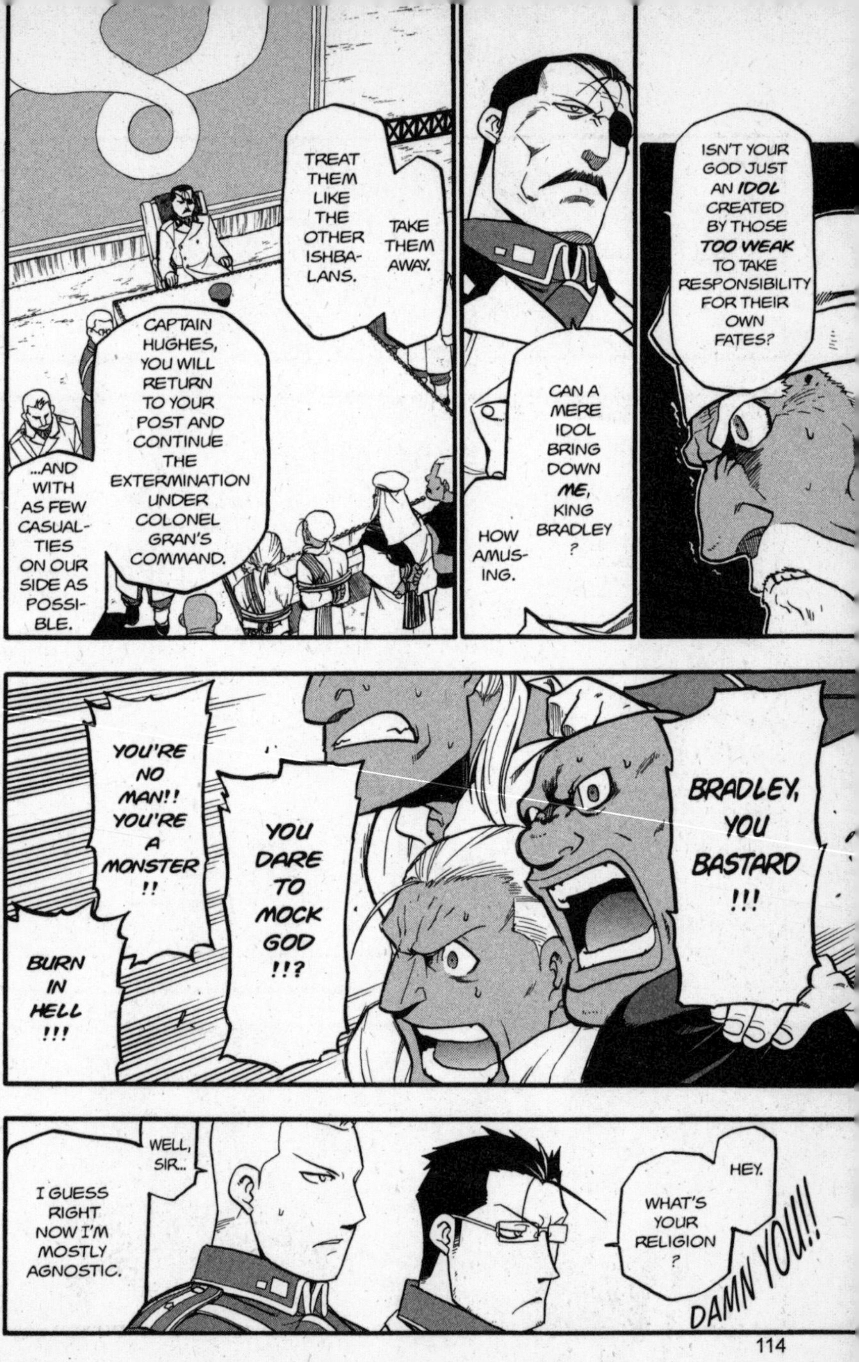
ISN'T YOUR GOD JUST AN IDOL CREATED BY THOSE TOO WEAK TO TAKE RESPONSIBILITY FOR THEIR OWN FATES?
CAN A MERE IDOL BRING DOWN ME, KING BRADLEY?
HOW AMUSING.
TAKE THEM AWAY.
TREAT THEM LIKE THE OTHER ISHBALANS.
CAPTAIN HUGHES, YOU WILL RETURN TO YOUR POST AND CONTINUE THE EXTERMINATION UNDER COLONEL GRAN'S COMMAND.
...AND WITH AS FEW CASUALTIES ON OUR SIDE AS POSSIBLE.
BRADLEY, YOU BASTARD!!!
YOU DARE TO MOCK GOD!!?
YOU'RE NO MAN!! YOU'RE A MONSTER!!
BURN IN HELL!!!
HEY.
WHAT'S YOUR RELIGION?
DAMN YOU!!
WELL, SIR...
I GUESS RIGHT NOW I'M MOSTLY AGNOSTIC.

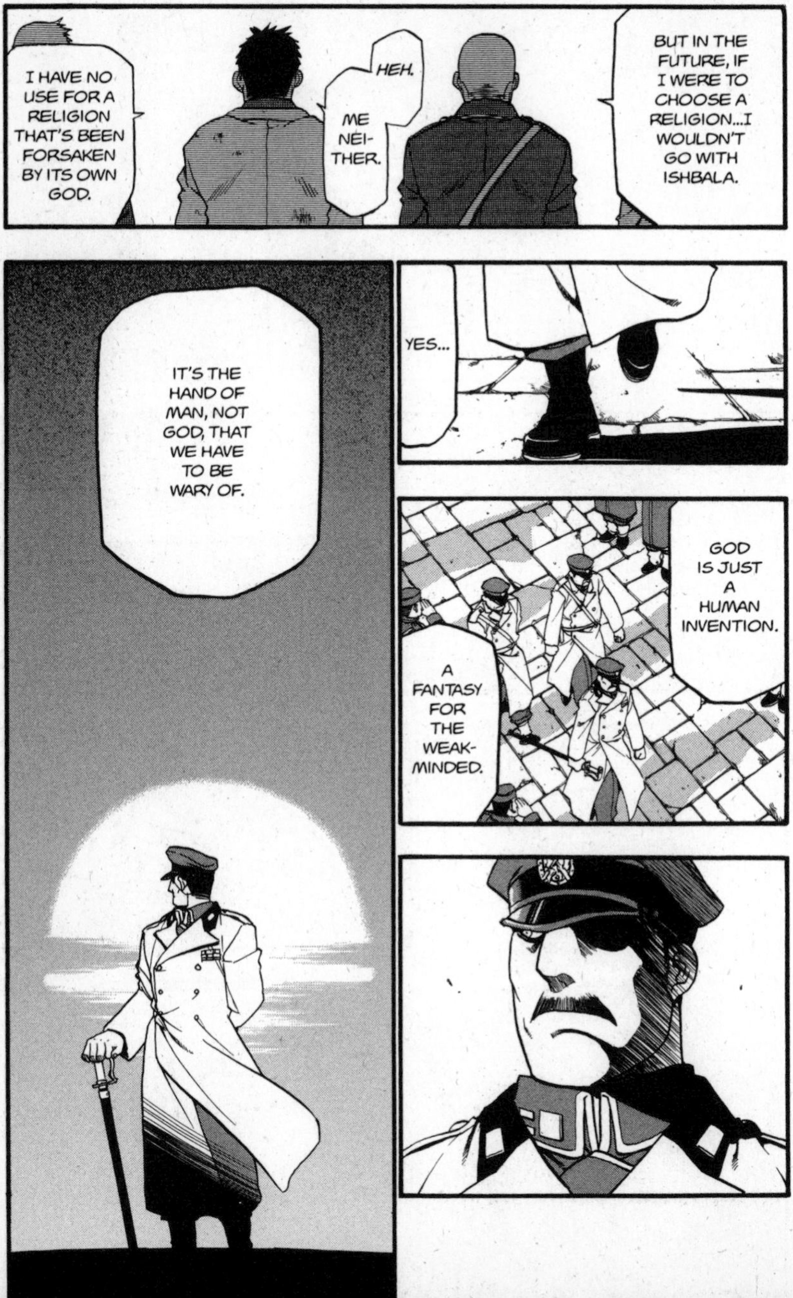
BUT IN THE FUTURE, IF I WERE TO CHOOSE A RELIGION...I WOULDN'T GO WITH ISHBALA.
HEH.
ME NEITHER.
I HAVE NO USE FOR A RELIGION THAT'S BEEN FORSAKEN BY ITS OWN GOD.
YES...
GOD IS JUST A HUMAN INVENTION.
A FANTASY FOR THE WEAK-MINDED.
IT'S THE HAND OF MAN, NOT GOD, THAT WE HAVE TO BE WARY OF.

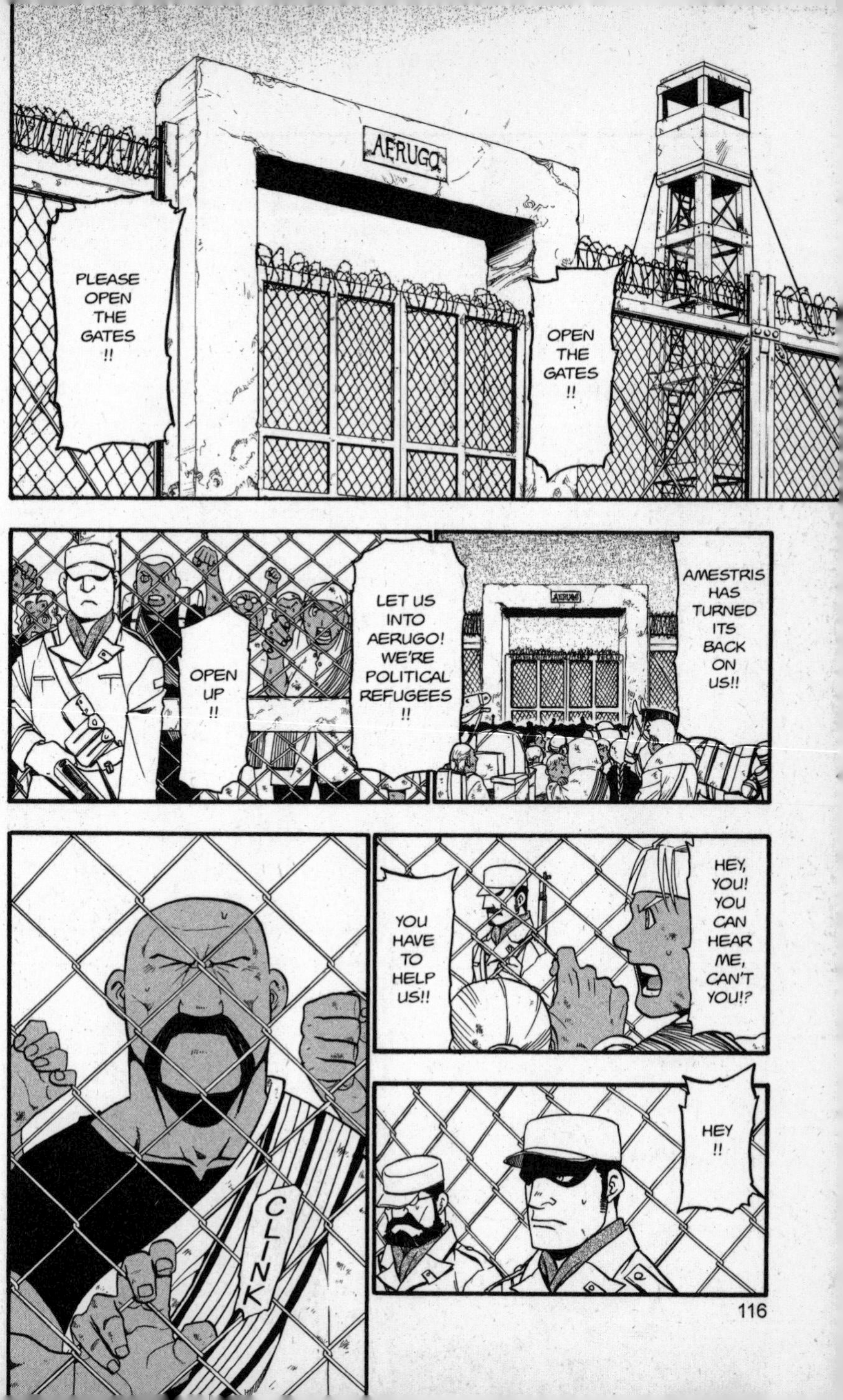
AERUGO
OPEN THE GATES!!
PLEASE OPEN THE GATES!!
AMESTRIS HAS TURNED ITS BACK ON US!!
LET US INTO AERUGO! WE'RE POLITICAL REFUGEES!!
OPEN UP!!
HEY, YOU! YOU CAN HEAR ME, CAN'T YOU!?
YOU HAVE TO HELP US!!
HEY!!
CLINK

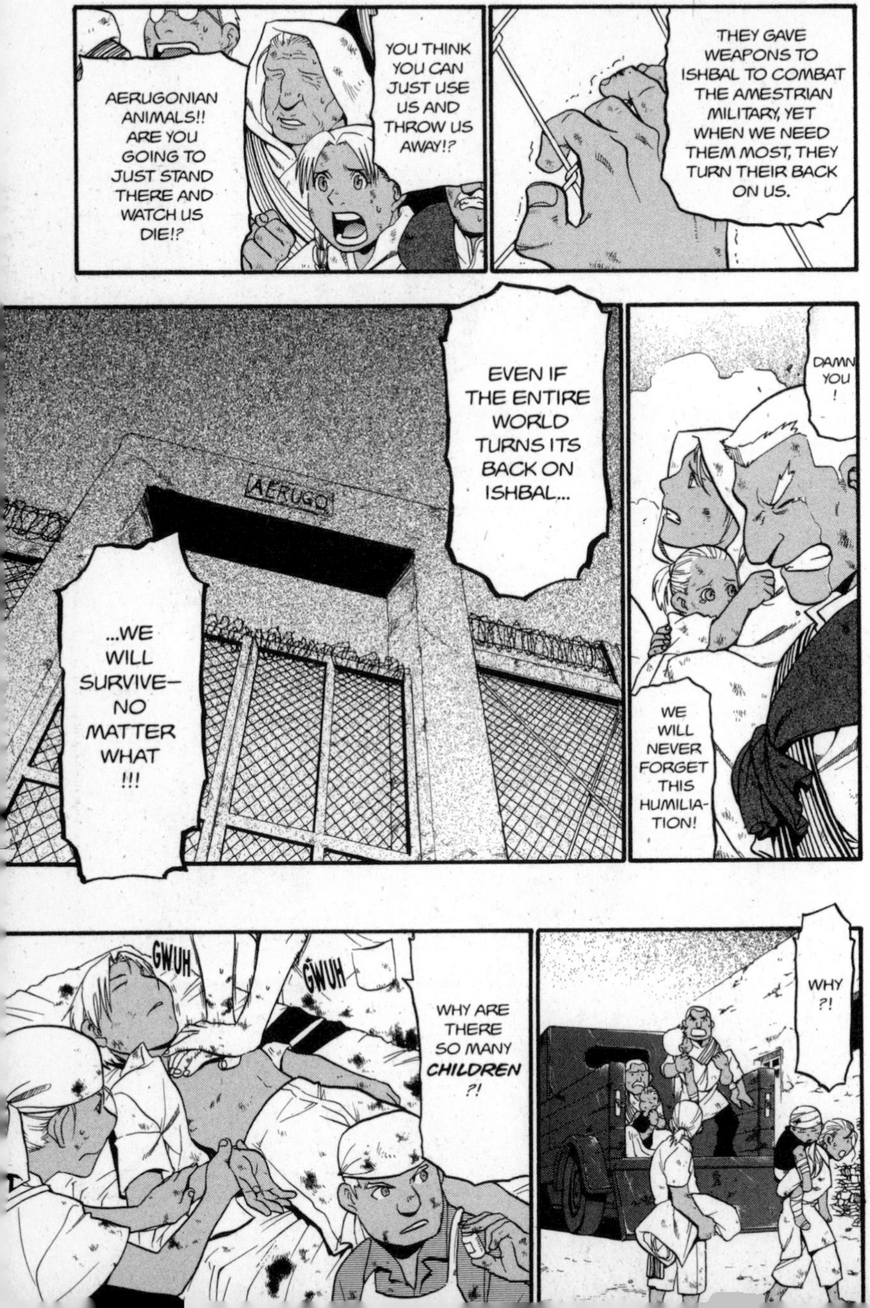
THEY GAVE WEAPONS TO ISHBAL TO COMBAT THE AMESTRIAN MILITARY, YET WHEN WE NEED THEM MOST, THEY TURN THEIR BACK ON US.
YOU THINK YOU CAN JUST USE US AND THROW US AWAY!?
AERUGONIAN ANIMALS!! ARE YOU GOING TO JUST STAND THERE AND WATCH US DIE!?
DAMN YOU!
WE WILL NEVER FORGET THIS HUMILIATION!
EVEN IF THE ENTIRE WORLD TURNS ITS BACK ON ISHBAL...
AERUGO
...WE WILL SURVIVE— NO MATTER WHAT!!!
WHY?!
WHY ARE THERE SO MANY **CHILDREN**?!
GWUH
GWUH

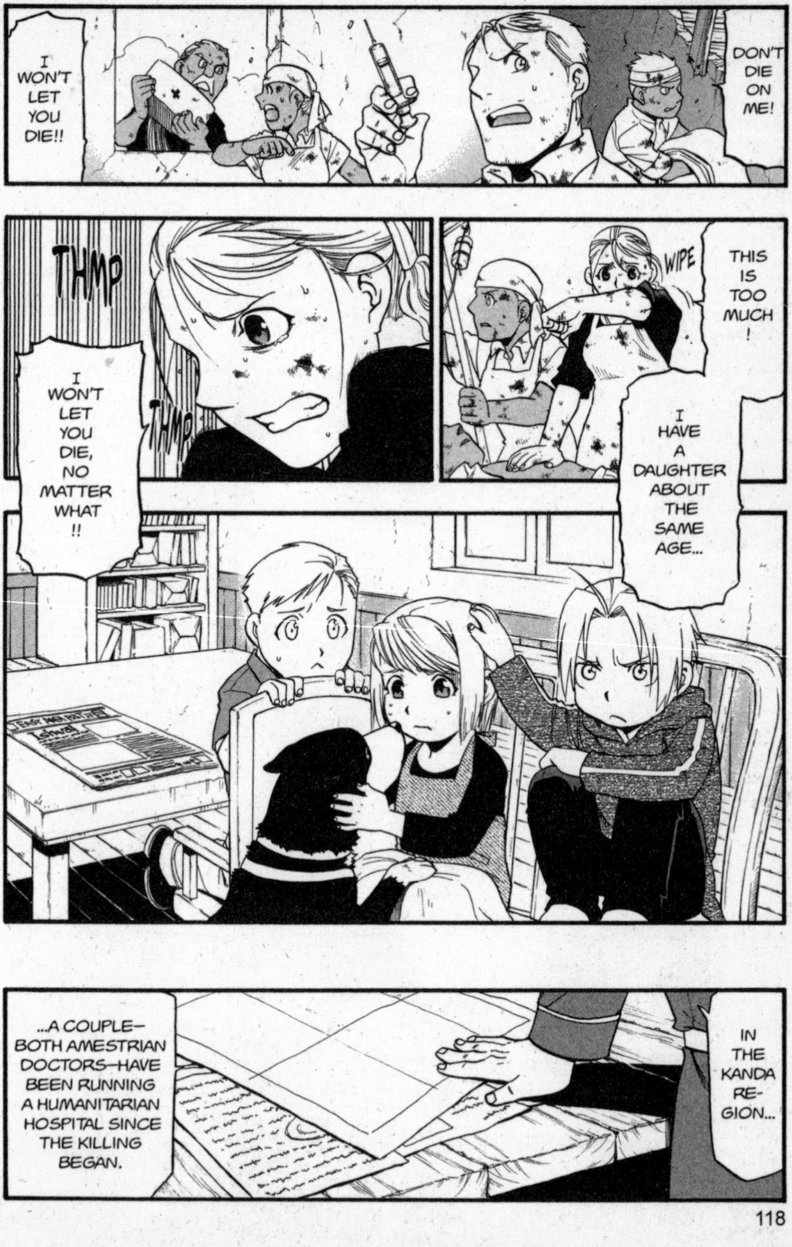
DON'T DIE ON ME!
I WON'T LET YOU DIE!!
WIPE
THIS IS TOO MUCH!
I HAVE A DAUGHTER ABOUT THE SAME AGE...
THMP
THMP
I WON'T LET YOU DIE, NO MATTER WHAT!!
IN THE KANDA RE-GION...
...A COUPLE—BOTH AMESTRIAN DOCTORS—HAVE BEEN RUNNING A HUMANITARIAN HOSPITAL SINCE THE KILLING BEGAN.

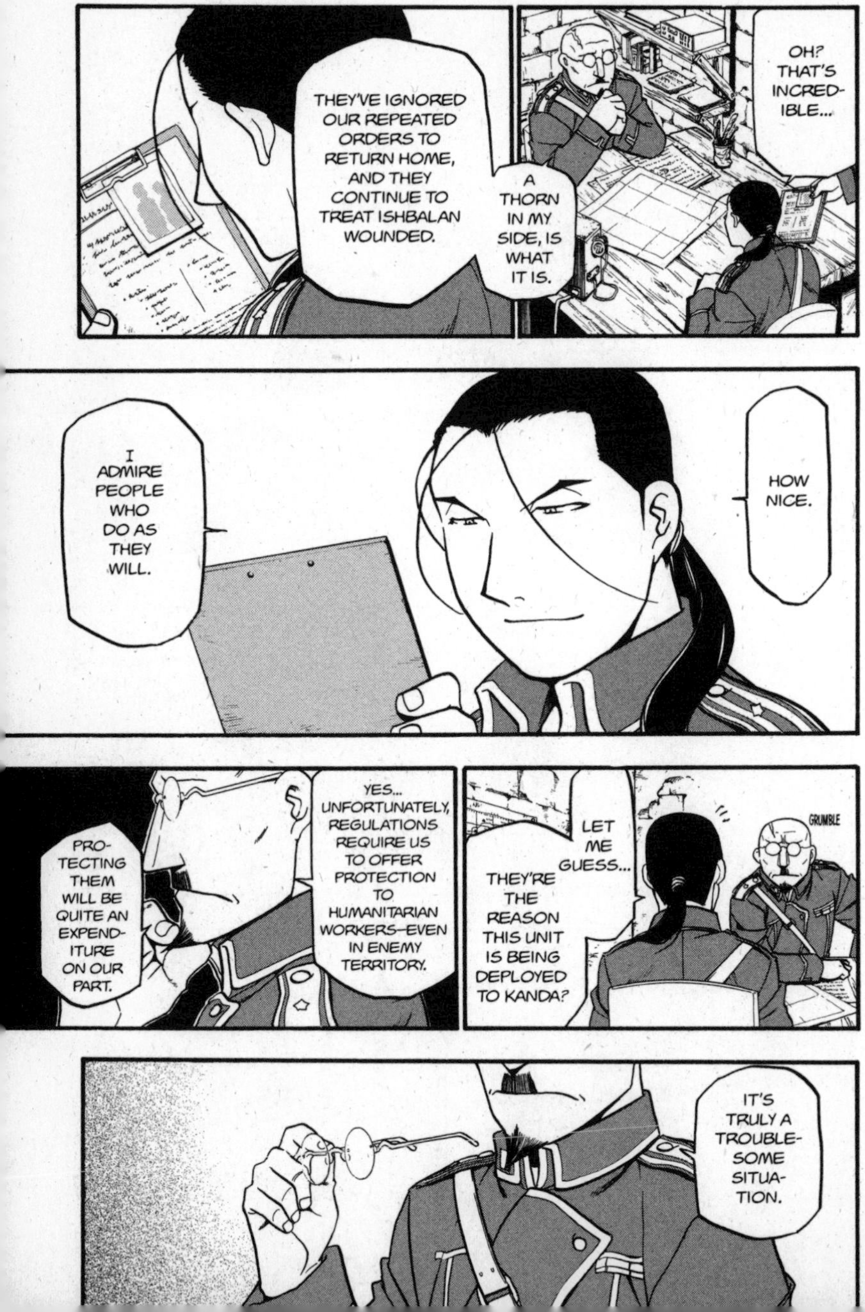
OH? THAT'S INCREDIBLE...
A THORN IN MY SIDE, IS WHAT IT IS.
THEY'VE IGNORED OUR REPEATED ORDERS TO RETURN HOME, AND THEY CONTINUE TO TREAT ISHBALAN WOUNDED.
HOW NICE.
I ADMIRE PEOPLE WHO DO AS THEY WILL.
GRUMBLE
LET ME GUESS...
THEY'RE THE REASON THIS UNIT IS BEING DEPLOYED TO KANDA?
YES... UNFORTUNATELY, REGULATIONS REQUIRE US TO OFFER PROTECTION TO HUMANITARIAN WORKERS—EVEN IN ENEMY TERRITORY.
PROTECTING THEM WILL BE QUITE AN EXPENDITURE ON OUR PART.
IT'S TRULY A TROUBLESOME SITUATION.

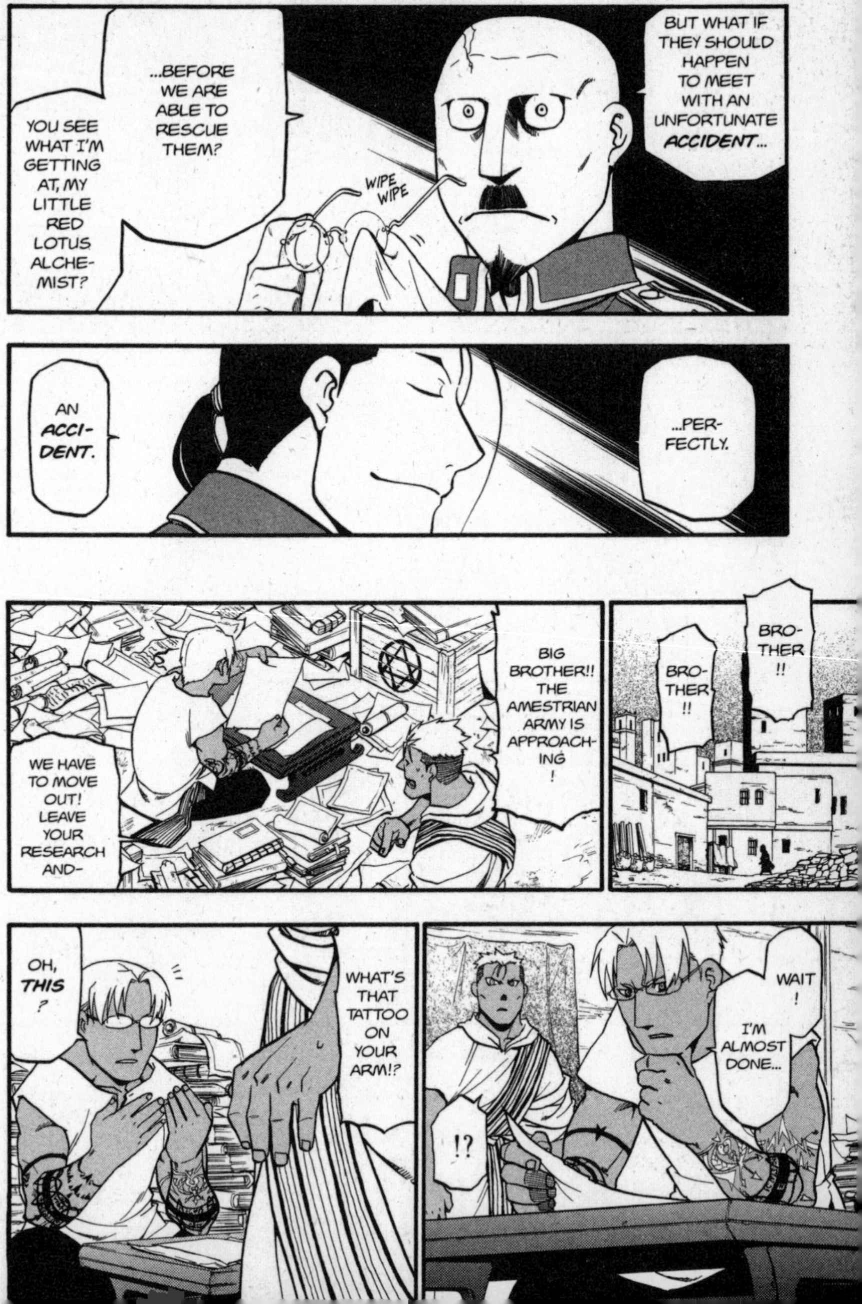

BUT WHAT IF THEY SHOULD HAPPEN TO MEET WITH AN UNFORTUNATE ACCIDENT...
...BEFORE WE ARE ABLE TO RESCUE THEM?
WIPE WIPE
YOU SEE WHAT I'M GETTING AT, MY LITTLE RED LOTUS ALCHEMIST?
...PERFECTLY.
AN ACCIDENT.
BROTHER!!
BROTHER!!
BIG BROTHER!! THE AMESTRIAN ARMY IS APPROACHING!
WE HAVE TO MOVE OUT! LEAVE YOUR RESEARCH AND-
WAIT! I'M ALMOST DONE...
!?
WHAT'S THAT TATTOO ON YOUR ARM!?
OH, THIS?

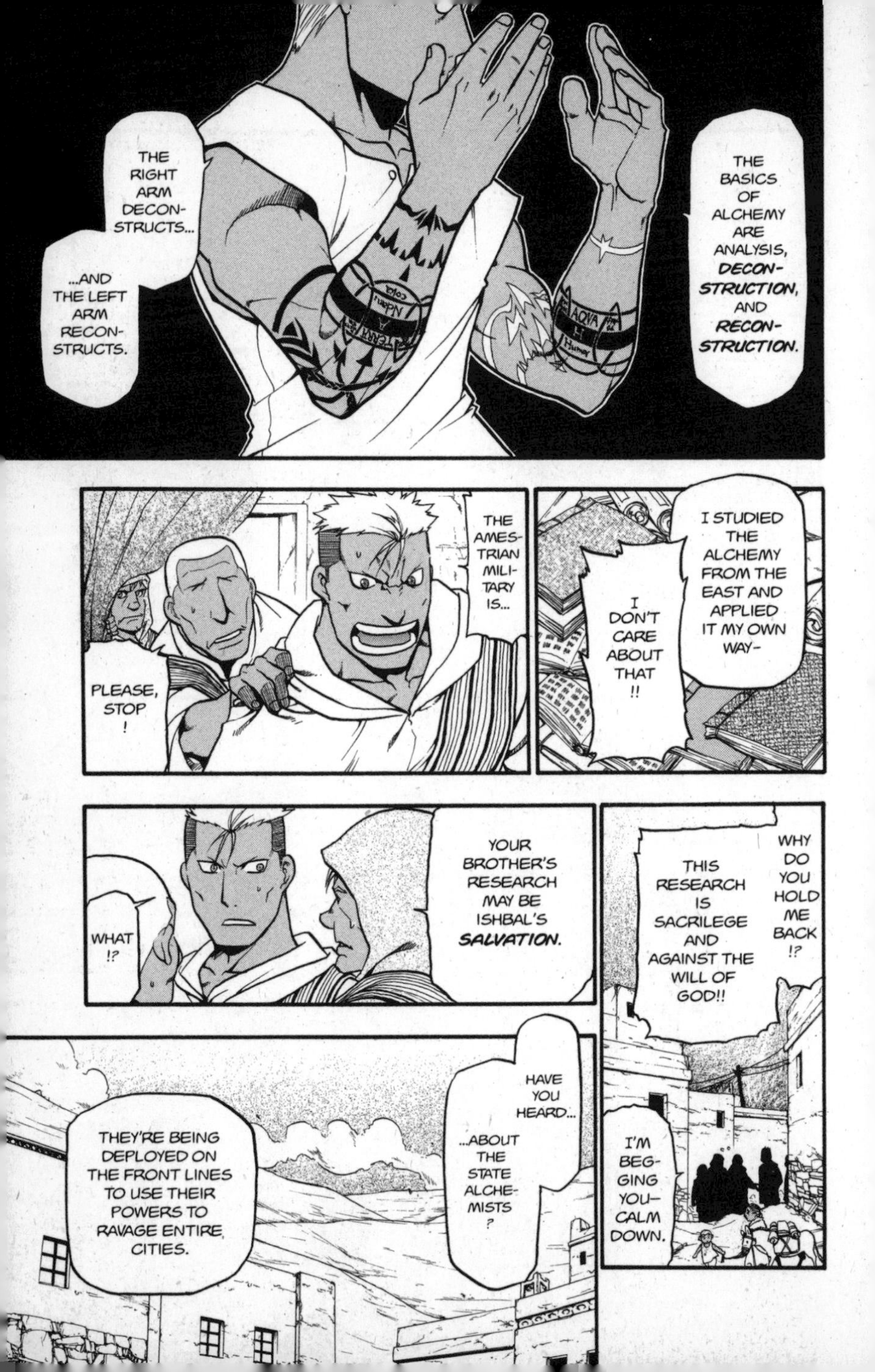

THE BASICS OF ALCHEMY ARE ANALYSIS, DECONSTRUCTION, AND RECONSTRUCTION.
THE RIGHT ARM DECONSTRUCTS...
...AND THE LEFT ARM RECONSTRUCTS.
I STUDIED THE ALCHEMY FROM THE EAST AND APPLIED IT MY OWN WAY-
I DON'T CARE ABOUT THAT!!
THE AMESTRIAN MILITARY IS...
PLEASE, STOP!
WHY DO YOU HOLD ME BACK!?
THIS RESEARCH IS SACRILEGE AND AGAINST THE WILL OF GOD!!
I'M BEGGING YOU—CALM DOWN.
YOUR BROTHER'S RESEARCH MAY BE ISHBAL'S SALVATION.
WHAT!?
HAVE YOU HEARD...
...ABOUT THE STATE ALCHEMISTS?
THEY'RE BEING DEPLOYED ON THE FRONT LINES TO USE THEIR POWERS TO RAVAGE ENTIRE CITIES.

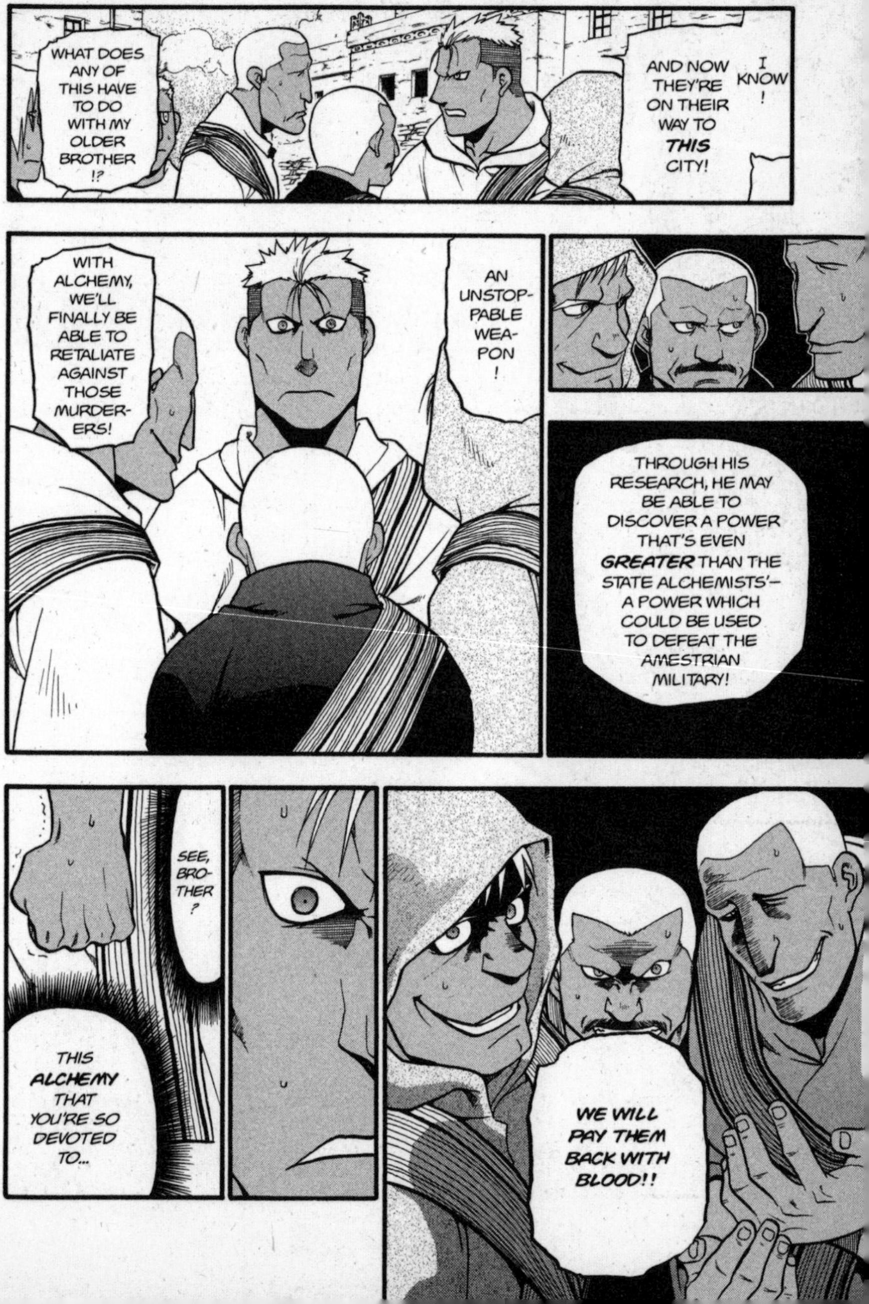
I KNOW!
AND NOW THEY'RE ON THEIR WAY TO **THIS** CITY!
WHAT DOES ANY OF THIS HAVE TO DO WITH MY OLDER BROTHER!?
THROUGH HIS RESEARCH, HE MAY BE ABLE TO DISCOVER A POWER THAT'S EVEN **GREATER** THAN THE STATE ALCHEMISTS'— A POWER WHICH COULD BE USED TO DEFEAT THE AMESTRIAN MILITARY!
AN UNSTOPPABLE WEAPON!
WITH ALCHEMY, WE'LL FINALLY BE ABLE TO RETALIATE AGAINST THOSE MURDERERS!
WE WILL PAY THEM BACK WITH BLOOD!!
SEE, BROTHER?
THIS ***ALCHEMY*** *THAT YOU'RE SO DEVOTED TO...*

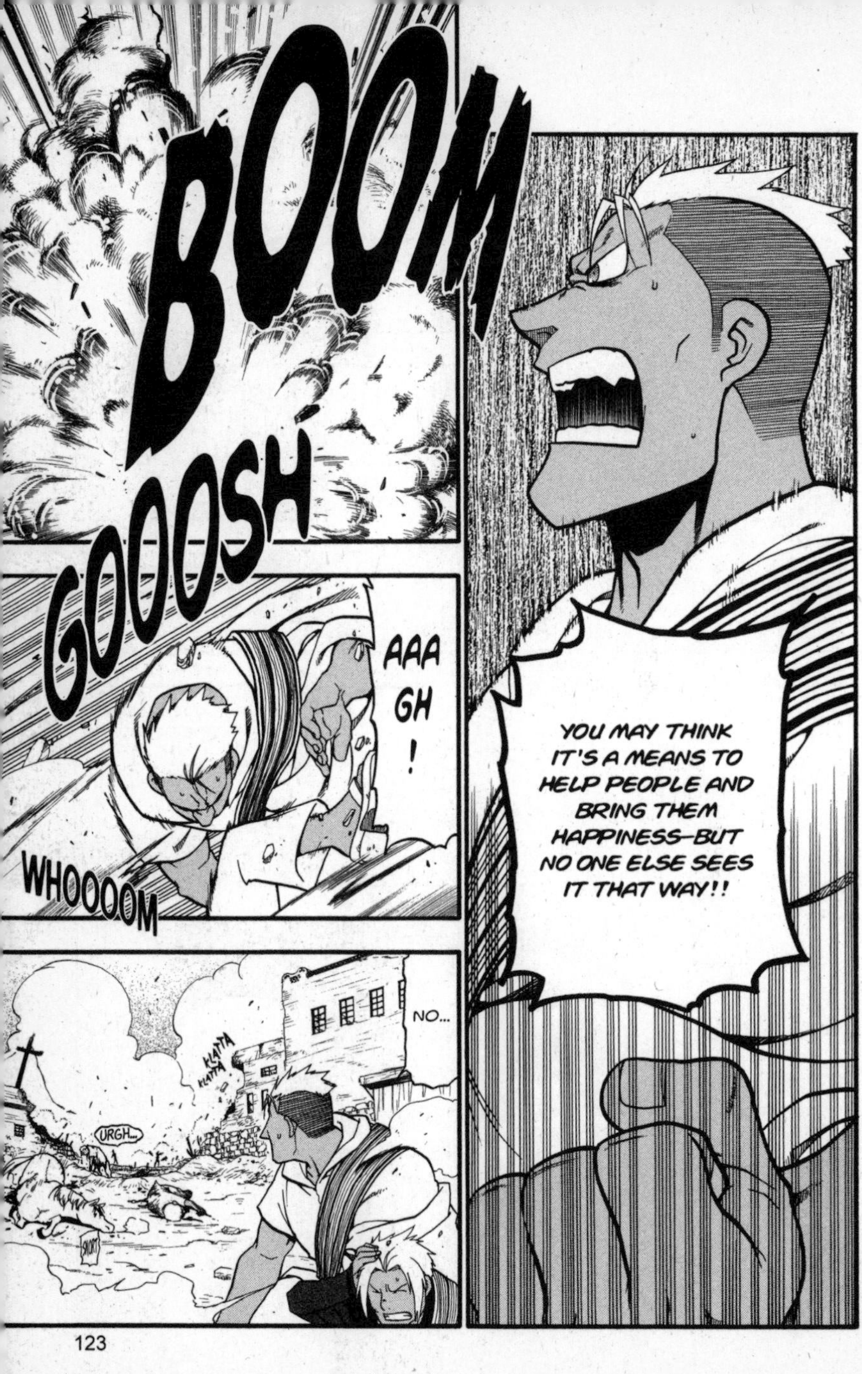
YOU MAY THINK IT'S A MEANS TO HELP PEOPLE AND BRING THEM HAPPINESS—BUT NO ONE ELSE SEES IT THAT WAY!!
BOOM
GOOOSH
AAAGH!
WHOOOOM
NO...
KLATTA KLATTA
URGH...

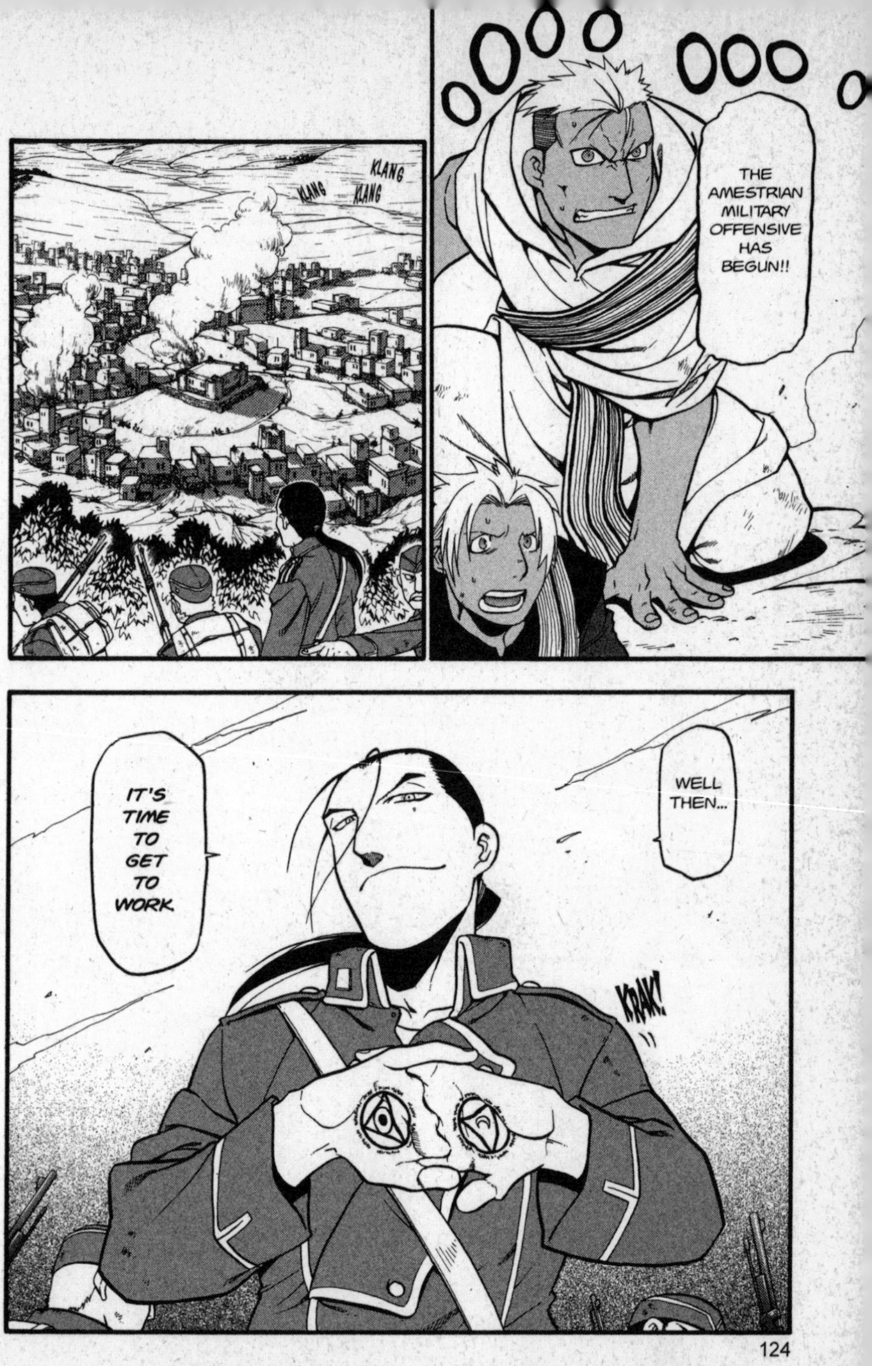
OOOO OOO O
THE AMESTRIAN MILITARY OFFENSIVE HAS BEGUN!!
KLANG
KLANG
KLANG
WELL THEN...
IT'S TIME TO GET TO WORK.
KRAK!

FULLMETAL
ALCHEMIST

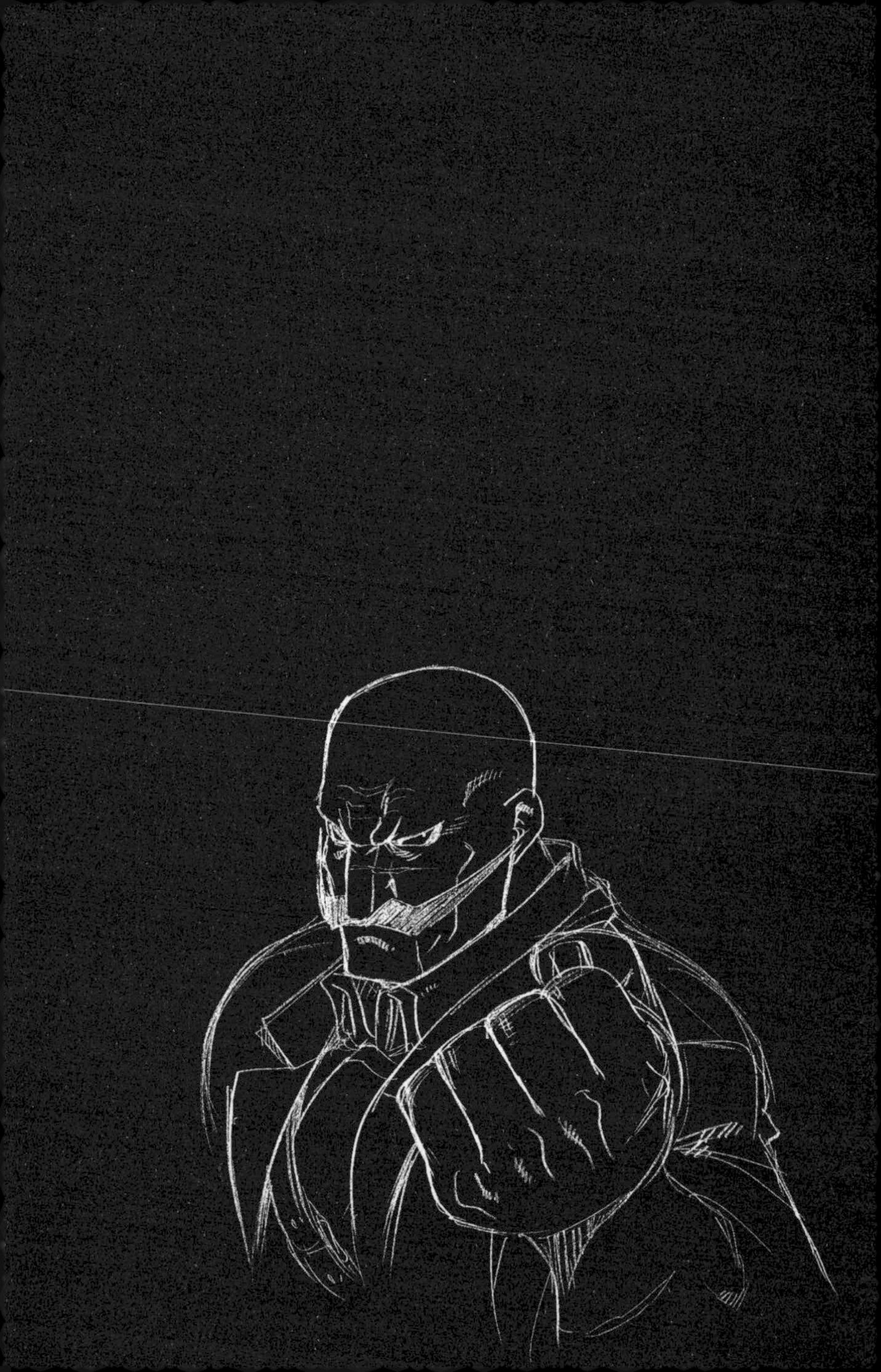

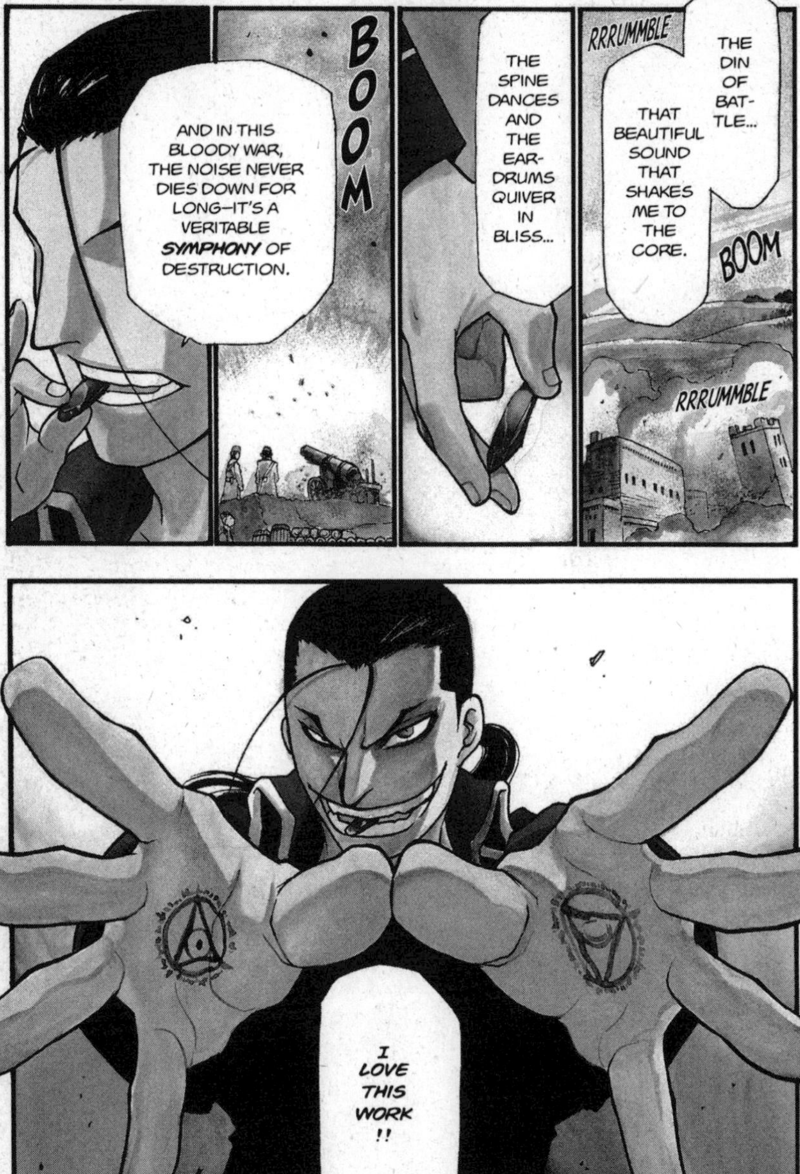

THE DIN OF BATTLE...
RRRUMMBLE
THAT BEAUTIFUL SOUND THAT SHAKES ME TO THE CORE.
BOOM
RRRUMMBLE
THE SPINE DANCES AND THE EARDRUMS QUIVER IN BLISS...
BOOM
AND IN THIS BLOODY WAR, THE NOISE NEVER DIES DOWN FOR LONG—IT'S A VERITABLE **SYMPHONY** OF DESTRUCTION.
I LOVE THIS WORK!!

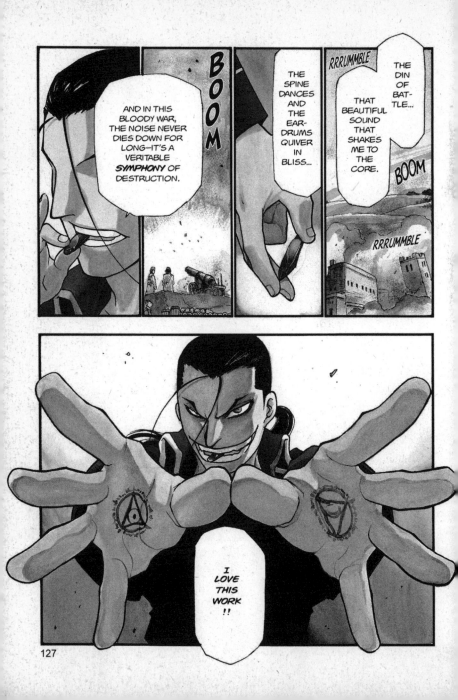

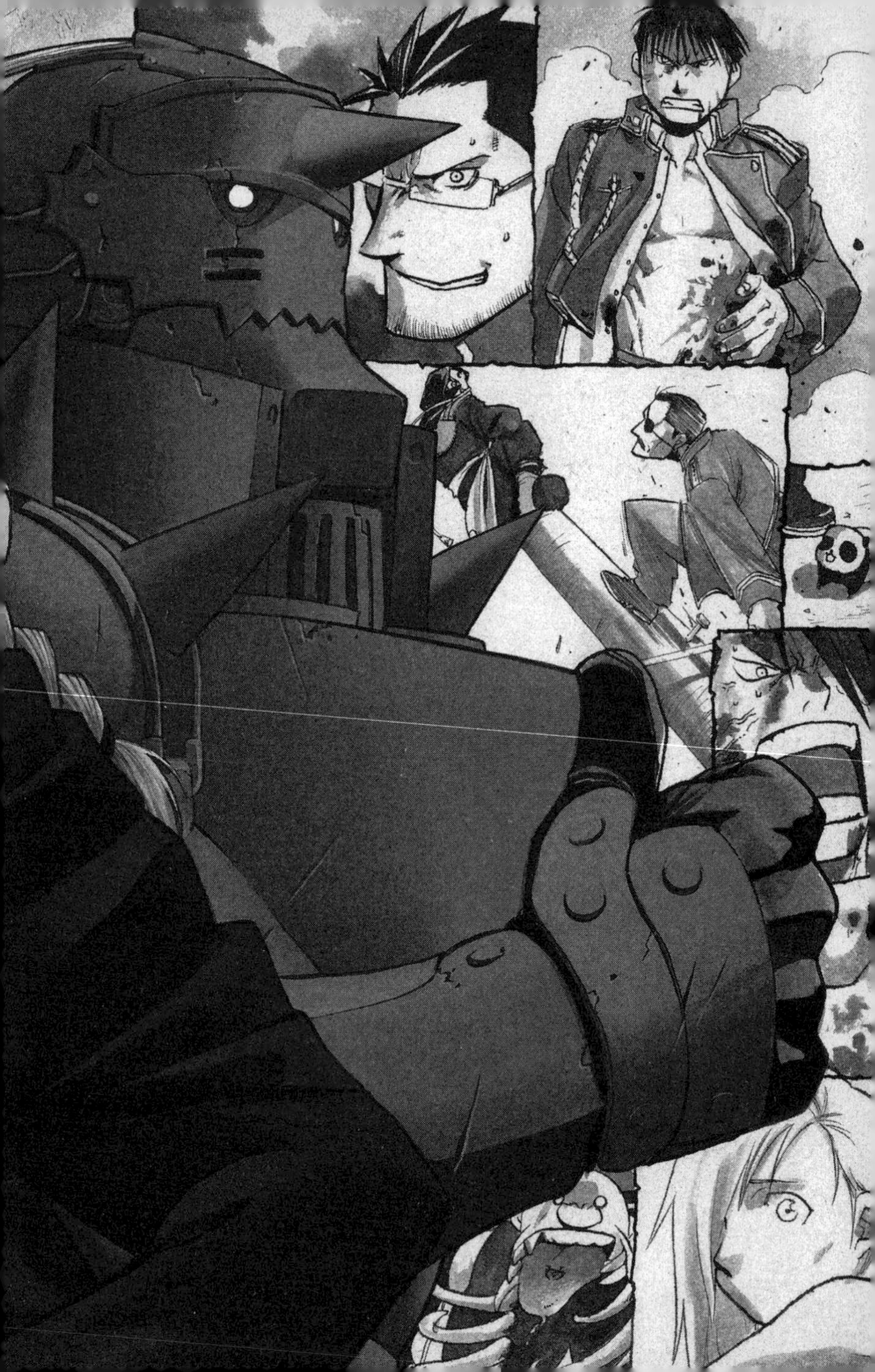

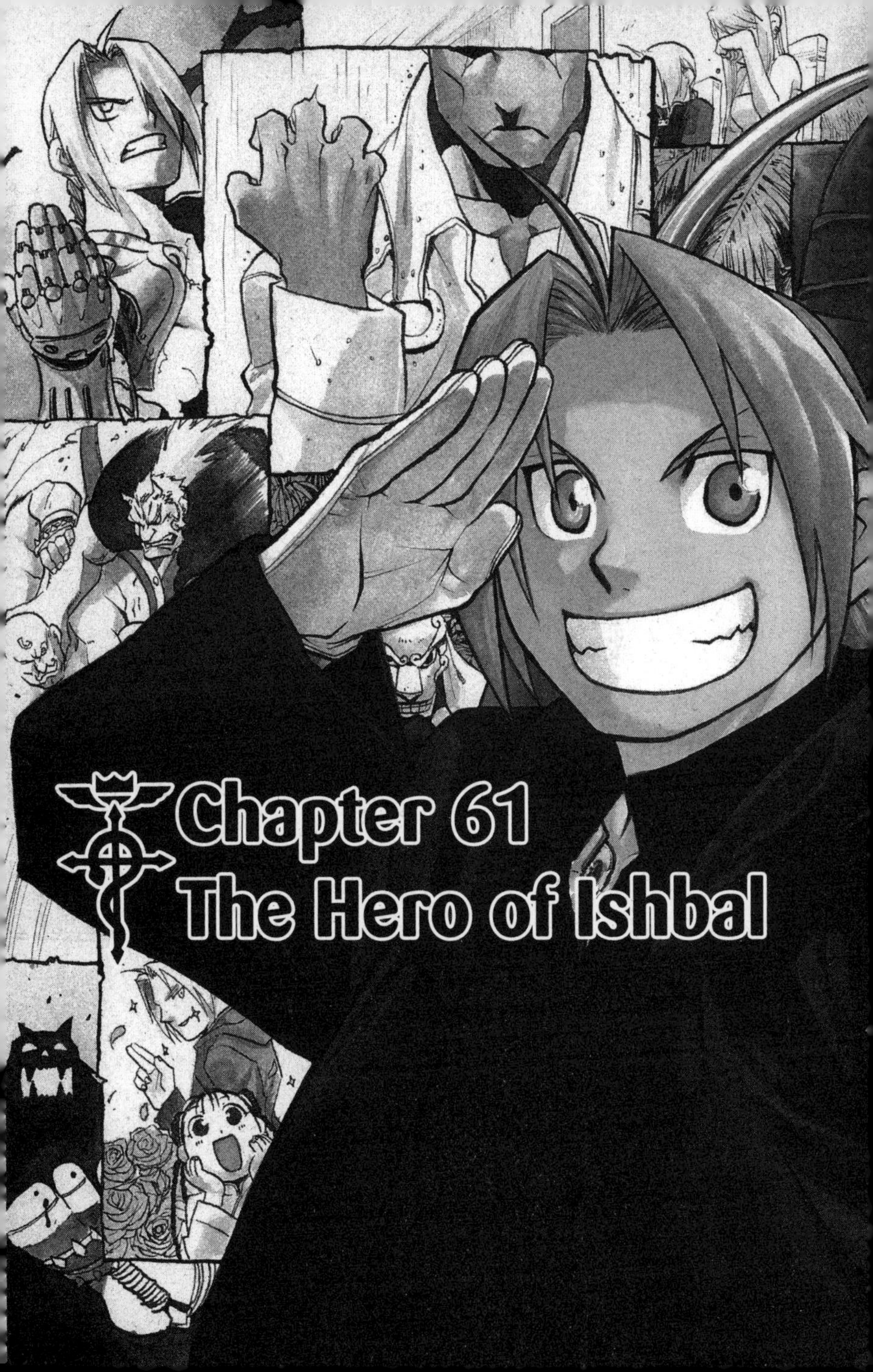
Chapter 61
The Hero of Ishbal

FULLMETAL
ALCHEMIST

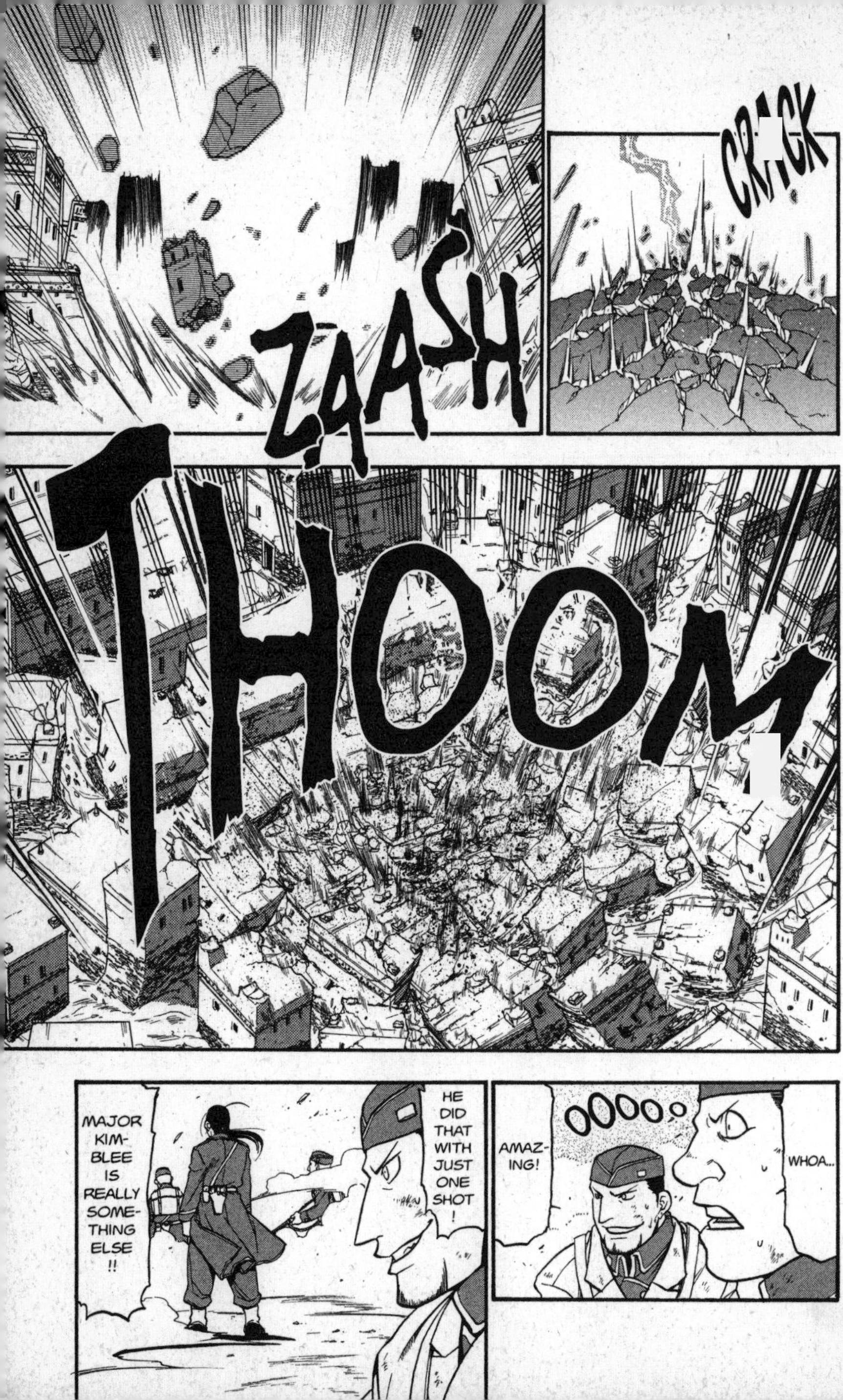
CRACK
ZAASH
THOOM
OOOOo
WHOA...
AMAZ-ING!
HE DID THAT WITH JUST ONE SHOT!
MAJOR KIM-BLEE IS REALLY SOME-THING ELSE!!

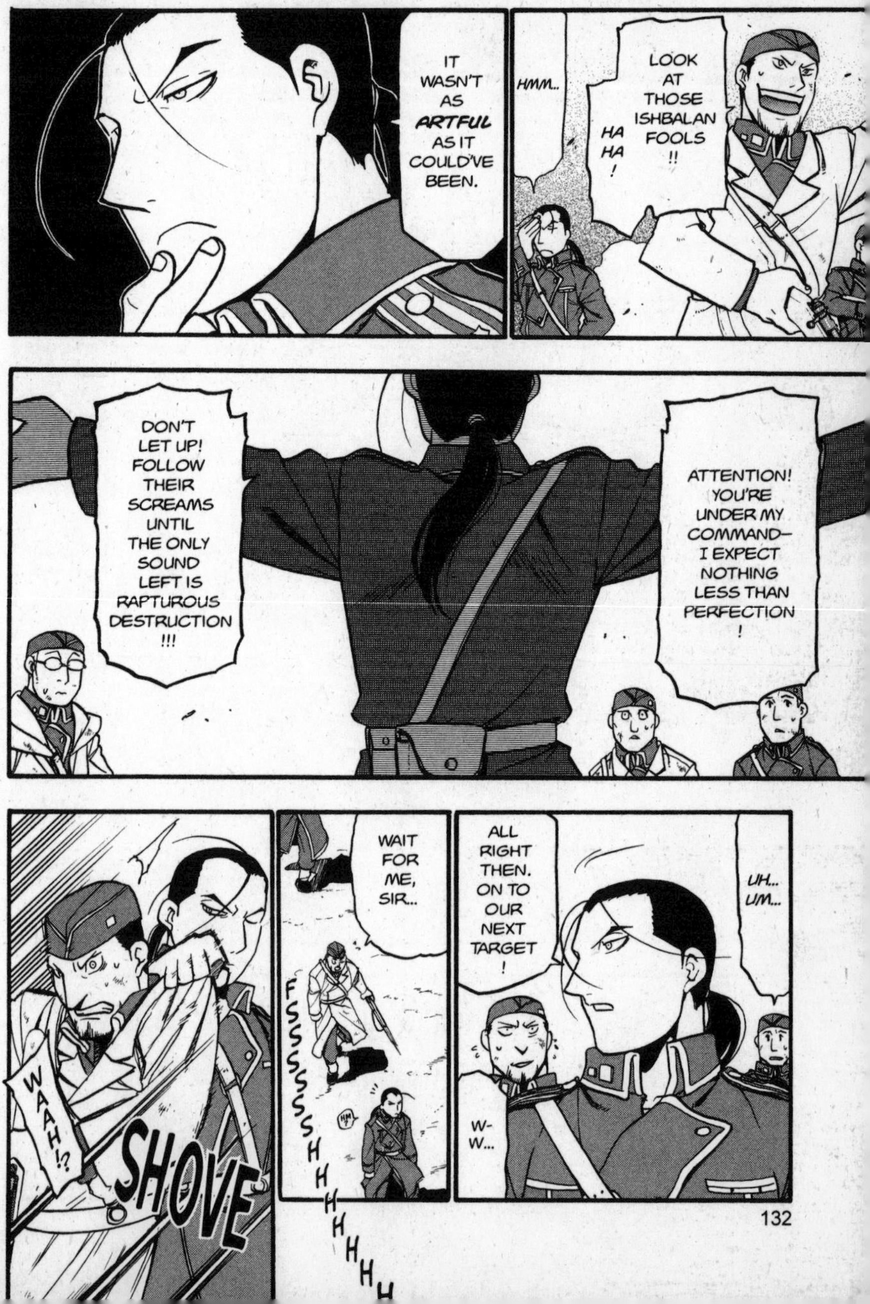

LOOK AT THOSE ISHBALAN FOOLS!!
HA HA!
HMM...
IT WASN'T AS *ARTFUL* AS IT COULD'VE BEEN.
ATTENTION! YOU'RE UNDER MY COMMAND— I EXPECT NOTHING LESS THAN PERFECTION!
DON'T LET UP! FOLLOW THEIR SCREAMS UNTIL THE ONLY SOUND LEFT IS RAPTUROUS DESTRUCTION!!!
UH... UM...
ALL RIGHT THEN. ON TO OUR NEXT TARGET!
W-W...
WAIT FOR ME, SIR...
FSSSSSHHHHHHH
HM?
SHOVE
WAAH!?

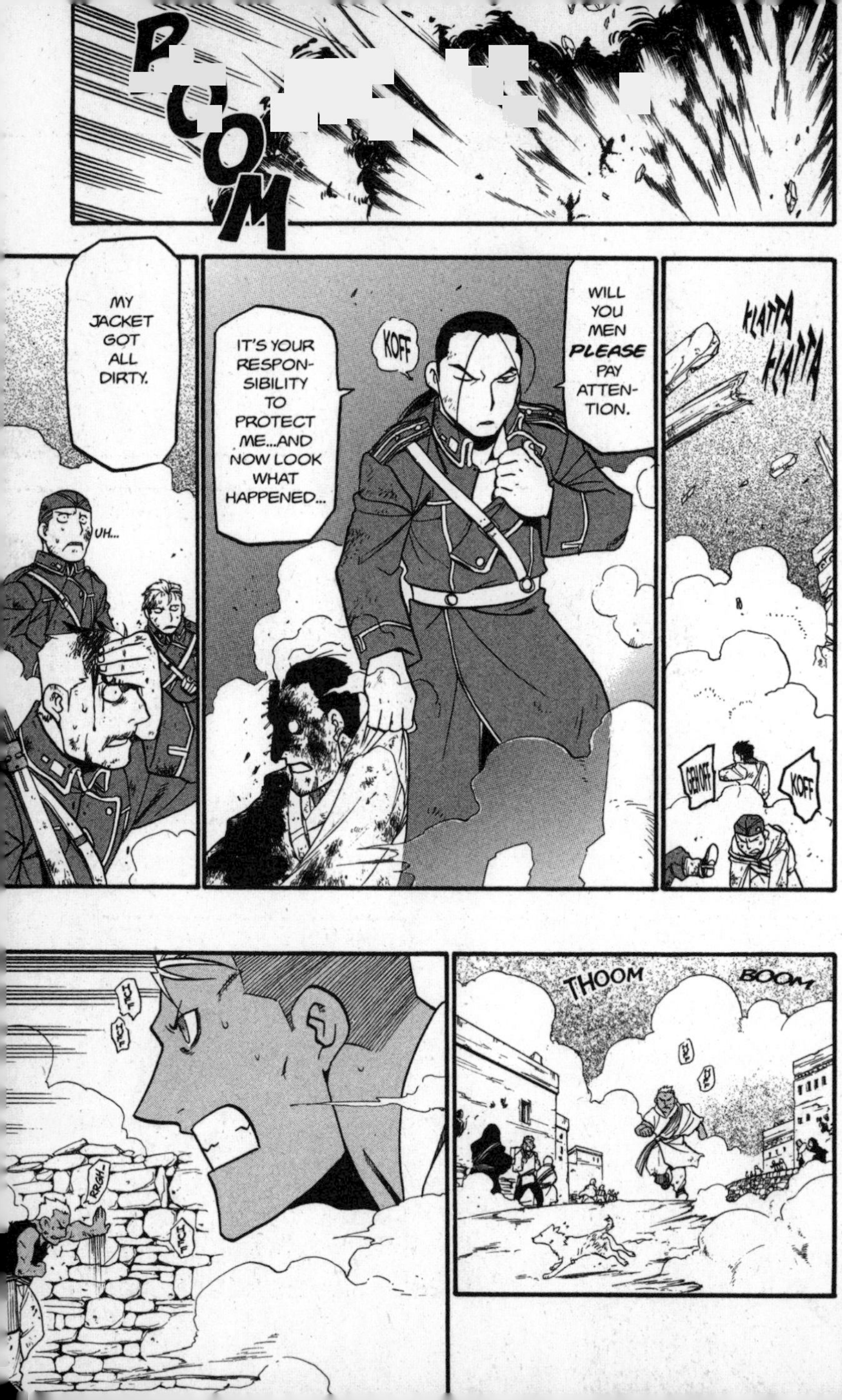
BOOM
KLATTA KLATTA
GEHOFF
KOFF
WILL YOU MEN **PLEASE** PAY ATTENTION.
KOFF
IT'S YOUR RESPONSIBILITY TO PROTECT ME...AND NOW LOOK WHAT HAPPENED...
MY JACKET GOT ALL DIRTY.
UH...
THOOM
BOOM
HUF
HUF
HUF
HUF
RRGH-
HUF

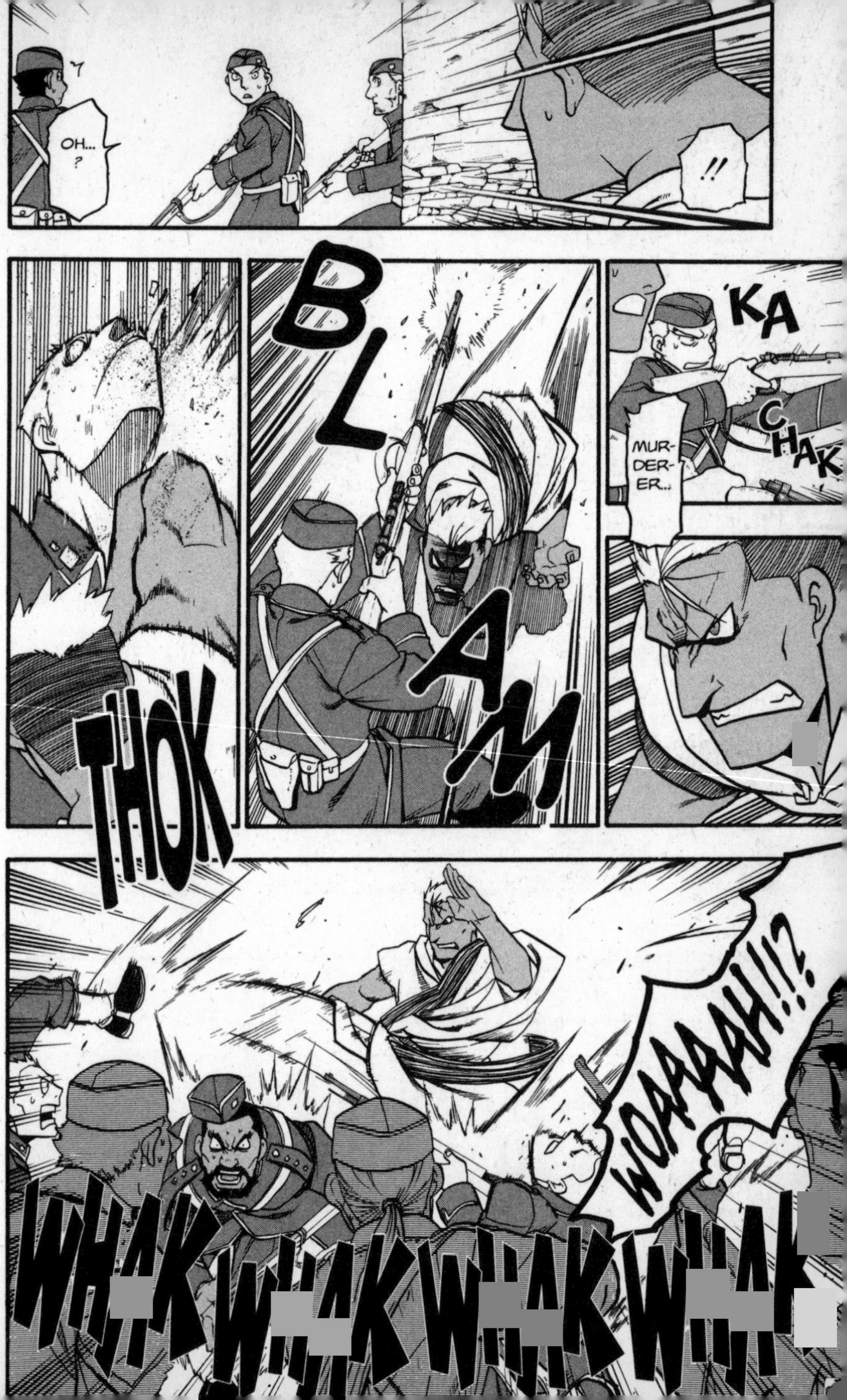
!!
OH... ?
KA CHAK
MURDERER...
BLAM
THOK
WOAAAH!!?
WHAK WHAK WHAK WHAK

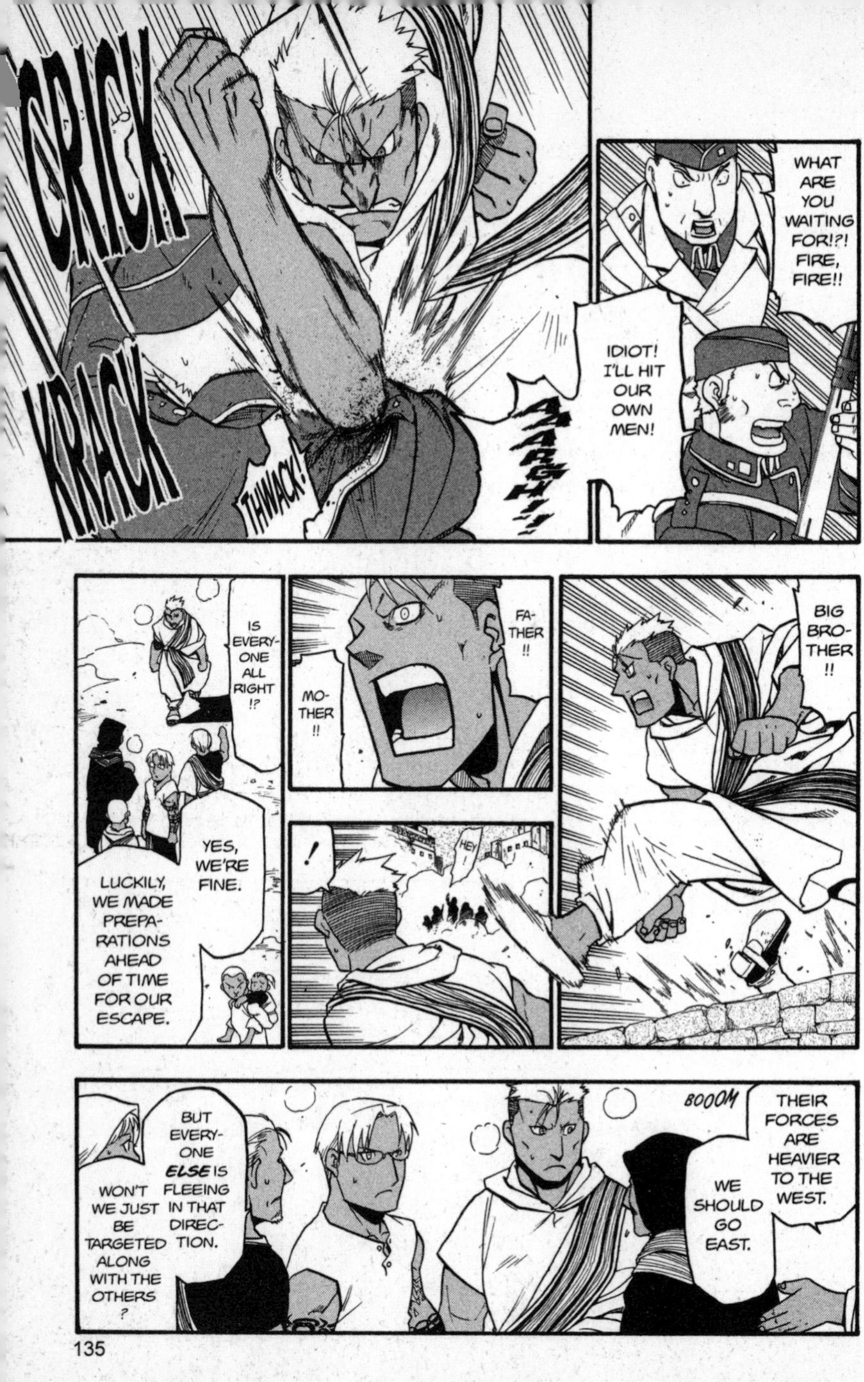
WHAT ARE YOU WAITING FOR!?! FIRE, FIRE!!
IDIOT! I'LL HIT OUR OWN MEN!
CRICK
KRACK
THWACK!
AAARGH!!
BIG BRO-THER !!
FA-THER !!
MO-THER !!
!
HEY
IS EVERY-ONE ALL RIGHT !?
YES, WE'RE FINE.
LUCKILY, WE MADE PREPA-RATIONS AHEAD OF TIME FOR OUR ESCAPE.
BOOOM
THEIR FORCES ARE HEAVIER TO THE WEST.
WE SHOULD GO EAST.
BUT EVERY-ONE ELSE IS FLEEING IN THAT DIREC-TION.
WON'T WE JUST BE TARGETED ALONG WITH THE OTHERS ?

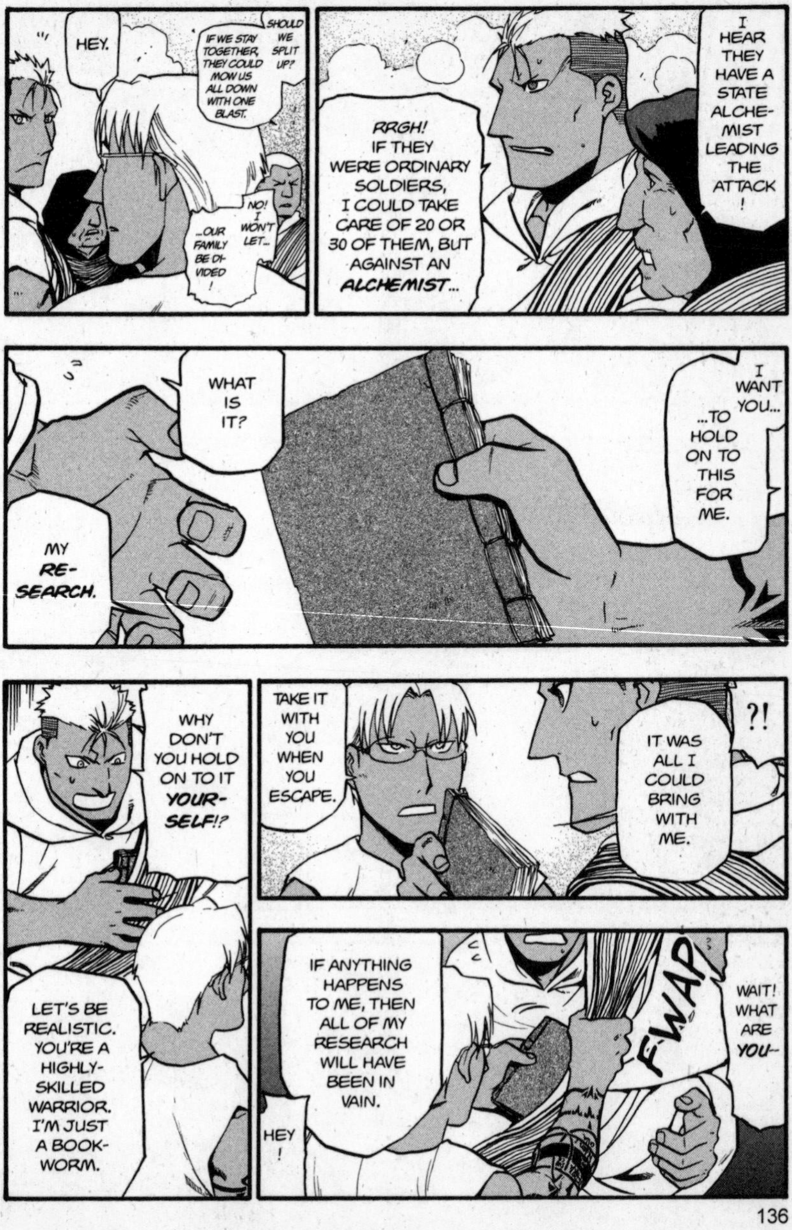
I HEAR THEY HAVE A STATE ALCHEMIST LEADING THE ATTACK!
RRGH! IF THEY WERE ORDINARY SOLDIERS, I COULD TAKE CARE OF 20 OR 30 OF THEM, BUT AGAINST AN ALCHEMIST...
SHOULD WE SPLIT UP?
IF WE STAY TOGETHER, THEY COULD MOW US ALL DOWN WITH ONE BLAST.
HEY.
NO! I WON'T LET...
...OUR FAMILY BE DIVIDED!
I WANT YOU...
...TO HOLD ON TO THIS FOR ME.
WHAT IS IT?
MY RESEARCH.
?!
IT WAS ALL I COULD BRING WITH ME.
TAKE IT WITH YOU WHEN YOU ESCAPE.
WAIT! WHAT ARE YOU-
FWAP
IF ANYTHING HAPPENS TO ME, THEN ALL OF MY RESEARCH WILL HAVE BEEN IN VAIN.
HEY!
WHY DON'T YOU HOLD ON TO IT YOURSELF!?
LET'S BE REALISTIC. YOU'RE A HIGHLY-SKILLED WARRIOR. I'M JUST A BOOKWORM.

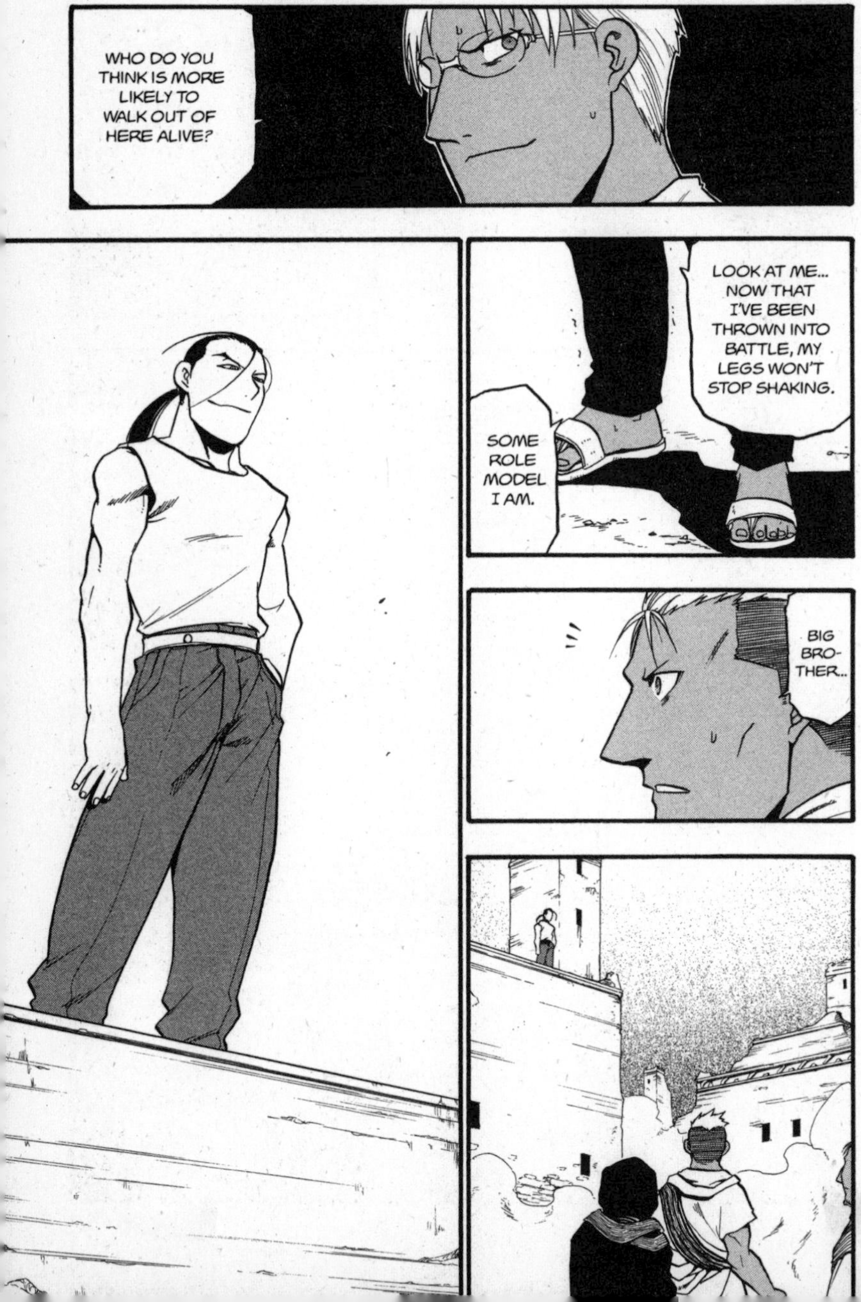
WHO DO YOU THINK IS MORE LIKELY TO WALK OUT OF HERE ALIVE?
LOOK AT ME... NOW THAT I'VE BEEN THROWN INTO BATTLE, MY LEGS WON'T STOP SHAKING.
SOME ROLE MODEL I AM.
BIG BRO-THER...

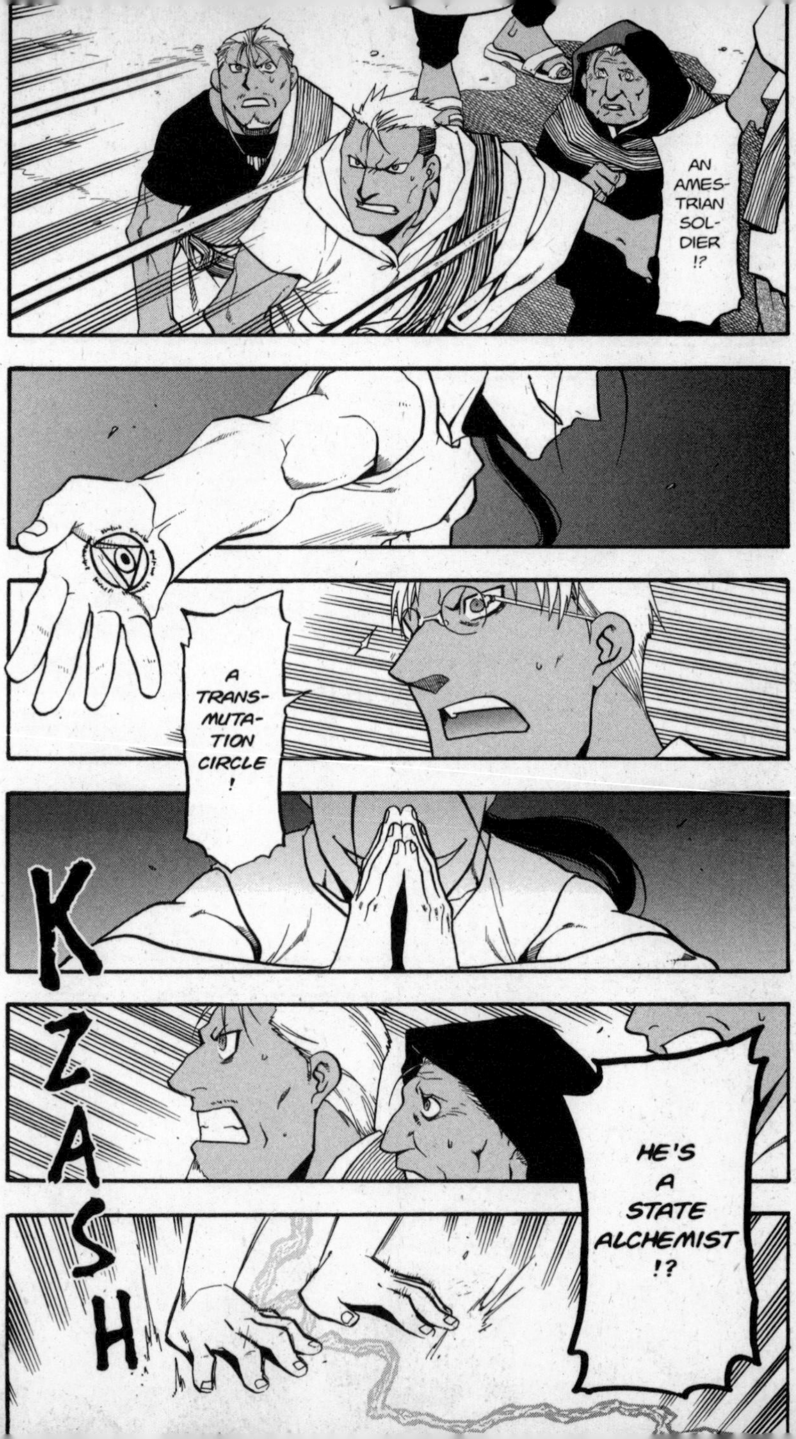
AN AMESTRIAN SOLDIER!?
A TRANSMUTATION CIRCLE!
KZASH
HE'S A STATE ALCHEMIST!?

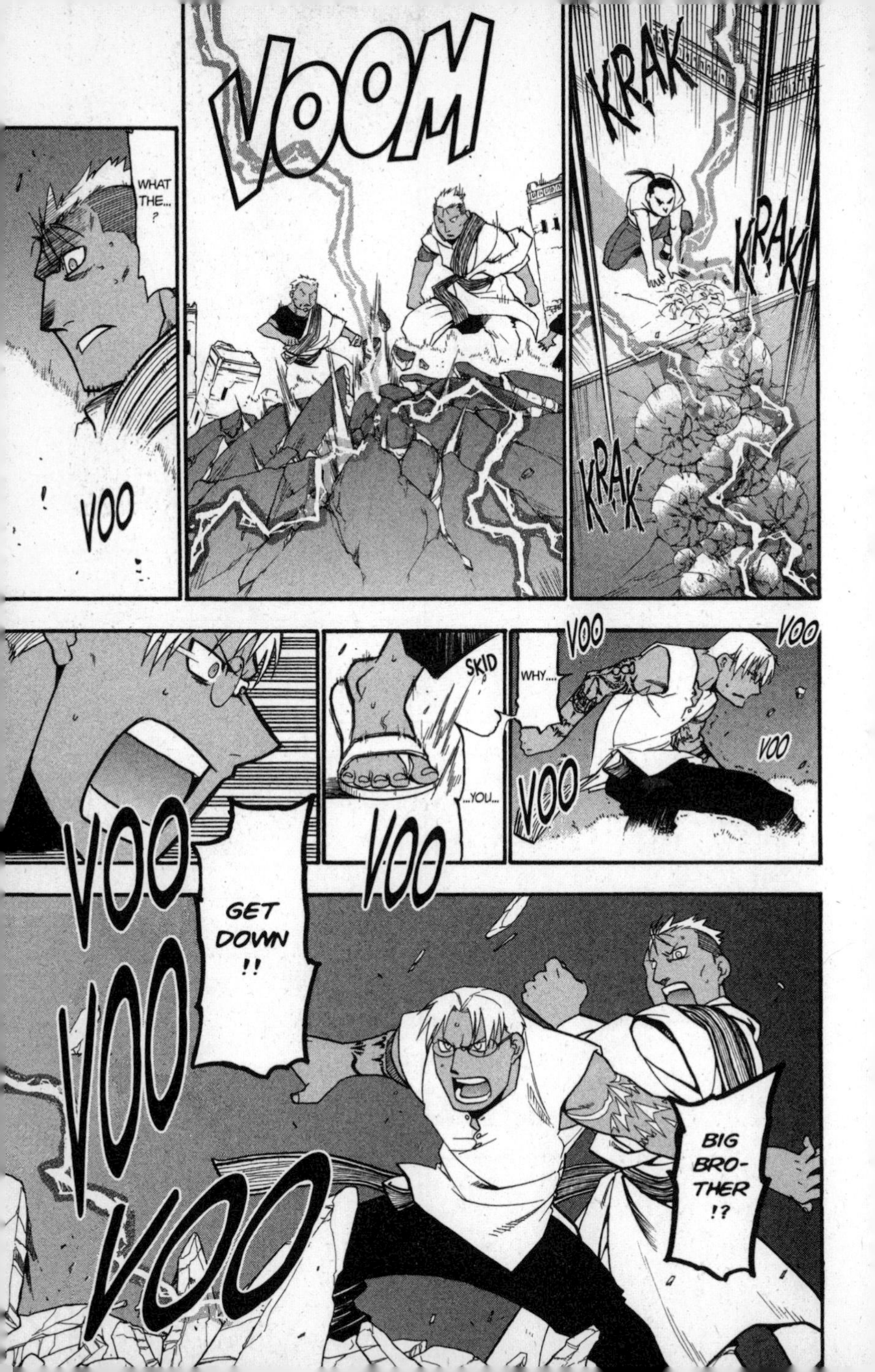
KRAK
KRAK
KRAK
VOOM
WHAT THE...?
VOO
VOO
WHY....
VOO
VOO
VOO
SKID
...YOU...
VOO
VOO
GET DOWN!!
BIG BRO-THER!?
VOO
VOO
VOO

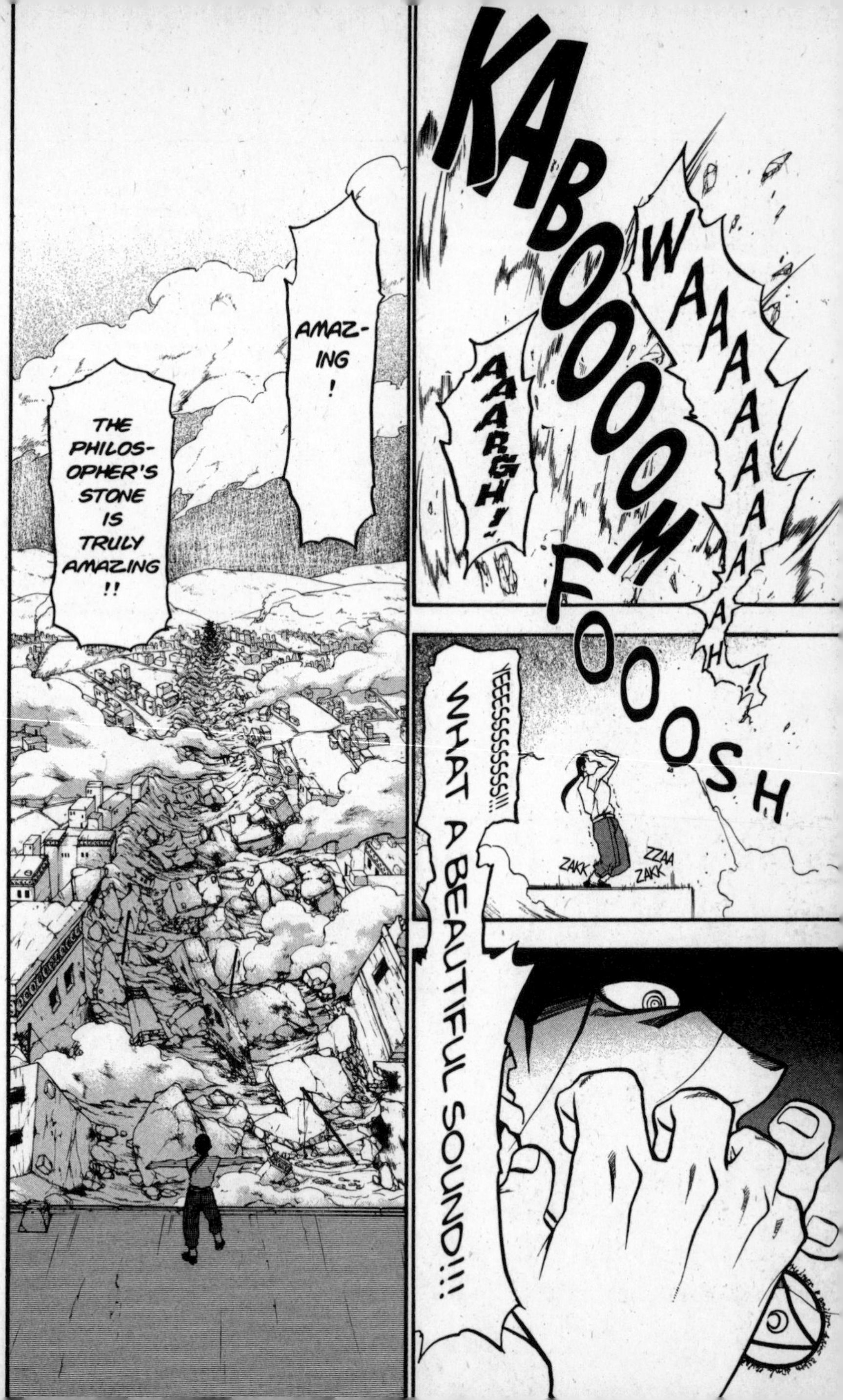
KABOOOOM
WAAAAAAAAAH!
AAARGH!
FOOOOSH
YEEESSSSSSS!!!
ZAKK
ZZAA
ZAKK
WHAT A BEAUTIFUL SOUND!!!
AMAZING!
THE PHILOSOPHER'S STONE IS TRULY AMAZING!!

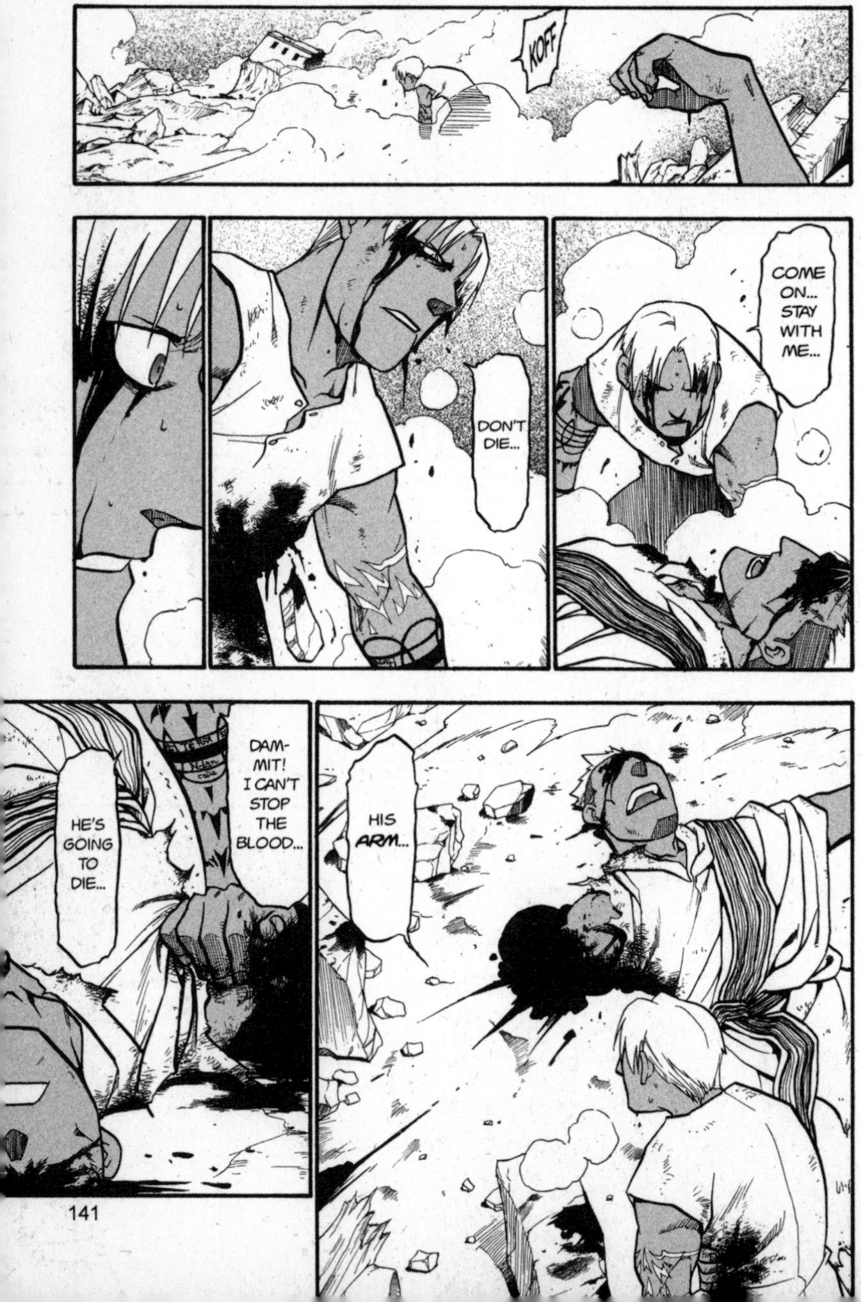
KOFF
COME ON... STAY WITH ME...
DON'T DIE...
HIS **ARM**...
DAM-MIT! I CAN'T STOP THE BLOOD...
HE'S GOING TO DIE...

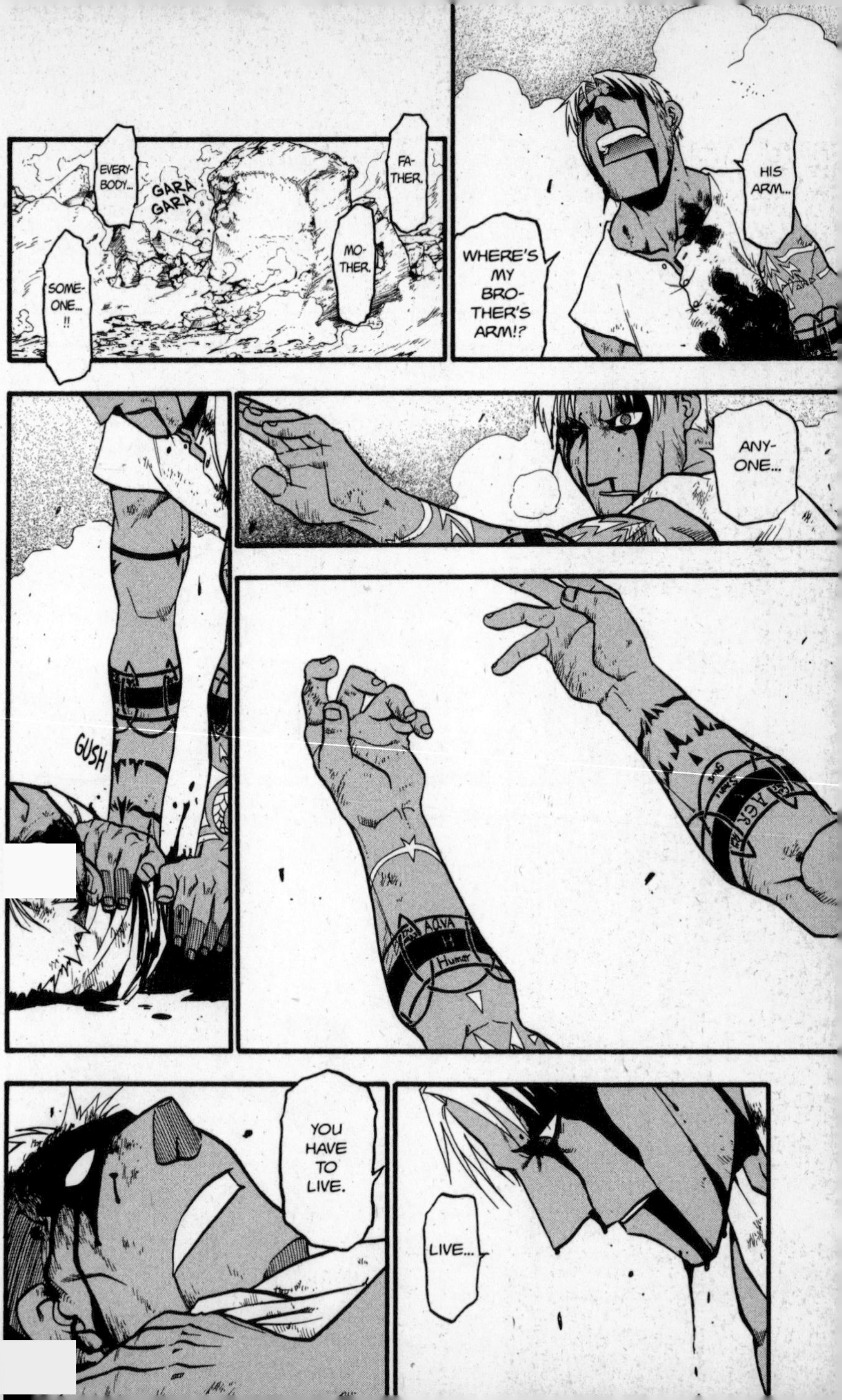
HIS ARM...
WHERE'S MY BRO-THER'S ARM!?
FA-THER.
MO-THER.
EVERY-BODY...
GARA GARA
SOME-ONE... !!
ANY-ONE...
GUSH
LIVE...
YOU HAVE TO LIVE.

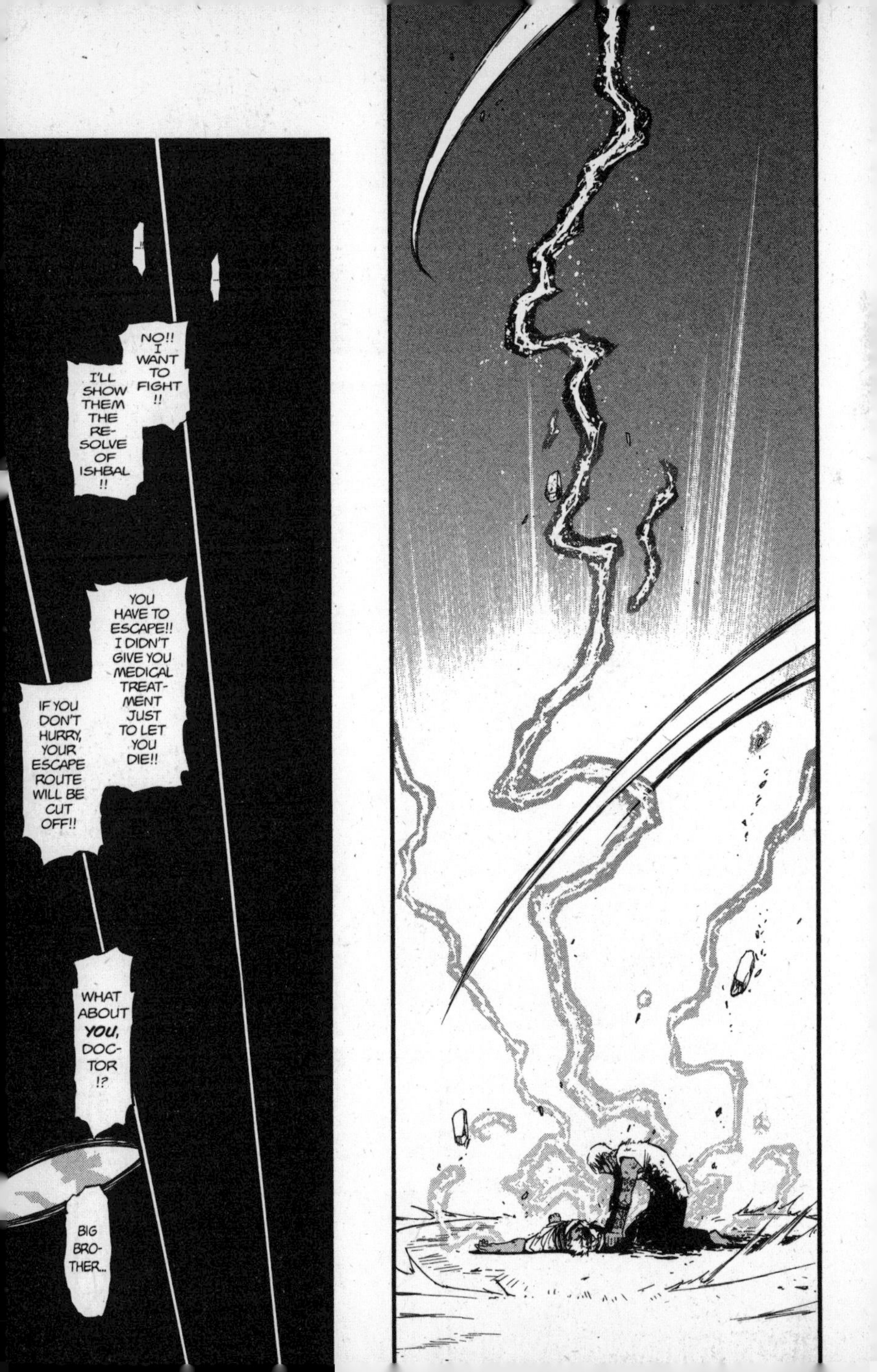
NO!! I WANT TO FIGHT!!
I'LL SHOW THEM THE RESOLVE OF ISHBAL!!
YOU HAVE TO ESCAPE!! I DIDN'T GIVE YOU MEDICAL TREATMENT JUST TO LET YOU DIE!!
IF YOU DON'T HURRY, YOUR ESCAPE ROUTE WILL BE CUT OFF!!
WHAT ABOUT ***YOU***, DOCTOR!?
BIG BROTHER..

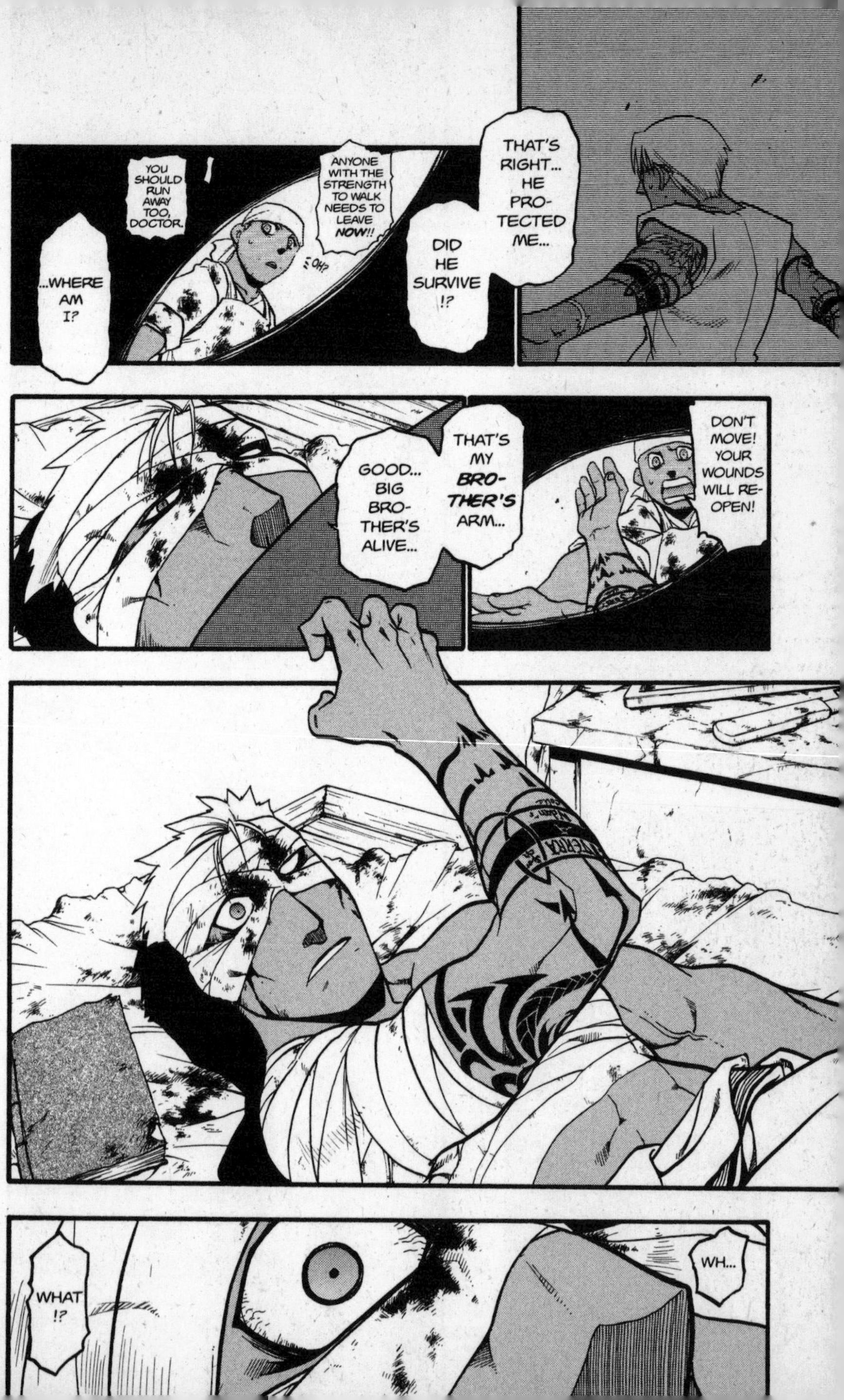
THAT'S RIGHT... HE PROTECTED ME...
DID HE SURVIVE!?
ANYONE WITH THE STRENGTH TO WALK NEEDS TO LEAVE NOW!!
OH?
YOU SHOULD RUN AWAY TOO, DOCTOR.
...WHERE AM I?
DON'T MOVE! YOUR WOUNDS WILL RE-OPEN!
THAT'S MY BROTHER'S ARM...
GOOD... BIG BROTHER'S ALIVE...
WH...
WHAT!?

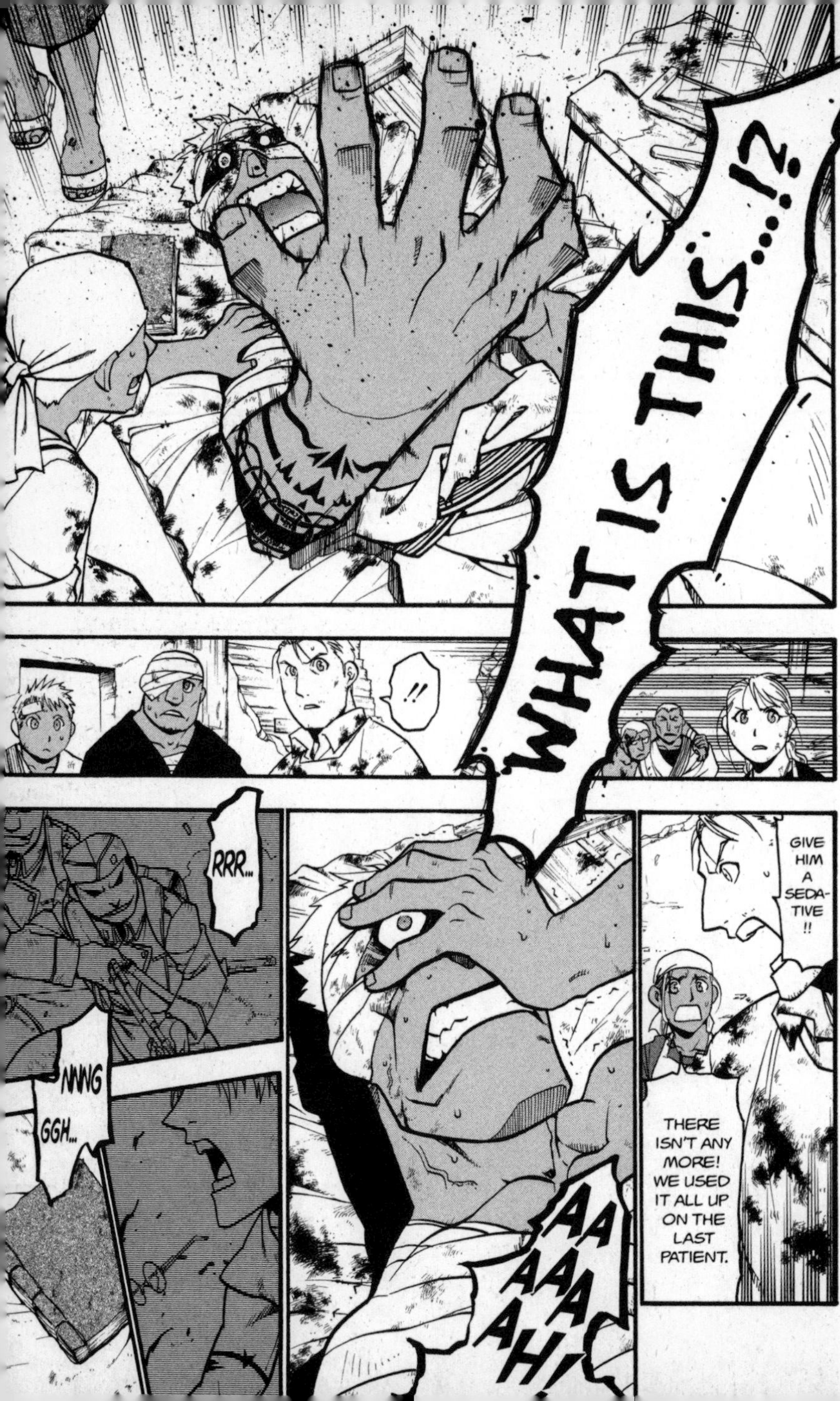
WHAT IS THIS...!?
!!
GIVE HIM A SEDATIVE!!
THERE ISN'T ANY MORE! WE USED IT ALL UP ON THE LAST PATIENT.
AAAAAAAH!
RRR...
NNNGGGH...

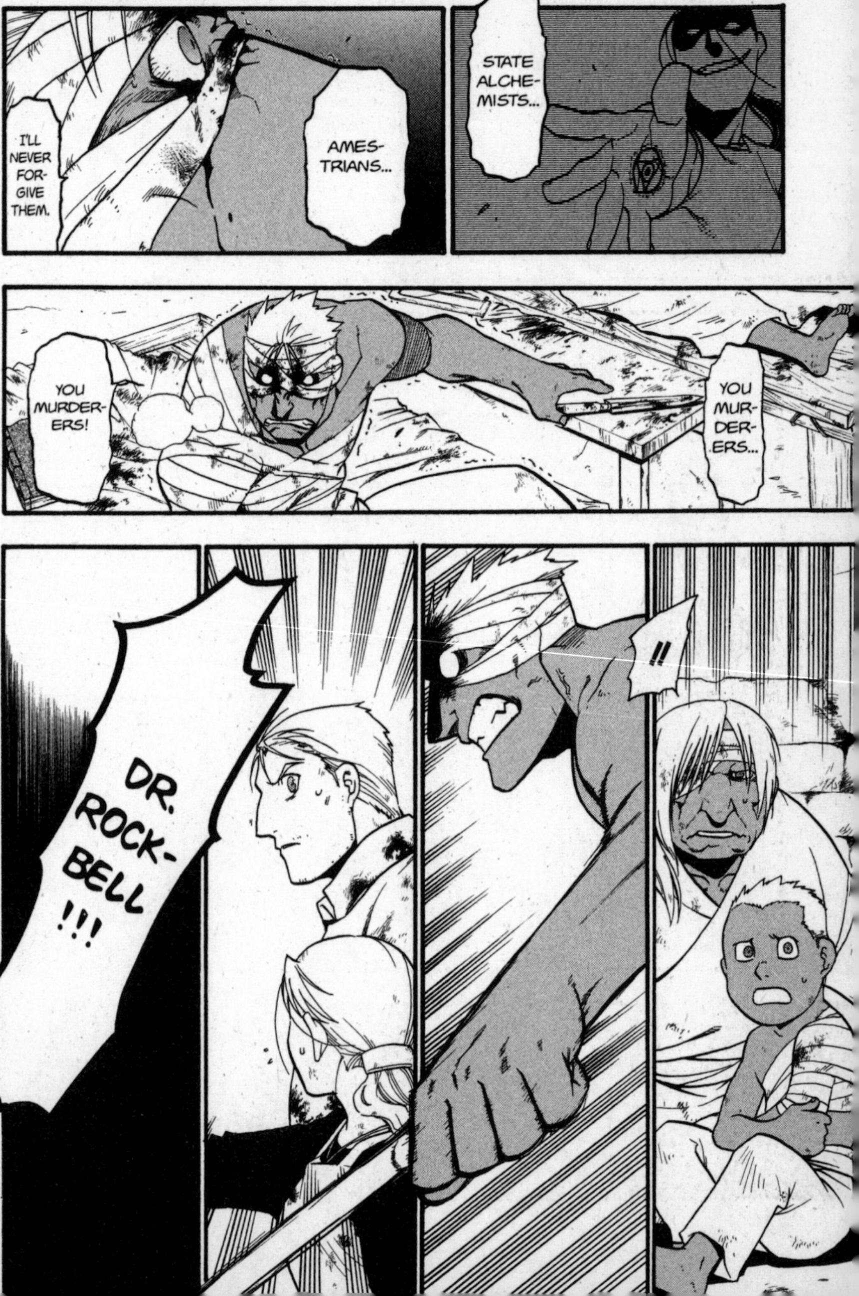
STATE ALCHE-MISTS...
AMES-TRIANS...
I'LL NEVER FOR-GIVE THEM.
YOU MUR-DER-ERS...
YOU MURDER-ERS!
!!
DR. ROCK-BELL !!!

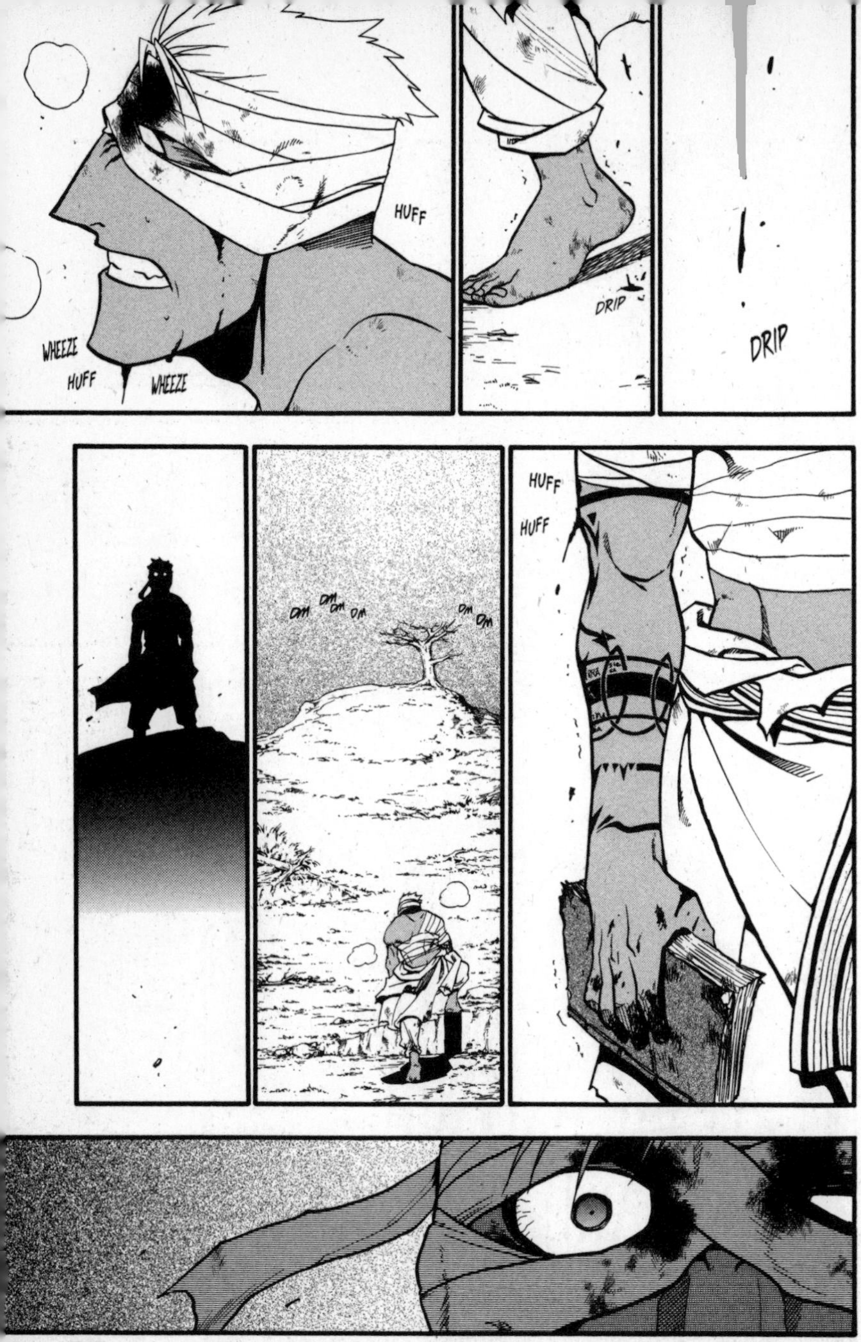
DRIP
DRIP
HUFF
WHEEZE
HUFF
WHEEZE
HUFF
HUFF
DM
DM
DM
DM
DM
DM

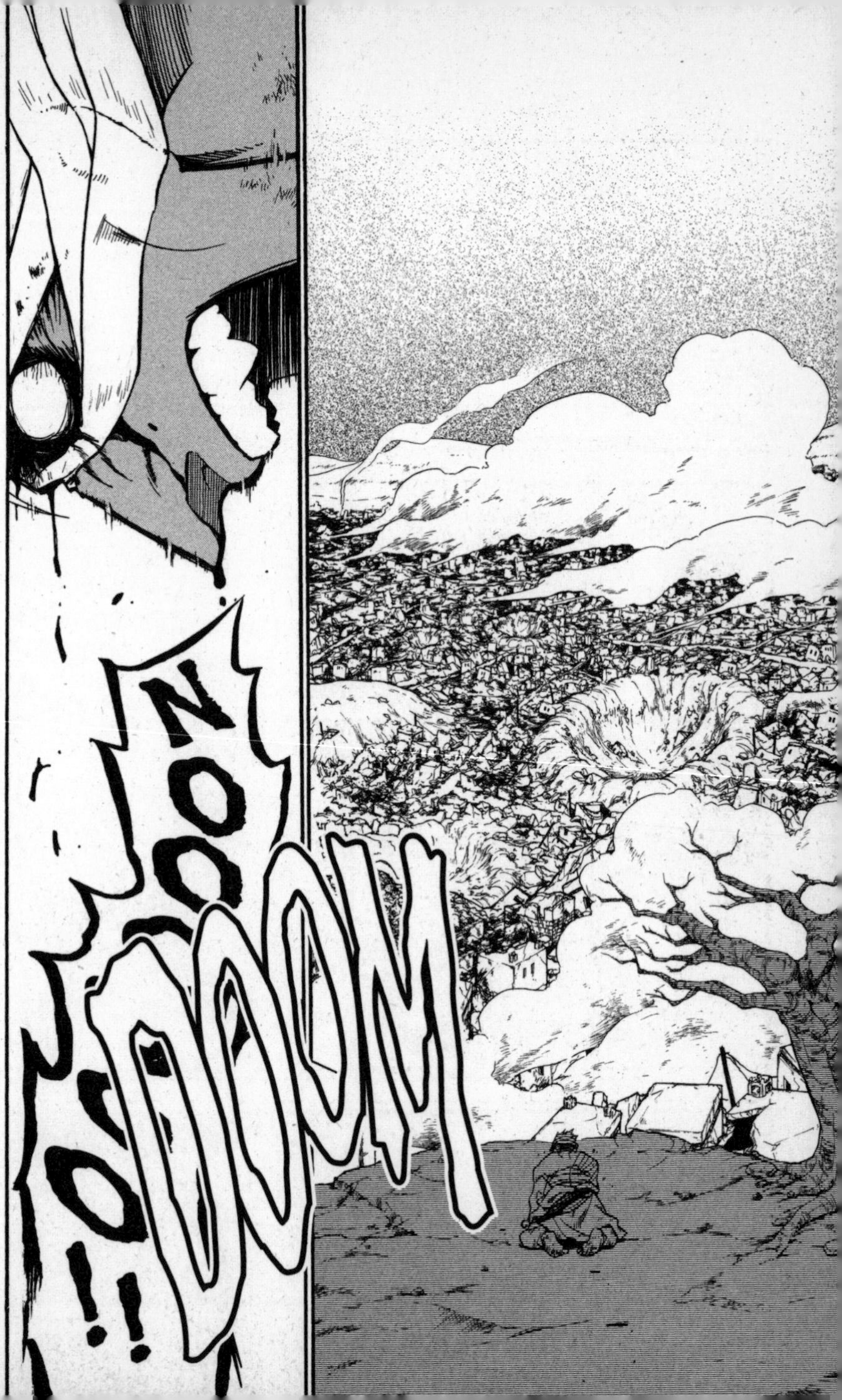
NOOOOO!!
DOOOM

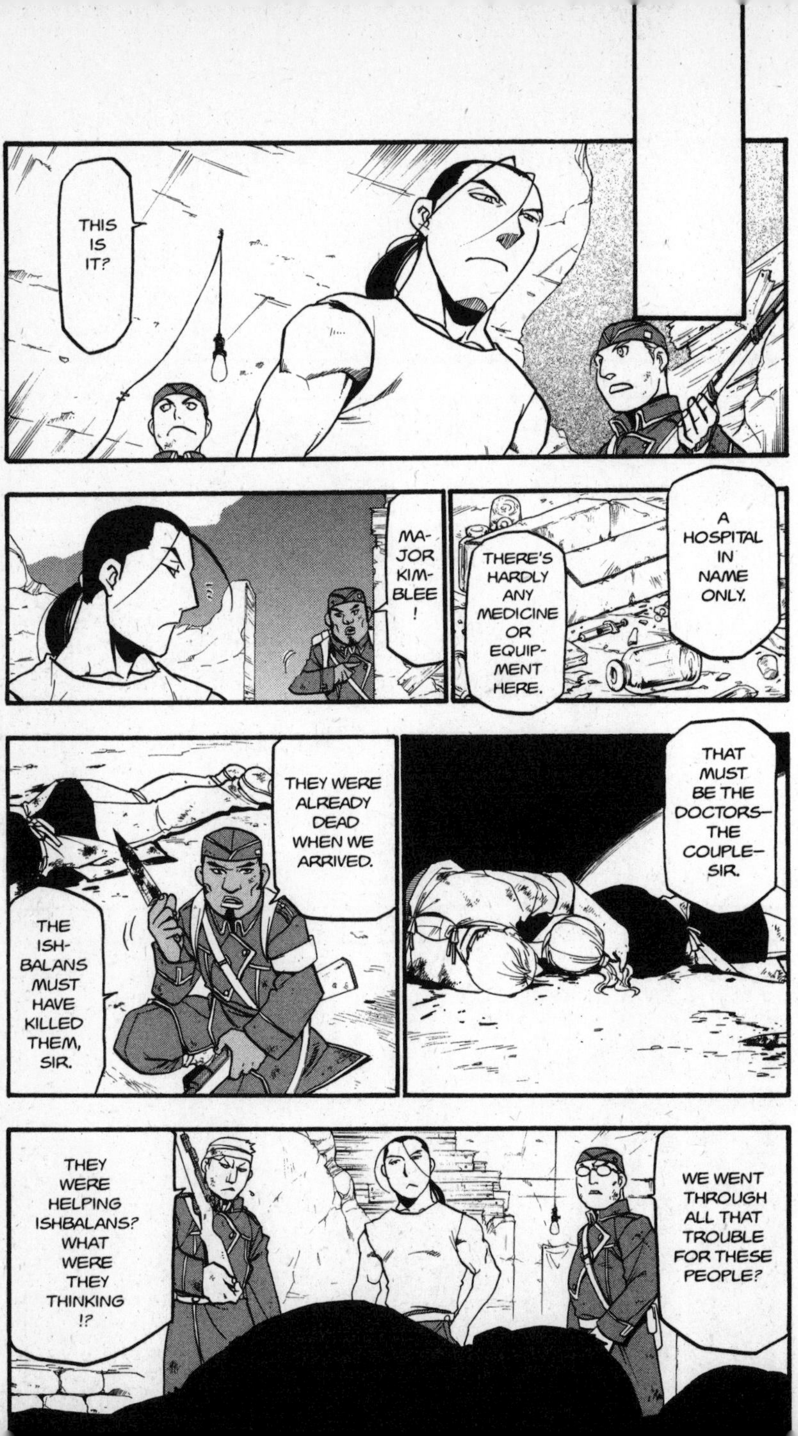
THIS IS IT?
A HOSPITAL IN NAME ONLY.
THERE'S HARDLY ANY MEDICINE OR EQUIPMENT HERE.
MAJOR KIMBLEE!
THAT MUST BE THE DOCTORS—THE COUPLE—SIR.
THEY WERE ALREADY DEAD WHEN WE ARRIVED.
THE ISHBALANS MUST HAVE KILLED THEM, SIR.
WE WENT THROUGH ALL THAT TROUBLE FOR THESE PEOPLE?
THEY WERE HELPING ISHBALANS? WHAT WERE THEY THINKING!?

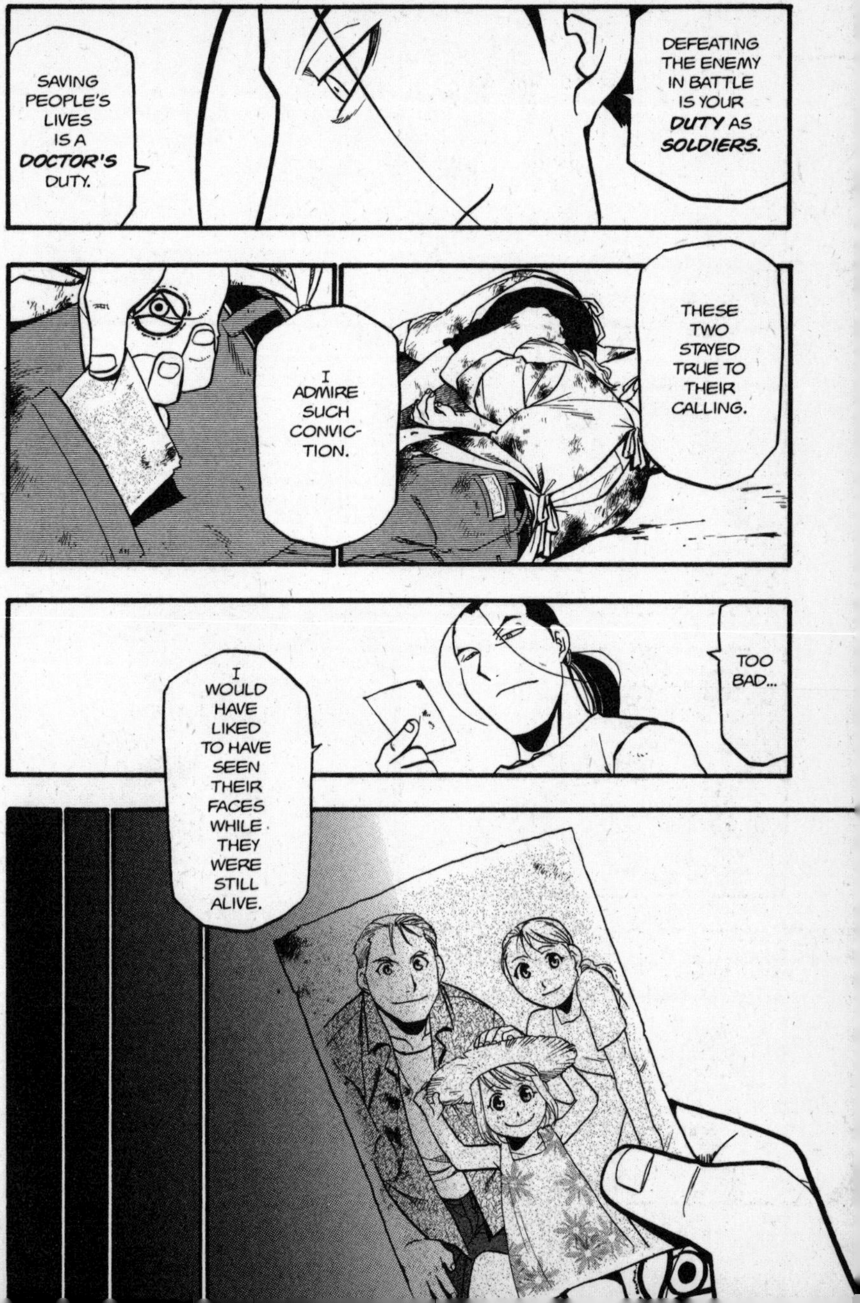
DEFEATING THE ENEMY IN BATTLE IS YOUR **DUTY** AS **SOLDIERS**.
SAVING PEOPLE'S LIVES IS A **DOCTOR'S** DUTY.
THESE TWO STAYED TRUE TO THEIR CALLING.
I ADMIRE SUCH CONVICTION.
TOO BAD...
I WOULD HAVE LIKED TO HAVE SEEN THEIR FACES WHILE THEY WERE STILL ALIVE.

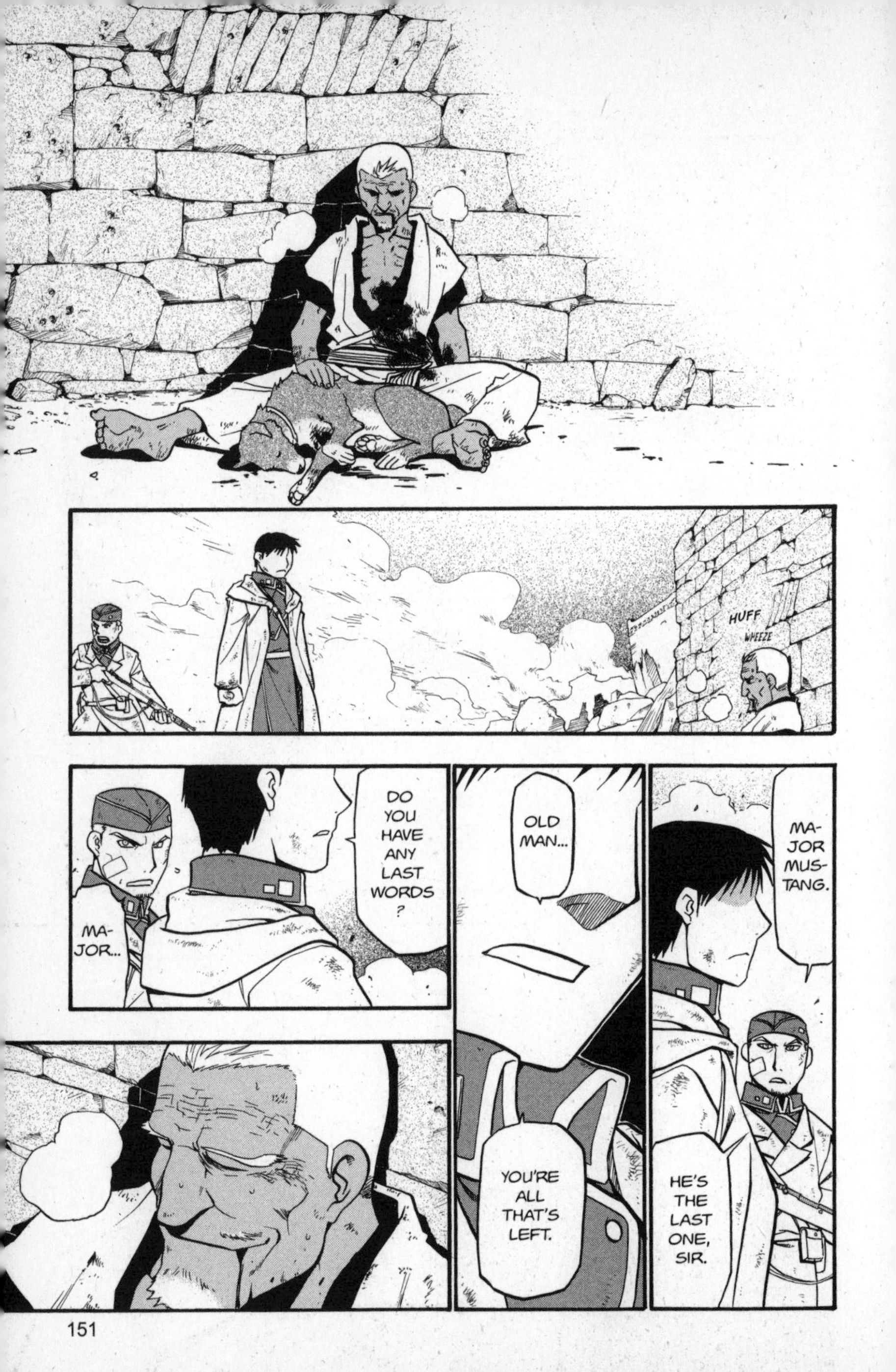
HUFF
WHEEZE
MAJOR MUSTANG.
HE'S THE LAST ONE, SIR.
OLD MAN...
YOU'RE ALL THAT'S LEFT.
DO YOU HAVE ANY LAST WORDS?
MAJOR...

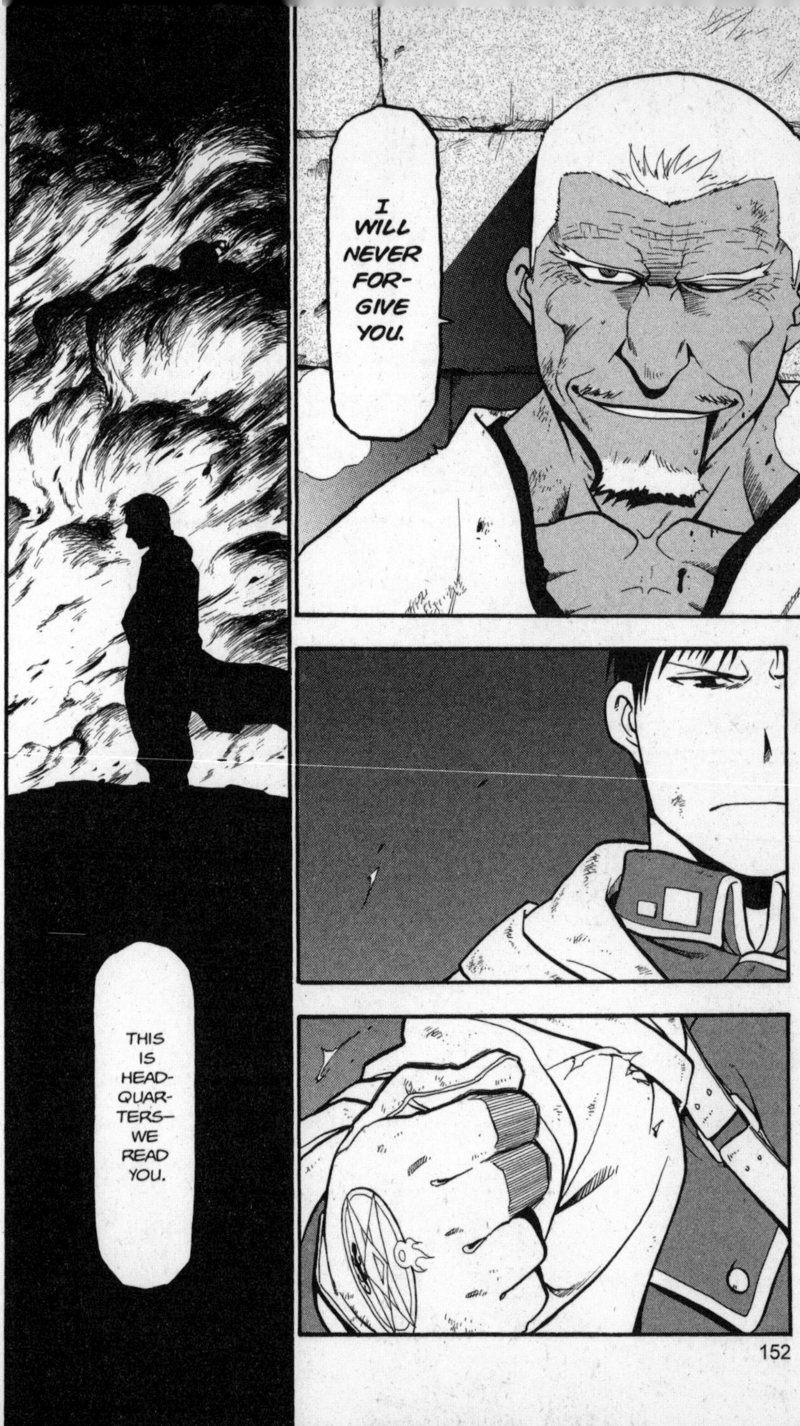
I WILL NEVER FORGIVE YOU.
THIS IS HEADQUARTERS—WE READ YOU.

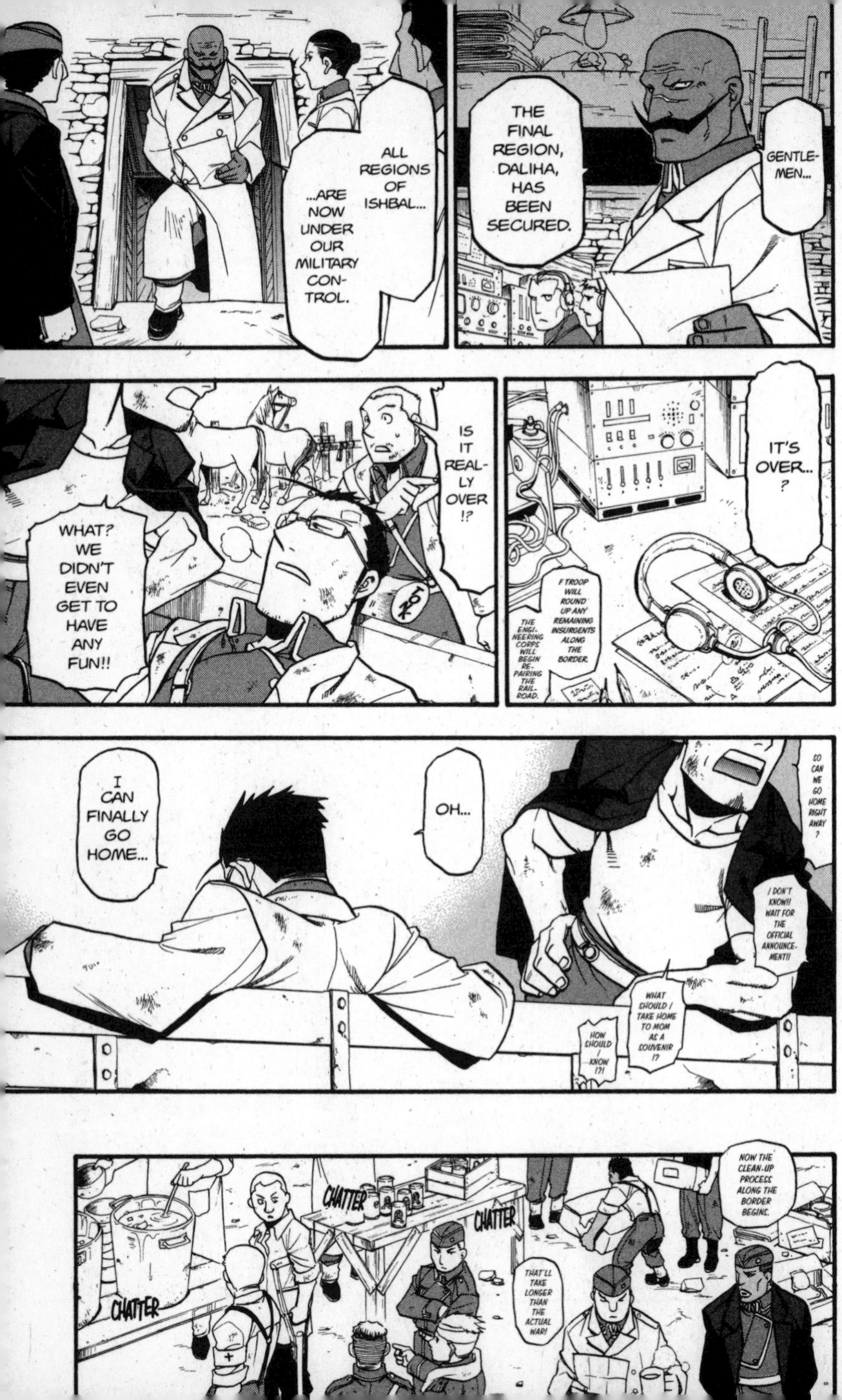
GENTLEMEN...
THE FINAL REGION, DALIHA, HAS BEEN SECURED.
ALL REGIONS OF ISHBAL...
...ARE NOW UNDER OUR MILITARY CONTROL.
IT'S OVER...?
F TROOP WILL ROUND UP ANY REMAINING INSURGENTS ALONG THE BORDER.
THE ENGINEERING CORPS WILL BEGIN REPAIRING THE RAILROAD.
IS IT REALLY OVER!?
TOK
WHAT? WE DIDN'T EVEN GET TO HAVE ANY FUN!!
SO CAN WE GO HOME RIGHT AWAY?
I DON'T KNOW!! WAIT FOR THE OFFICIAL ANNOUNCEMENT!!
WHAT SHOULD I TAKE HOME TO MOM AS A SOUVENIR!?
HOW SHOULD I KNOW!?!
OH...
I CAN FINALLY GO HOME...
NOW THE CLEAN-UP PROCESS ALONG THE BORDER BEGINS.
CHATTER
THAT'LL TAKE LONGER THAN THE ACTUAL WAR!
CHATTER
CHATTER

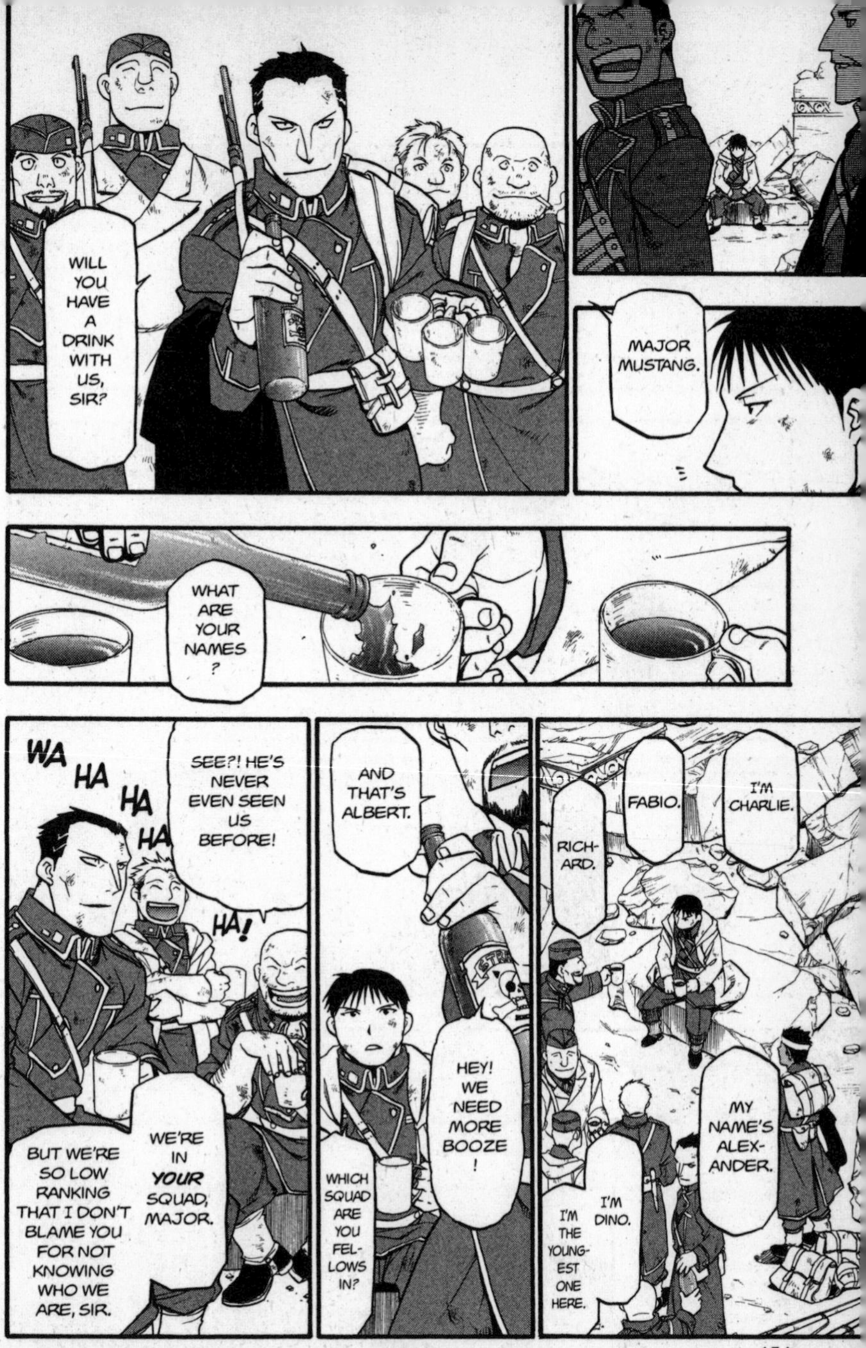
MAJOR MUSTANG.
WILL YOU HAVE A DRINK WITH US, SIR?
WHAT ARE YOUR NAMES?
I'M CHARLIE.
FABIO.
RICHARD.
MY NAME'S ALEXANDER.
I'M DINO.
I'M THE YOUNGEST ONE HERE.
AND THAT'S ALBERT.
HEY! WE NEED MORE BOOZE!
WHICH SQUAD ARE YOU FELLOWS IN?
SEE?! HE'S NEVER EVEN SEEN US BEFORE!
WA HA HA HA HA!
WE'RE IN *YOUR* SQUAD, MAJOR.
BUT WE'RE SO LOW RANKING THAT I DON'T BLAME YOU FOR NOT KNOWING WHO WE ARE, SIR.

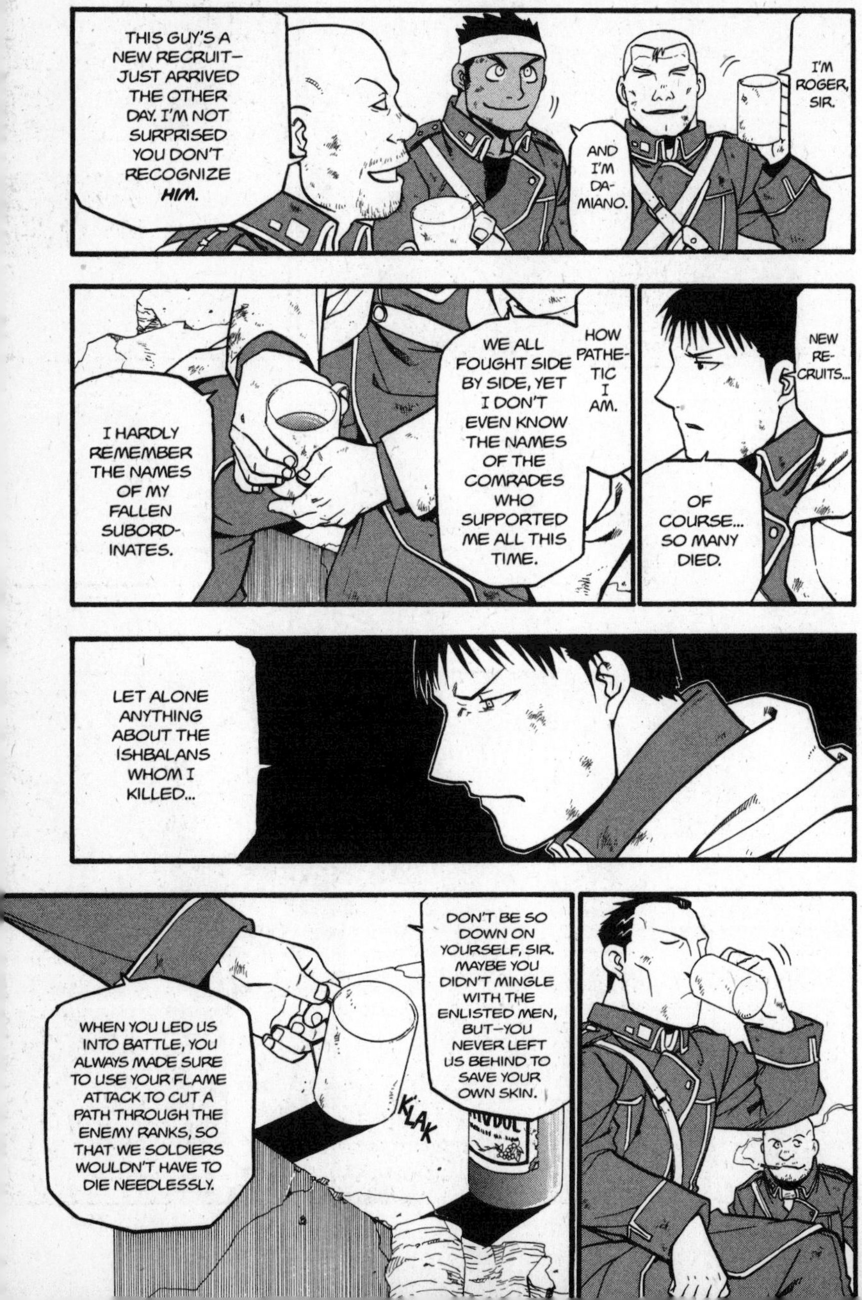
I'M ROGER, SIR.
AND I'M DAMIANO.
THIS GUY'S A NEW RECRUIT—JUST ARRIVED THE OTHER DAY. I'M NOT SURPRISED YOU DON'T RECOGNIZE ***HIM.***
NEW RECRUITS...
OF COURSE... SO MANY DIED.
HOW PATHETIC I AM.
WE ALL FOUGHT SIDE BY SIDE, YET I DON'T EVEN KNOW THE NAMES OF THE COMRADES WHO SUPPORTED ME ALL THIS TIME.
I HARDLY REMEMBER THE NAMES OF MY FALLEN SUBORDINATES.
LET ALONE ANYTHING ABOUT THE ISHBALANS WHOM I KILLED...
DON'T BE SO DOWN ON YOURSELF, SIR. MAYBE YOU DIDN'T MINGLE WITH THE ENLISTED MEN, BUT—YOU NEVER LEFT US BEHIND TO SAVE YOUR OWN SKIN.
KLAK
WHEN YOU LED US INTO BATTLE, YOU ALWAYS MADE SURE TO USE YOUR FLAME ATTACK TO CUT A PATH THROUGH THE ENEMY RANKS, SO THAT WE SOLDIERS WOULDN'T HAVE TO DIE NEEDLESSLY.

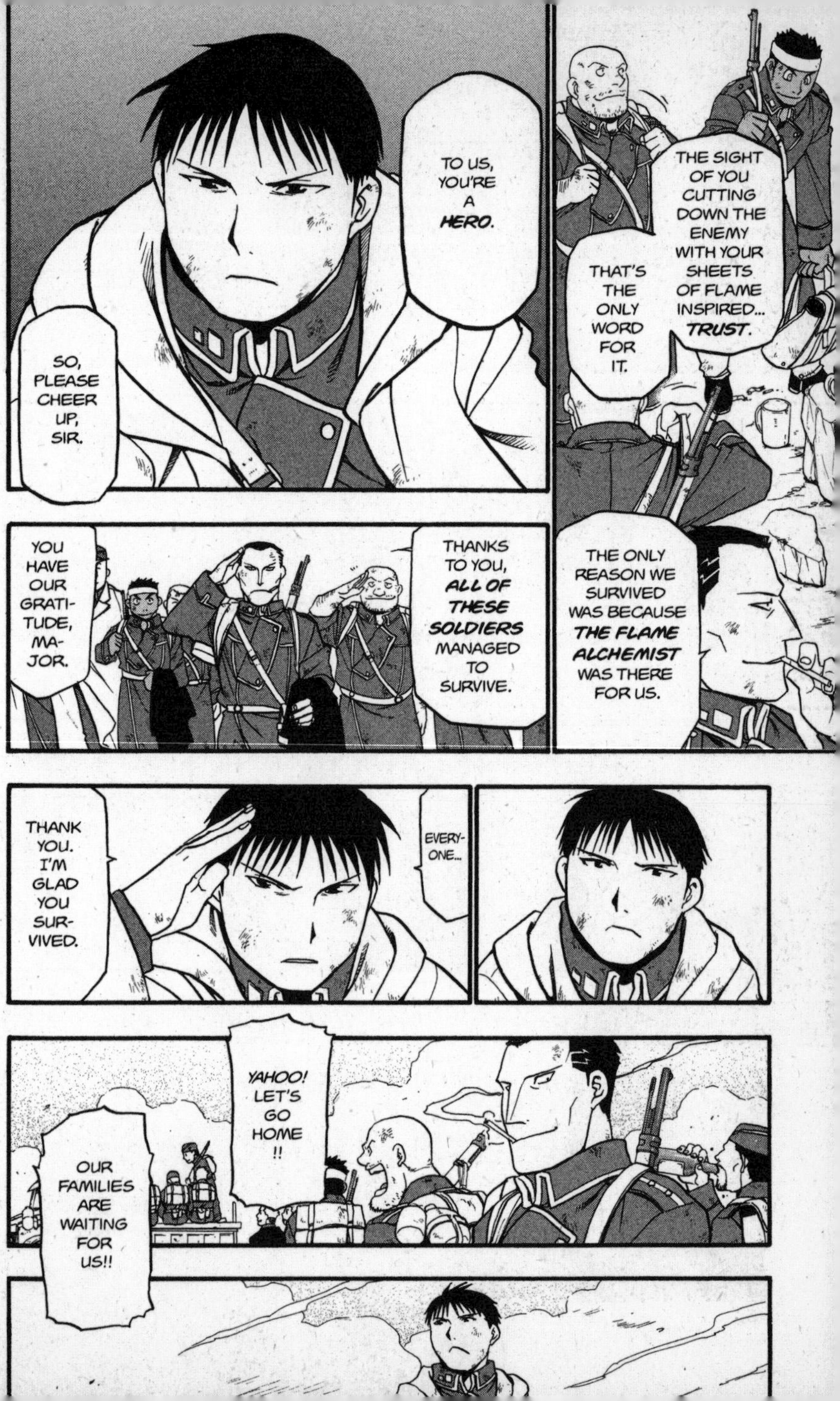
THE SIGHT OF YOU CUTTING DOWN THE ENEMY WITH YOUR SHEETS OF FLAME INSPIRED... TRUST.
THAT'S THE ONLY WORD FOR IT.
THE ONLY REASON WE SURVIVED WAS BECAUSE THE FLAME ALCHEMIST WAS THERE FOR US.
TO US, YOU'RE A HERO.
SO, PLEASE CHEER UP, SIR.
THANKS TO YOU, ALL OF THESE SOLDIERS MANAGED TO SURVIVE.
YOU HAVE OUR GRATITUDE, MAJOR.
EVERY-ONE...
THANK YOU. I'M GLAD YOU SURVIVED.
YAHOO! LET'S GO HOME!!
OUR FAMILIES ARE WAITING FOR US!!

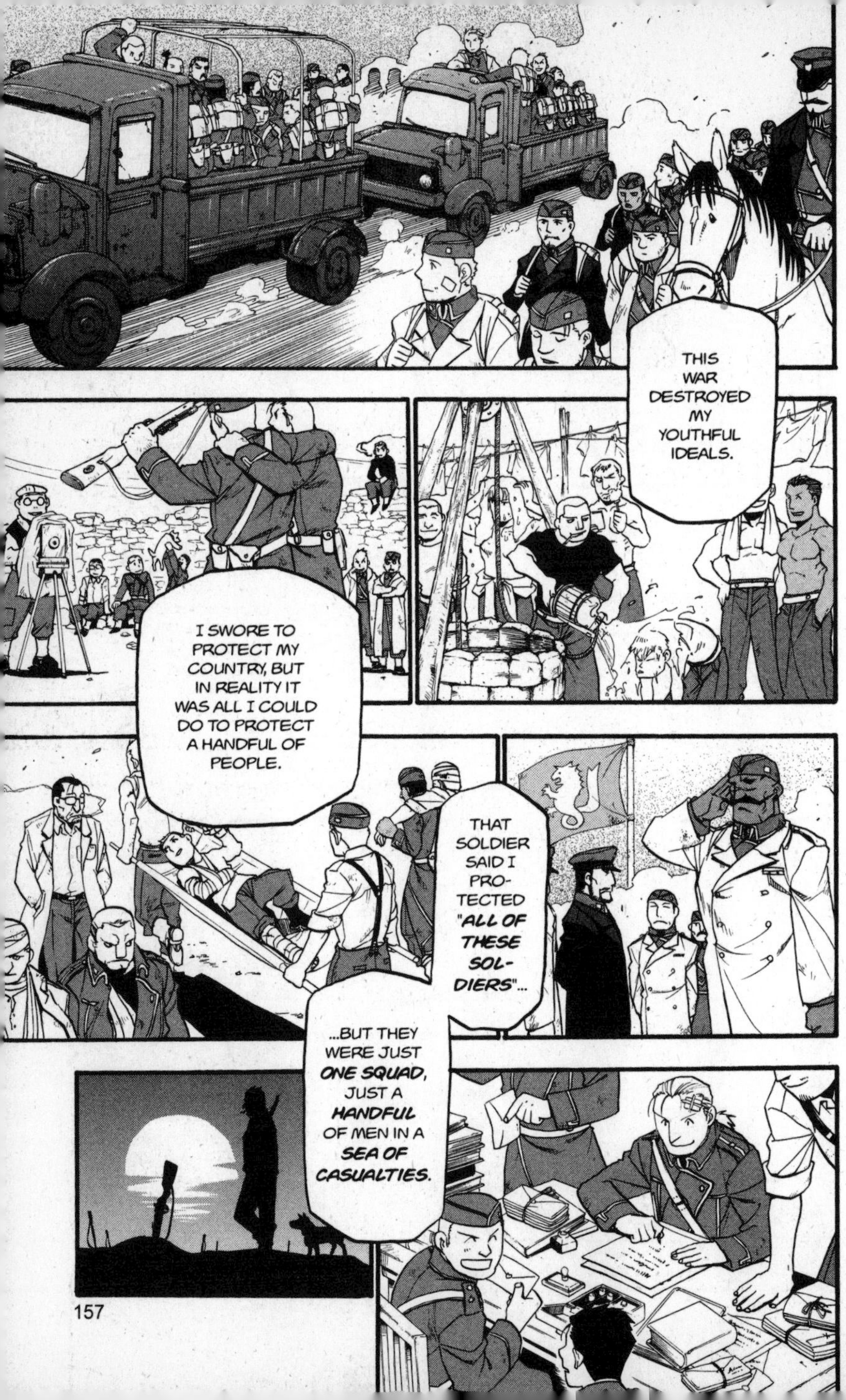
THIS WAR DESTROYED MY YOUTHFUL IDEALS.
I SWORE TO PROTECT MY COUNTRY, BUT IN REALITY IT WAS ALL I COULD DO TO PROTECT A HANDFUL OF PEOPLE.
THAT SOLDIER SAID I PRO-TECTED "ALL OF THESE SOL-DIERS"...
...BUT THEY WERE JUST ONE SQUAD, JUST A HANDFUL OF MEN IN A SEA OF CASUALTIES.

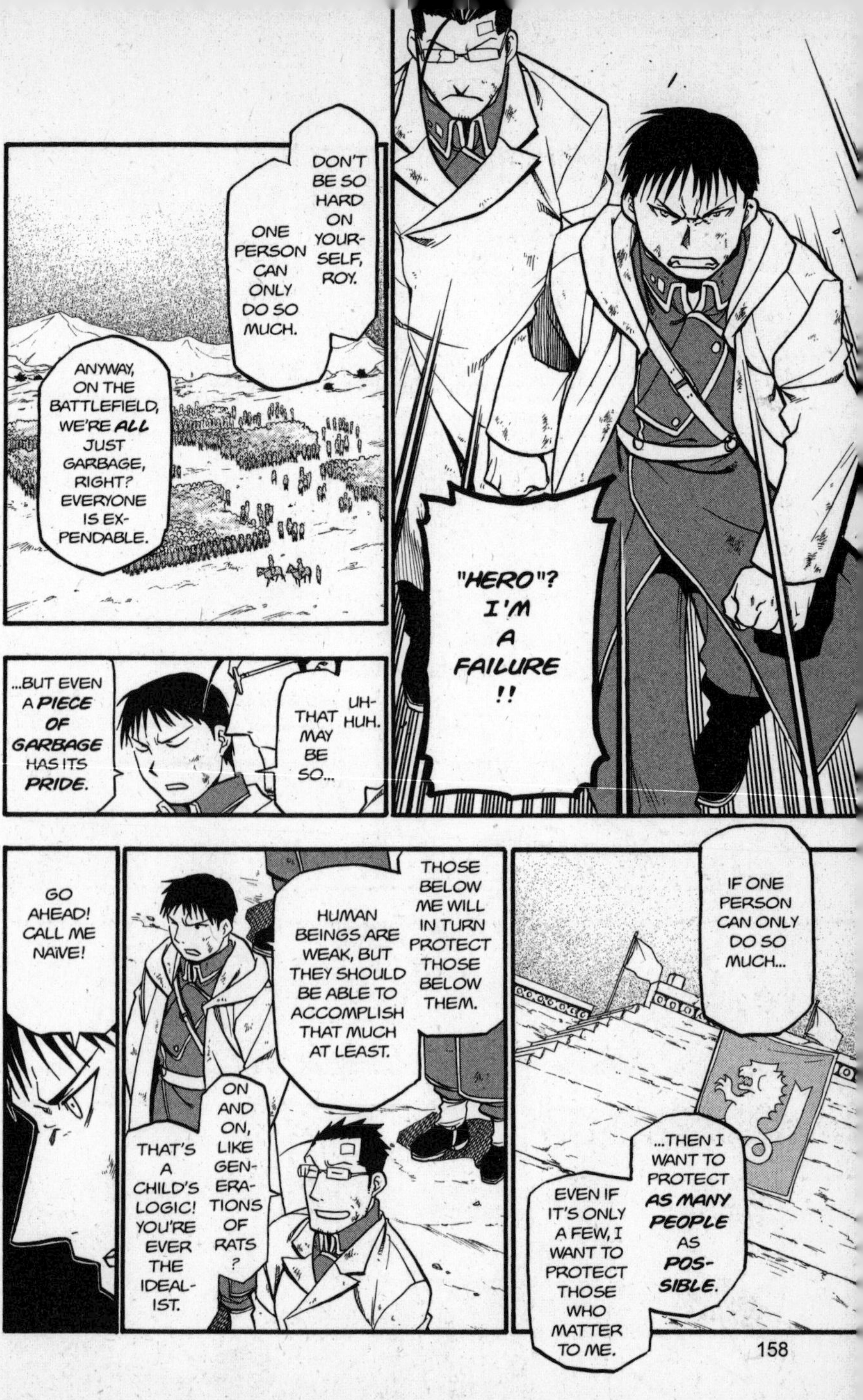
"HERO"? I'M A FAILURE!!
DON'T BE SO HARD ON YOURSELF, ROY.
ONE PERSON CAN ONLY DO SO MUCH.
ANYWAY, ON THE BATTLEFIELD, WE'RE ALL JUST GARBAGE, RIGHT? EVERYONE IS EXPENDABLE.
UH-HUH.
THAT MAY BE SO...
...BUT EVEN A PIECE OF GARBAGE HAS ITS PRIDE.
IF ONE PERSON CAN ONLY DO SO MUCH...
...THEN I WANT TO PROTECT AS MANY PEOPLE AS POSSIBLE.
EVEN IF IT'S ONLY A FEW, I WANT TO PROTECT THOSE WHO MATTER TO ME.
THOSE BELOW ME WILL IN TURN PROTECT THOSE BELOW THEM.
HUMAN BEINGS ARE WEAK, BUT THEY SHOULD BE ABLE TO ACCOMPLISH THAT MUCH AT LEAST.
ON AND ON, LIKE GENERATIONS OF RATS?
THAT'S A CHILD'S LOGIC! YOU'RE EVER THE IDEALIST.
GO AHEAD! CALL ME NAIVE!

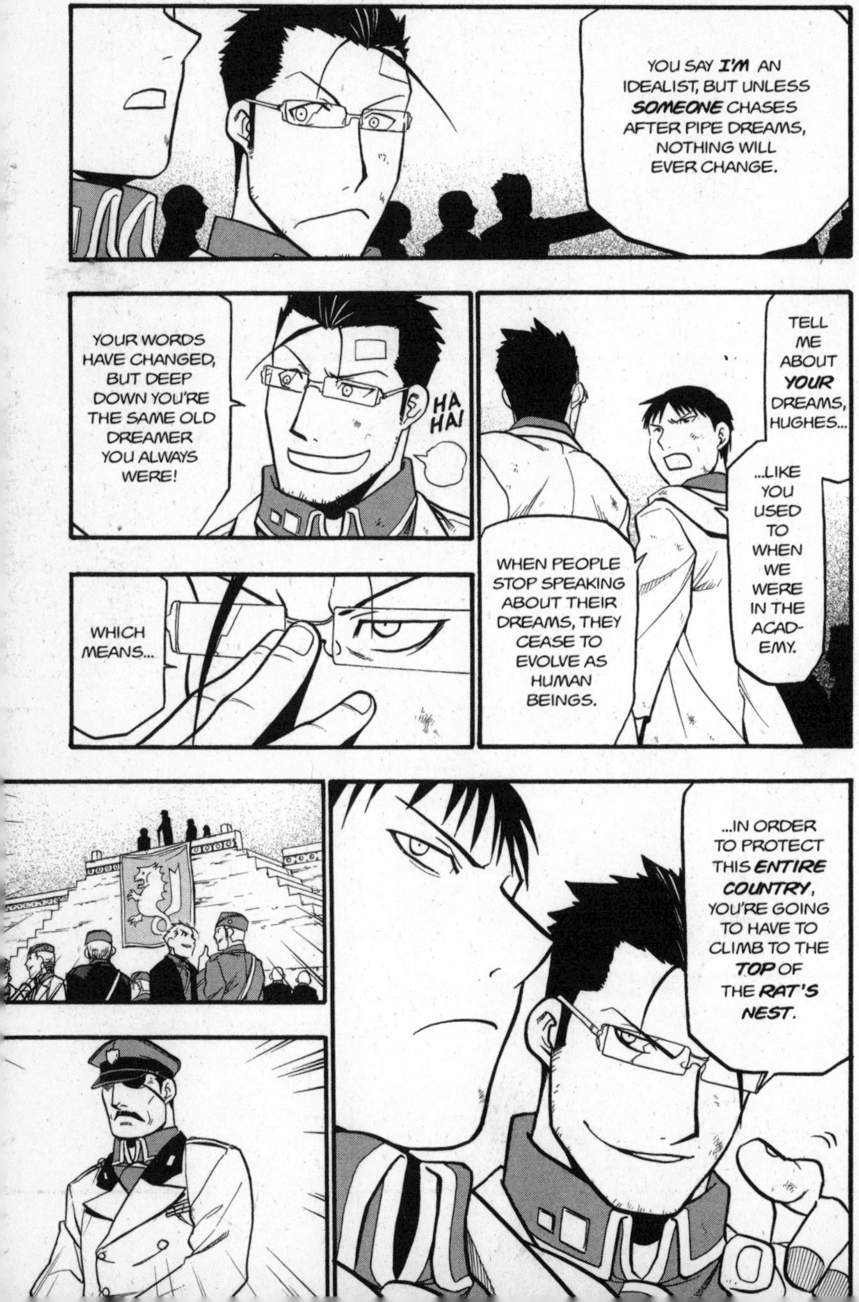
YOU SAY I'M AN IDEALIST, BUT UNLESS SOMEONE CHASES AFTER PIPE DREAMS, NOTHING WILL EVER CHANGE.
TELL ME ABOUT YOUR DREAMS, HUGHES...
...LIKE YOU USED TO WHEN WE WERE IN THE ACAD-EMY.
WHEN PEOPLE STOP SPEAKING ABOUT THEIR DREAMS, THEY CEASE TO EVOLVE AS HUMAN BEINGS.
YOUR WORDS HAVE CHANGED, BUT DEEP DOWN YOU'RE THE SAME OLD DREAMER YOU ALWAYS WERE!
HA HA!
WHICH MEANS...
...IN ORDER TO PROTECT THIS ENTIRE COUNTRY, YOU'RE GOING TO HAVE TO CLIMB TO THE TOP OF THE RAT'S NEST.

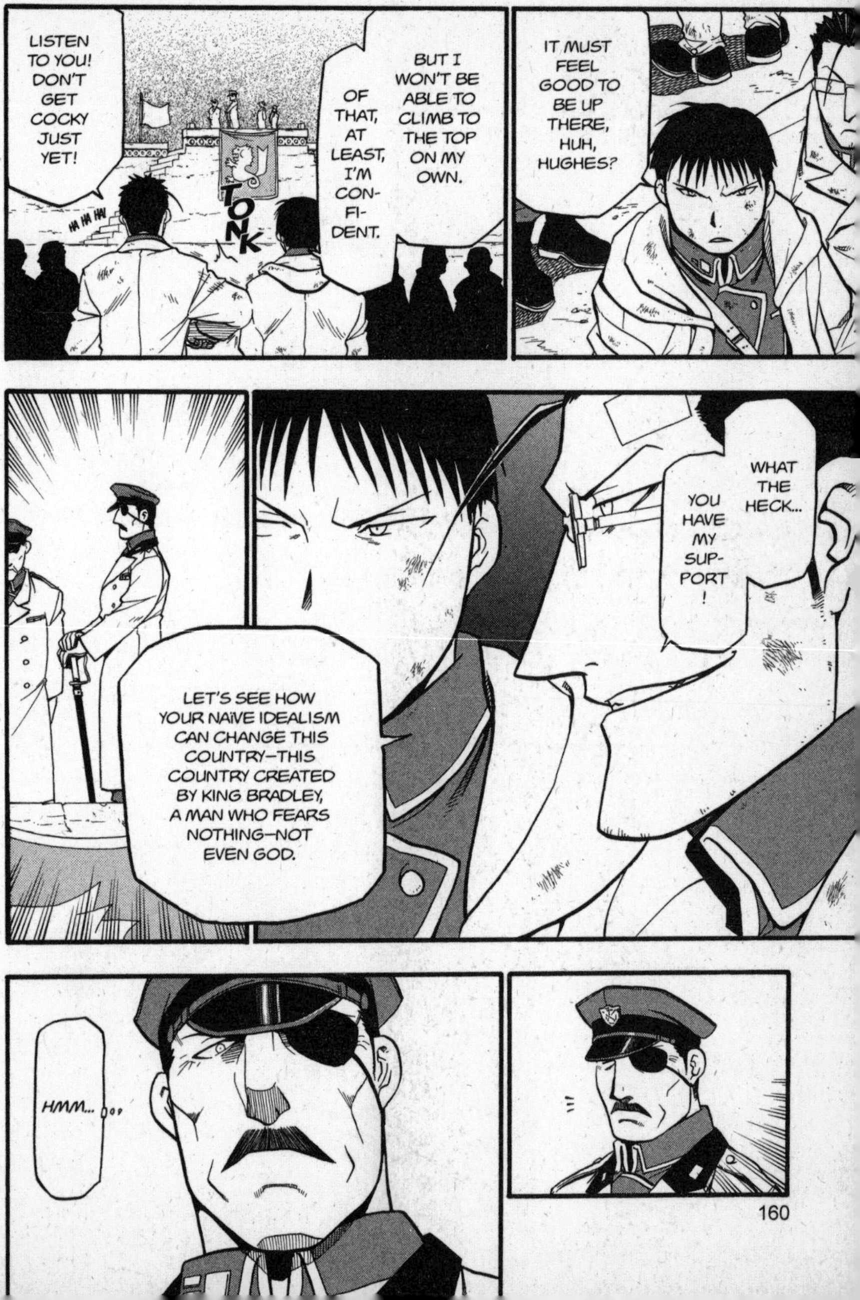
IT MUST FEEL GOOD TO BE UP THERE, HUH, HUGHES?
BUT I WON'T BE ABLE TO CLIMB TO THE TOP ON MY OWN.
OF THAT, AT LEAST, I'M CON-FI-DENT.
TONK
LISTEN TO YOU! DON'T GET COCKY JUST YET!
HA HA HA!
WHAT THE HECK...
YOU HAVE MY SUP-PORT!
LET'S SEE HOW YOUR NAÏVE IDEALISM CAN CHANGE THIS COUNTRY—THIS COUNTRY CREATED BY KING BRADLEY, A MAN WHO FEARS NOTHING—NOT EVEN GOD.
HMM...

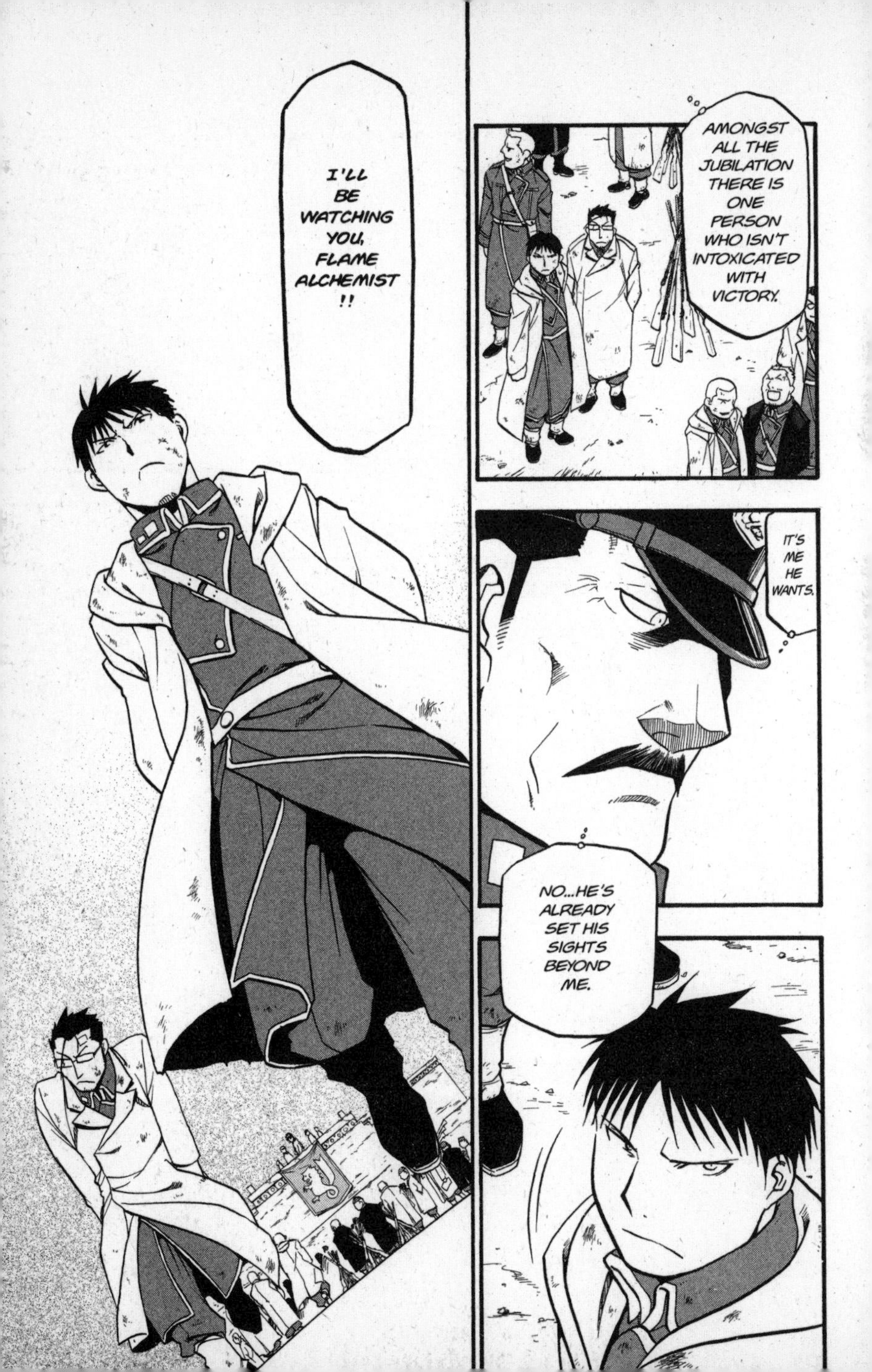
AMONGST ALL THE JUBILATION THERE IS ONE PERSON WHO ISN'T INTOXICATED WITH VICTORY.
IT'S ME HE WANTS.
NO...HE'S ALREADY SET HIS SIGHTS BEYOND ME.
I'LL BE WATCHING YOU, FLAME ALCHEMIST!!

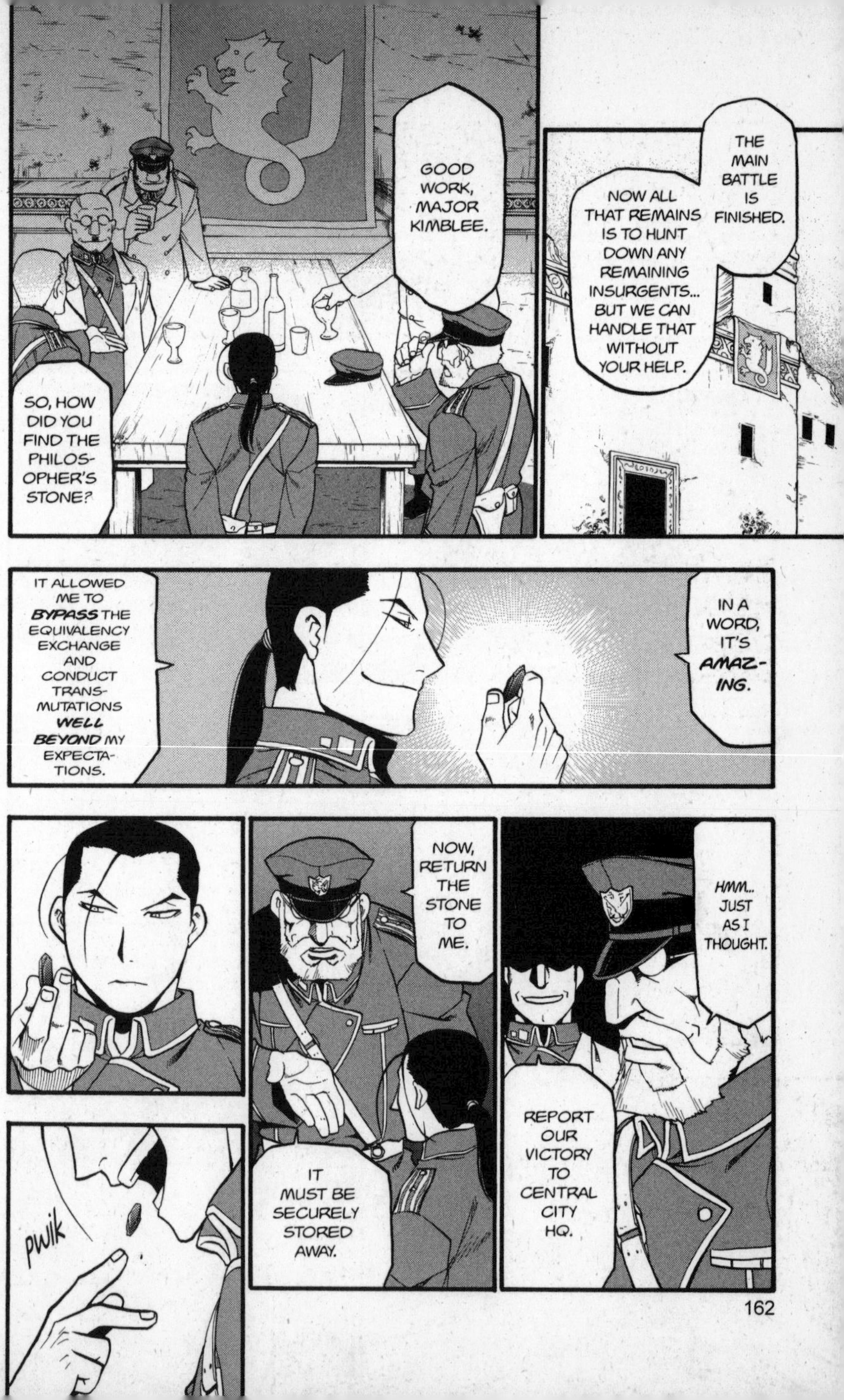
THE MAIN BATTLE IS FINISHED.
NOW ALL THAT REMAINS IS TO HUNT DOWN ANY REMAINING INSURGENTS... BUT WE CAN HANDLE THAT WITHOUT YOUR HELP.
GOOD WORK, MAJOR KIMBLEE.
SO, HOW DID YOU FIND THE PHILOSOPHER'S STONE?
IN A WORD, IT'S **AMAZING.**
IT ALLOWED ME TO **BYPASS** THE EQUIVALENCY EXCHANGE AND CONDUCT TRANSMUTATIONS **WELL BEYOND** MY EXPECTATIONS.
HMM.. JUST AS I THOUGHT.
REPORT OUR VICTORY TO CENTRAL CITY HQ.
NOW, RETURN THE STONE TO ME.
IT MUST BE SECURELY STORED AWAY.
pwik

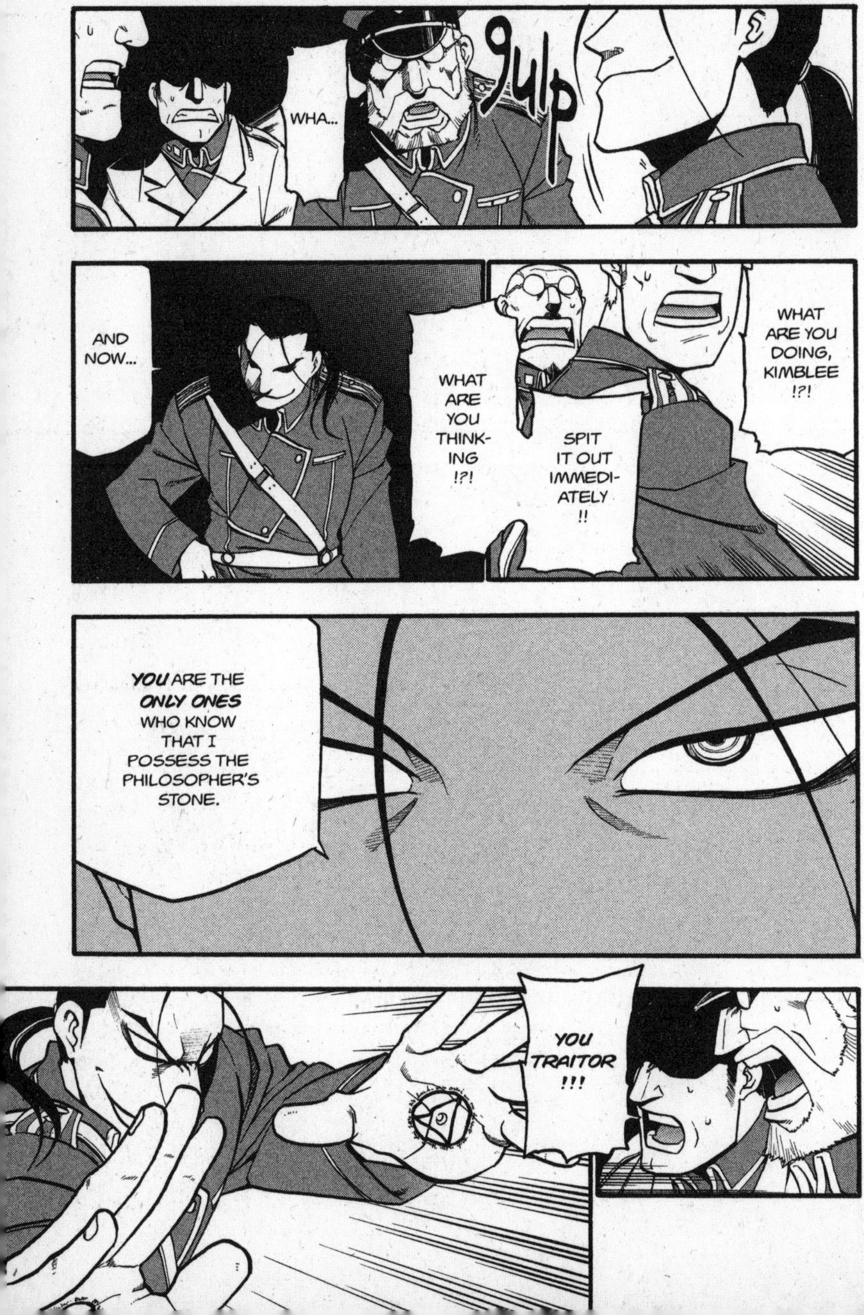
gulp
WHA...
WHAT ARE YOU DOING, KIMBLEE !?!
SPIT IT OUT IMMEDIATELY !!
WHAT ARE YOU THINKING !?!
AND NOW...
YOU ARE THE ONLY ONES WHO KNOW THAT I POSSESS THE PHILOSOPHER'S STONE.
YOU TRAITOR !!!

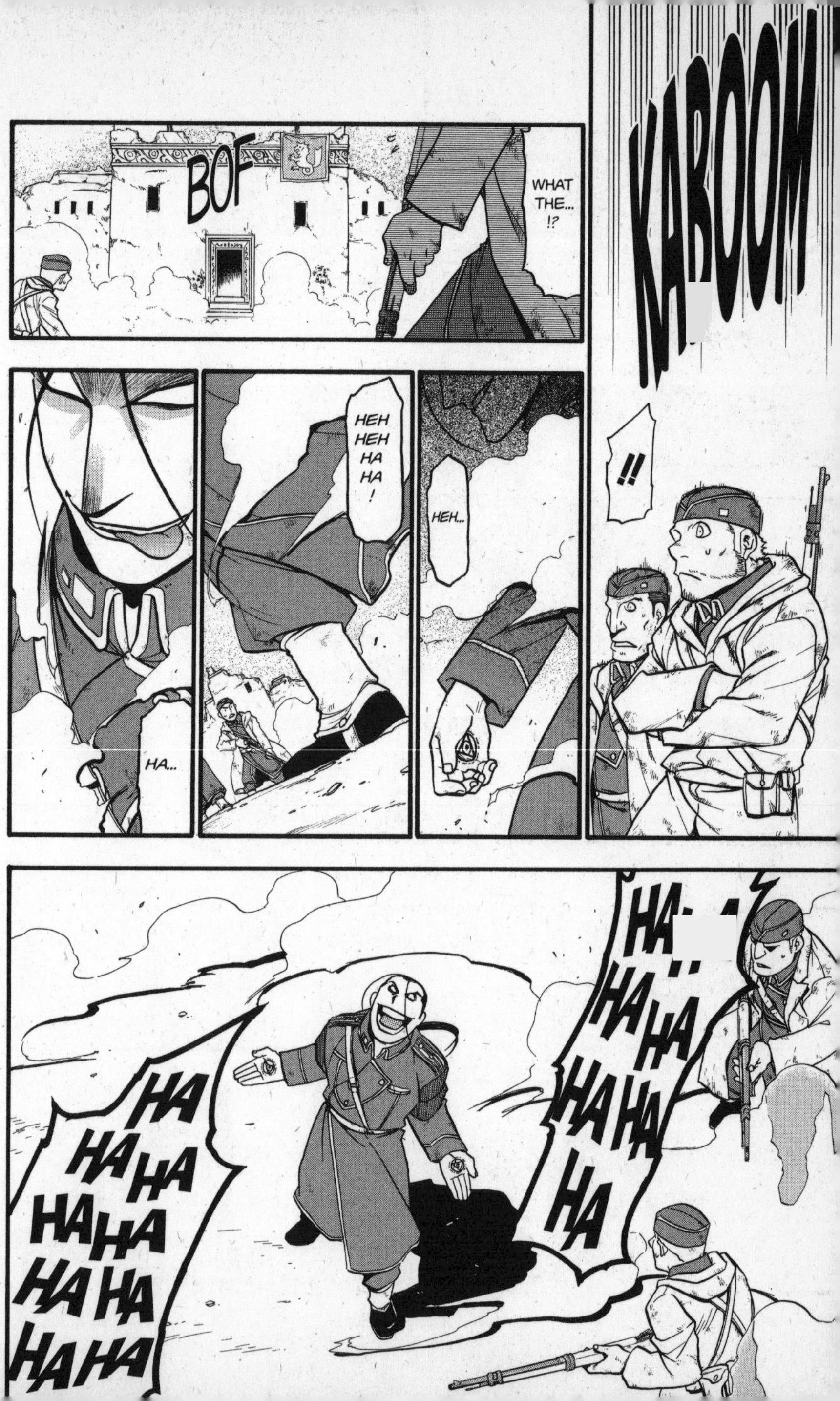
KABOOM
!!
BOF
WHAT THE... !?
HEH...
HEH HEH HA HA!
HA...
HA HA HA HA HA HA HA HA HA HA
HA HA HA HA HA HA HA HA HA HA HA

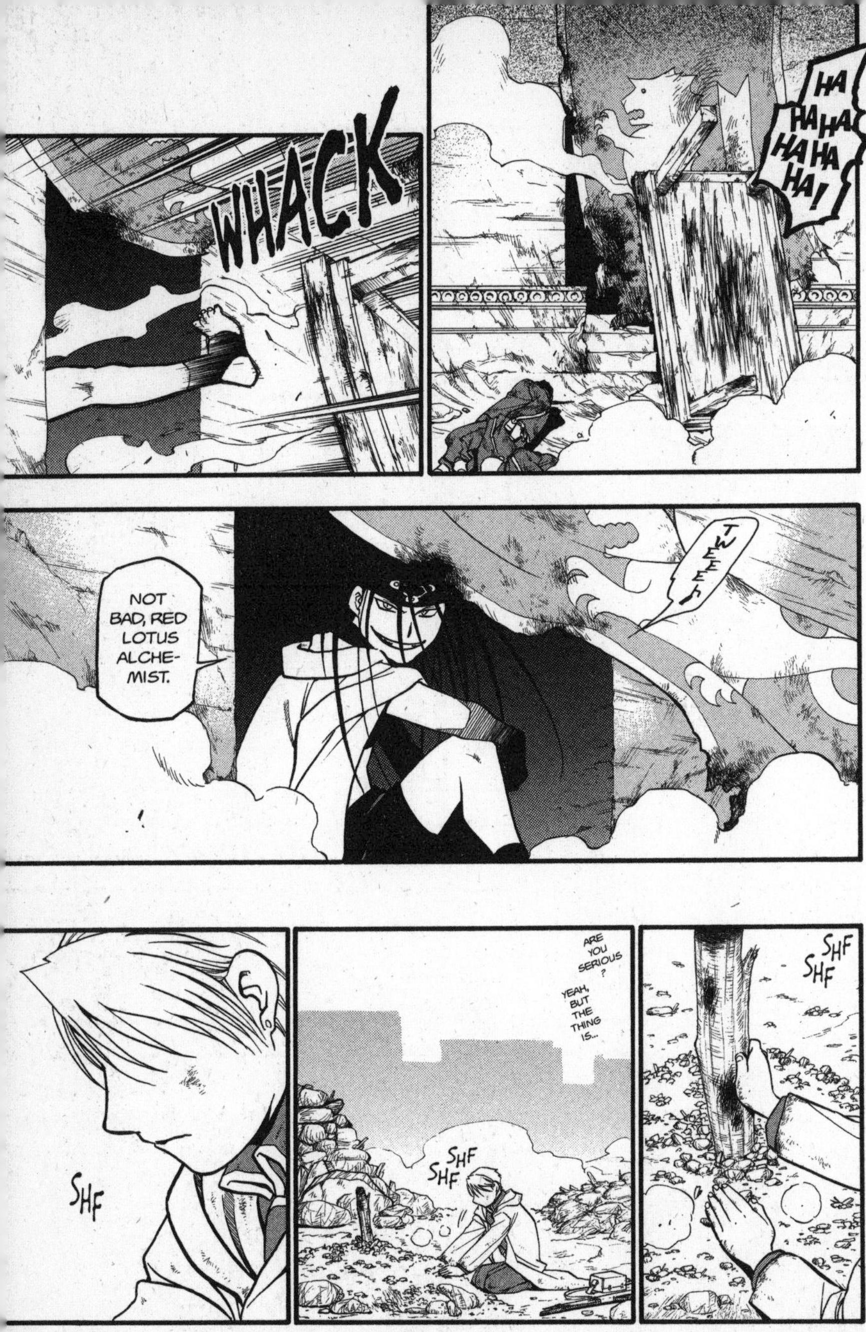
HA HA HA HA HA HA HA!
WHACK
TWEEE
NOT BAD, RED LOTUS ALCHEMIST.
SHF SHF
ARE YOU SERIOUS?
YEAH, BUT THE THING IS...
SHF SHF
SHF

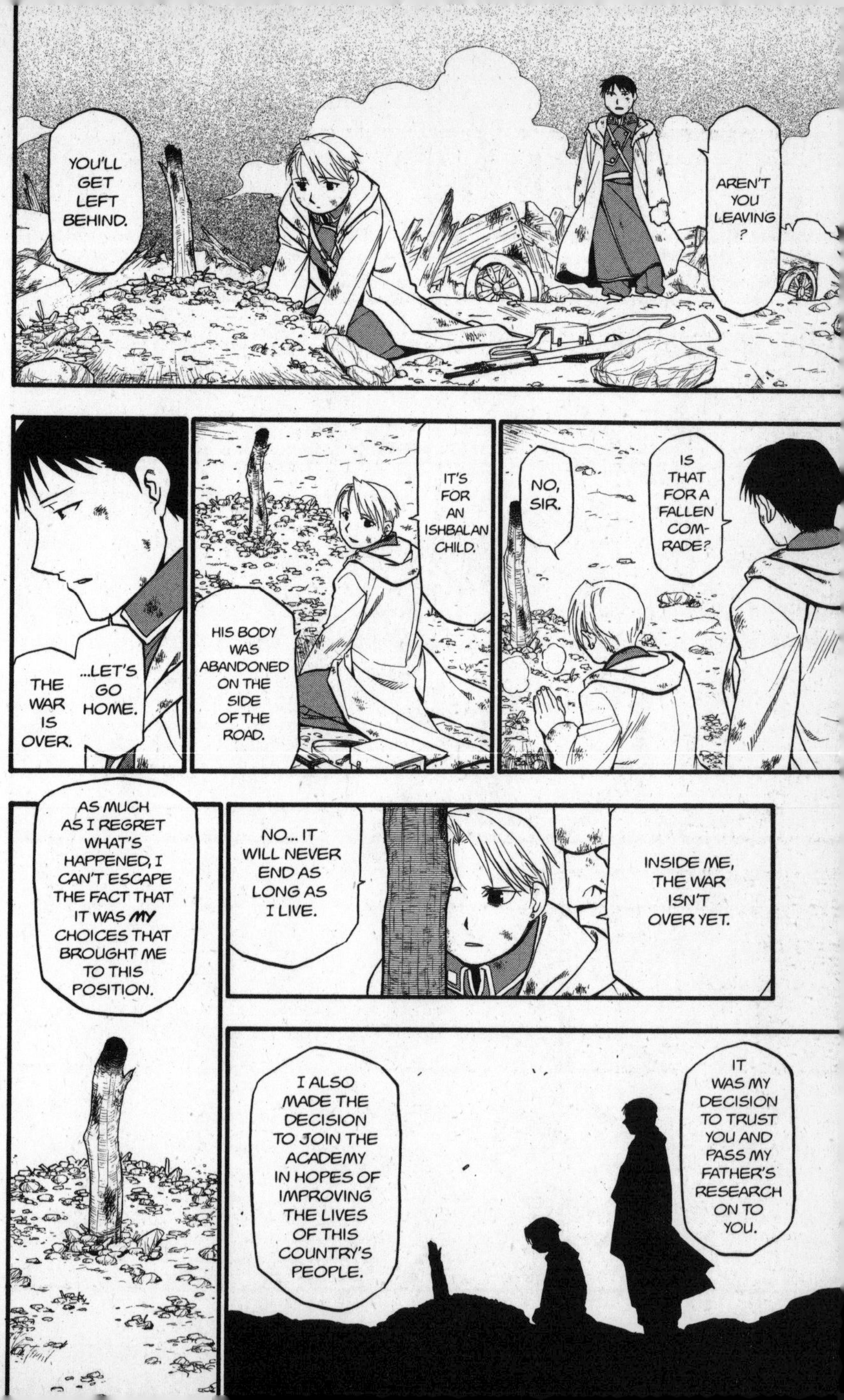
AREN'T YOU LEAVING?
YOU'LL GET LEFT BEHIND.
IS THAT FOR A FALLEN COMRADE?
NO, SIR.
IT'S FOR AN ISHBALAN CHILD.
HIS BODY WAS ABANDONED ON THE SIDE OF THE ROAD.
...LET'S GO HOME.
THE WAR IS OVER.
INSIDE ME, THE WAR ISN'T OVER YET.
NO... IT WILL NEVER END AS LONG AS I LIVE.
IT WAS MY DECISION TO TRUST YOU AND PASS MY FATHER'S RESEARCH ON TO YOU.
I ALSO MADE THE DECISION TO JOIN THE ACADEMY IN HOPES OF IMPROVING THE LIVES OF THIS COUNTRY'S PEOPLE.
AS MUCH AS I REGRET WHAT'S HAPPENED, I CAN'T ESCAPE THE FACT THAT IT WAS MY CHOICES THAT BROUGHT ME TO THIS POSITION.

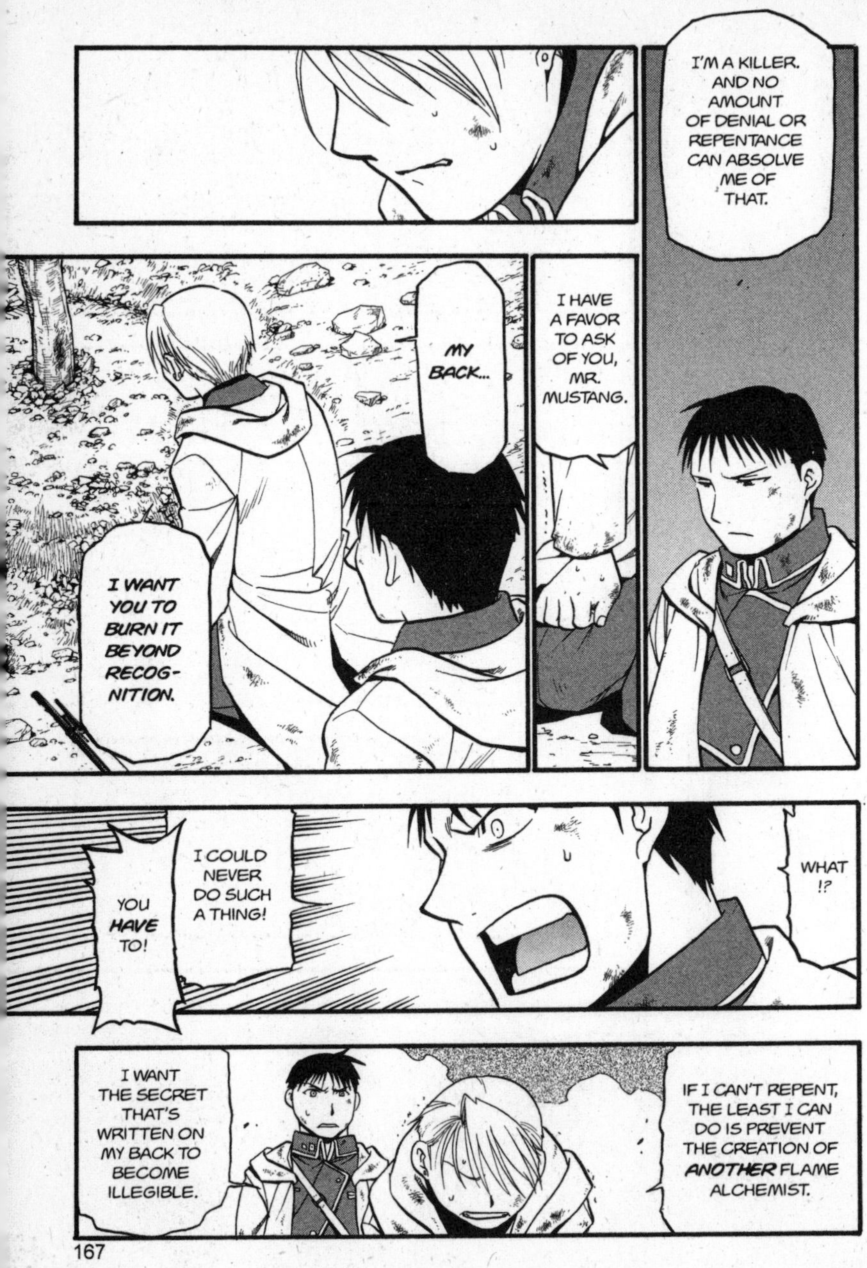
I'M A KILLER. AND NO AMOUNT OF DENIAL OR REPENTANCE CAN ABSOLVE ME OF THAT.
I HAVE A FAVOR TO ASK OF YOU, MR. MUSTANG.
MY BACK...
I WANT YOU TO BURN IT BEYOND RECOG-NITION.
WHAT!?
I COULD NEVER DO SUCH A THING!
YOU HAVE TO!
IF I CAN'T REPENT, THE LEAST I CAN DO IS PREVENT THE CREATION OF ANOTHER FLAME ALCHEMIST.
I WANT THE SECRET THAT'S WRITTEN ON MY BACK TO BECOME ILLEGIBLE.

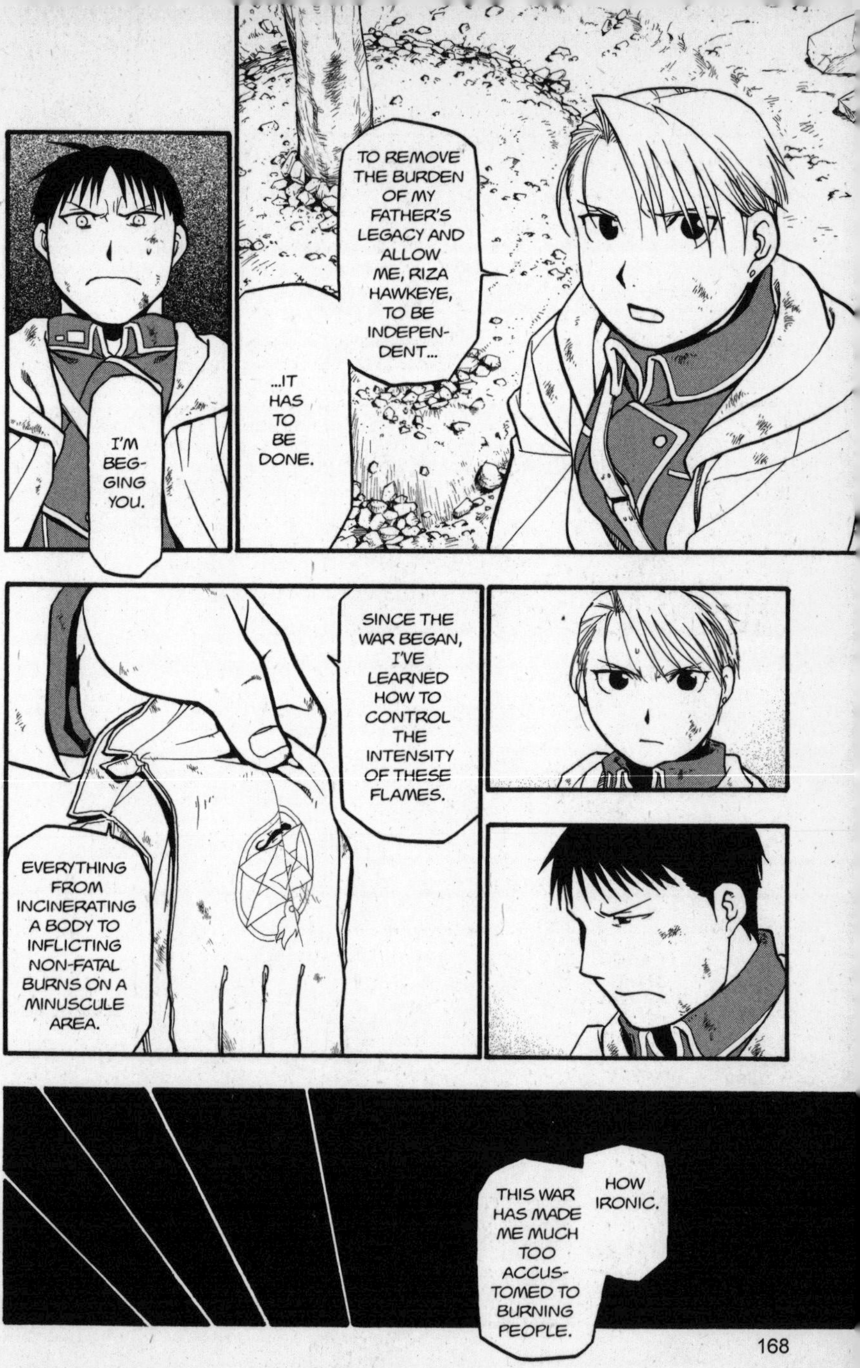
TO REMOVE THE BURDEN OF MY FATHER'S LEGACY AND ALLOW ME, RIZA HAWKEYE, TO BE INDEPEN-DENT...
...IT HAS TO BE DONE.
I'M BEG-GING YOU.
SINCE THE WAR BEGAN, I'VE LEARNED HOW TO CONTROL THE INTENSITY OF THESE FLAMES.
EVERYTHING FROM INCINERATING A BODY TO INFLICTING NON-FATAL BURNS ON A MINUSCULE AREA.
HOW IRONIC.
THIS WAR HAS MADE ME MUCH TOO ACCUS-TOMED TO BURNING PEOPLE.

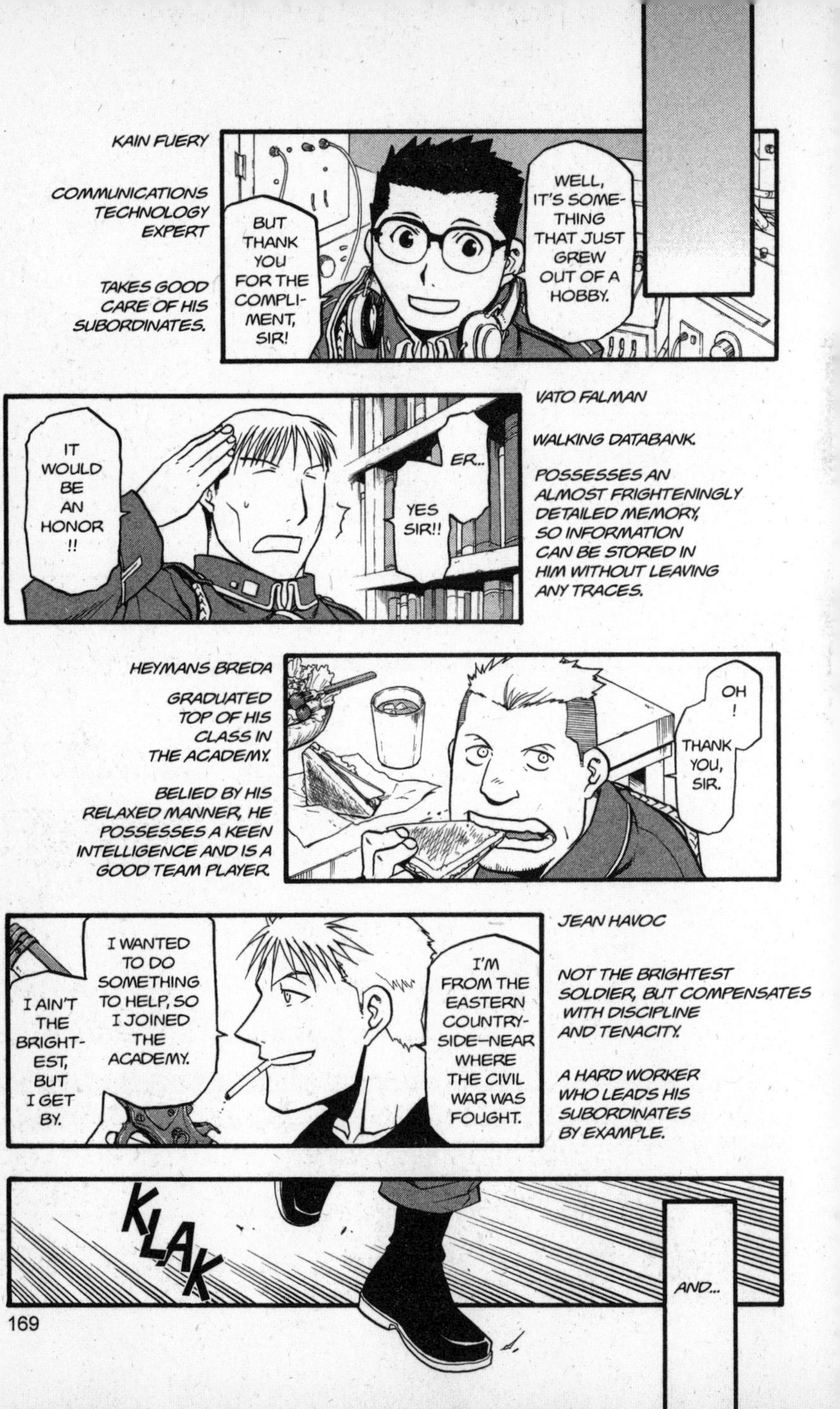
WELL, IT'S SOMETHING THAT JUST GREW OUT OF A HOBBY.
BUT THANK YOU FOR THE COMPLIMENT, SIR!
KAIN FUERY
COMMUNICATIONS TECHNOLOGY EXPERT
TAKES GOOD CARE OF HIS SUBORDINATES.
VATO FALMAN
WALKING DATABANK.
POSSESSES AN ALMOST FRIGHTENINGLY DETAILED MEMORY, SO INFORMATION CAN BE STORED IN HIM WITHOUT LEAVING ANY TRACES.
ER...
YES SIR!!
IT WOULD BE AN HONOR!!
OH! THANK YOU, SIR.
HEYMANS BREDA
GRADUATED TOP OF HIS CLASS IN THE ACADEMY.
BELIED BY HIS RELAXED MANNER, HE POSSESSES A KEEN INTELLIGENCE AND IS A GOOD TEAM PLAYER.
JEAN HAVOC
NOT THE BRIGHTEST SOLDIER, BUT COMPENSATES WITH DISCIPLINE AND TENACITY.
A HARD WORKER WHO LEADS HIS SUBORDINATES BY EXAMPLE.
I'M FROM THE EASTERN COUNTRYSIDE—NEAR WHERE THE CIVIL WAR WAS FOUGHT.
I WANTED TO DO SOMETHING TO HELP, SO I JOINED THE ACADEMY.
I AIN'T THE BRIGHTEST, BUT I GET BY.
AND...
KLAK

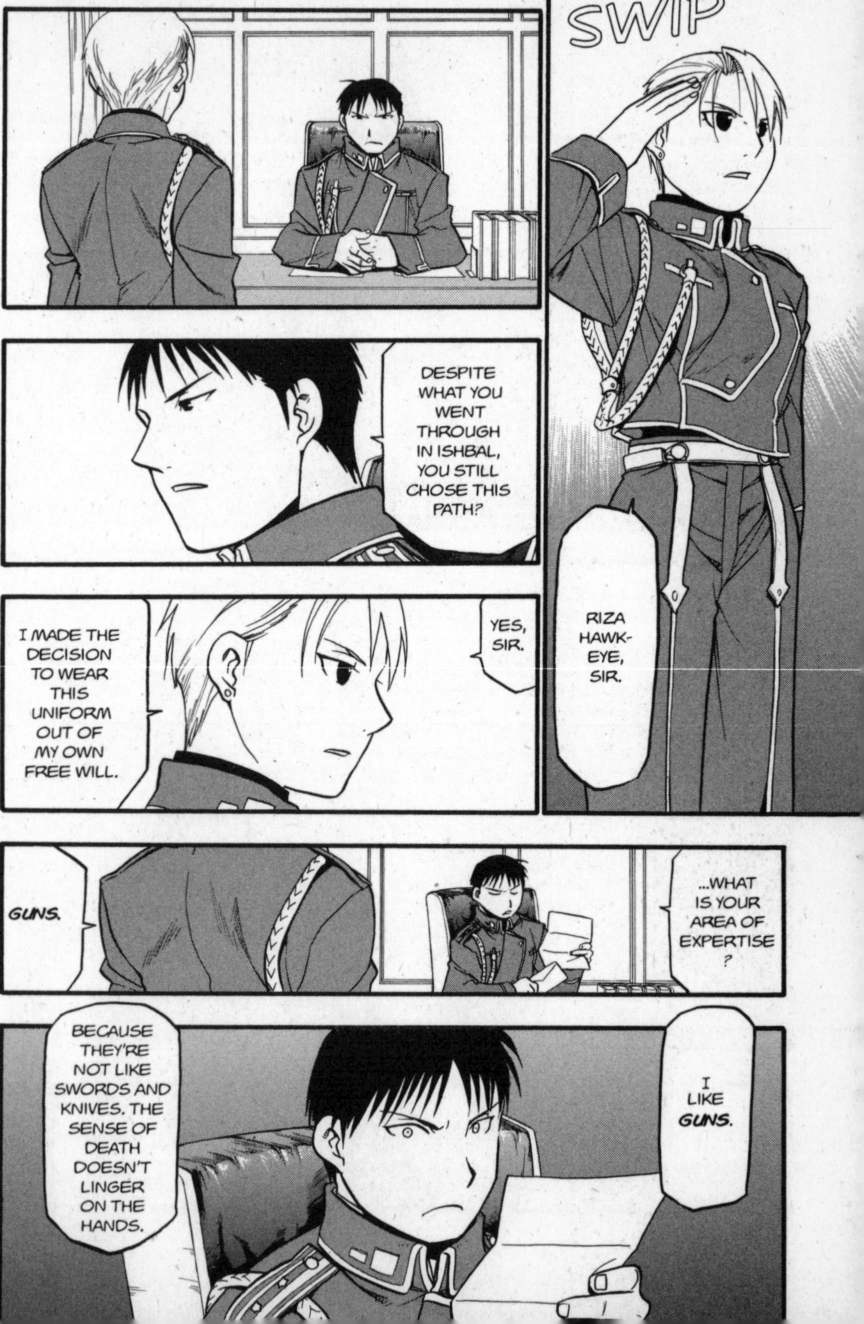
SWIP
RIZA HAWKEYE, SIR.
DESPITE WHAT YOU WENT THROUGH IN ISHBAL, YOU STILL CHOSE THIS PATH?
YES, SIR.
I MADE THE DECISION TO WEAR THIS UNIFORM OUT OF MY OWN FREE WILL.
...WHAT IS YOUR AREA OF EXPERTISE?
GUNS.
I LIKE GUNS.
BECAUSE THEY'RE NOT LIKE SWORDS AND KNIVES. THE SENSE OF DEATH DOESN'T LINGER ON THE HANDS.

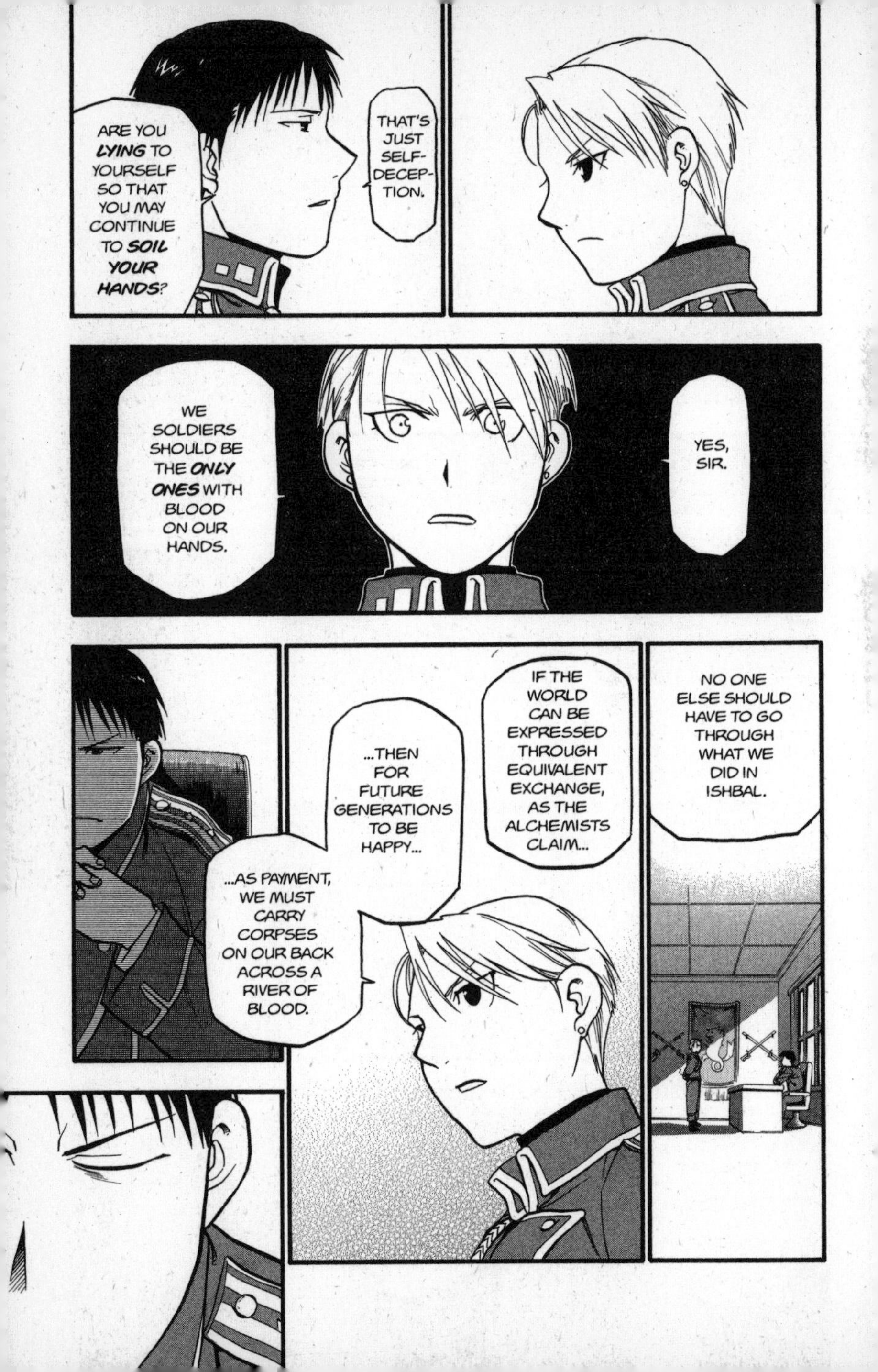
THAT'S JUST SELF-DECEPTION.
ARE YOU LYING TO YOURSELF SO THAT YOU MAY CONTINUE TO SOIL YOUR HANDS?
YES, SIR.
WE SOLDIERS SHOULD BE THE ONLY ONES WITH BLOOD ON OUR HANDS.
NO ONE ELSE SHOULD HAVE TO GO THROUGH WHAT WE DID IN ISHBAL.
IF THE WORLD CAN BE EXPRESSED THROUGH EQUIVALENT EXCHANGE, AS THE ALCHEMISTS CLAIM...
...THEN FOR FUTURE GENERATIONS TO BE HAPPY...
...AS PAYMENT, WE MUST CARRY CORPSES ON OUR BACK ACROSS A RIVER OF BLOOD.

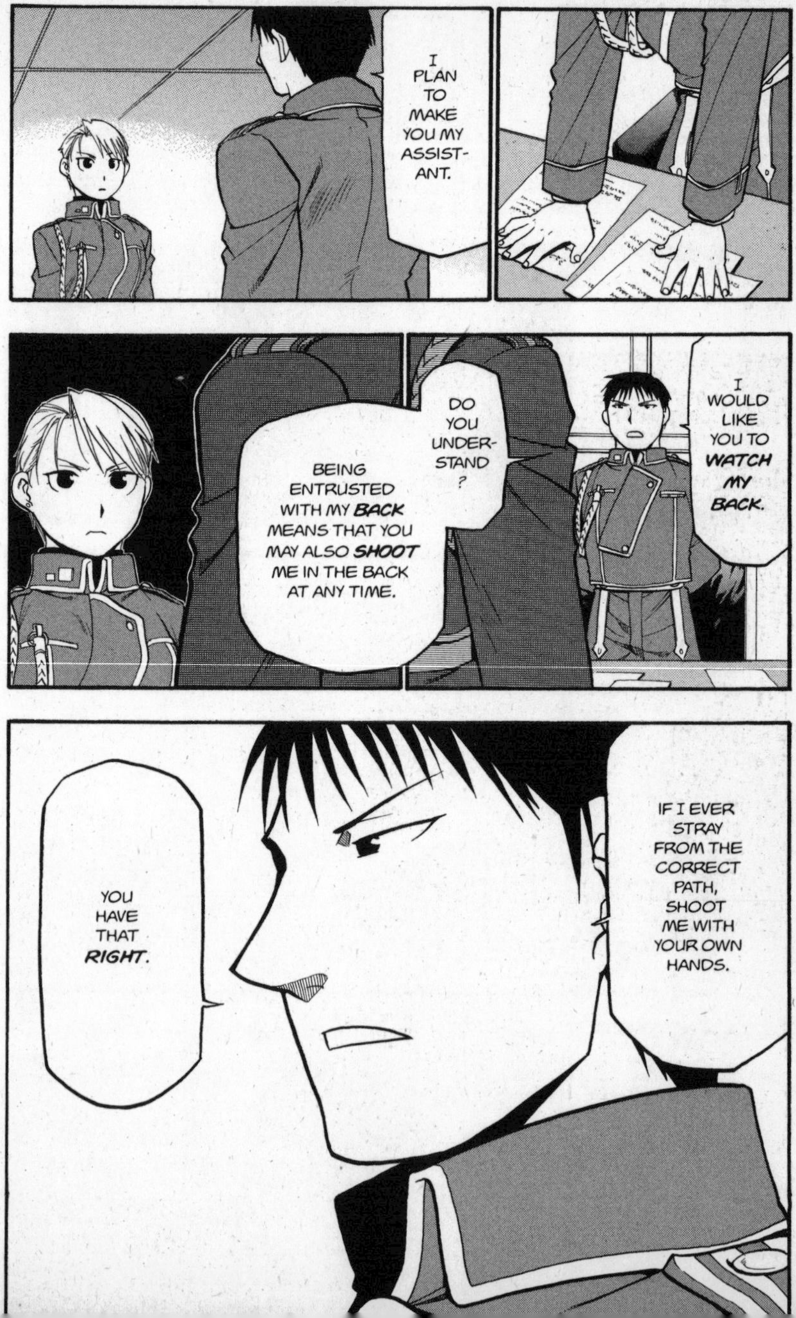
I PLAN TO MAKE YOU MY ASSISTANT.
I WOULD LIKE YOU TO WATCH MY BACK.
DO YOU UNDERSTAND?
BEING ENTRUSTED WITH MY BACK MEANS THAT YOU MAY ALSO SHOOT ME IN THE BACK AT ANY TIME.
IF I EVER STRAY FROM THE CORRECT PATH, SHOOT ME WITH YOUR OWN HANDS.
YOU HAVE THAT RIGHT.

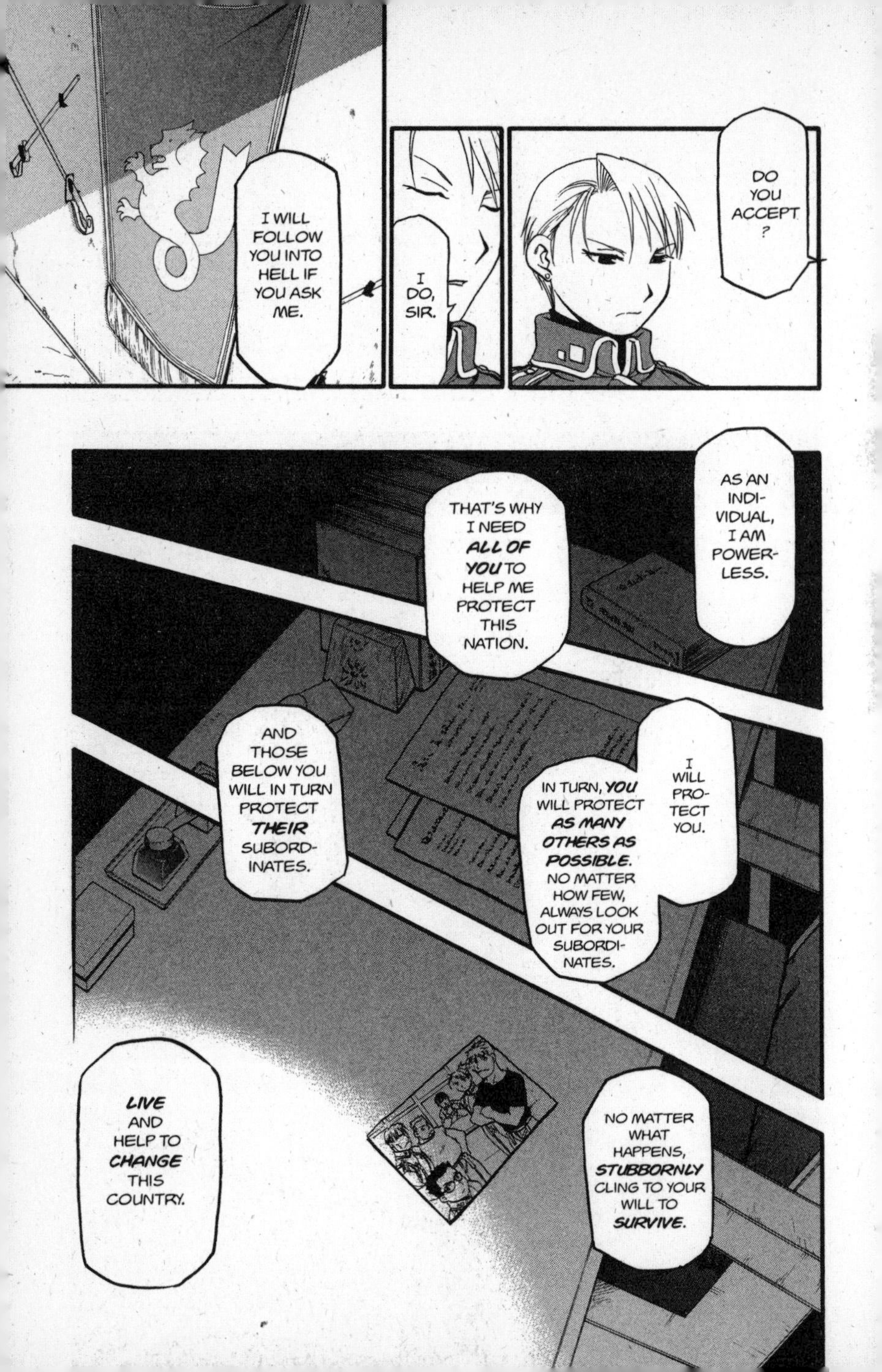
DO YOU ACCEPT?
I DO, SIR.
I WILL FOLLOW YOU INTO HELL IF YOU ASK ME.
AS AN INDIVIDUAL, I AM POWERLESS.
THAT'S WHY I NEED ALL OF YOU TO HELP ME PROTECT THIS NATION.
I WILL PROTECT YOU.
IN TURN, YOU WILL PROTECT AS MANY OTHERS AS POSSIBLE. NO MATTER HOW FEW, ALWAYS LOOK OUT FOR YOUR SUBORDINATES.
AND THOSE BELOW YOU WILL IN TURN PROTECT THEIR SUBORDINATES.
NO MATTER WHAT HAPPENS, STUBBORNLY CLING TO YOUR WILL TO SURVIVE.
LIVE AND HELP TO CHANGE THIS COUNTRY.

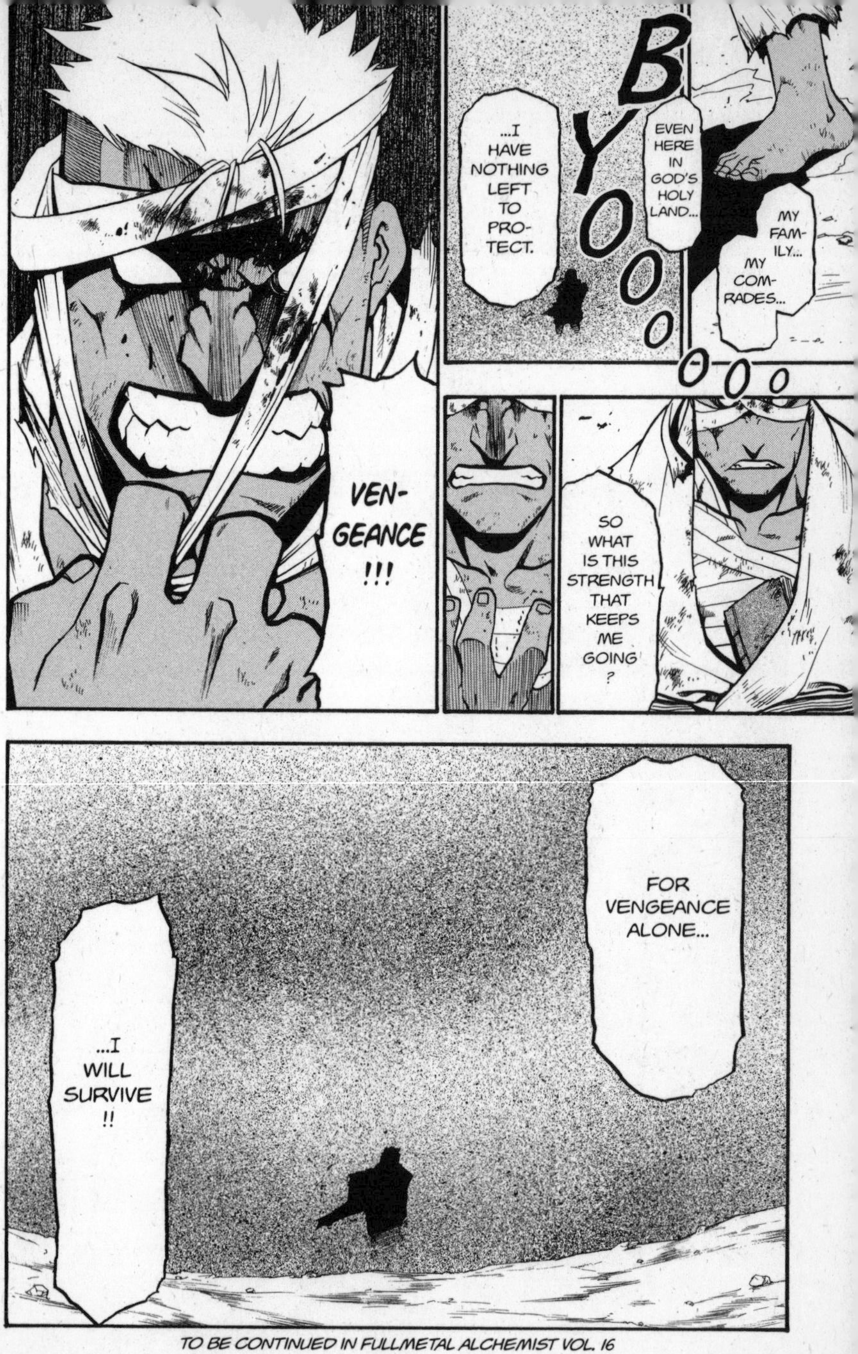
MY FAMILY... MY COMRADES...
EVEN HERE IN GOD'S HOLY LAND...
...I HAVE NOTHING LEFT TO PROTECT.
BYOOOOOO
SO WHAT IS THIS STRENGTH THAT KEEPS ME GOING?
VENGEANCE!!!
FOR VENGEANCE ALONE...
...I WILL SURVIVE!!

TO BE CONTINUED IN FULLMETAL ALCHEMIST VOL. 16

EXTRAS

SCAR
FROM
CHAPTER
61

THIS
IS WHY
YOU
SHOULD
NEVER
FALL
ASLEEP
AROUND
YOUR
SO-CALLED
"FRIENDS."

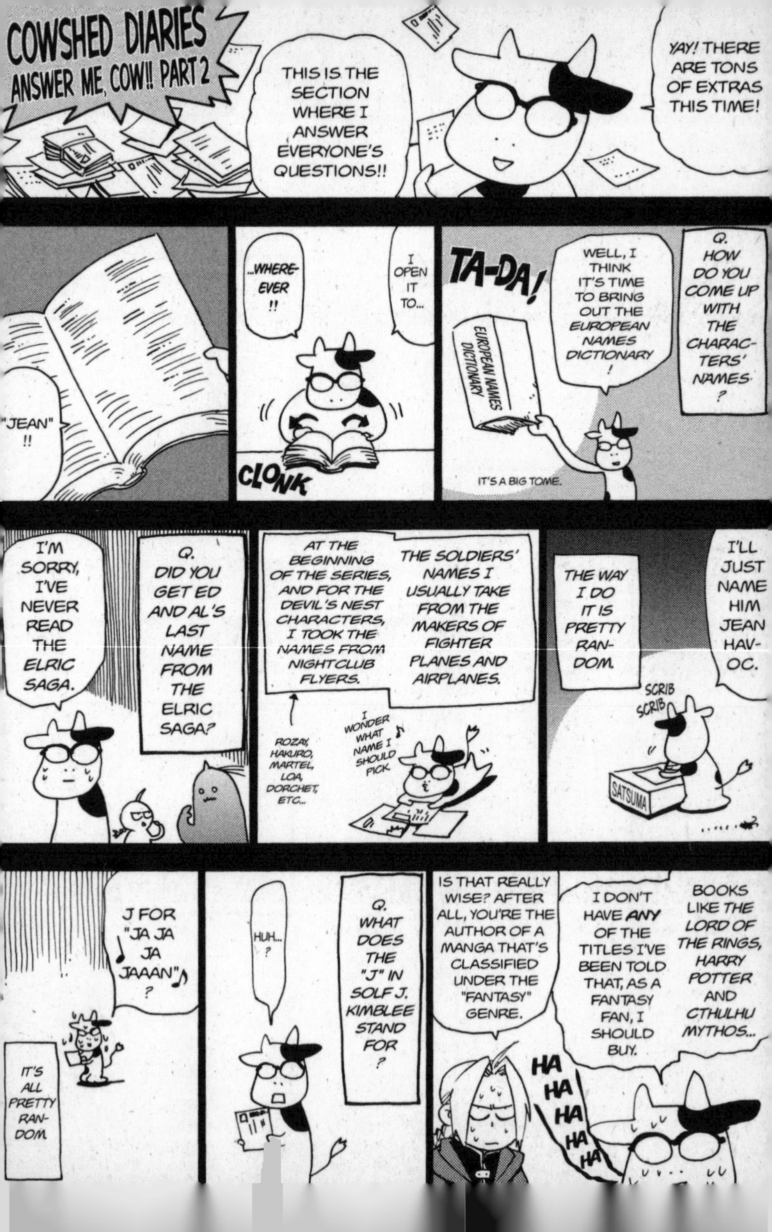
COWSHED DIARIES
ANSWER ME, COW!! PART 2
YAY! THERE ARE TONS OF EXTRAS THIS TIME!
THIS IS THE SECTION WHERE I ANSWER EVERYONE'S QUESTIONS!!
Q. HOW DO YOU COME UP WITH THE CHARACTERS' NAMES?
WELL, I THINK IT'S TIME TO BRING OUT THE EUROPEAN NAMES DICTIONARY!
TA-DA!
EUROPEAN NAMES DICTIONARY
IT'S A BIG TOME.
I OPEN IT TO...
...WHEREEVER!!
CLONK
"JEAN"!!
I'LL JUST NAME HIM JEAN HAVOC.
THE WAY I DO IT IS PRETTY RANDOM.
SCRIB SCRIB
SATSUMA
THE SOLDIERS' NAMES I USUALLY TAKE FROM THE MAKERS OF FIGHTER PLANES AND AIRPLANES.
AT THE BEGINNING OF THE SERIES, AND FOR THE DEVIL'S NEST CHARACTERS, I TOOK THE NAMES FROM NIGHTCLUB FLYERS.
I WONDER WHAT NAME I SHOULD PICK
ROZAY, HAKURO, MARTEL, LOA, DORCHET, ETC...
Q. DID YOU GET ED AND AL'S LAST NAME FROM THE ELRIC SAGA?
I'M SORRY, I'VE NEVER READ THE ELRIC SAGA.
BOOKS LIKE THE LORD OF THE RINGS, HARRY POTTER AND CTHULHU MYTHOS...
I DON'T HAVE ANY OF THE TITLES I'VE BEEN TOLD THAT, AS A FANTASY FAN, I SHOULD BUY.
IS THAT REALLY WISE? AFTER ALL, YOU'RE THE AUTHOR OF A MANGA THAT'S CLASSIFIED UNDER THE "FANTASY" GENRE.
HA HA HA HA HA
Q. WHAT DOES THE "J" IN SOLF J. KIMBLEE STAND FOR?
HUH...?
J FOR "JA JA JA JAAAN"?
IT'S ALL PRETTY RAN-DOM.

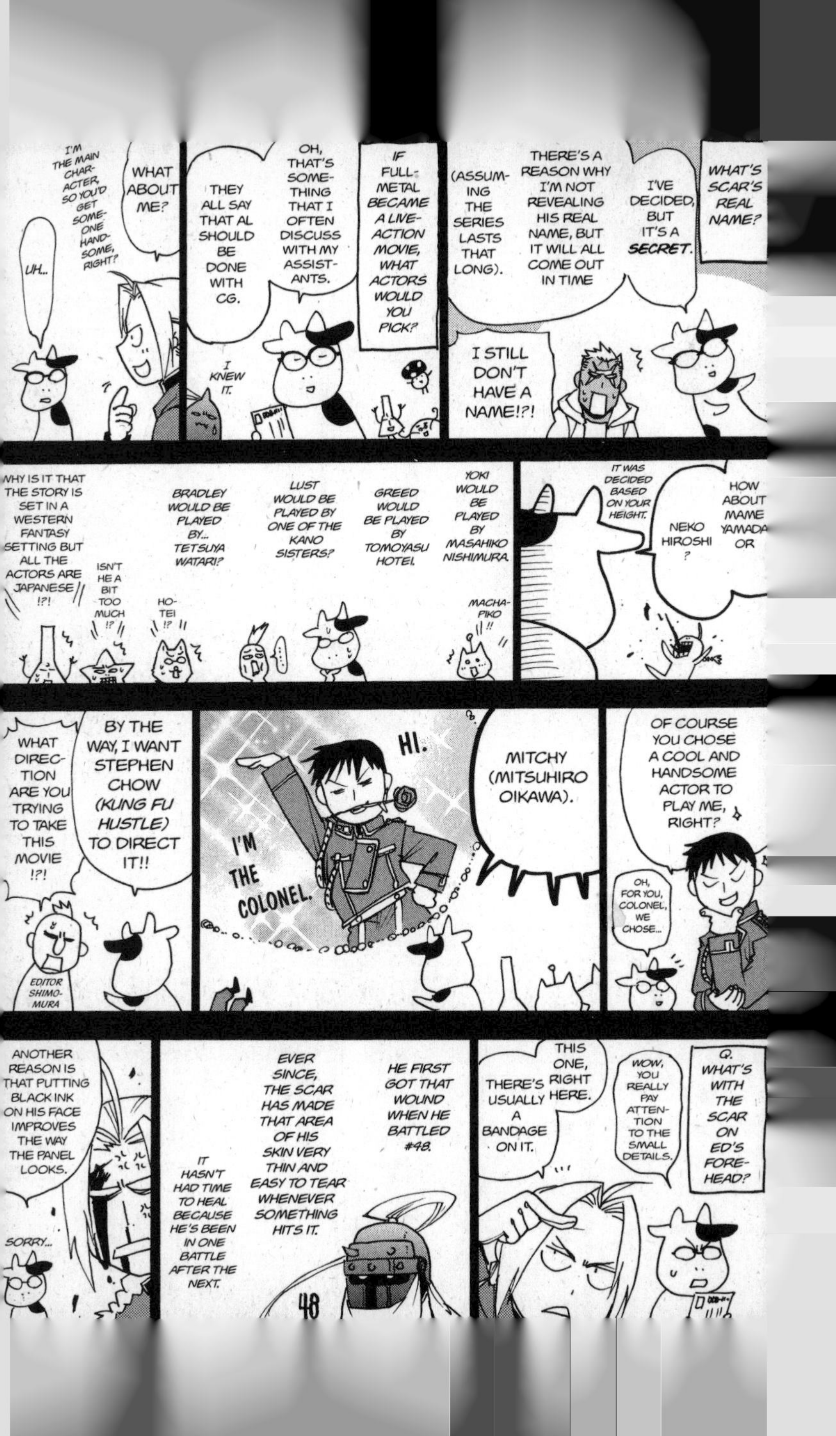
WHAT'S SCAR'S REAL NAME?
I'VE DECIDED, BUT IT'S A SECRET.
THERE'S A REASON WHY I'M NOT REVEALING HIS REAL NAME, BUT IT WILL ALL COME OUT IN TIME
(ASSUMING THE SERIES LASTS THAT LONG).
I STILL DON'T HAVE A NAME!?!
IF FULL-METAL BECAME A LIVE-ACTION MOVIE, WHAT ACTORS WOULD YOU PICK?
OH, THAT'S SOMETHING THAT I OFTEN DISCUSS WITH MY ASSISTANTS.
THEY ALL SAY THAT AL SHOULD BE DONE WITH CG.
I KNEW IT.
WHAT ABOUT ME?
I'M THE MAIN CHARACTER, SO YOU'D GET SOMEONE HANDSOME, RIGHT?
UH...
HOW ABOUT MAME YAMADA OR NEKO HIROSHI?
IT WAS DECIDED BASED ON YOUR HEIGHT.
YOKI WOULD BE PLAYED BY MASAHIKO NISHIMURA.
MACHAPIKO!!
GREED WOULD BE PLAYED BY TOMOYASU HOTEI.
LUST WOULD BE PLAYED BY ONE OF THE KANO SISTERS?
BRADLEY WOULD BE PLAYED BY... TETSUYA WATARI!?
HOTEI!?
ISN'T HE A BIT TOO MUCH!?
WHY IS IT THAT THE STORY IS SET IN A WESTERN FANTASY SETTING BUT ALL THE ACTORS ARE JAPANESE!?!
OF COURSE YOU CHOSE A COOL AND HANDSOME ACTOR TO PLAY ME, RIGHT?
OH, FOR YOU, COLONEL, WE CHOSE...
MITCHY (MITSUHIRO OIKAWA).
HI.
I'M THE COLONEL.
BY THE WAY, I WANT STEPHEN CHOW (KUNG FU HUSTLE) TO DIRECT IT!!
WHAT DIRECTION ARE YOU TRYING TO TAKE THIS MOVIE!?!
EDITOR SHIMOMURA
Q. WHAT'S WITH THE SCAR ON ED'S FOREHEAD?
WOW, YOU REALLY PAY ATTENTION TO THE SMALL DETAILS.
THIS ONE, RIGHT HERE.
THERE'S USUALLY A BANDAGE ON IT.
HE FIRST GOT THAT WOUND WHEN HE BATTLED #48.
EVER SINCE, THE SCAR HAS MADE THAT AREA OF HIS SKIN VERY THIN AND EASY TO TEAR WHENEVER SOMETHING HITS IT.
IT HASN'T HAD TIME TO HEAL BECAUSE HE'S BEEN IN ONE BATTLE AFTER THE NEXT.
ANOTHER REASON IS THAT PUTTING BLACK INK ON HIS FACE IMPROVES THE WAY THE PANEL LOOKS.
SORRY...

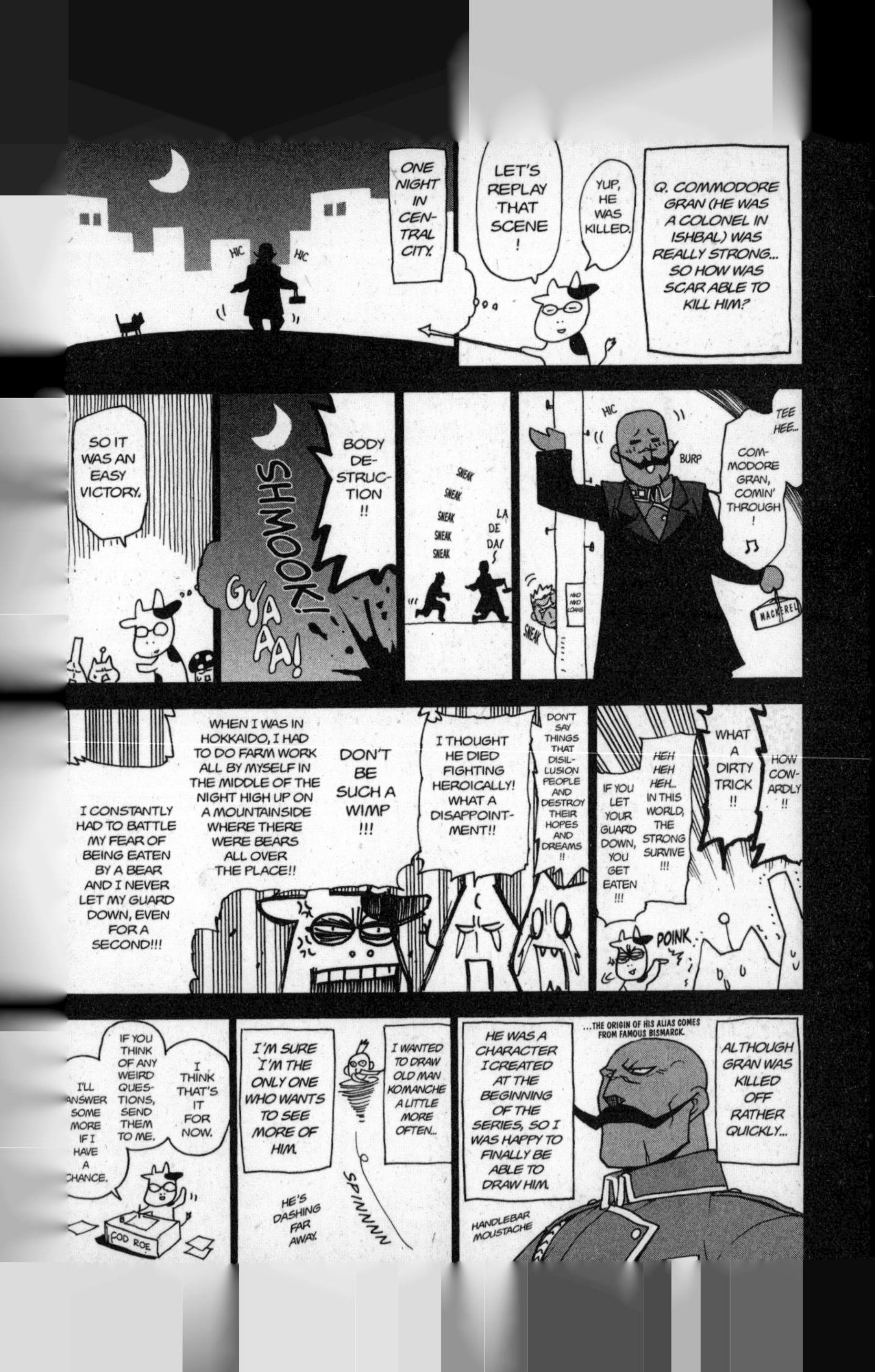
Q. COMMODORE GRAN (HE WAS A COLONEL IN ISHBAL) WAS REALLY STRONG... SO HOW WAS SCAR ABLE TO KILL HIM?
YUP, HE WAS KILLED.
LET'S REPLAY THAT SCENE!
ONE NIGHT IN CENTRAL CITY.
HIC
HIC
TEE HEE...
COMMODORE GRAN, COMIN' THROUGH! ♪
HIC
BURP
MACKEREL
NIKO NIKO LOANS
SNEAK
LA DE DA
SNEAK SNEAK SNEAK SNEAK SNEAK
BODY DESTRUCTION!!
SHMOOK!
GYAAA!
SO IT WAS AN EASY VICTORY.
HOW COWARDLY!!
WHAT A DIRTY TRICK!!
HEH HEH HEH... IN THIS WORLD, THE STRONG SURVIVE!!!
IF YOU LET YOUR GUARD DOWN, YOU GET EATEN!!!
POINK
DON'T SAY THINGS THAT DISILLUSION PEOPLE AND DESTROY THEIR HOPES AND DREAMS!!
I THOUGHT HE DIED FIGHTING HEROICALLY! WHAT A DISAPPOINTMENT!!
DON'T BE SUCH A WIMP!!!
WHEN I WAS IN HOKKAIDO, I HAD TO DO FARM WORK ALL BY MYSELF IN THE MIDDLE OF THE NIGHT HIGH UP ON A MOUNTAINSIDE WHERE THERE WERE BEARS ALL OVER THE PLACE!!
I CONSTANTLY HAD TO BATTLE MY FEAR OF BEING EATEN BY A BEAR AND I NEVER LET MY GUARD DOWN, EVEN FOR A SECOND!!!
ALTHOUGH GRAN WAS KILLED OFF RATHER QUICKLY...
...THE ORIGIN OF HIS ALIAS COMES FROM FAMOUS BISMARCK.
HE WAS A CHARACTER I CREATED AT THE BEGINNING OF THE SERIES, SO I WAS HAPPY TO FINALLY BE ABLE TO DRAW HIM.
HANDLEBAR MOUSTACHE
I WANTED TO DRAW OLD MAN KOMANCHE A LITTLE MORE OFTEN...
I'M SURE I'M THE ONLY ONE WHO WANTS TO SEE MORE OF HIM.
SPINNNN
HE'S DASHING FAR AWAY.
I THINK THAT'S IT FOR NOW.
IF YOU THINK OF ANY WEIRD QUESTIONS, SEND THEM TO ME.
I'LL ANSWER SOME MORE IF I HAVE A CHANCE.
COD ROE

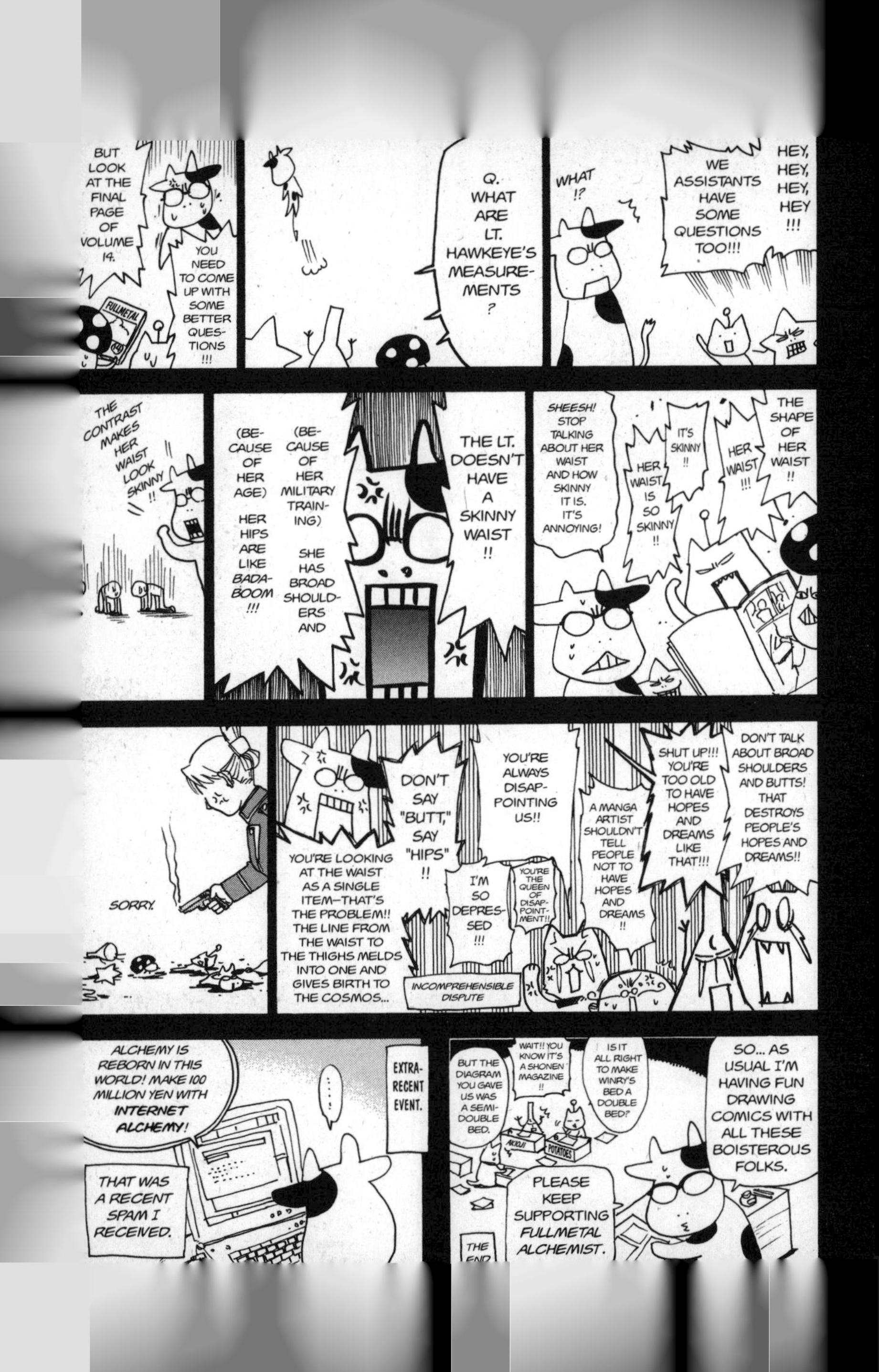
HEY, HEY, HEY, HEY!!!
WE ASSISTANTS HAVE SOME QUESTIONS TOO!!!
WHAT!?
Q. WHAT ARE LT. HAWKEYE'S MEASUREMENTS?
BUT LOOK AT THE FINAL PAGE OF VOLUME 14.
YOU NEED TO COME UP WITH SOME BETTER QUESTIONS!!!
FULLMETAL
THE SHAPE OF HER WAIST!!
HER WAIST!!!
IT'S SKINNY!!
HER WAIST IS SO SKINNY!!
SHEESH! STOP TALKING ABOUT HER WAIST AND HOW SKINNY IT IS. IT'S ANNOYING!
THE LT. DOESN'T HAVE A SKINNY WAIST!!
(BECAUSE OF HER MILITARY TRAINING) SHE HAS BROAD SHOULDERS AND
(BECAUSE OF HER AGE) HER HIPS ARE LIKE BADA-BOOM!!!
THE CONTRAST MAKES HER WAIST LOOK SKINNY!!
DON'T TALK ABOUT BROAD SHOULDERS AND BUTTS! THAT DESTROYS PEOPLE'S HOPES AND DREAMS!!
SHUT UP!!! YOU'RE TOO OLD TO HAVE HOPES AND DREAMS LIKE THAT!!!
A MANGA ARTIST SHOULDN'T TELL PEOPLE NOT TO HAVE HOPES AND DREAMS!!
YOU'RE ALWAYS DISAPPOINTING US!!
YOU'RE THE QUEEN OF DISAPPOINTMENT!!
I'M SO DEPRESSED!!!
DON'T SAY "BUTT," SAY "HIPS"!!
YOU'RE LOOKING AT THE WAIST AS A SINGLE ITEM—THAT'S THE PROBLEM!! THE LINE FROM THE WAIST TO THE THIGHS MELDS INTO ONE AND GIVES BIRTH TO THE COSMOS...
INCOMPREHENSIBLE DISPUTE
SORRY.
SO... AS USUAL I'M HAVING FUN DRAWING COMICS WITH ALL THESE BOISTEROUS FOLKS.
IS IT ALL RIGHT TO MAKE WINRY'S BED A DOUBLE BED?
WAIT!! YOU KNOW IT'S A SHONEN MAGAZINE!!
BUT THE DIAGRAM YOU GAVE US WAS A SEMI-DOUBLE BED.
POTATOES
PLEASE KEEP SUPPORTING FULLMETAL ALCHEMIST.
THE
EXTRA-RECENT EVENT.
ALCHEMY IS REBORN IN THIS WORLD! MAKE 100 MILLION YEN WITH INTERNET ALCHEMY!
......
THAT WAS A RECENT SPAM I RECEIVED.

EDWARD AND THE MAGIC LAMP

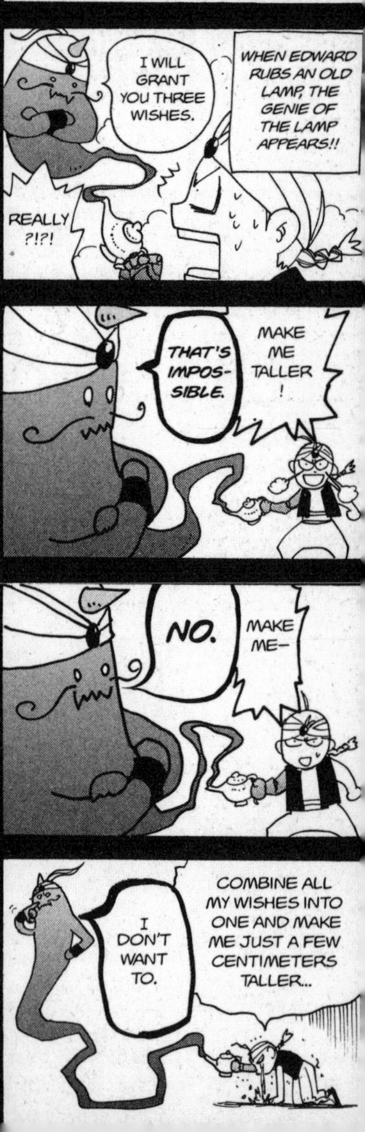
WHEN EDWARD RUBS AN OLD LAMP, THE GENIE OF THE LAMP APPEARS!!
I WILL GRANT YOU THREE WISHES.
REALLY ?!?!
MAKE ME TALLER !
THAT'S IMPOSSIBLE.
MAKE ME—
NO.
COMBINE ALL MY WISHES INTO ONE AND MAKE ME JUST A FEW CENTIMETERS TALLER...
I DON'T WANT TO.

FOR YOUR EYES...

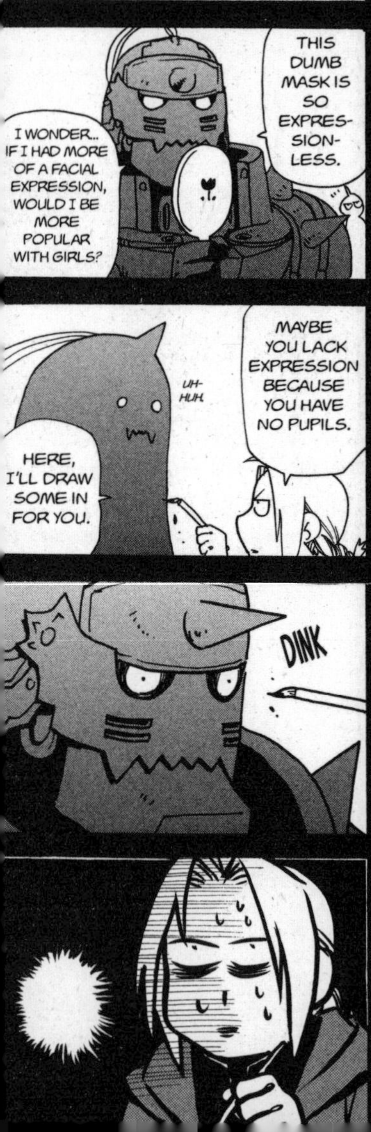
THIS DUMB MASK IS SO EXPRES-SION-LESS.
I WONDER... IF I HAD MORE OF A FACIAL EXPRESSION, WOULD I BE MORE POPULAR WITH GIRLS?
MAYBE YOU LACK EXPRESSION BECAUSE YOU HAVE NO PUPILS.
UH-HUH.
HERE, I'LL DRAW SOME IN FOR YOU.
DINK

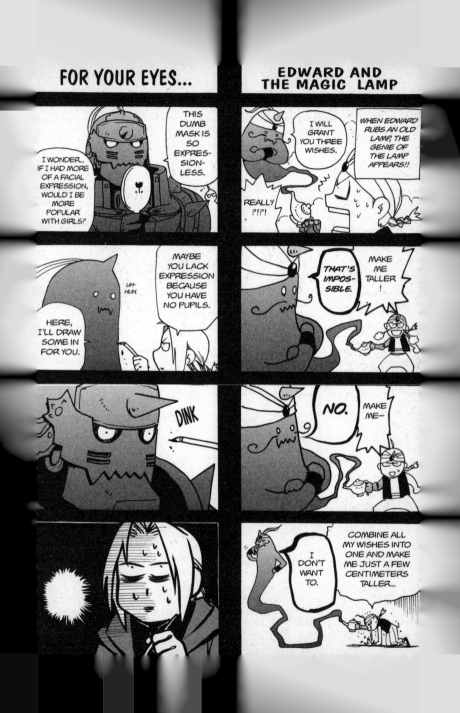

OLDER BROTHER'S WISH

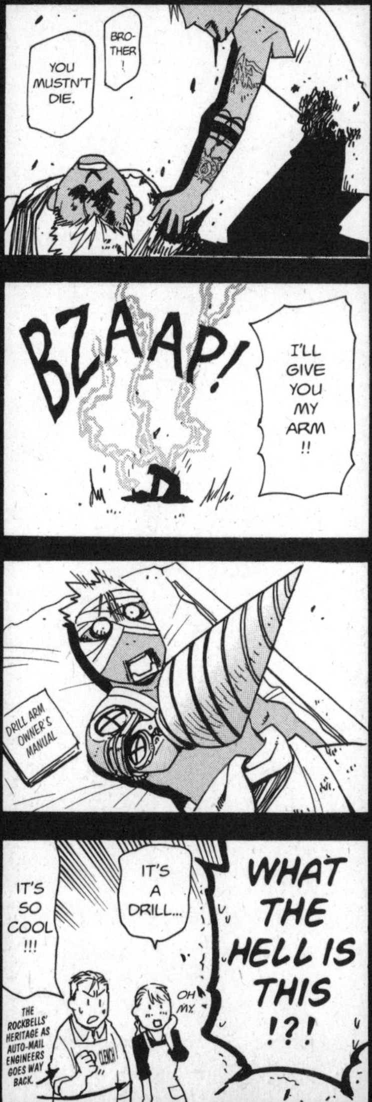
BROTHER!
YOU MUSTN'T DIE.
I'LL GIVE YOU MY ARM!!
BZAAP!
DRILL ARM OWNER'S MANUAL
WHAT THE HELL IS THIS!?!
IT'S A DRILL...
IT'S SO COOL!!!
OH MY.
CLENCH
THE ROCKBELLS' HERITAGE AS AUTO-MAIL ENGINEERS GOES WAY BACK.

PLEASE LET ME USE YOUR RESTROOM!

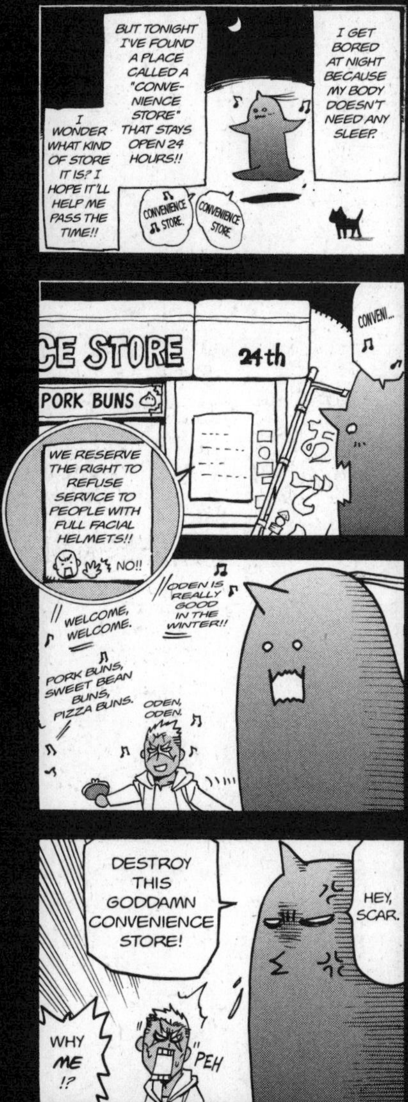
I GET BORED AT NIGHT BECAUSE MY BODY DOESN'T NEED ANY SLEEP.
BUT TONIGHT I'VE FOUND A PLACE CALLED A "CONVENIENCE STORE" THAT STAYS OPEN 24 HOURS!!
I WONDER WHAT KIND OF STORE IT IS? I HOPE IT'LL HELP ME PASS THE TIME!!
CONVENIENCE STORE.
CONVENIENCE STORE.
CONVENI...
CE STORE
24th
PORK BUNS
WE RESERVE THE RIGHT TO REFUSE SERVICE TO PEOPLE WITH FULL FACIAL HELMETS!!
NO!!
ODEN IS REALLY GOOD IN THE WINTER!!
WELCOME, WELCOME.
PORK BUNS, SWEET BEAN BUNS, PIZZA BUNS.
ODEN, ODEN.
HEY, SCAR.
DESTROY THIS GODDAMN CONVENIENCE STORE!
WHY ME!?
PEH

ADDITIONAL FEE REQUIRED IF YOU WANT TO SEE MORE

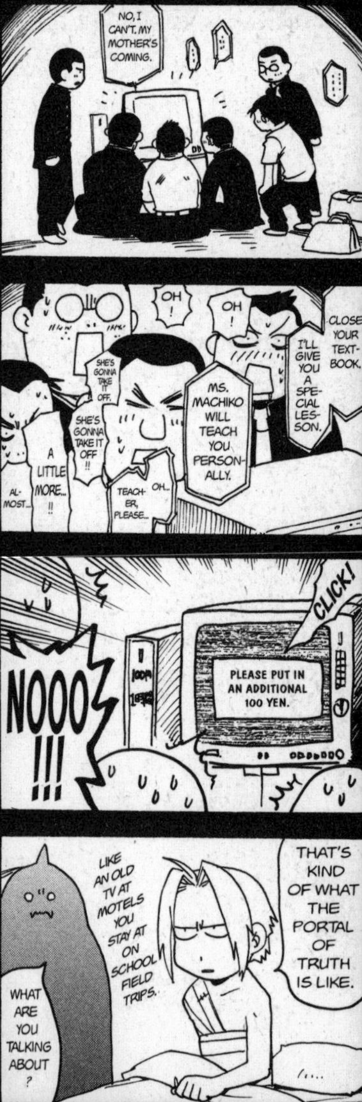
NO, I CAN'T. MY MOTHER'S COMING.
CLOSE YOUR TEXT-BOOK.
I'LL GIVE YOU A SPE-CIAL LES-SON.
OH!
OH!
MS. MACHIKO WILL TEACH YOU PERSON-ALLY.
SHE'S GONNA TAKE IT OFF.
SHE'S GONNA TAKE IT OFF!!
OH..
TEACH-ER, PLEASE...
A LITTLE MORE...!!
AL-MOST...
CLICK!
PLEASE PUT IN AN ADDITIONAL 100 YEN.
NOOO!!!
THAT'S KIND OF WHAT THE PORTAL OF TRUTH IS LIKE.
LIKE AN OLD TV AT MOTELS YOU STAY AT ON SCHOOL FIELD TRIPS.
WHAT ARE YOU TALKING ABOUT?

HARD-BOILED

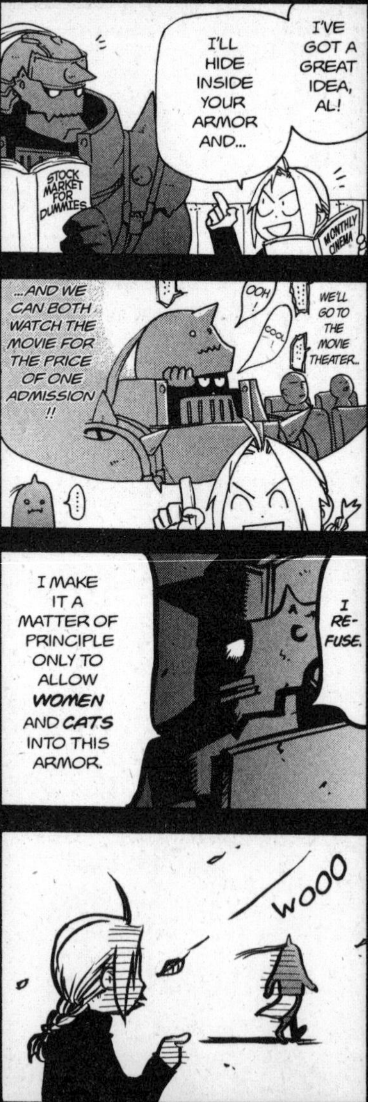
I'VE GOT A GREAT IDEA, AL!
I'LL HIDE INSIDE YOUR ARMOR AND...
MONTHLY CINEMA
STOCK MARKET FOR DUMMIES
WE'LL GO TO THE MOVIE THEATER..
OOH!
COOL!
...AND WE CAN BOTH WATCH THE MOVIE FOR THE PRICE OF ONE ADMISSION!!
I REFUSE.
I MAKE IT A MATTER OF PRINCIPLE ONLY TO ALLOW WOMEN AND CATS INTO THIS ARMOR.
WOOO

HUMAN VS. ARTIFICIAL HUMAN

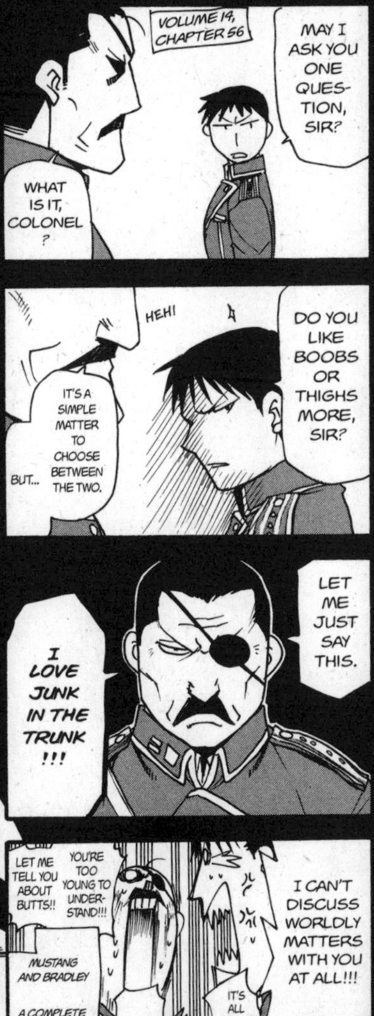
VOLUME 14, CHAPTER 56
MAY I ASK YOU ONE QUESTION, SIR?
WHAT IS IT, COLONEL?
DO YOU LIKE BOOBS OR THIGHS MORE, SIR?
HEH!
IT'S A SIMPLE MATTER TO CHOOSE BETWEEN THE TWO.
BUT...
LET ME JUST SAY THIS.
I LOVE JUNK IN THE TRUNK!!!
I CAN'T DISCUSS WORLDLY MATTERS WITH YOU AT ALL!!!
YOU'RE TOO YOUNG TO UNDERSTAND!!!
LET ME TELL YOU ABOUT BUTTS!!
IT'S ALL ABOUT THE THIGHS!!
MUSTANG AND BRADLEY
A COMPLETE DIFFERENCE IN OPINION.
WHAAAT!?!
ROOOOOAR!

FULLMETAL ALCHEMIST 15

SPECIAL THANKS to:

KEISUI TAKAEDA
SANKICHI HINODEYA
JUN TOHKO
AIYABALL
NONO
YOICHI KAMITONO
MASASHI MIZUTANI
SAKAMAKI
COUPON
SAORI TAKAGI
MASANARI YUZUKA sensei
MANAGER MR. YOICHI SHIMOMURA

AND YOU!!

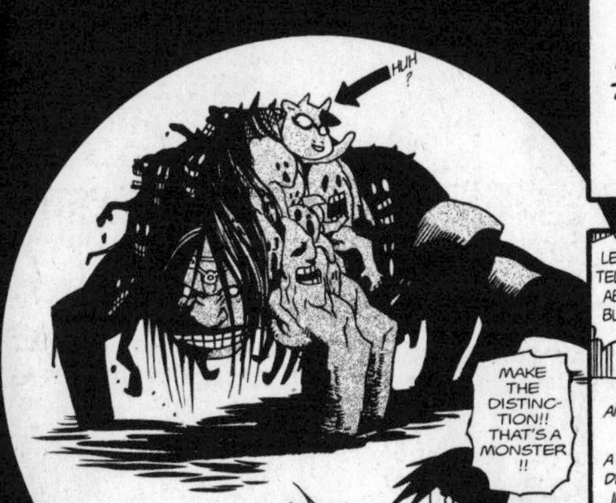
HUH?
MAKE THE DISTINCTION!! THAT'S A MONSTER!!
OKAY

NOW THE STORY CONTINUES...

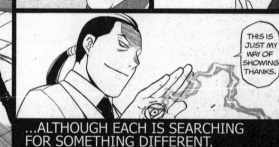

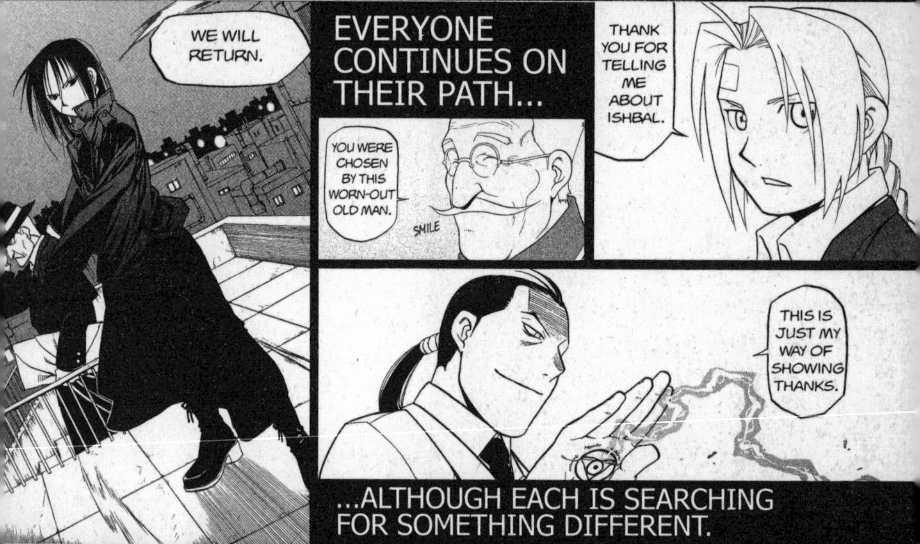

EVERYONE CONTINUES ON THEIR PATH...
THANK YOU FOR TELLING ME ABOUT ISHBAL.
YOU WERE CHOSEN BY THIS WORN-OUT OLD MAN.
SMILE
THIS IS JUST MY WAY OF SHOWING THANKS.
...ALTHOUGH EACH IS SEARCHING FOR SOMETHING DIFFERENT.
WE WILL RETURN.

SCAR'S OLDER BROTHER DECLARED, **"THERE'S SOMETHING STRANGE ABOUT THIS COUNTRY'S ALCHEMY!!"** WHAT IS THE MEANING BEHIND HIS WORDS?! AS THE ACTION HEADS NORTH, THE CHARACTERS CONVERGE FOR A NEW CONFLICT. KIMBLEE IS RELEASED FROM INCARCERATION, AND A **NEW CHARACTER** MAKES AN APPEARANCE! WHO IS GENERAL ARMSTRONG?!

FULLMETAL ALCHEMIST 16 ON SALE NOW!

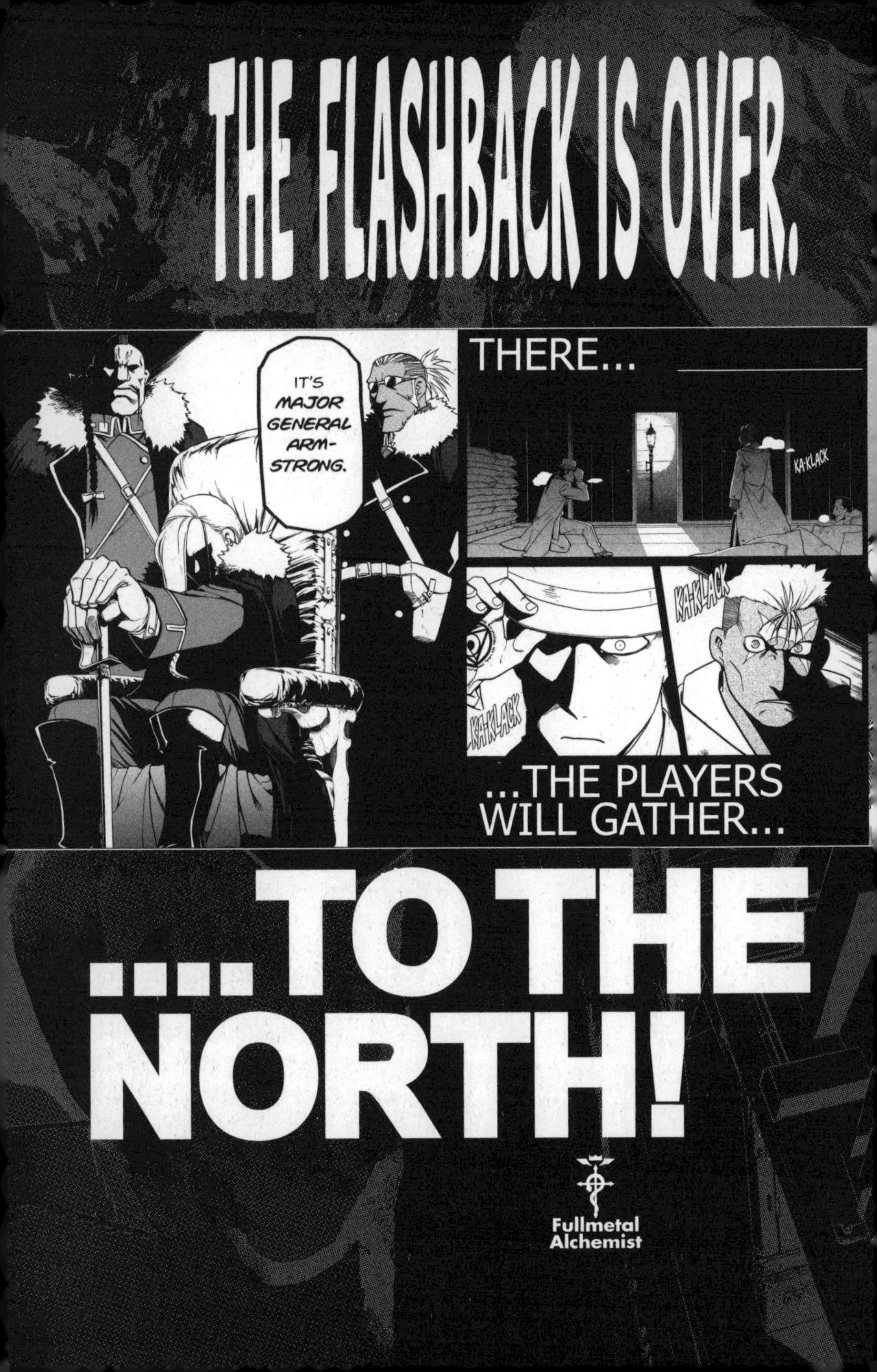
THE FLASHBACK IS OVER.
THERE...
KA-KLACK
KA-KLACK
KA-KLACK
...THE PLAYERS WILL GATHER...
IT'S MAJOR GENERAL ARM-STRONG.
....TO THE NORTH!
Fullmetal Alchemist

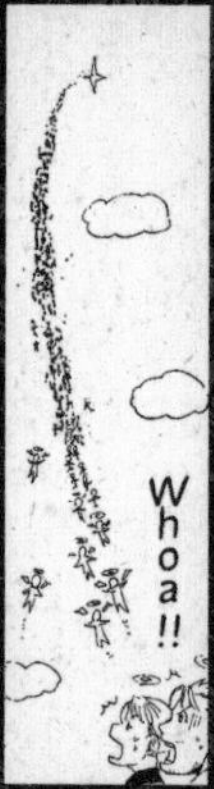
Whoa!!

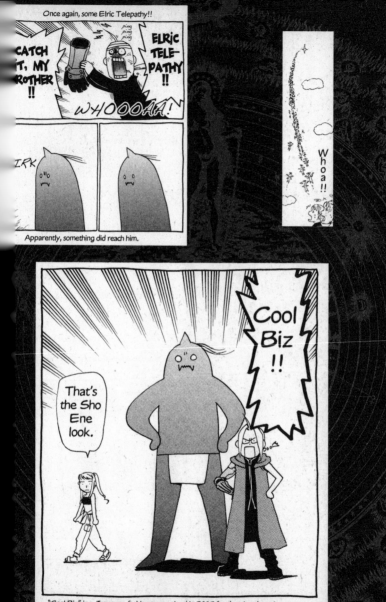

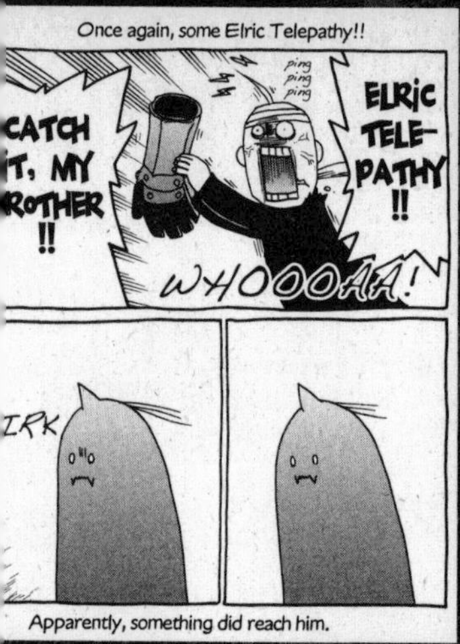
Once again, some Elric Telepathy!!
ELRIC TELE-PATHY !!
ping ping ping
CATCH T, MY ROTHER !!
WHOOOAA!
IRK
Apparently, something did reach him.

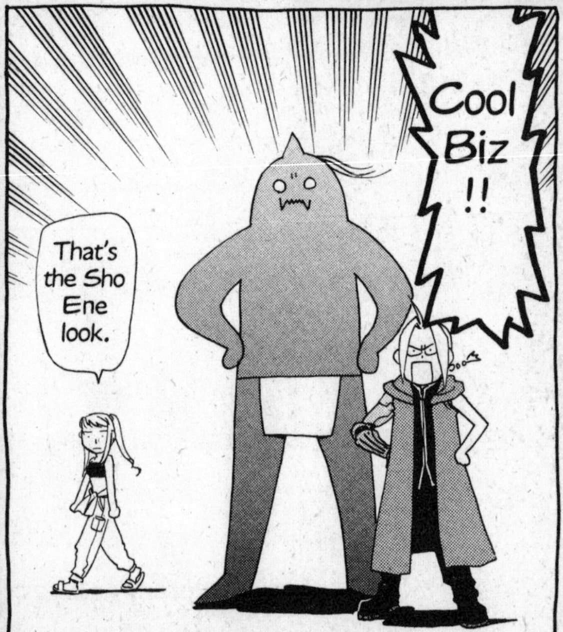
Cool Biz !!
That's the Sho Ene look.

"Cool Biz" is a Japanese fashion term coined in 2005 for dressing down in cooler/lighter business attire in order to cut down on air conditioning. "Sho Ene" was a similar attempt at energy-saving fashion from the '70s that bombed with consumers.

Fullmetal Alchemist Profiles

Get the background story and world history of the manga, plus:

- Character bios
- New, original artwork
- Interview with creator Hiromu Arakawa
- Bonus manga episode only available in this book

Fullmetal Alchemist Anime Profiles

Stay on top of your favorite episodes and characters with:

- Actual cel artwork from the TV series
- Summaries of all 51 TV episodes
- Definitive cast biographies
- Exclusive poster for your wall

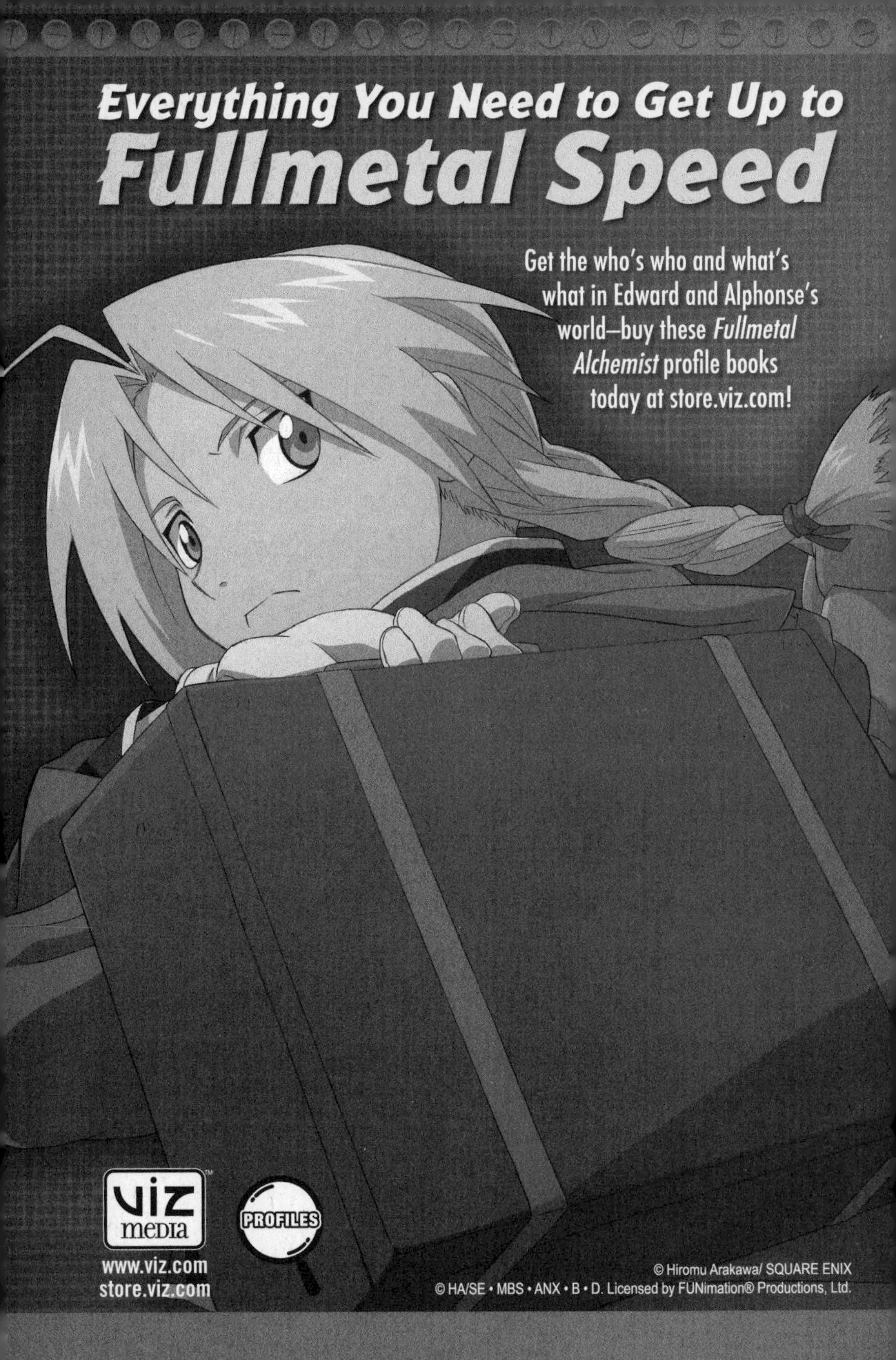
Everything You Need to Get Up to
Fullmetal Speed
Get the who's who and what's what in Edward and Alphonse's world—buy these Fullmetal Alchemist profile books today at store.viz.com!
VIZ media
PROFILES
www.viz.com
store.viz.com
© Hiromu Arakawa/ SQUARE ENIX
© HA/SE • MBS • ANX • B • D. Licensed by FUNimation® Productions, Ltd.

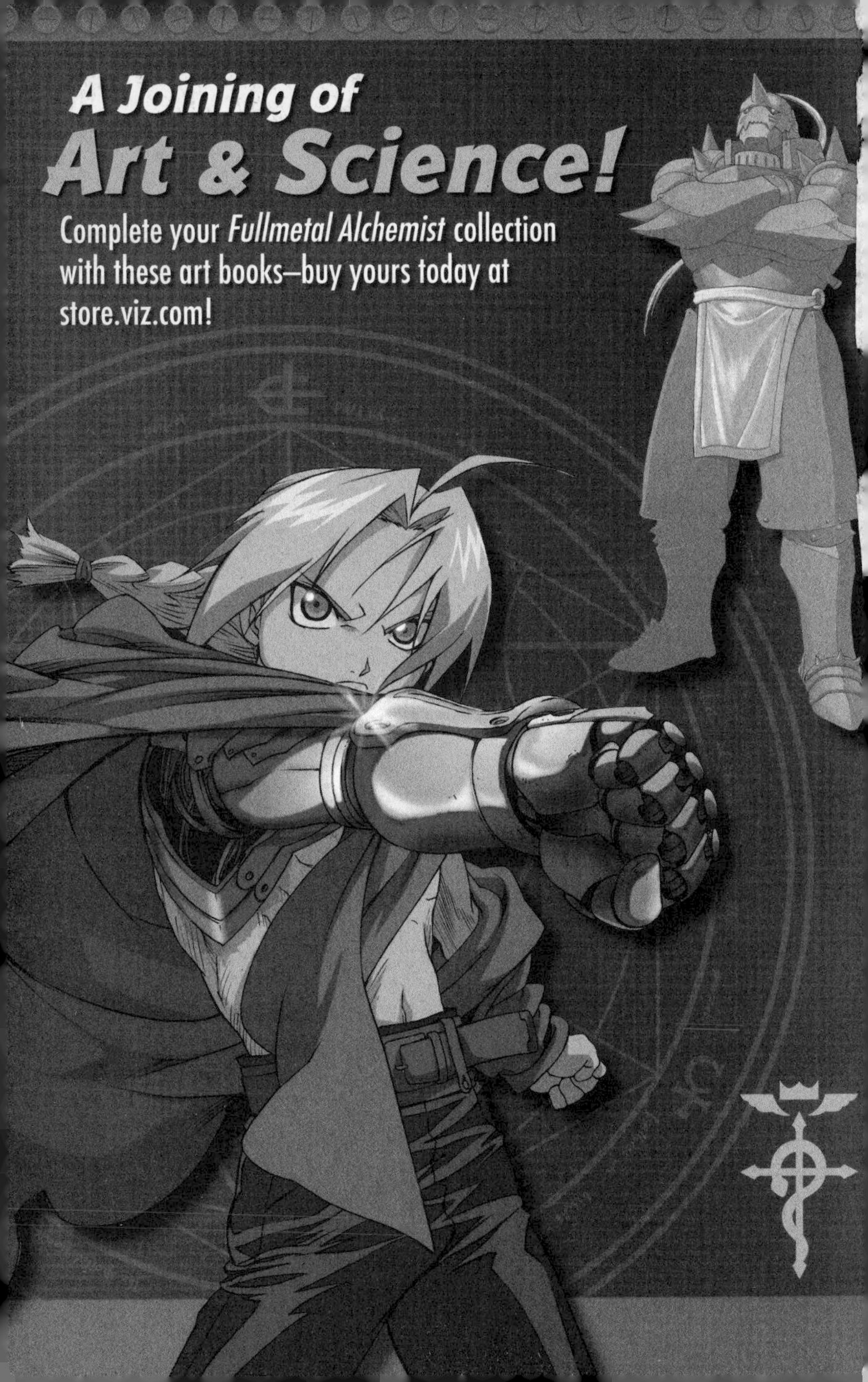
A Joining of
Art & Science!
Complete your *Fullmetal Alchemist* collection with these art books—buy yours today at store.viz.com!